Mashya and Mashyana Unearthed

First having arrived in the realm of the inanimate,
From the inanimate to the vegetal they moved.

For years they lived as vegetal,
And yet stubbornly they could not recall the inanimate.

When from the vegetal to the animal they moved,
They could not recall the vegetal.

Except for this desire they have towards it –
Especially during the springtime and fresh vegetation.

Just like the desire of children with their mothers –
They know not the secret of their longing in their lips.

Yet again from the animal towards the human
Draws them the Creator whom you know.

Thus from domain to domain they went
Until they got to be so intelligent and clever.

They cannot recall their earlier reasons –
Though from this reasoning too they shall evolve.

Until they are delivered from this avaricious, unstable reason –
To witness hundreds of thousands of other reasons ...

Until they are awaken from this slumber
So they'd laugh at their own predicament.

Until suddenly the Day of Resurrection will dawn –
So they'd be delivered from the darkness of all false and flawed consciousness.

Rumi, *Masnavi (1258–73)*

Mashya and Mashyana Unearthed

Myth, Metonymy and the Unknowing Subject

Hamid Dabashi

EDINBURGH
University Press

Edinburgh University Press is one of the leading university presses in the UK. We publish academic books and journals in our selected subject areas across the humanities and social sciences, combining cutting-edge scholarship with high editorial and production values to produce academic works of lasting importance. For more information visit our website: edinburghuniversitypress.com

Edinburgh University Press Ltd
13 Infirmary Street
Edinburgh EH1 1LT

First published in hardback by Edinburgh University Press 2024

Typeset in 10/12 EB Garamond by
Cheshire Typesetting Ltd, Cuddington, Cheshire, and
printed and bound by CPI Group (UK) Ltd, Croydon, CR0 4YY

A CIP record for this book is available from the British Library

ISBN 978 1 3995 1794 2 (hardback)
ISBN 978 1 3995 1795 9 (paperback)
ISBN 978 1 3995 1796 6 (webready PDF)
ISBN 978 1 3995 1797 3 (epub)

Contents

Figures

Figures

Introduction
The World of Pure Verisimilitude

I've often noticed that we are not able to look at what we have in front of us, unless it's inside a frame.[1]

Abbas Kiarostami

I was recently watching a major Iranian film I had not seen before. While watching the film on my laptop from a DVD that had been sent to me by the director, I was also text-messaging on WhatsApp with a young filmmaker friend in Iran. The film I was watching was Nasser Taghva'i's *Kaghaz-e Bi-Khat/Unruled Paper* (2002), which was widely popular at the time of its initial release. Among other things, I was discussing with this friend the trouble with the ruling censorship laws in Iran where the appearance of a male and a female actor in the same frame is deeply troublesome for the custodians of public chastity in the Islamist government. They get very nervous if a man and a woman, even when playing a married couple, or perhaps particularly when playing a married couple, would appear in the same frame. They do not like it, and they do not allow the slightest suggestion of bodily contact or, God forbid, physical intimacy. It is an utter calamity, I was telling my friend, to see otherwise very gifted actors appearing in the same frame, and the paralysing fear of the censorial eyes of the Islamist government frightens them and their director out of their wits and deeply affects their performances. Just a minute earlier the two actors, Khosrow Shakiba'i and Hedyeh Tehrani, among the best of their generation, were doing perfectly fine interacting with their children and friends and older family members, but as soon as they appear in the same frame together, their voices begin to change, their body language becomes deformed and contorted, and their acting degenerates into the most amateurish and pedantic. Truly calamitous to watch.

The film ended, as did my long-distance conversation with my friend. But my mind remained focused on the question of gender and performance and obviously back to Judith Butler's seminal text *Gender Trouble: Feminism and the Subversion of Identity* (1990) to which I had briefly referred while texting with my friend on WhatsApp. I had just discussed Butler's text in my 'Critical Theory: A Global Perspective', a course I teach at Columbia, in which I had included it for quite some time, and it was fresh on my mind. The trouble with Judith Butler's *Gender Trouble*, I have always thought, is as with all other such high theory speculations: its Euro-Universalism – namely, precisely its point of strength.[2] Their insights are empowered by their blindness. I should have perhaps started first by saying I immensely like this book, have read and taught it many times, and the more I do so the more I realise how strange and alien, how limited and limiting, to my world this book is. It is too thinly abstract, too philosophically immaterial in an irredeemably Eurocentric way, too preoccupied with other European and North American theorists and philosophers and critical thinkers, and by the same self-assured measures too much confined by the European provincialism of its points of references. I do read and enjoy all such texts, but more as a spectator who has no dog in the fight or horse in the race, as it were. I am a postcolonial person – deeply rooted in the project to decolonise the mental universe European thinkers invented so their rulers could rule better. To critical thinkers like me, the provincialism that so energises their false universalism is at once the frame of their insights and the limits of their imagination and therefore their global irrelevance. Above all, the trouble with texts such as *Gender Trouble* is that they lack any serious or tangible archive, and thus frame of reference. It does not work with any significant archive of literature, film, fiction, drama and the like. They just work with, through and in conversation with other self-universalising philosophers. Their 'Western' provenance, as they say, gives them a false sense of confidence and assurance. They just put their theoretical speculations up against other theoretical speculations before them, which is fine, but in the end it becomes a closed-circuited amusement park for a while, until their merry-go-round spins into vertiginous boredom. My habitual preference is to think with other works of art, film, fiction, poetry and so on, for they offer better occasions for critical thinking, or in short, they *frame* theoretical speculations in very specific and concrete material, sources, evidence, which others can read to agree, or disagree, and move forward. Both Butler and her philosophical parentage in Derrida and others traffic in a certain limited number of epistemic allusions familiar to them and yet speak with an entirely unwarranted metaphysical certainty. As I said, I am intellectually entertained by reading them, as I would be by watching an American basketball game with renowned athletes. I enjoy the spectacle but really could not care less about who wins and who loses the game they play, for the global and comparative irrelevance of that eventual outcome is a foregone conclusion for me.

From Truth to Verisimilitude

I can put this cognitive dissonance between the sorts of prose Butler and other Eurocentric philosophers like her put forward and in which they beautifully thrive and my own theoretical predilection in a language familiar to theirs but foreign to their false self-universalisation. *Performance* and *repetition* are indeed fine and insightful ways of seeing the social construction of gender and sexuality, of 'the feminine' and 'the masculine', but so is *framing* as an additional factor ranging from the censorial terror of political pressure to its exact opposite – the opening vistas of aesthetic emancipation. What is the difference between *performance* in a daily social setting and *performance* under political pressure or in front of an audience or a camera? By their mandatory clothing codes and *mis-en-scène*, for example, actors can be effectively de-gendered, de-sexed and de-sexualized, as if two men are acting, or two women, and now if we see them that way, the game becomes quite subversive in a different homoerotic way. In other words, when performance is *framed* sarcastically, the whole episteme of gender and sexuality constructions falls flat on its belly. There is a popular joke about Tehran airports after the Islamisation of the Iranian revolution of 1977–79, when the authorities had imposed a separate entrance for men and women. A man enters the terminals and sees this gender apartheid, turns to a security official and says to him: 'Brother, this is a very brilliant rule you have created. Men and women should indeed enter from separate doors, traffic in different terminals, board different planes, fly to different destinations. And you know what, while you are at it, men might as well just marry other men, and women marry other women to make things really and completely separate and thoroughly Islamic!'

The brilliance of this joke is precisely in its realistic premise and subversive punchline in those tyrannical circumstances where its unreal conclusions seemingly carry *ad absurdum* the prospect of homoerotic horizons in an Islamic Republic. Dismantling the ruling violence in patriarchy, theocracy and heteronormative sexuality can scarcely be done with more economy of wits and brevity. Lacking the prospects of such subversive *moments*, not *disciplines*, Butler's elaborate and quite brilliant arguments still remain boldly subversive, and as a philosophical project with a potent political edge quite revolutionary. But, alas, it remains so very much limited within the confines of her theoretical cohorts. In *Gender Trouble*, to this day her best work, Butler has indeed successfully de-naturalised the presumed coherence of the categories of sex, gender and sexuality, proposing that it is the *repetition* of stylised acts that constitutes such social constructs. Sex and gender are as much *performative* as the act of sex itself. Assumptions of binary sex and gender are powerful social and ideological constructs, she tells us, and it makes perfect sense. The desiring subjects, thus constituted, are therefore integral to the regulative discourses that enable such preconditioned and limited subjectivities. Such patterns of intelligibility and disciplinary regimes of useful knowledge are the forestructure of power that pre-fabricates and legislates desires. It is much easier to see the logic of Butler's argument if we just translate it from gender and sexuality into race and racism, as well as the invention of 'the White' and 'the Black' people very much into the model of 'men' and 'women'. Naturalised binary sexes determine naturalised binary gender and sexuality the same way that the colours 'White' and 'Black' determine racialised biology of power and domination – White in this simile is Male, Black is Female, and the structure of patriarchy deeply resembles the structure of racism. Heterosexuality is therefore as power-based as the racialised colour codification of power. Sex is produced by discourse, and so is gender and sexuality, as is colour and race. Butler goes in for the kill when she dismantles the feminist argument for equality, in fact, taking this fabrication for granted, as, we might add beyond Butler's concerns, racial equality cross-authenticates race. The structure of power is therefore consolidated, not subverted by such discourses of equality between races and genders. Identity as free-floating and gender as a performance thus subvert the very foundation of power – that keeps codifying itself in terms of colours and races and genders and classes.

I merely extended Butler's apt argument regarding gender and sex to race and racism, just to show the larger social construction framing of her references. What in effect Butler is theorising is quite simple and yet utterly subversive in her immediate cultural context where heteronormative gender formations and sexual politics rule supreme. We are not *men* or *women*, she tells Americans and Europeans. It is our habit of acting that way that makes us that way. As men we do not desire women, or as women men, but we have been conditioned to act that way. Men could be women, women men, men could desire men, women could desire women. Men could wake up one day and feel like a woman, or women like men, and yet go back to sleep feeling differently. They may even opt to do physical surgeries and psychological counselling to have their bodies and souls correspond to the body and soul that they think best represents them. The free-floating ballet of sex, gender and sexuality could thus unfold into a beautiful choral of possibilities. The proposition is emancipatory and even exhilarating. The traumatised and stigmatised LGBTQ+ community in particular suddenly finds in Butler's ideas a moment of euphoric liberation, that there is nothing wrong with them, that indeed there is something wrong with their detractors and accusers. Judith Butler's powerful theoretical position thus perfectly dovetails with a social condition where the stigmatised and brutalised gay and lesbian communities can heave a sigh of relief now that they have a solid philosophical argument behind them. Butler is justly and deservedly loved and admired as a philosophical liberator of an entire category of existence, a whole different mode of being. Yes, in the ideas of Derrida and Foucault much of what Butler proposes had been germinating for a while, but she brought them all to good and effective fruition.

Butler is therefore all good and well as far as she goes – until we invite her to sit with us in front of a masterpiece by Abbas Kiarostami and ask her if we might for a moment check her books at the door and begin to meditate on the much richer and more fluid possibilities of our being-in-the-world, not just as men and women, or both, or neither, but as the *verisimilitude* of the changing truth that hangs on our gendered politics. Here is where philosophy (particularly European and Europeanised philosophy) must sit politely in the presence of art and learn how to stop thinking and start watching. If Butler were to meet Kiarostami and chat, as they regularly do in my own imagination, she would much love and admire his art, and he would have not only no objection to her propositions that genders and sexualities are fluid but in fact take it for a ride into his own cinema. Kiarostami is not into who and what we are, but who and what we *appear* to be in a *frame* he places around us. Butler can give him any fluidity of the gender she wishes to mark a radical turn in her philosophy. Kiarostami will make the solidity of that philosophical position start singing and dancing to a different tune, by framing it one way as opposed to another. We can *perform* and *iterate* all we want or just stay still until hell freezes over. Kiarostami will have no objection. He will just put a frame around and about us and then a camera in front of who and what we think we are, and we see all our identities and alterities starting to metamorphose into each other. We are not what we perform, we are what those performances become when looked at from the reverse angle of a camera which the world places in front of us and which Kiarostami's camera best mimics.

Butler deciphers the depth of our being in the acts we perform. Kiarostami places the surfaces of those acts in front of an inquisitive camera to reverse its gaze. In that reversal, being male, female, or anything else in between fades out into the simulacrum of pure verisimilitude. Truth suspends itself here, and verisimilitude takes over to redefine the world. In Kiarostami's camera, Butler becomes a veritable metaphysician, all her postmodernist protestations notwithstanding. To be sure, Butler's propositions are quite serious and seriously subversive. But her philosophy is limited in imagination, her theoretical insights blinded by her own rushed desires. Next to Kiarostami, Butler becomes, how shall we put it, quite a retrograde and even reactionary metaphysician who can only liberate in metaphysical terms. She is still into sex, gender and sexuality. She just tosses them into the air and juggles with them, and she juggles well. But she is still after the truth of our sex, gender and sexuality, thought into the fluidity of what we are. So she is not into ice; she breaks the ice into particles and particles into running water and sets sail on that water which is quite cool. But Kiarostami takes a snapshot of that running water, or even a seashore, as he did in his *Five Dedicated to Ozu* (2003), and teases it into the verisimilitude of itself, where representation has bid farewell to all acts of representing any truth. He freezes Butler's juggling of gender and sexuality, pictures it in a matrix of self-sublation and sends her a postcard bidding her metaphysics farewell.

Butler thinks (and rightly so) that by releasing the world from the manufactured binary of a male-female dichotomy she has reached a truly revolutionary goal – and of course she is right to think that way, so far as we are still operating within the confines of what they call 'Western Metaphysics' where not just two but multiple and floating subjects are at work. But that form of subjection still remains confined within the metaphysics of authenticity that has now been set up for a delightful juggling – still seeking to release truth from its fetters of social constructions. But here in the domain of Abbas Kiarostami we have altogether abandoned the dream of truth for a vision of verisimilitude. Kiarostami does not posit an 'Eastern Metaphysics', Heavens Forbid, to mirror and counter 'the Western metaphysics'. His aesthetic intuition of transcendence generates and dismantles its own, as it does all other metaphysics.

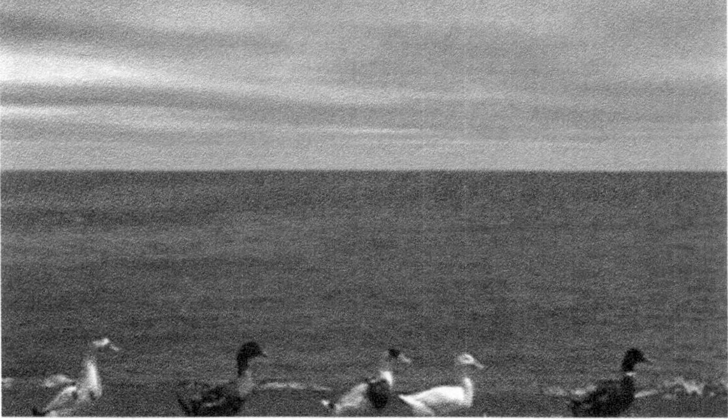

Figure I.1 *A shot from Abbas Kiarostami's* Five Dedicated to Ozu *(2003), Number 4. (Photo: Courtesy of Kiarostami Foundation)*

So: not performance but framing, not truth but verisimilitude, not names but metonyms – and, above all, not speculative shop-talk among European and Europeanised philosophers, but factual evidence from the liberating world of art where frivolous facts have become playful with truth.

Under the Debris of the Fourth Wall

Let us get more specific now – we are onto something between truth and verisimilitude, between fact and fantasy (I have called this premise *factasy*), and, above all, between names and metonyms.

In a signature shot of Abbas Kiarostami's *Certified Copy* (2010), we see a close-up of Juliette Binoche/Elle making herself up as if she were looking into a mirror while, in fact, she is looking into Kiarostami's camera as if it were the mirror. Kiarostami has done this shot before in his previous films, in *The Wind Will Carry Us* (1999), and also in a slightly different way in his *Shirin* (2008), as well as in his version of *Ta'ziyeh* (2003). In all these cases, his camera is looking at people looking at something else – sometimes at themselves. His camera studies their faces as their faces are studying something else – in this case she is examining her own face. But, and there is the rub, through the camera she is also looking back at us, subjecting our gaze to her own gaze – quite an unnerving staring down the spectators. Is she looking at herself in the mirror, or is she looking at us through the camera? The exchange is quite disconcerting because it effectively breaks the Fourth Wall, as Juliette Binoche/Elle's gaze crosses through it and generates a bizarre sense of the Brechtian 'Estrangement Effect/ Verfremdungseffekt'.[3]

Breaking the Fourth Wall overrides the power of the gaze that underscores the *performativity* and *iteration* of just about anything, including sex and gender.

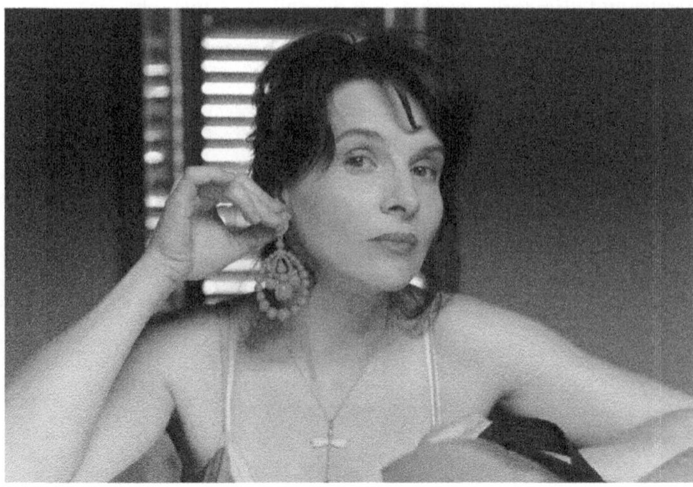

Figure I.2 *Juliette Binoche in Abbas Kiarostami's* Certified Copy *(2010). (Photo: Courtesy of Kiarostami Foundation)*

Performance is for others to watch and to affirm. We are at the mercy of the look of the Other, as Jean-Paul Sartre pointed out in his *L'Être et le Néant/Being and Nothingness* (1943). What if the very corridor of communication between the vulnerability of my performance and your self-empowering spectatorship is dismantled by dismantling the Fourth Wall that is supposed to separate the stage of my performances and the anonymity of your spectatorship? Breaking the Fourth Wall is just the opening door here aesthetically to de-authenticate any claim to the metaphysical certainty of truth and celebration of its verisimilitude, of fact and fiction, of reality and irreality, of the authentic and the inauthentic, of phenomenon and representation – and therefore of name and metonym. This broken wall dismantles any and all acts of representations. Nothing can be represented anymore; everything is pure representation now – including truth *itself*. Truth and verisimilitude collapse under the ruins of this collapsed wall. The identity and alterity of truth and verisimilitude have 'infected' each other, and truth and narrative have morphed into one another. The relation between truth and verisimilitude is no longer metaphoric for they have become metamorphic – as the name that stands for any fact or phenomenon has become metonymic onto itself. As under the debris of the Fourth Wall performance has become truth, so has truth become narrative, the verisimilitude of itself.

That brings us to the subject of Kiarostami's *Certified Copy* – the film itself, its storyline. What is the story of the film, what is the film about, as it were? The entire encounter between the man (William Schimell/James Miller) and the woman (Juliette Binoche/Elle) at the centre of the film surrounds the question of the authentic and fake versions of a work of art; everything is fake, and everything is authentic, at one and the same time, while the haphazard encounter between the man and the woman eventually dissolves into scenes from a failed or failing marriage. In a subsequent interview, Kiarostami has also interpreted his own film as a study of how *misunderstanding* is the very essence of love, of people becoming attracted to each other because they don't know each other, and the more they know each other the faster their love disappears. This dissolution of the *authentic* and *inauthentic*, of the unfamiliar familiarity, of the real and the fake, and the performance of the two characters from complete strangers into a married couple in effect mirrors the central function of that seminal close-up of Juliette Binoche staring through Kiarostami's camera at her audience, making them uncomfortable and thus staring them down to create a tertiary space where truth and verisimilitude, the performer and the performance, the name and the metonym collide, collude, come together and sublate into the condition of complete and pure verisimilitude. The breakdown of the Fourth Wall here is a passage to the dissolution of any truth-claim, to mere and remorseless verisimilitude.

This effective visual breaking of the Fourth Wall happens in a few other films of Kiarostami, but their recent cinematic origins might be traced back to another iconic figure in Iranian cinema: Bahram Beiza'i's revolutionary cut in his masterpiece *Travelers* (1990) where he both visually and verbally breaks the Fourth Wall by having his lead actress Homa Rusta as Mahtab Davaran in the very first sequence of the film stare right into the camera and tell the audience while still in character as Mahtab

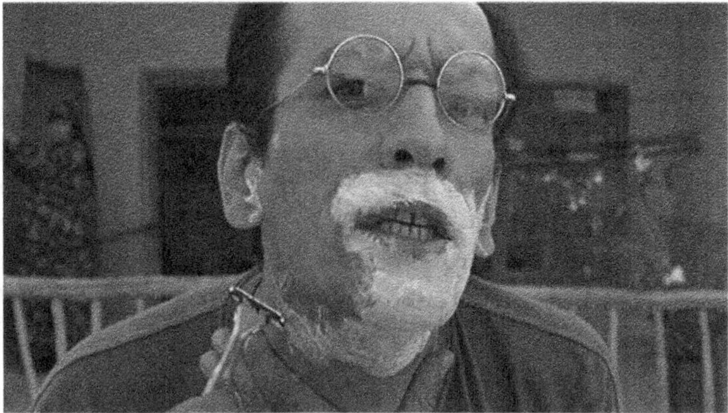

Figure I.3 *Behzad Dorani in Abbas Kiarostami's* The Wind Will Carry Us *(1999). (Photo: Courtesy of Kiarostami Foundation)*

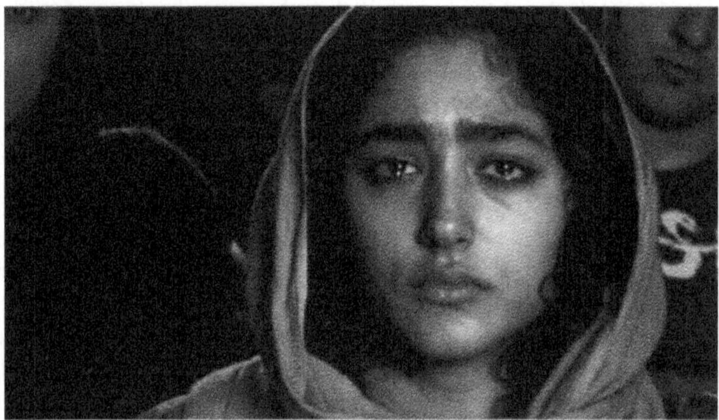

Figure I.4 *Golshifteh Farahani in Abbas Kiarostami's* Shirin *(2008). (Photo: Courtesy of Kiarostami Foundation)*

Davaran that she and her family are on their way to Tehran for her sister's wedding, but they will not get there, for on their way they will have an accident and die. The entirety of the film thus begins with this startling breaking of the Fourth Wall, and at the very end in the last sequence of the film it ends with a classic case of Deus ex Machina, when the dead family returns to life and comes to the sister's wedding, bringing the family mirror as they had promised. In between two pronounced acts of *Verfremdungseffekt* at the beginning and *Deus ex Machina* at the end, Beiza'i tells his story with verve and precision. Here too we are placed in the midst of cinematic space where two theatrical devices suspend the Aristotelian bifurcation between truth and verisimilitude, and the transfusion of the two places us onto what in Islamic philosophy at least since Shahab al-Din Yahya Suhrawardi (1154–91) we have known as *Alam-e Mithal*, meaning the

Realm of Archetypal Images. What is crucial here is that Homa Rusta is not breaking the Fourth Wall as Homa Rusta, but as Mahtab Davaran, the character that she plays. Soon after, they all board the car and just before they have the predicted automobile accident and die, all other members of her family in the car, plus the driver and a young woman they have picked up on their way, all introduce themselves to the camera (to us) as their characters. In other words, the characters break the Fourth Wall, not the actors. This adds yet another astonishing twist to the act of *Verfremdungseffekt*, which launches the whole film into the realm of pure verisimilitude – not by virtue of the names of the actors, but the verisimilitude of their characters.

The world of *Hurqalya* as the philosophical *locus classicus* of this idea of pure verisimilitude I propose here has a long and elaborate history in Islamic philosophy.[4] It refers to the *Alam-e Mithal*, or the Realm of Archetypal Images, as best described by Shahab al-Din Yahya Suhrawardi (1154–91) in the twelfth century and after him by Mulla Sadra (ca 1572–1640) in the sixteenth and seventeenth centuries, continuing with other philosophers all the way to the nineteenth and twentieth centuries. *Hurqalya* is imagined as a liminal space between material sense perceptions and intellectual abstractions. It is a transmaterial abode of these archetypes, a spatial location of *Barzakh*, somewhere between the material and immaterial worlds. The nineteenth-century Sheikhi school of philosophy, named after Shaykh Ahmad al-Ahsa'i (1753–1826), expanded this concept further from Mulla Sadra and Suhrawardi. The philosophical domain of *Hurqalya* as conceptualised in this particular trajectory from Suhrawardi to Mulla Sadra to Sheikh Ahmad Ahsa'i is the philosophical foregrounding of what I propose here as the aesthetic space of pure verisimilitude, where the fusion of fact and fantasy, what in my previous work on Iranian cinema I have called 'factasy', is made possible. As such, the verisimilitude staged in the realm of *Hurqalya* facilitates the correspondence between the realm of the named and their metonymic representations. In its original context, the realm of *Hurqalya* was to account for three thorny theological issues – Bodily Resurrection on the Day of Judgement, the Mi'raj of the Prophet, and the Occultation of the Twelfth Imam – which are here presumed to be all through *Badan Hurqalya'i*, the *Hurqalya'i* Body, which here might be translated as the Ethereal Body. I am extending that deep-rooted Islamic philosophical concept to the predicate of the cinematic universe in which the visions of the invisible are made possible.

Predicated on the sustained course of this idea of *Hurqalya* in Islamic philosophy, aesthetic imagination, or aesthetic reason, emerges as the domain of the sublime and the beautiful, entirely adjacent to the scholastic and metaphysical domain of the nonaesthetic reason or the true. It is crucial to keep in mind at this point that this aesthetic reason is philosophically achieved entirely independent of any traceable cultural heritage of Greek, Indian, Iranian, or Islamic origins.

To understand the way these visual indirections of verisimilitude, emanating from the cinematic subconscious of *Hurqalya*, as it were, work we might compare these formidable shots of Kiarostami and Beiza'i with the globally celebrated pictures of Shirin Neshat, most recently in her *Book of Kings* (2012) or *Our House is on Fire* (2013), in which the flat-figured and platitudinous look of the photographed subjects

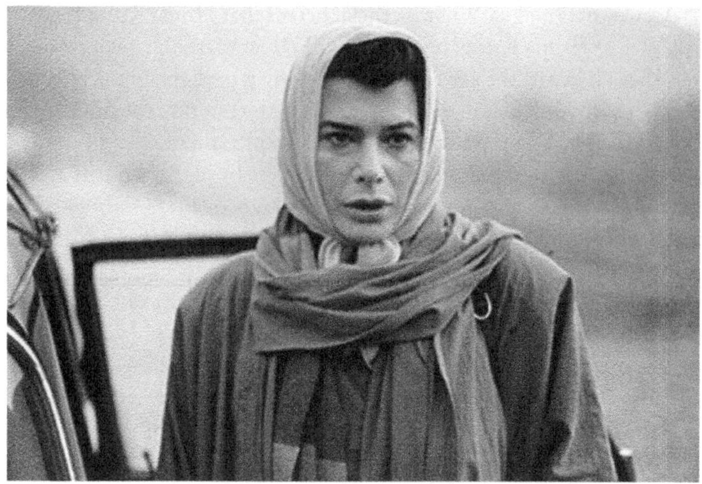

Figure I.5 *Homa Rusta in Bahram Beiza'i's* Travelers *(1991). (Photo: Courtesy of Bahram Beiza'i)*

stares into the vacuity of Shirin Neshat's lens, further fortifying the Fourth Wall. The calligraphic simulacra of verbal superimpositions further exacerbate this crowded confusion of multiple and conflated signs, effectively turning the staged subjects into inmates of a four-walled prison house of captured signs unable to breathe, let alone escape or mean. The calligraphic letters here look like barbed wire, placing the subjects inside a fortress impossible to reach from this side or escape from the other. Neshat became a justly celebrated name outside Iran, and her aesthetics was informed by a self-professed *exilic* anxiety to mean specific things in a tightly sealed hermetic cell. In a globalised world where no one is any longer at any 'home', she continues to insist she is 'in exile' – while taking full advantage of a systemic self-Orientalisation. The photographic appeal of Neshat's work is a particular feature of a captured imagination unable to dwell in the moral and aesthetic imagination of her own homeland, which she left decades ago, while equally unable to be liberated in her adopted environs. In this state of limbo, which is the trademark of Shirin Neshat's artworld, the Fourth Wall is in fact fortified into a fortress. Be that as it may, Neshat's aesthetic formalism may have had a crucial impact on Kiarostami soon after they met in New York City in the 1990s. The poetic underpinning of Neshat's video installations soon began to have a palpable presence of patient poetic implosions and in-dwelling in Kiarostami's subsequent and mature works that had begun in his own photographic work and now culminated in his final films such as *Ten* (2002), *Five* (2003), *10 on Ten* (2004) and then especially *24 Frames* (2014). Impervious to any false notion of 'exile', Kiarostami in effect liberated Neshat's 'captured imagination' and let it loose into his own far more confident and emancipated imageries. The more Kiarostami's artworld moved onto the fertile ground of pure verisimilitude, the more the aesthetic emancipation of his visual imagination became a reality *sui generis*.[5]

The spectrum of this *in-dwelling* and *enframing* where signs and signifiers, facts and their fictions, begin to become permeable is far beyond the works of Kiarostami or Neshat, or any other single artist. We might trace the poetic origin of all these visual speculations evident in the works of Kiarostami and Beiza'i by framing them with a beautiful stanza from Forough Farrokhzad's signature poem '*Tavallodi Digar*/ Another Birth' (1962), where she says:

In a room that is the size of a solitude,
My heart, which is as spacious as love,
Looks at the simple excuses of its happiness:
At the beautiful decay of flowers in the vase,
At the small sapling you have planted
In our garden,
While listening to the songs of the canaries
singing at the limits of my window –

Oh, this is my fair share –
This is my fair share
My share is a sky
That is taken away from me at the drop of a curtain –
My share is descending a flight of forsaken stairs
And connecting to something in decay and solitude –
My fair share is a stroll in the sad garden of my reminiscences
And my despair
As I hear the voice that tells me:
'I love your hands!'[6]

Phrases like 'the size of a solitude', 'as spacious as love', 'flowers in the vase', 'a small sapling in the garden', canaries 'singing at the limits of my window', 'a sky / That is taken away from me at the drop of a curtain' and so on are all framing phrases, staccatos of instances when *totality* is interrupted by *infinity*, if we were to use Emmanuel Levinas' notions, and where *enframing* and *in-dwelling* in fact paradoxically delimit the totality of experience to mark the infinity that enables it. The poetic interplay between totality and infinity here in Farrokhzad's poem has left behind veritable evidence of how the reservoir of pure verisimilitude has thematically sustained itself.

We might also find an even deeper and still more philosophical origin of this proposition in Mulla Sadra's notion of '*Ittihad-e Aqil wa Ma'qul*/Unification of the Intellectual and the Intellection', in which the knower, the knowable and the act of knowing, or the intellectual, the intellection and the intellect, all come together to form a veritable unit, which here I call *pure verisimilitude*, and where Kiarostami's cinema characteristically marks and envisions.[7] My point here is to identify the poetic, the aesthetic and the philosophical contours of an idea that finds its fortuitous cinematic character in Kiarostami's work.

Here an element of intertextuality between two or more of Kiarostami's films suggests itself, such as if we place two similar shots of two of his different films on a filmic

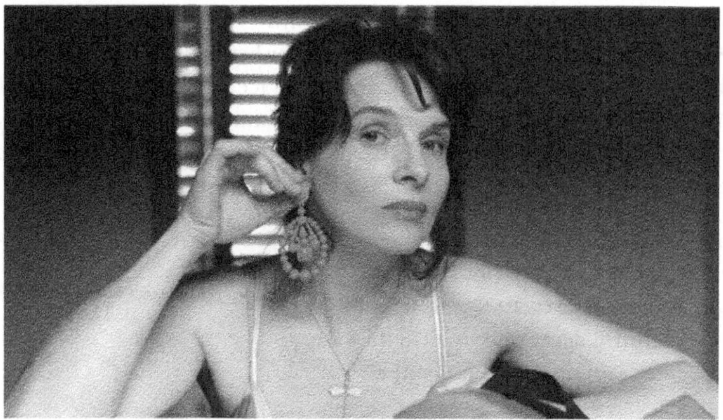

Figure I.6 *Juliette Binoche in Abbas Kiarostami's* Certified Copy *(2010). (Photo: Courtesy of Kiarostami Foundation)*

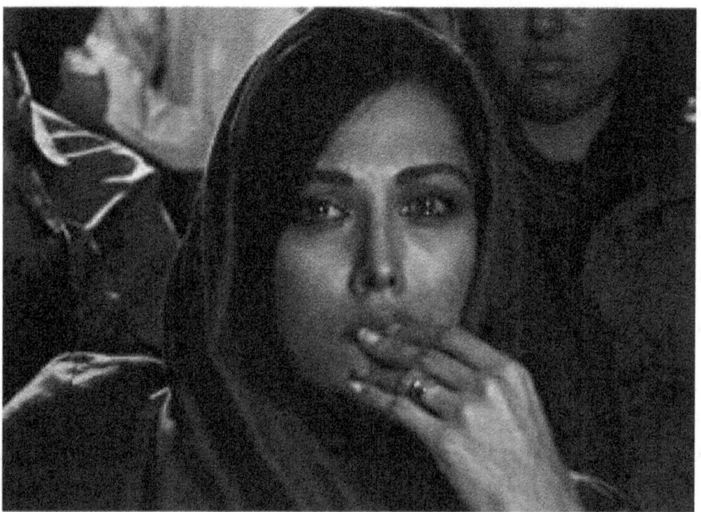

Figure I.7 *Mahtab Keramati in Abbas Kiarostami's* Shirin *(2008). (Photo: Courtesy of Kiarostami Foundation)*

montage outside their respective texts and thus reframe them differently, such as these two shots from two of his films, *Certified Copy* and *Shirin*. Thus co-framed, the result makes it look as if Mahtab Keramati in Abbas Kiarostami's *Shirin* (2008) is looking at her own self-projection onto Juliette Binoche in Kiarostami's *Certified Copy* (2010). Keep in mind that the French actress Juliette Binoche is also included in Kiarostami's *Shirin*, sitting in the audience with other Iranian actresses for Kiarostami's camera to examine their faces as they watch a romantic movie, of which we only hear the soundtrack. Onto the screen of Kiarostami's film shot in Italy far away from the censorial policies of the ruling Islamic state he can project the image of a woman as she is making herself up as she wishes – as millions of Iranian women do far away from a chastised camera. The two shots from the two different films here come together to frame the intertextual implications of the two shots in an act of framing, not done by Kiarostami himself but enabled by his entire oeuvre. The suggested gaze enables an enframing different from the one we see separately in these two different films. The intertextual implication is thus enabled by the fact that in his three components of his Koker trilogy he was actively involved precisely in the same intertextual cross-references. This intertextuality also allows for the in-dwelling of loosened mimetic gestures beyond the captured imagination of one storyline from one story or another. Here, no iteration or repetition can constitute any identity, for everything always points to an alterity about, always about, to happen. Here, we therefore move away from any and all metaphysics of identity into which Butler's liberating hermeneutics is trapped, towards an aesthetics of alterity that Kiarostami's cinema enables. Juliette Binoche is in Mahtab Keramati's mind when Kiarostami films them both – and *vice versa*. This can only happen under the debris of the Fourth Wall and in the purgatorial space of the *Hurqalya* where pure verisimilitude overrides any act of framing with reframing.

Ostranenie and the Arrested Mimesis of the Body

To sum up until this point: I am proposing a semiotic proximity between the world of pure verisimilitude and the metonymic allusions of a cinematic universe where works of art mean with a non-committal aesthetic reason. But why do I do that?

Things in Kiarostami's cinema, with its roots in other major works of film, fiction and poetry, compromise, overcome and dismantle themselves in a creatively subversive way that the Russian formalist theorist Viktor Shklovsky calls *Ostranenie*, where every fact overturns against itself, in and of itself.[8] The playful act never allows for a metaphysics of authenticity of any sort – sex, gender, race, identity – to find a firm ground. Every claim to identity becomes a prelude to alterity. At strategic moments, the Fourth Wall is broken, the door of reality and irreality open onto each other, truth and verisimilitude meet and allow for pure verisimilitude to take over, where everything becomes representation, where mimesis takes over and all allusions of all signifiers to any signified are categorically dismantled. We have entered the absolute realm of liberation from all signs signalling anything. They just signate. We are in the world of *Alam-e Mithal* – where facts and fiction, truth and narrative, names and metonyms have collapsed onto each other.

Let me shift gear here to a different prose to make my point clearer. In *Asrar al-Tawhid fi Maqamat al-Sheikh Abi Said* (composed ca 117), a masterpiece of classical Persian Sufi hagiography, we read how Sheikh Abu Said, the chief protagonist of the stories, was passing by a small village where a local saintly dignitary was his host. The host did not believe in the Sufi practice of *Sama'*/Sacred Dance for he considered it blasphemous. Sheikh Abu Said asks for an attendee to recite a poem; he does, and the Sheikh feels ecstatic and gets up and starts dancing. The host is made uncomfortable. The Sheikh holds his hand and asks him to get up and dance with him; the host is reluctant, the Sheikh then points outside their abode and tells him to look; he looks, and he sees all the trees and mountains and buildings dancing in harmony with the Sheikh. The host involuntarily starts dancing and equally tells his brother, 'Oh brother, come and join us, we are no match for this master'.[9]

This is the prose from which Kiarostami's cinematic poetry in part derives – and for that he did not need either Brecht or Shklovsky to theorise any sense of *Verfremdungseffekt* or *Ostranenie* for him. A saint starts dancing, and by the gift of his grace the trees and mountains and building start dancing in harmony. Where are we then? Are we with the historical and factual figure of Sheikh abi Sa'id abi al-Kheyr, or are we in the world of mystical and mysterious *Karamat*/Miraculous Deeds – the world of pure verisimilitude, where anything is possible? There is no answer to that question. There need not be a response to that question. For the fusion of fact and fiction have already created a veritable world of their own. My point of contention here is that the whole production of gender and sexuality in Butler's project and the gender theorists who come before and after her is too sedate to be stable, too structural-functional, too solid. To be sure, in her own areas of studies and reflections she is quite a revolutionary thinker – but when we move to slightly different areas around the world, the whole production of these feminists becomes positively provincial – divorced from any larger frame of reference, especially in far more complicated domains of sex and gender politics and practices that are seriously more fluid and casual. There is a certain 'Christian morality' at work here, against which people like Butler or even Foucault before her rightly revolt. But that Christian morality has never been a hurdle to other cultures, say, in China, Japan, India, Iran, or Africa. But my point here is not a comparative cultural analysis. My point is to see how the world of pure verisimilitude completely dismantles any identity formation by *ipso facto* positing its alterity – whereby the nonaesthetic reason yields to the aesthetic reason.

I do wish to appeal to alternative particularities (and the universalities they entail) that are embedded in much wider cultural and even civilisational framings – more specifically to Persian and Islamic references. But in this book, I have no desire or appetite for the very distant past. There is a radical contemporaneity to this book working mostly with film, fiction and poetry, with occasional excursions into Islamic philosophy – though, as you will soon see, I have a very distant mythic past to invoke in my arguments. This leads me to refer to Joseph Massad's seminal text, *Desiring Arabs* – as a contrapuntal document *vis-à-vis* Butler's. I have nothing to add or detract from Massad's central argument that the rise of gay rights in the Arab and Muslim world is integral to the larger Orientalist and colonial project of European self-universalisation, and that it imposes a particular kind of homoeroticism at the cost of concealing or denying others. I have already written briefly on this and demonstrated how in the Iranian context there are varieties of homoerotism that do not necessarily fit with what today we witness in the LGBQT+ movement – perfectly legitimate and timely in its own context. My point is rather the vast topography of literary and historical evidence that Massad marshals to make his case for an alternative mode of eroticism in the Arab and Muslim world. I have neither the contentious position of Massad nor the hobby horse of Western Orientalism and colonialism to bring out for yet another beating. I have deep admiration for Butler and have learned much from her and consider much of her insights in fact remarkably accurate wherever we look. My purpose here is to draw attention to the two issues of *performance* and *iteration* into a larger and more compelling issue of *framing* that is both theoretically and thematically absent from her work, while crucially present in the work of Erving Goffman whose much earlier and more compelling work I find immensely significant for what I am about to write about the formation of selves and societies in Iranian film and fiction. Questions of gender and sex to me here are particularities of the larger issues of the dialectic between self and society – which is always mitigated through the aesthetic functions of verisimilitude and metonymic allusions, impossible to register without the central role of what Shklovsky called *Ostranenie*.

This move to the Iranian scene entails both its insights and its blindness. Let me turn around and do a reverse shot, as it were, to make my point clearer. The trouble with Iranian cinema, which is the key subject of my thinking here, is that it is hard at work trying to convert a basically verbal tapestry deeply informed by poetic imageries into a visual culture, with a heavily censured body at the epicentre of its perils and promises. Iran has a rich and powerful visual culture of its own, from ancient reliefs over manuscript illustrations and coffee house painting to later royal portraits and ultimately its share of abstract and conceptual art of the last century. It took generations of filmmakers and visual artists leading to Abbas Kiarostami, Amir Naderi, Rakhshan Bani-Etemad, Shirin Neshat and Bahram Beiza'i to cultivate finally that cinematic language in multiple and rich registers. But for a variety of reasons that language stutters when it comes to the human body. Coming to terms with that arrested mimesis of the body is a key element of understanding the manner in which the estrangement effect works.[10]

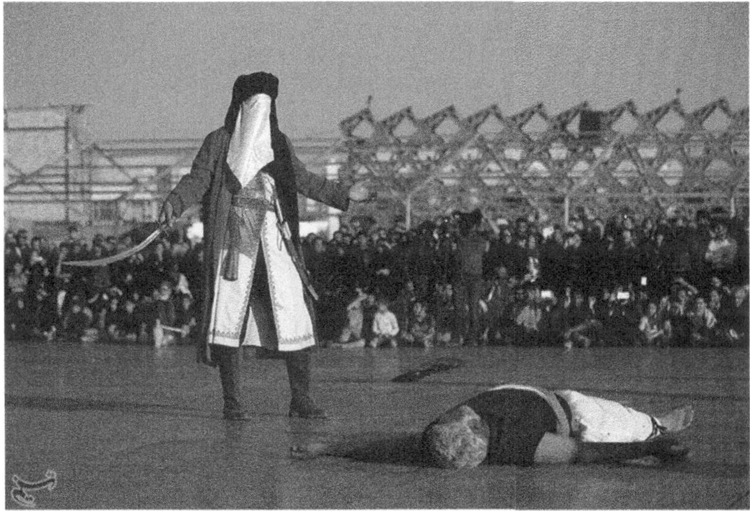

Figure I.8 Ta'ziyeh *passion play performed at Tehran's Imam Hussein Square, 15 October 2015. (Photo: Tasnim New Agency, photo by Hossein Zohrvand)*

This bodily predicament brings us back to *Ta'ziyeh*, a rooted and rich theatrical tradition whose origins are lost in time immemorial, and which has its own visual and performing assemblage of mimetic representations, entirely independent of what Shklovsky and Brecht had theorised as the practice of *estrangement* or *alienation*. The verbal passion evident in this dramaturgical tradition does not translate into visual performance of the body. Very much concealed under heavy costumes and formalised gestures, akin to what we see in Indian, Chinese or Japanese theatrical traditions, the body has to be covered and turned iconic and the face either completely veiled or heavily made up to allow for the power of the verbal passion to express, perform and articulate itself.[11]

The liberation of the body from that corporeal entrapment within a heavily formalised theatrical tradition and the performing culture it has informed happened in the rebellious poetry of Forough Farrokhzad (1934–67) where the physical body begins to explore its earthly desires in specifically bodily (Bakhtinian) terms. In a stanza in her '*Fath-e Bagh*/Conquest of the Garden', she writes:

Sokhan az Peyvand-e sost-e do nam ...

We're not talking about the unstable union of two names
And of lovemaking in the aging pages of a book –
We're talking about the blissful happiness of my hair
And the burnt anemones of your kisses
And the sincerity of our bodies in stealing each other
And the shimmering glow of our nakedness
Just like the fish scale in water
We're talking about the silvery life of a song
That early in the morning the little fountain was singing.[12]

She then becomes far more specific in her legendary poem '*Asheqaneh*/Lovingly':

Ah Ay ba jan-e man amikhteh

Oh, you intertwined with my soul
You who resurrected me from my grave ...
With you my loneliness disappeared
My body smelled of lovemaking
You the water in the dried brooks of my chest
The flood in my veins ...
Ay you stranger to my shirt
Familiar with the pastures of my body ...[13]

The distance between the liberated and confident body in Forough Farrokhzad's erotic poetry and the staged formalism of the performing bodies was never covered – could never be covered. This uncovered distance makes the staging of the performing body an impossibility – except through a hidden but effective memorial recollection. In the 1950s and 1960s, the so-called '*Filmfarsi*' (very popular melodramas) bordered on soft porn, but the whole genre was a transgressive space where the ritualised underclass (the Jahili culture) was staged only to be denounced to define the bourgeois morality of the middle class. This 'European' (effectively Christian) bourgeois morality soon took over where Shi'i mimesis had left off and disallowed for the preforming bodies to learn how to frame and stage their desires. This discrepancy between erotic memories and arrested bodies generated a mimetic crisis for the body, hidden under multiple and self-conflating veils. When he left Iran, the leading Iranian filmmaker Mohsen Makhmalbaf tried to explore this arrested body in two of his films, *Sex va Falsafah/ Sex and Philosophy* (2005) and *Faryad-e Moorchehgan/Cries of Ants* (2005), but the result was an unqualified disaster. The mimetic arrest of the desiring body became a signature of Iranian visual and performing arts, to this day, so much so that, even when Sohrab Shahid-Saless or Abbas Kiarostami (before their passing), or Amir Naderi or Bahram Beiza'i, the very best of Iranian filmmakers, left Iran and could make films the way they wished without fear of censorship, they still had no clue or even desire how to film the human body, especially the feminine body. By now, the sense of self-estrangement had become definitive to the human body as perceived through the Iranian cinematic practices.

Soon a new generation of younger filmmakers emerged, born or raised in Iran or abroad, and although the experiments were limited, they were still promising. A gifted young filmmaker, Maryam Keshavarz, in her *Circumstance* (2011) tried to explore the optic possibilities of homosexuality between two lesbians in Iran. The film had its perils and promises, but the Orientalist gaze she solicited from her European and US film critics killed the prospect and prevented any more serious encounter with her work. Far more successful was Ana Lily Amirpour's *A Girl Walks Home Alone at Night* (2014). She banked on the vampire genre and recast the chador in a boldly reimagined iconography. But by the same logic the genre had delimited her creative imagination of the body. All one had to do was to compare these experiments with Rakhshan Bani-Etemad's *Banu-ye Ordibehesht/The May Lady* (1998) to see the widening discrepancies between films shot inside or outside Iran – one rooted in the visual impossibilities of the body, and the other liberated into the wayward precarity of the genres.[14]

Two other experiments with animation are crucial here. First is Marjane Satrapi's *Persepolis*, as an autobiographical series of *bandes dessinées* (2000–4) and then as an animated film (2007). The other is Ali Soozandeh's *Tehran Taboo* (2017), a German-Austrian animated attempt to deal with social malice in the director's homeland. Both these cases are remarkably successful experiments with the virtual simulacrum of the body which, in turn, is compromised precisely by their evident irreality. Compare these two films with the late Sohrab Shahid-Sales' (1944–2008) film and television features he made during his sojourn in Germany. The exilic condition of his alienation had placed Shahid-Saless squarely in the immigrant communities in Europe, with all traces of his bodily presence erased. Or else compare them with Shirin Neshat's first feature film, *Women without Men* (2009), or any of her video installations, where the body remains as sedate and arrested. All of these cases exude an inability to film the body in its defiant desires. This mimetic arrest of the body is where the verbal eloquence of the poetic and literary art finds itself in a purgatory. Compare these with the story of Seyavash and Sudabeh in Ferdowsi's *Shahnameh*, or his story of Bizhan and Manizheh in the same epic. Examples abound in classical Persian poetry. But it is in Forough Farrokhzad's contemporaneously bold, brilliant and defiant erotic poetry that the colonial consciousness of gendered bifurcations and the heteronormative bourgeois morality it entails are all poetically dismantled.

In the Eurocentric context that Judith Butler's defiant theorisation of the gendered body best represents, *truth* (whether we are male or female) is conflated with *performance* and *fact* with *iteration*. This works perfectly fine for the limited provincialism of Eurocentric philosophising. On the much wider postcolonial sites farthest removed from Butler's analytics, we might posit *truth* (whether we are male or female) as a particular take, a variation, on a verisimilitude allusion to that truth. This is made possible, I have argued, from the vantage point of a purgatorial space we call *Alam-e Mithal* – the realm of Archetypal Images somewhere between the material world of our corporeal bodies and the conceptual world of intellection where we theorise our bodies. I have also put forward the idea that through the estrangement effect (Brecht's *Verfremdungseffekt* or Schklovsky's *Ostranenie*) and the practice of breaking the Fourth Wall, truth claims and their varied verisimilitudes collide, collude and come together and become one and the same thing. What complicates the matter is how through the visually arrested body that collusion is interrupted and broken. But that is not the end of the story. We have a way out.

When in the poetry of Forough Farrokhzad the erotic body is liberated from its arrested mimesis, then again representation becomes possible, truth and verisimilitude come back to coagulate and collude, and thereby metonymy and its pronominal allusions equally collide and collude – and thus truth becomes tantamount to all its narrative. Farrokhzad's liberation of the erotic body made it a living organism, at once truthful and yet pure verbal verisimilitude – as the pronominal and the metonymic in her poetry come together and as the truth of the erotic body yields to its poetic narratives. The ruling Islamist censorship may not allow bodily contact between male and female actors, but in the minds of those very actors Forough Farrokhzad is always already singing her poetry to the pulse of their aroused bodies. The ruling Islamist censorship may ban or censor Farrokhzad's poetry, as they often do, but these actors are the very product of those erotic poems Farrokhzad had occasioned in their parents' youthful bodies. The older editions of Farrokhzad's books are kept as mementos of those passionate memories their parental generations shared, and now they recite and remind them to their children. This is no mere cultural resistance to totalitarian and disciplined tyranny – something far more serious is at work here. These actors enter the scene having already seen and sensed their bodies in Farrokhzad's poetry. The censorship may not allow them to perform those richly poeticised bodies in front of a camera, but they still see, sense and feel those bodies in the privacy of their bedrooms and the publicity of their censored but memorial bodies and excited imagination. What is at stake here is the sustained course of the interface between the truth of their bodies – *samimiat tanhaman dar tarrari*/the sincerity of our bodies in their acts of thievery, as Forough Farrokhzad called it – and the verisimilitude of their recollections and representations – between their pronominal identities and their metonymic alterities, surface between the potent forces active in their cinematic *Hurqalya* or *Alam-e Mithal*, the very topography of the world of verisimilitude. The Eurocentric and even Christian Christological emphasis on performance and repetition – both dramaturgical – are all fine and well, but also distortive of the poetic prosody, the aesthetic framing and the moral imaginary at work in the architectonic of truthful verisimilitude. I am therefore proposing here a renewed conception of *Alam-e Mithal* that constitutes the cinematic subconscious of the visual and performing arts – where truth and verisimilitude, fact and fiction, pronominal and metonymic allusions all freely frequent each other's respective spaces and dwell in theirs otherwise.

My point here is to draw attention to and suggest the way out of what I have called the arrested mimesis of the body, where the body has not yet explored visually the verbal growth of the language, where language has already bordered on chaos. The link I propose between *Ostranenie* and the arrested mimesis of the body brings us to the threshold of pure verisimilitude, achieved through breaking the Fourth Wall. But the arrested mimesis of the body remains otherwise paralysed on the stage or else concealed behind a double veil, one imposed by the Islamist regime and the other self-imposed involuntarily and unawares. The interface and the tension between the pure verisimilitude of the enframing and the arrested mimesis of the body is the central creative crisis of Iranian visual and performing arts, liberated through the memorial evidence of the erotic body. This breaking of the Fourth Wall in Kiarostami's cinema, we must keep in mind, generates a 'fifth wall', for by breaking the Fourth Wall he turns the entire spectacle of filming itself into a spectacle. The double mirroring effect becomes infinite, just as Shamlou says in a poem:

> *Man barmikhizam* ...
>
> I rise
> Holding a light in my hand
> And a light in my heart –
> I polish the rust on my soul,
> I place a mirror in front of your mirror
> To turn you into an infinity.[15]

Framing the Performances, Spacing Performativity

The origin of Butler's insights into gender as performance might be traced back to Erving Goffman's *Presentation of Self in Everyday Life*, and so is my introduction of the question of 'framing', which was also developed in the classical text *Frame Analysis* by Goffman, a Canadian anthropologist who was at the University of Pennsylvania when I was a graduate student there. I never managed to take any courses with him because I was soon drawn to Philip Rieff and because the trajectory of my theoretical work found a different direction. But without being his direct student, I was attracted to his work which has remained very close to my own thinking.

Goffman's *Presentation of Self in Everyday Life* (1956) was a pioneering study of our lived experiences as theatrical performances whereby we seek to control the different impressions we leave on others we encounter through a dramaturgical exercise in our character and public demeanour. Goffman rightly saw a semblance between what we do in our daily encounters and what actors do on stage. The dramaturgical performances turn the whole life into a performing spectacle. Very early in his preface, Goffman writes:

> The perspective employed in this report is that of the theatrical performance; the principles derived are dramaturgical ones. I shall consider the way in which the individual in ordinary work situations presents himself and his activity to others, the ways in which he guides and controls the impression they form of him, and the kinds of things he may and may not do while sustaining his performance before them.[16]

This perspective, minus Goffman's dramaturgical twist, might be traced back to the sociological school of 'symbolic interactionism' and the works of George Herbert Mead and Herbert Blumer before Goffman. The key feature of Goffman's theory is this idea of 'self-presentation', evident in the very title of his book, 'presentation of the self', which in dramaturgical terms becomes tantamount to self-representation. There seems to be nothing ingrained, metaphysical, enduring, or even sustainable about this self, which becomes almost like a chameleon negotiating a camouflaged presence in multiple publics. What in Goffman's theory is of interest to me here is the spontaneity of the performance he theorises. This is how he puts it:

> We find, then, that when the individual is in the immediate presence of others, his activity will have a promissory character. The others are likely to find that they must accept the individual on faith, offering him a just return while he is present before them in exchange for something whose true value will not be established until after he has left their presence.[17]

The entire project of Goffman's seminal text is thus geared towards a dialogical interface between a self and the others they encounter. There is a dynamic to this interface set in a fixed position but still malleable to dramaturgical influences. My point here is not to reduce Butler to Goffman. There are serious differences between them, especially in the distinction between *performance* and *performativity*. Jen A. Zelezny (2010) traces Butler back to John Langshaw Austin's work from the 1950s and after that to Jacques Derrida's critique of Austin in the 1960s, and then brings the theory forward to performance theorist Richard Schechner.[18] The point that Butler makes and Zelezny emphasises is crucial for assimilating performativity backward to performance, and it compromises Butler's crucial turn to argue for continuous subjectivity, the way a subject is in a constant state of formation and production. There is a presumption of agency in Goffman that Butler would not grant.

Keeping this crucial distinction that philosophers make between performance and performativity in mind, I still draw attention to Goffman's other major work, *Frame Analysis: An Essay on the Organization of Experience* (1974), where he tries to show how conceptual frames organise social experiences. For Goffman a picture frame is an example of a primary frame that makes what it holds meaningful. He posits two general kinds of primary frames: natural and social. This is how he puts it in the first chapter of his book, which calls 'Primary Frameworks':

> When the individual in our Western society recognizes a particular event, he tends, whatever else he does, to imply in this response (and in effect employ) one or more frameworks or schemata of interpretation of a kind that can be called primary. I say primary because application of such a framework or perspective is seen by those who apply it as not depending on or harking back to some prior or 'original' interpretation; indeed, a primary framework is one that is seen as rendering what would otherwise be a meaningless aspect of the scene into something that is meaningful.[19]

Goffman is obviously self-conscious that his theorisation is very much limited to what he calls 'our Western society', which oddly enough remains constant, stable and almost metaphysical precisely at a time when he had just theorised the multivariance of self-representation. But this reference to 'our Western society' could also be understood precisely as a frame he is interjecting for his theorisation, lest the open-ended reading of it becomes entirely untenable. What overcomes this paradox is much later in his text, in his Chapter Five, which he calls 'The Theater Frame', where he says: 'The argument, then, is that the theatrical frame is something less than a benign construction and something more than a simple keying'.[20] Predicated on this premise, Goffman makes a crucial observation about spatial boundaries of the stage:

> The spatial boundaries of the stage sharply and arbitrarily cut off the depicted world from what lies beyond the stage line. (Many other social activities are, of course, restricted to a particular roped-off or elevated space, but with the possible exception of ritual, these activities are conducted as though events outside the boundary were of the same general order of being as those within. Not so in theatrical staging.) Further, the endings of a drama can follow somewhat the possible endings in real life; the beginnings of a play don't seem to have much of a parallel in unstaged activity. For typically the curtains open on an episode in progress, with no attention given by the characters to the fact that they have suddenly come into view. Movies, incidentally, can effect a more gradual introduction of the realm the onlookers will enter.[21]

We might here also think of Derrida's idea of '*Différance*' which in his speculation points at the heterogeneous framings that determine the production of textual meaning – not just by what they mean, but more by what they do not mean and from which they differ and thus defer. This perpetual deferring of the meaning becomes the frame.

We can even go further back to George Herbert Mead and Max Scheler and their philosophies of intersubjectivity in the constitution of subjectivity, which is inevitably predicated on the formation of an alienated and generalised Other which is always already outside the First World theorist. This hidden or manifest Other is both the *bête noire* and the Achilles' Heel of 'the First World' theorists and philosophers. In a cogent and brilliant critique, 'The Secularity of Empire, the Violence of Critique: Muslims, Race, and Sexuality in the Politics of Knowledge-Production', Sunera Thobani has turned Judith Butler upside down, exposing her unexamined (fanatical) secularism bordering uncomfortably on a bizarre Islamophobia.[22] Thobani exposes the discursive strategies that work systematically 'to Westernize feminist-queer scholars/hip and activism as these enact the very relations of power they set out to question and possibly undo'.[23] What seems to have agitated Butler here is the prospect of Islamic violence matching colonial violence, but disqualifying her to claim any theoretical authority in understanding let alone philosophising it.

The issue, however, is much larger and more widespread than merely in Butler. In 'Patterns of Intersubjectivity in the Constitution of Subjectivity: Dimensions of Otherness', Nelson Ernesto Coelho Jr and Luís Claudio Figueiredo go into extensive philosophical, sociological and psychological details as to why and how 'dimensions of otherness [...] never occupy the field of human experience'.[24] Here is the key conclusion of the essay:

> ... traumatic intersubjectivity is indispensable for the emergence of a subjective singularity from the primordial trans-subjective soil. Thus it is that in Heidegger, as in Merleau-Ponty, there is a reference to the absolutely other in me, to an 'outside the world' and 'outside the being', without which nothing could be experienced beyond oneself. It is in Levinas, however, that this 'otherwise than being' takes shape as radical otherness. On the other hand, the mere externalness of the other would never result in subjectivization unless in this other there were also found a welcome and a living-space, and unless something of this previous experience of inclusion were not constantly operating in every encounter, whether marked by traumatism or by complementarity.[25]

The latter part of the passage, beginning with 'On the other hand', is completely wishful-thinking liberal and Christian charity, and it has nothing to do with the authors' precise and damning conclusion that in the constitution of the (European) subject – all these philosophers they examine are European and white American – this absolute otherness is 'indispensable for the emergence of a subjective singularity from the primordial trans-subjective soil'. The rest of us, the wretched of the earth to Europeans, are condemned and exiled to the abode of 'the absolutely other in' them, we are 'outside the world', 'outside the being' – in fact, we are 'otherwise than being'. We do not exist, we cannot exist, for our very existence is philosophically inhibited, prohibited, made impossible in their philosophies. This is what the brilliant essay of Sunera Thobani on Butler reveals.

From Goffman's nervous tic, 'in our Western society', to Butler's Islamophobia when she is caught red-handed by Thobani, and from there to the entire philosophical and theoretical pedigree they both represent and where non-Europeans cannot think, we have the decisive framing of a form of subjectivity that must by necessity posit itself against its non-Europe.[26] To see how that works not so paradoxically we need to go to two other European philosophers, Heidegger and Agamben, and consider how they see *Enframing* (*Gestell*) as the very machinery (apparatus) of knowledge production – before we reframe them all in Abbas Kiarostami's simple assertion that nothing makes sense outside a frame. In 'Question Concerning Technology' (1954), Heidegger had suggested considering the very essence of technology as Enframing/*Gestell* – not as a means to an end but as a mode of existence. 'Technology is therefore no mere means. Technology is a way of revealing. If we give heed to this, then another whole realm for the essence of technology will open itself up to us. It is the realm of revealing, i. e., of truth'.[27] From this premise Heidegger then concludes: 'We now name that challenging claim which gathers man thither to order the self-revealing as standing-reserve: Ge-stell [Enframing]'.[28] Following this position and that of Foucault's articulation of 'apparatus', Agamben in his *What is an Apparatus* (2006) proposes:

> What is common to all these terms [Hegel's positivity, Heidegger's *Gestell*, Foucault's Apparatus] is that they refer back to this Oikonomia, that is to a set of practices, bodies of knowledge, measures, and institutions that aim to manage, govern, control, and orient – in a way that purports to be useful – the behaviors, gestures, and thoughts of human beings.[29]

In a short essay on cinema, 'For an Ethics of Cinema', Agamben considers cinema an apparatus or *Gestell* since films capture and record the gestures of human beings.[30] The Enframing therefore is where 'a set of practices, bodies of knowledge, measures, and institutions that aim to manage, govern, control, and orient – in a way that purports to be useful – the behaviors, gestures, and thoughts of human beings'. Enframing therefore becomes the condition of constituting the subject, the omnipotent, omniscient, omnipresent European subject.

Let us now turn to Kiarostami from whom we learn how Enframing is in fact far more central to formation of subjectivity than repetition and performativity – an enframing that leads us to the world of pure verisimilitude, the *Alam-e Mithal*. As Kiarostami puts it:

> I've often noticed that we are not able to look at what we have in front of us, unless it's inside a frame. So I took my car windscreen as a frame, and I turned off the windscreen wipers so as not to wipe off the rain – I wanted the raindrops to remain on the glass. Everything we can see in the photographs – the yellow-brown, the green, the black – we owe to the light. It's the reflection of the light on the raindrops that gives the pictures these subtleties and nuances.[31]

This Enframing (without which we are blinded to what we see) therefore becomes that proverbial Fourth Wall through which we exit the scene and enter and access the world of pure verisimilitude, and where we begin to see the visions of the otherwise invisible, and where now all life begins to make sense, and that who begins thus to see and make sense of the world becomes an unknowing subject.

The Liberating World of Pure Verisimilitudes

Kiarostami returned to this world of pure verisimilitude in his very last masterpiece *24 Frames* (2017), released soon after his passing in July 2016 and featured in the 70th Anniversary Events section at the 2017 Cannes Film Festival. On the premise of this world of pure verisimilitude evident in the entirety of this masterpiece, we face the active suspending of any and all truth-claims and all their metaphysics of authenticity, where representation becomes all that is and all that matters, liberating all evident phenomena from any pretence to foundational truth or all its beguiling variations. What is evident in Kiarostami's *24 Frames* in particular is the way he minds the manners and frames the form so emphatically and unapologetically that the visible bodies – trees, roads, snow, animals, trees – no longer matter in and out of themselves, but the communion of their corporeal bodies and the aesthetic congregation they occasion and form do. Take the frames of these visual events off, and there is nothing to watch – everything melts into oblivion. Put the frames back, and a whole commotion of agitated worlds is visibly at work. The frame turns the invisible not just visible but eventful.

Now recall how in *Bodies That Matter: On the Discursive Limits of 'Sex'* (1993) Judith Butler takes performativity as the volatile framing of the enactment of sex and gender – performativity as iterability as citationality as habitual and regulated repetitions of the normative. This iterability is the *conditio sine qua non* of the subject who becomes a knowing and knowable subject through his engendering the normative as heteronormative. Subjection therefore is made possible only through gendering – a paradoxical proposition that both suppresses and enables at one and the same time. This is how she puts it:

> This repetition is not performed by a subject; this repetition is what enables a subject and constitutes the temporal condition for the subject. This iterability implies that 'performance' is not a singular 'act' or event, but a ritualized production, a ritual reiterated under and through constraint, under and through the force of prohibition and taboo, with the threat of ostracism and even death controlling and compelling the shape of the production, but not, I will insist, determining it fully in advance.[32]

Compared to the bodies that Butler marks as those that matter, these acts of pure verisimilitude evident in the way Kiarostami stages them in *24 Frames* mark the bodies that do not matter, for they are visually absolved into the ideas that carry them from their cradle to their graves – for as Rumi says in his *Masnavi* – and the echoes at the back of Kiarostami's visual mind:

> *Ay Baradar to hameh andisheh'i ...*
>
> Oh, brother you're all pure thoughts –
> The rest of you just bone and cartilage –
> If your thoughts are made of flowers then you're a flowerbed,
> If they're made of thorns then you're fuel for fire,
> If you're made of rose water they sprinkle you on their sleeves
> And if you're made of excrement they then eject you![33]

The immaterial (*Hurqalya'i*) body is not subject to generation, growth and decay, for it is 'the spiritual body upon a celestial earth', as Henry Corbin would summarise the core of a sustained philosophical course of Islamic thinking in his famous treatise *Spiritual Body and Celestial Earth* (1960). Rooted in the material, the immaterial body is visible only in the mirror of pure verisimilitude, the visual and performing arts at work within the three walls of stage and translucent through the Fourth Wall. These are the bodies that do not matter, meaning they do not coagulate in one gender or another. They flow from one to another and back. In my *Corpus Anarchicum* (2012), I have mapped out a posthuman body that is no longer subject to generation, growth and decay.[34] Here, however, I am making a similar argument through the visual articulation of the cine-aesthetic of the immaterial body.

Since subjection is contingent on gendering on the European (colonial) gendered model, then the precolonial dynamics of gendering become troublesome to the project. There are serious scholarly discussions that the figure of the beloved in Persian poetry is actually an expression of homosexuality.[35] There are two major flaws in this argument. First, by homosexuality they mean only men and boys' homoeroticism, not women and girls' homoeroticism, and second, they disregard the overwhelming evidence that, because in Persian we do not have gender-specific pronouns, these references, even when today they may appear as referencing young boys, are entirely ambivalent and undecidable – it could be men and boys' homoeroticism, and it could mean women and girls' homoeroticism, and there is nothing there that precludes heteronormative sexuality either. There is a bourgeois morality that informs and titillates this literature, and the prose of its scholarship is in the mode of scandal – lo and behold, we have homoeroticism in the form of *shahed-bazi*/pederasty. This seriously compromises this body of otherwise learned literature in which we have much evidence of male-to-male homoerotism, which is a truism; then, they jump the gun that the figure of the beloved in Persian is entirely male, which is categorically flawed, as it could be male to male, female to female (which they completely disregard), or potentially male to female or female to male. The point being the fluidity of the sex and gender formation here opens up the articulation of subjectivity to unforeseen and unlegislated dimensions.

This leads us to the prospect of a reading of the emblematic designations of Men, Women, etcetera by way of en/framing the differences. If we now look back at Juliette Binoche's picture, we see how it stages the breaking of the Fourth Wall as she looks at and through the camera that is there to look at her. This breaking of the Fourth Wall brings Truth and Verisimilitude deeply into each other. Looking at a fictive mirror by way of looking at and through the camera is a far more effective, powerful and subversive way of breaking the Fourth Wall than looking at the audience and addressing them, or else looking at the camera and speaking to the audience, as we see in Beiza'i's *Mosaferin/Travelers*. The second effective way is when the camera catches you looking at something else, something we cannot see, something we are barred from seeing, something the selfsame camera has barred us from seeing, something we cannot see what it is but we can hear what it is, as we do in Kiarostami's *Shirin*, a pre-cinematic moment we must now share with postmodern cinema, that moves to instrumentalise the self-consciousness of camera itself. The third comes when we see in person the performance similar to what the filmed persons were looking at, as in Kiarostami's *Ta'ziyeh* performance, which turns the spectators to spectacles themselves. One can even imagine Kiarostami filming his audience in Palermo or anywhere else watching Iranians watching *Ta'ziyeh* as they try to watch the *Ta'ziyeh*, too.

This is another threesome convulsion of spectatorship, just like the Koker trilogy. This successive interpolation of spectatorship draws the visible and the visitor into a specular triumvirate that leads straight to the domain of pure verisimilitude.

We therefore have multiple ways of en/framing the spectacle and the spectator, the seer and the seen, which puts a new spin on the famous Latin motto *Quis custodiet ipsos custodes*/Who watches the watcher? Among the intention of the author/*intentio auctoris*, the intention of the reader/*intentio lectoris* and the intension of the text/*intentio operis* (to use Umberto Eco's hermeneutic theory), here we have entered a common ground.[36] Kiarostami has done the same thing in his Koker trilogy, too, when in a single shot he brings the three films together – with all the three directors, himself and the two actors who play him as directors are caught in on circular shot, and thus their three films have also thematically come together. The trilogy as a result emerges as a collated triumvirate – first filming *Where is the Friends House* (1987), then looking for the actors of that film in *Life and nothing Else* (1992) and, finally, in a film about the filming of the second when a love story emerges in *Through the Olive Trees* (1994). The trilogy thus becomes a virtuoso performance and a master class in staging pure verisimilitude. What is happening here is reality uplifting itself as truth before sublating into pure verisimilitude. Verisimilitude here is no longer verisimilar to truth, it has absolved truth of that formal pretence and responsibility. This is where Brecht, Shklovsky and Butler are all invited to sit in the front row of a master class of Kiarostami, to lead them into the uncharted territories where we are no longer watching film, fiction, or poetry, but where we are as we are the subject of their specular observations. We have been drawn into the play, into the hyperspace of being-there. Next to Abbas Kiarostami, Butler here becomes a veritable metaphysician, limited in their philosophical imagination as to what is possible as she just turns the binary into multiple, floating, non-binary possibilities, like a juggler throwing not two but five, six, or ten balls into the air and creating the illusion of freedom from gravity. She, in fact, exacerbates and reaffirms what postmodern European philosophers habitually call and seek to dismantle as 'Western metaphysics'.

Structural freedom on the colonial edges of European modernity is when truth and all its verisimilitudes trade places and when we no longer know which is which, and this is made possible by playfully reframing the un/knowing subject on the premise of a radically different domain of knowing and being. I first articulated this prospect in my book *Truth and Narrative* (1990) almost a quarter of a century ago – when I read the monumental work of the Persian philosopher-mystic Ayn al-Qudat al-Hamadhani in a decidedly counterintuitive way. Now in this book I wish to expand that argument into a longer frame of more contemporary references in film, fiction, poetry, politics and philosophical treatises embracing the visual and performing arts. The sorts of Euro-universalism in which philosophers like Butler are trapped has a false sense of unframed universalism, and as such it has lost touch with any enabling archive outside their imagination – an archive they dismiss as 'anthropological' because they are ignorant of its philosophical disposition and because that ignorance frightens their theoretical confidence. Such nervous reactions feed into its own provincialising abstractions for it has no world to which it can belong and theorise its worldliness. By exercising my own theoretical reflexes within a specific frame of archival evidence, I wish to unearth, unchain and unbound the worldliness of a world hitherto anthropologised and Orientalised and thus dismissed by way of falsely universalising a self-forgetful archive that has ceased to articulate its own particular worldliness. My turn to the iconic references of Women, Men, Etcetera, and my reframing of their differences frames the formations of selves and their societies in terms irreducible to outdated Euro-universalism.

Self-consciously enframing, as Kiarostami does in his artworld, formally destructs the false solidity of the Fourth Wall, enables access to the mirroring world of pure verisimilitude where immaterial bodies are liberated to a renewed re-subjection as decolonised, nomadic subjects – unknowing to themselves, unbeknownst to the world – cast upon a newly realisable world.

Mashya and Mashyana Unearthed

My texting with the Iranian friend on WhatsApp had remained at the back of my mind while I began thinking through the formation of the world of pure verisimilitude as the literary conduit in the constitution of selves and society in an assemblage of Iranian film, fiction and poetry. In the midst of all these contemporary materials that had now begun drawing my attention to their layered significance, the archetypal figures of Man and Woman that had started emerging through these reflections led me back to the sacred and mythic sources that had inaugurated them all in the figures of Adam and Eve in the Qur'an or the Bible, and from there to the even more ancient archetypes of Mashya and Mashyana in Persian mythologies. What is a Man, what is a Woman, what do they mean, how do they signify, where do they meet and mingle, and how could their sex and gender have been fixated one way or another? Here I began to realise that throughout these reflections I was in search of how the iconic figures of Man and Woman (forcefully fixated) were being reconceived in Iranian film, fiction and poetry – almost unbeknownst to themselves. Much older and far more deeply rooted than the Qur'an, or even the Bible, according to the Zoroastrian myth of creation as described in the *Bundahishn*, as Ahura Mazda's sixth creation stood Kayumars who was neither male nor female. The Evil Spirit or Ahriman (Angra Mainyu) dwelt in the Absolute Darkness, seeking to destroy all that Ahura Mazda had created. It sent the demoness Jeh to kill Kayumars. Upon its death, the moon captured his seed. From Kayumars' corpse grew a tree, the seeds of which were the origin of all plant life, and from the branches of which grew Mashya and Mashyana. How did that myth of origin survive, thrive, transmutated, sublated, and finally reach us in concealed and enabling terms?

In Iranian mythology, Kayumars is considered 'the sixth of the heptad in Mazdaian myth of creation, the protoplast of man, and the first king in Iranian mythical history'.[37] In the surviving Zoroastrian tradition, he is 'a primordial giant, the first man from whom mankind descends. In the Avesta, Gayōmard is shown to be the beginning of this world, just as Sōšāns represents the end, and he is often accompanied by the sole-created Ox'. From Kayumars then emerges Mashya and Mashyana – but the epic rise of the two archetypes is first predicated on a traumatic event:

> In the end, in accordance with the aspect of his horoscope [...] Gayōmart succumbed to his injuries and passed away, while his sperm was in two parts purified by the rays of the sun and entrusted for safe-keeping to the deity Nēryōsang and in one part fell upon the earth and was received by Spandārmad, his creator and mother. His seed remained for forty years in the earth, out of which slowly grew the rhubarb plant, the stem of which developed into the first human couple, Mašīa and Mašīānag, the progenitors of all human races, the ten species of mankind *that* inhabit the Xwanīrah, the central continent of the earth.[38]

I read and think through these two intertwined mythic figures of Mashya and Mashyana the way dramatists from Aeschylus (ca 524–455 BC) to Shelly (1792–1822) have read the myth of Prometheus. Percy Bysshe Shelley's *Prometheus Unbound* (1820) is a lyrical drama that recasts the Greek mythological figure of Prometheus in a radically romanticised light, while in classical antiquity in Aeschylus' *Prometheia*, or *Prometheus Bound*, the full ironic tragedy of the mythic is far more lucidly evident. I use the term 'unearthed' rather than 'un/bound' plays. Prometheus was bound to a rock, where each day an eagle came to eat his liver, which would then grow back overnight to be eaten again the next day. This was a punishment for Prometheus having stolen fire to give it to humanity. But in the case of Mashya and Mashyana they were bound together as two vegetables and later animals, held together at their hips and groins, but separated for the divine purpose of copulation. Initially they were sexless and desireless, but eventually they desired each other and became fruitful. They loved their first children so much that they did not know what to do with them, so they ate them. But then their love for their children was eventually tempered, and they began to raise them and care for them. I also find it quite serendipitous that in the most recent scholarship offered by Scott D. de Hart in his *Shelley Unbound: Discovering Frankenstein's True Creator* (2013) we learn that the authorship of an iconic text is actually by a couple rather than one or the other of them.

To sum up before we begin our journey: the central ideas of *verisimilitude, estrangements, metonymic gestations, unknowing subject* and *framing* are central to my turn to and through an interface between aspects of Iranian visual and performing arts that critically question the received notions of aesthetic mimesis. Here, my argument is ultimately rooted in the ancient Iranian myth of origin, beginning with the creation of Kayumars (whose name means 'Mortal Life') from whose semen a plant of rhubarb is believed to have grown, which in turn becomes the origin of Mashya and Mashyana, the first proto-human couple who father and mother our humanity. Kayumars was created by Ahura Mazda and lived alone in the mountains for thirty years, and upon his death his semen was ejaculated from his body and purified by the sun for forty years – it is from that semen that the rhubarb plant eventually emerges, as the fauna and flora of living organisms coalesce. There is no idea of any original sin in this creation myth – nor indeed the gendered opposition between Adam and Eve. This inaugural moment of the birth of humanity remains definitive to the rest of my book. The point of this introductory chapter is to map out in some detail the intermediary function of metonymic tropes in the visual and performing arts, facilitating the mnemonic interface between hidden ancient myths and manifest modern arts that effectively recast this myth of origin in effervescent gestations. These works of art that I plan to examine closely throughout this book will function as the purgatorial conduits between the mythic foregrounding of deeply distanced cultures and their metonymic resurrections and recasting towards a renewed intuition of aesthetic transcendence. This creative dialectic between ancient myths and modern metonyms becomes the aesthetic domain where the postcolonial philosophy of the unknowing subject will be placed and posited. That entire mythic history of the material transubstantiation of consciousness comes together in this seminal poem of Forough Farrokhzad, 'Another Birth' (1962):

Hameh-ye Hasti-ye Man ...

My entire existence is a dark verse
That repeating you in itself
Carries you to the morning moment
Of all the everlasting blossoming and growing –
In this verse I have sighed you,
O have I sighed you!
In this verse I have rooted you
In tree, water, and fire ...
I plant my hands in the garden
I'll blossom I know –
O I know I know I know:
And sparrows will nest in the grooves in between my fingers.[39]

PART I

MEN AND WOMEN

1

Men without Women

Amma hamisheh dar havashi-ye meydan-ha ...

But always in the vicinity of city squares
You could spot these little criminals
Standing idly by and staring
At the overflowing of the fountains –
Perhaps still
Behind the crumpled eyes and in the depth of coldness
Something half alive but confused had remained intact ...[1]

Forough Farrokhzad, '*Ayeh-ha-y Zamini*/Earthly Verses' (1962)

In 1963, Ali Akbar Akbari published a major sociological examination of the phenomenon of lumpenism in Iran. In this pioneering study, Akbari extensively discussed the social, political and cultural dimensions of this rampant phenomenon.[2] In 1964, he added a special section to this study in which he examined the prevalence of lumpenism in Iranian cinema. As the concept is used at this time and by this critical assessment, 'lumpenism' had entered Iranian critical vocabulary through the specifically Marxist concept of '*Lumpenproletariat*', referring to what Marx and Engels considered the underclass that was devoid of any class consciousness and therefore subject to exploitation by reactionary forces. Akbari's attention to this social phenomenon is a pioneering examination of a problem that has far-reaching but twisted roots in Iranian patriarchy. Although the economic roots of this social malaise are immediately evident in the class formations of the more recent colonial and postcolonial developments in the Iranian petite-bourgeoisie, its cultural origins go far deeper into the specifics of Iranian patrimonialism. Although Akbari does not develop his examination of the Iranian cinema in this respect far enough to investigate the ideological implications of a culture of lumpenism, we can clearly see through his study the significance of a popular art form in facilitating the legitimacy and endurance of a particularly pathological aspect of the ruling sentiments of colonially calibrated patriarchy.

As an art form, cinema establishes what Mas'ud Zavvarzadeh has called an 'imaginary relation between the spectator (the subject) and the world'.[3] Cinema is therefore one of the most crucial mechanisms of constituting the spectator as a knowing subject, placing them in a universe of signification called culture. Through the active constitution of such 'imaginary relations' between the subject and the world, Zavvarzadeh adds, 'the discourses of ideology turn the opacity of the world into a luminous intelligibility that not only makes sense of the reality "out there" but also, and more important, creates meaning for the film's viewer, who becomes in this process a knowing subject'.[4] The transmutation of the opacity of the world, even its being called 'the world', into parameters of a 'luminous intelligibility', however, does not take place *ex nihilo*, or solely in and through cinema. There is an active correspondence between the dominant and received parameters of a culture and the modes of intelligibilities that the discourses of ideology entail, generate and sustain. These discourses are in effect at the service of that particular juncture where the self-perpetuating forces of the operative culture and the economic necessity of the discourses of ideology meet. Iranian lumpenism, as it is evident through Akbari's study, is a clear example of this concurrence.

Akbari's principal proposition in this book is that, in the absence of a strong and self-consciously progressive bourgeoisie, and equally in the absence of a strong and self-consciously revolutionary working class, the size and social significance of the Iranian petite-bourgeoisie have been extraordinarily vital in modern social history. Akbari attributes an altogether counter-revolutionary weight to this class.[5] The peculiar socio-economic characteristic of Iranian lumpenism, Akbari argues, is its precarious attachments to the lowest strata of the working class. This proposition is particularly plausible in view of the fact that, because of its retarded capitalist developments as well as its domination by colonial forces, Iran has never had a full-fledged and self-consciously revolutionary working class to which the lumpenproletariat can be linked. The Iranian version of lumpenism, however we may choose to hypothesise and hyphenate them, is economically most unproductive while culturally reactionary and regressive. As much as economically they represent the direst consequences of a jaundiced national bourgeoisie and a debilitating colonial condition, culturally they constitute the most retrograde traits of Iranian patrimonialism. Even under the conditions of a thriving bourgeoisie and a revolutionary working class in the Europe of Marx's time, he called them in *The Communist Manifesto* 'the "dangerous class", the social scum, that passively rotting mass thrown off by the lowest layers of old society, may, here and there, be swept into the movement by a proletarian revolution; its conditions of life, however, prepare it far more for the part of a bribed tool of reactionary intrigue'.[6] How it is that lumpens are more prone to revolutionary assimilation or more drawn to reactionary intrigue will take us to the relation of Iranian intellectuals in general and Iranian filmmakers in particular to this underclass.

Lumpens, Intellectuals, Clerics

One of the most insightful observations of Akbari about the nature and function of Iranian lumpenism is their relationship with other social classes and groupings, and with the intellectuals in particular. The artists and the literati, the law-enforcement officers and the administrative apparatus of the state bureaucracy are in constant contact with the lumpens. The speech pattern and mannerism of the lumpens have thus entered the cultural repertoire of the intellectuals. Inorganic and drawn from various segments of the bourgeoisie, the Iranian intellectuals have confused their false identification with a non-existent revolutionary working class with adopting the mannerism of the lumpens. 'These kinds of intellectuals', as Akbari puts it, 'who are inadvertently drawn to the life and characteristics of the lumpens think they have come close to the living condition of the working class'.[7] Akbari's condemnation of the intellectuals is in very strong terms:

> By far the most ludicrous aspect of these intellectuals is their ridiculous imitation of the lumpens' speech pattern. On every occasion, in utter stupidity and ignorance, they try to talk like them. In addition, because the majority of the athletes, especially the wrestlers, come from the lower classes of the society and have grown up in petite-bourgeois and lumpen environments, they share the principal characteristics of lumpenism. Certain segments of intellectuals who are attracted to sports and to athletes are under the impression that they have come close to the working class.[8]

Akbari is equally insightful about the proclivity of the lumpens towards religion, particularly towards the popular aspects of Sufism. But the word 'popular' here is not accurate enough. What we observe about the Iranian lumpens of the 'Jahel' type in particular is a constitutionally corrupt form of the medieval conceptions of 'manliness', as evident in the phenomenon of *ayyari*, *javanmardi*, or *futuwwah*,[9] all of them meaning 'chivalry', with their roots in practical Sufism.[10] In this corrupted contemporary form, all the noble qualities of *futuwwah* seem to have disappeared, and the ideal has become a kind of brutish machismo that only remotely resembles its classical counterpart. Be that as it may, the lumpen degeneration of *futuwwah* does share certain character traits with its classical antecedents. These character traits have to do with genuine asceticism (which the lumpens feign), respect and dignified treatment of others (which the lumpens express in the form of exaggerated and fake humility). The female members of a friend of a lumpen's family are instantly treated as 'mothers and sisters', in order to proclaim in public that they have no sexual intentions towards them, whereas the same female members of a foe's family are treated as whores and prostitutes, and as such become the targets of verbal sexual abuse, in order to humiliate in public their male relations. Misogynistic tendencies of the most pathological forms are constitutional to the lumpen state of mind and socio-pathological behaviour.

The structural link between lumpens, intellectuals and the Shi'i clergy remains a crucial factor in the unfolding history of Iran between the Constitutional Revolution of 1906–11 and the Islamic Revolution of 1977–79. That link, however, has deeper roots that help us understand its paradoxical fruits.

Searching for Deeper Roots

Despite his insights into the contemporary social functions of lumpenism, Akbari falls quite short of the fuller dimensions of his own observations. The athletic ethics that Akbari identifies principally among the wrestlers is also the historically modulated version of the classical Iranian practice of *ayyari*, or *javanmardi*, which ostensibly celebrates a form of chivalry but in effect embodies the full dimensions of a masculinist culture and a thinly disguised homoerotic proclivity. Power of the most brutish sort is at the root of this ethics. Today, curses that are constitutional to this ethics without any exception have to do with the raping of the female members of the person's family. The word '*gheyrat*' is particularly important here. *Gheyrat*, literally meaning 'honour', is something that only 'real men' have, but paradoxically its location is in the sexual organs of their female relatives. If someone as much as looks at their mother or sisters or, *horribile dictu*, wife, that 'honour' is instantly jeopardised, and the man is accused of not having *gheyrat*. *Gheyrat* and *mardanegi* ('manhood') are interchangeably used to designate the highest and most praised characteristics in a man. The *locus classicus* of the man's honour is in the sexual organs of his female relatives, to the possession of which he is either born or else entitled by having married/purchased it. The idea and social function of *gheyrat* reveals as much about the misogynistic culture of masculinist domination as it paradoxically reveals about the homoerotic space of manliness that entails it.

Both *gheyrat* and *mardanegi*, as the defining traits of masculinist manhood, point to the origin of these attributes in the ancient practice of *ayyari*. By far the most famous literary example of the practice of *ayyari* is the book of *Samak Ayyar* by Faramarz ibn Khodadad ibn Abdullah al-Kateb al-Arjani, with no certain date of composition, but certainly after the thirteenth century.[11] The origin of the story is pre-Islamic, and prior to and after its textual rendition, it has been a widely known folk-tale with extensive popular reception.[12] *Samak Ayyar* is the story of the hero Samak who is the son of the king of Aleppo and an Iraqi princess. Samak falls in love with the daughter of the Chinese emperor, and his adventures thereafter lead him all the way to what today we might consider to be Japan (Machin = the land beyond China). *Samak Ayyar* is the oldest and most significant textual evidence we have of the practice of *ayyari*, or chivalry, in popular Persian literature. Tracing the origin of *ayyari* all the way back to the thirteenth century textually, we can see the even older roots of the practice in more ancient times. Parviz Natel Khanlari, who has conducted an extensive study of the history of *ayyari*, believes that the origin of this particular mode of chivalry goes back to pre-Islamic periods. Both *ayyari* and its synonym *javanmardi* point to a manly practice of chivalry in which the specifics of the masculine virtues are celebrated. *Ayyari* seems to have been a specific cultic practice, in which men participated and in which the virtues of masculine chivalry were actively ritualised and cherished.[13] The homosociality of the literary and social space that the idea and practice occupy at once conceals and yet implicates its homoerotic disposition.

The cultic character of *ayyari* was closely linked to the institution of Sufism, and the two webs of affiliation intensified each other's patriarchal and homoerotic nature and disposition. It is from the depth of this ancient tradition of Iranian chivalry, constituted by generations of presuppositions predicated one on the other, that all positive human attributes have been considered to be *manly*. It is *manly* to tell the truth, to keep a friend's secret, to be generous, to come to the help of the needy, or to be devoted to a noble cause. If women ever do partake in these qualities, they do so by being 'men-like', and thus they achieve the status of being called '*javan-mard*' ('heroic-man').[14] In turn, the misogynistic traits of *ayyari* have a variety of manifestations. Here, we need to pay particular attention to words that designate 'chastity', 'honour' and 'dignity'. '*Effat*' is one of these words. '*Effat*' literally means 'chastity'. But it has a range of connotations far beyond that. '*Effat*' also means mastery over one's carnal soul. The world, women of the world, in particular, are full of temptations. The true man is he who can resist such temptations.[15] For Samak, as the prototype of all Persian literary and cultural heroes, women are the singular source of salacious temptation – as perhaps best exemplified in the case of Sudabeh in the *Shahnameh* when she tries to seduce the chaste Seyavash, her stepson. The heroes demonstrate their chivalrous and manly characters by either resisting the temptation of having sex with them, or else adopting them as their 'sisters'.[16] There were ritualistic ceremonies of adopting women as their 'sister' among the *ayyars*. Through this ritual, the sexual temptations suspected in women are thus presumably neutralised. Moreover, the women are rendered '*mahram*', or ritually 'close' and thus sexually 'closed' and 'forbidden' to the hero. To have a sexual attraction to a woman without being properly wedded to her is to be a '*na-javan-mard*' (literally = 'not-heroic-man'), or even a '*haram-zadeh*' (a 'bastard' – having been born out of wedlock). To look at a woman with sexual intention is to have a '*chashm-e khata*' (a 'mischievous eye'). The Iranian heroic models believe that 'God holds me dearly because I have never done anything that would appease Satan, nor will I ever do an improper act'.[17] The result of such active demonisation of women as all the source of evil in part is the metaphoric representation of feminine beauty in the aesthetic culture of Persian literary chivalry in a range of misogynistic traits. These metaphors are either *militaristic* – the hair is like a lasso, the eyebrow is like a bow, the eye-lashes are like sharp arrows, the nose is like a dagger – or *edible* – the breasts are like a pair of pomegranates, the belly as if having been massaged with almond oil – or else *monetary* – the mouth is like a precious coin, the face is as white as silver, the breast is like a plate of silver, the feet are like ivory. Militaristic, monetary and edible, the metaphorics of femininity posit women as something to be purchased, devoured, or defeated.

The patriarchal constitution and privileging of 'the masculine' as true and right simultaneously constitutes and second-sexes 'the feminine' in entirely negative terms – while at the same time revealing the thinly disguised homoeroticism of that masculine space. The feminist critic of the patriarchally constituted masculinity has long since noted this historical formation of 'the manliness'. In her essay on 'Imperialism and Sexual Difference', Gayatri Chakravorty Spivak, taking her cue from Paul de Man, argues that 'the basis of a truth-claim is no more than a trope',[18] suggesting that 'to take the privileged male of the white race as a norm for universal humanity is no more than a politically interested figuration. It is a trope that passes itself off as truth and claims that women or the racial other is merely a kind of troping of that truth of man – in the sense that both must be understood *as* unlike (non-identical with) it and yet *with* reference to it'.[19] The constitution and second-sexing of 'the feminine' is, as we see in the case of medieval Persian notions of chivalry, quintessential to the theoretical unwrittenness of the patriarchal order. In the Iranian patriarchal order, in particular, the heroic deeds of masculine characters have in effect written the patrimonial anxiety into the very letter of history. In reading that masculine history, the persistent dismantling of the father-figure may prevent the 'blindness' against which Spivak warns. Playing on the title of Paul de Man's essay 'Blindness and Insight', Spivak suggests that 'the price of the insight into the tropological nature of a truth-claim is the blindness of truth-telling'.[20] The active re-subjection of 'the feminine' and the corollary detailing of the homoerotic foregrounding of 'the masculine' therefore needs to be conscious of that tropological trap. 'As we feminist critics discover the troping error of the masculinist truth-claim to universality or academic objectivity', Spivak warns, 'we perform the lie of constituting a truth of global sisterhood ...'[21] The warning is crucial to point to 'our performance of certain imperialist ideological structures even as we deconstruct the tropological error of masculism'.[22] Spivak's apt and timely warning is doubly true when we work on the premise of the colonial citations of such tropologies – where the constitution of the gender partitions is a decidedly colonial construct in the best interests of capitalist modernity.

From Lumpenism to Fascism

The tropological error of masculism, however, is the truth-claim of all historical narratives hitherto written in patriarchal terms. Contemporary lumpenism, with its distorted cultural roots in the ancient Persian practices of chivalry, underlines a whole set of parameters at the political basis of persistent populist and proto-fascist traits in modern Iranian history. In his examination of the relation between lumpenism and fascism, Akbari anticipated in the early 1970s what was to come in the early 1980s when the official and unofficial organs of the Islamic Republic actively began to recruit members of the lumpens as *Ansar-e Hezbollah*, or 'The Companions of the Party of God' (a Qur'anic phrase), as a paramilitary force to crush every form of political protest. Ayatollah Khomeini was a master practitioner in speaking the language of these lumpens and exciting their basest sentiments, their *gheyrat*, in particular, to crush political dissent against his regime. A campaign of terror and intimidation was launched against all forms of political protest. The champion of these lumpens in the early years of the Islamic Revolution in Tehran was, paradoxically, a woman, a certain 'Zahra Khanom', who led bands of hooligans against any kind of political gathering that the ideologues of the Islamic Republic deemed counter-revolutionary – but who were, in fact, revolutionaries of a different sort. Some of Akbari's observations about the reasons for the attraction of the lumpens to proto-fascistic practices are prophetic for having been made about two decades before their precise realisation by the organised strike forces that in the aftermath of the Islamic Revolution terrorised political activists and innocent citizens alike:

> By accepting the lumpens and giving them dangerous and adventurous tasks to perform, fascistic parties and reactionary forces generate a sense of pride and character in them. Whereas they were totally disregarded and looked down at by other classes and progressive forces, the lumpens begin to interfere directly in adventurous political activities and thus feel a sense of pride and power.[23]

To be sure, by the time Akbari was writing these words in the 1960s, the experience of the US- and UK-led coup of 1953 to bring the runaway monarch back to power was of course paramount on his mind. In this case, the mobilisation of the lumpens led by a prominent thug known as Sha'ban the Brainless was instrumental in bringing the Shah back to power. What remains common between the coup of 1953 and the revolution of 1979 was the active mobilisation of this substrata of the rootless lumpens at the service of one sort of fascism or another. The ruling intellectuals at the service of the Pahlavi regime and the clerical cadre ruling the Islamic republic that succeeded it were identical in their appeals to the masculinist proclivities of this underclass.

Inorganic Intellectuals

The identification of Iranian intellectuals (as a *bona fide* category) with the lumpens and lumpenism, as Akbari best describes it, points to a peculiar kinds of patriarchal hegemony which needs to be noted carefully.[24] The inorganic nature of the Iranian intellectuals, the fact that they come from diverse social strata and lack any organic link to either a progressive national bourgeoisie or a revolutionary working class, has made them particularly susceptible to whimsical identification with what they consider to be the working class, and they are, in fact, the worst elements among the lumpens. The patriarchal traits constitutional to these lumpens who are precariously linked to the lowest strata of the petite-bourgeoisie thus find a particularly powerful medium of expression among the intellectuals. The inorganic Iranian intellectuals as a result (consciously or otherwise) become the spokesmen for the most reactionary forces operative among the lumpenist elements of the petite-bourgeoisie. The patriarchal forces operative among the basest forces of the petite-bourgeoisie thus tend to perpetuate their enduring presence in Iranian culture through the artistic medium at the disposal of Iranian inorganic intellectuals. Inorganic intellectuals and rootless lumpens thus in effect share a common sociological formation – one in practice, the other in sympathy. The cinema of lumpenism, or '*Film Jaheli*', as it is called, has been by far the most consistent medium of this continuity through a much-celebrated cinematic lumpenism.

Gramsci believed that one of the principal functions of the intellectuals was to link organically and thus resolve the constitutional differences between what he called the *alta cultura*, or the culture of the high bourgeoisie, and the *cultura popolare*, or the culture of the subaltern classes. But like most other observations of Gramsci, they are specifically applicable to advanced capitalist economies – and as such require critical adjustments on the more naked colonial sites.[25] In the Iranian case, as indeed in the case of much of the colonised world, the absence of an advanced and progressive bourgeoisie has meant a total absence of what Gramsci calls *alta cultura*, except in literary abstractions and erudite traditions. The inorganic Iranian intellectuals, as a result, could never speak, or organise the culture, as Gramsci would put it, for any *alta cultura*, or facilitate its hegemonic links to the Iranian *cultura popolare*. What has happened instead is a group of inorganic intellectuals giving voice and legitimacy to the basest aspects of *cultura popolare*, the lumpenist traits of it, to be more specific, thinking that they are speaking for the aspirations of the working class. But the catastrophic irony of this phenomenon has been that the lumpenist traits with which the Iranian intellectuals have actively identified are precisely those patriarchal forces that have sustained both the Persian monarchy and Shi'i clericalism alike. The most enduring traits of patrimonialism were thus sustained by the basest strata of the petite-bourgeoisie and, through the identification of the intellectuals with them, re-narrated into a hegemonic force that sustained the most enduring forces of anti-modernity (in a total absence of a legitimate critique of colonial modernity). The affirmation and articulation of the patrimonial traits operative in both Persian monarchy and Shi'i clericalism by the ostensibly alienated intellectuals were the most paradoxical aspect of their false but effective identification with the lumpens.

The inorganic nature of Iranian intellectuals is constitutional to their inadvertently sub-serving the proto-fascistic tendencies in Iranian patrimonialism – monarchic or clerical. The practice, in fact, may lead to a reconsideration of what even Gramsci himself called 'traditional' intellectuals,[26] which is in fact the indication of precisely classical bourgeois proclivities to universalise its own particulars. 'Since these various categories of traditional intellectuals', Gramsci noted, 'experience through an "*esprit de corps*" their uninterrupted historical continuity and their special qualification, they thus put themselves forward as autonomous and independent of the dominant social group'.[27] But whether from the bourgeois or working class, the organic intellectuals represent in theoretical and cultural terms the material presence of their function within a specific social formation. In the absence of the formation of these classes, under colonial conditions that did not figure in Gramsci's formulations, it is the inorganic intellectuals who tend to universalise their function and thus blind themselves to their reactionary consequences. What we gather from Gramsci's conception of *organic intellectuals* is that they perform a historically significant mediating factor in galvanising the material forces of their time and leading them towards their emancipatory potentials. These 'emancipatory potentials', however, are not of a trans-historically valid sort, as the bourgeois, or occasionally even the working-class intellectuals assume. They are specific to the material and social basis of their constitutional formations. Nevertheless, they do push the revolutionary potentials of their class to logical and rhetorical ends. In the case of Iranian intellectuals, however, they have failed to do any such revolutionary galvanising, precisely because of their inorganic links to the most reactionary (petite-bourgeoisie) classes. Weak class formations at both the bourgeois and the working-class basis have effectively been translated to even weaker and more inorganic intellectuals, principally engaged in abstractions and false affiliations – ultimately resulting in a false, reactionary consciousness.

In classical Social Democratic (Karl Kautsky) terms, the bourgeois intellectuals were in effect betraying their own class interests by joining force with the interests of the working class when they provided them with theoretical and organisational leadership towards class struggle and revolutionary consciousness. In the course of the revolutionary movements of the late nineteenth and early twentieth centuries in Europe and Asia, and later in the century in Africa and Latin America, the historical fusion between the working class and the strategically de-classified bourgeois intellectuals led to the inevitable conclusion that the ideology and leadership of the revolutionary movements could be the unanticipated consequences of ideas and sentiments generated within the general body of intellectuals, whether from the bourgeois or the working class. Gramsci's idea of the organic intellectual came at the conclusion of these earlier developments, insisting, however that only through an organic membership in the material condition of the working class can a body of intellectuals produce ideas and provide leadership that can lead to progressive and liberating revolutionary movements. Under the circumstances that advanced capitalist economies produce both bourgeois and working-class consciousness, organic intellectuals are formed within both of these social groupings. Whereas Gramsci considered, because of his own obvious political concerns, 'organic' intellectuals almost exclusively within its working-class environment, his own theory entails a similar formation among the bourgeoisie. Under the condition of advanced capitalist economies, where both the bourgeois and the working class have been actively formed and self-consciously theorised, 'progressive' ideas are the exclusive prerogative of neither the bourgeois nor the working-class organic intellectuals. 'Progressive' and 'liberating' ideas are, instead, the dialectical outcome of the clash of political cultures underlying the epistemic assumptions of both these perspectives – of the bourgeois and the working-class intellectuals. 'Every social group, coming into existence on the original terrain of an essential function in the world of economic production', Gramsci pointed out, 'creates together with itself, organically, one or more strata (*ceti*) of intellectuals which give it homogeneity and an awareness of its own function not only in the economic but also in the social and political fields'.[28]

Totally absent from Gramsci's analysis, however, are the colonial circumstances in which the colonised intellectuals are de-classified. Under the controlling circumstances of colonialism and the impoverished domestic economic conditions conducive to it, there is no active formation of either a progressive national bourgeoisie or a revolutionary working class to produce their organic intellectuals. Beyond these two classes constitutional to the global capitalist economies, one can also look at the peasantry for an alternative social grouping to provide potentially revolutionary leadership. But here we need to note that, as Gramsci was first to realise, not all social groupings, even those that are highly productive in economic terms, are conducive to producing their own organic intellectuals. Gramsci noted, for example, that 'the mass of the peasantry, although it performs an essential function in the world of production, does not elaborate its own "organic" intellectuals, nor does it "assimilate" any stratum of "traditional" intellectuals, although it is from the peasantry that other social groups draw many of their intellectuals and a high proportion of traditional intellectuals are of peasant origin'.[29] This assertion testifies that the function of organic intellectuals, in multiplicity and plurality, has far-reaching implications beyond their respective presence in a specific social grouping. But by the same token, inorganic intellectuals of the colonised societies remain both economically and theoretically divorced from any revolutionary potential beyond their obvious anti-colonialism. Top-ranking intellectuals, such as the eminent novelist Mahmoud Dolatabadi (born 1940), could (and did), of course, use peasant and nomadic rebellions against feudal tyranny, as in the setting of his monumental epic *Kelidar* (1978–84).

The fact that, once they join rank with other social groupings, the intellectuals of peasant origin lose their organic links to their own class is a clear indication that there is an elective affinity between the intellectuals and their material or moral interests in a class. Moreover, the process of urbanisation and the formation of the 'leisure class' (Thorstein Veblen) is quintessentially related to the formation of a creative impulse in the person of the intellectual that can organically or non-organically produce revolutionary and emancipatory ideas. 'The category of ecclesiastics', Gramsci noted, 'can be considered the category of intellectuals organically bound to the landed aristocracy. It had equal status juridically with the aristocracy, with which it shared the exercise of feudal ownership of land, and the use of state privileges connected with property'.[30] The same can obviously be said of the organic intellectuals linked either to the bourgeoisie or to the working class, because in both cases they are the simultaneous beneficiaries of their own class interests. But none of these attributes is applicable to the inorganic intellectuals, precisely because they lack such vested interests and thus their moral and ideological persuasions remain on abstract theoretical planes.

There is a revolutionary potential to Edward Said's conception of the exilic intellectual that can be the saving sign of the inorganic intellectuals and their stated ideals. In a piece of evident self-theorisation, Said has noted that ...

> ... while it is an actual condition, exile is also [...] a metaphoric condition. [...] Even intellectuals who are lifelong members of a society can, in a manner of speaking, be divided into insiders and outsiders: those on the one hand who belong fully to the society as it is, who flourish in it without an overwhelming sense of dissonance or dissent, those who can be called yea-sayers; and on the other hand, the nay-sayers, the individuals at odds with their society and therefore outsiders and exiles so far as privileges, power, and honors are concerned.[31]

To be sure, Said's conception of the exilic marginality does not totally redeem the inorganic intellectual. In fact, one may argue that intellectuals in exile are inorganic in a double sense – a case of dual marginality in fact. They are removed from both class affiliation and national context. But under the circumstance of global capitalism, when the search for cheap raw material and labour, as well as for lucrative markets, has collapsed the boundaries of national economies, there is no reason why at once inorganic and exilic intellectuals could not perform their potentially revolutionary functions from beyond their political boundaries – or alternatively incorporated into the propaganda machinery of the ruling class. As I have argued and demonstrated extensively in my *Brown Skin White Masks* (2011), the very cadre of the exilic intellectuals that Said thought would be revolutionary can, in fact, turn out to be entirely reactionary, as in the case of Foad Ajami and Azar Nafisi and countless other comprador intellectuals who put their active services at the disposal of American imperial projects in the Arab and Muslim world.[32] Be that as it may, admitting an inorganic status can be liberating in the marketplace of ideas. Accepting the exilic tangentiality can indeed be quite emancipatory. The revolutionary potentials of the exilic intellectuals can perhaps be best grasped when compared to the corrupting influences of domesticity and nativism, as perhaps best exemplified by Akbari's insight into the identification of Iranian intellectuals with lumpenism. But by the same token, neither should the mutation of exilic intellectuals into guns for hire be neglected.

Lumpenism in Cinema

The focal point of Akbari's diagnosis, and by far the most significant aspect of his extraordinary study, is his careful attention to lumpenism in Iranian cinema. Having been published in 1973, the section on cinema is fully cognizant of the positive development in Iranian cinema. Mehrju'i's *Cow* (1969) Akbari singles out as 'the most significant Iranian film and one of the best films of the world'.[33] But then he dismisses with a precision and authority that stems from his study of lumpenism such films as *Qeysar* (1969), *Reza Motori* (1970) and *Dash Akol* (1971), all by the doyen of Iranian cinema Mas'ud Kimia'i and all the most technically advanced cinematic celebration of Iranian lumpenism – though, in their cases, with a crucial twist that Akbari fails to notice. Akbari's harsh judgment is that 'the Iranian cinema reflects only the life of lumpens and to some extent of the petite-bourgeoisie and nothing of other social classes [for example, landlords, peasants, capitalists, workers, intellectuals]. In effect, Iranian cinema is the cinema of lumpens and to some extent the petite-bourgeoisie'.[34] Although this assessment is largely applicable to the Iranian cinema until the late 1960s, much of Akbari's observations are still applicable in more recent developments, even among some of the art films that are critically acclaimed. Certainly, until the early 1960s, as Akbari has documented his assertions, the overwhelming majority of Iranian films had to do with melodramatic tales of good luck, haphazard accidents, fate and serendipity. Usually, a wealthy young woman falls in love with a member of the lumpens, and after a dramatic interlude they finally get married and live happily ever after. Wealth is always coveted by these lumpens, but wealthy people are depicted as corrupt and sick. Poverty is escaped like a plague, and yet it is conceitedly celebrated as a virtue. Asceticism is ostensibly celebrated, while with a persistent *resentment* wealth is also very much coveted. No sustained energy is directed towards a goal, and only chance and good luck are believed to be the key to success. There is a pervasive fatalism evident in these stories: fate dictates everything. Lumpens are celebrated for their honesty, sincerity, fidelity, the virtues which in reality they lack.

Esma'il Kushan's *Kolah Makhmali* (*The Velvety Hat*, 1962) is in many respects a prototypical example of *Film Jaheli*, the genre devoted to the celebration of lumpenism. Nasser Malak Moti'i (1930–2018), a leading Iranian actor who appeared as the lead character, defined the genre as the male protagonist who personified the lumpen ideals. The title role referred to a special kind of hat made of velvet (*makhmal*) that became the iconic symbol of this type.[35] The hat had to be worn with a studied kind of casualness. The character type was then identified with the hat he wore. Kolah Makhmali, or the Velvety Hat, personified a whole series of attributes. In this particular case, we see Kolah Makhmali having just been released from prison. But, as always, he has been imprisoned falsely and really is innocent. He seeks revenge on those who unjustly framed him. But yet again, he is trapped by them and made to look like a drug dealer. Kolah Makhmali runs away, and a peasant who looks like him is captured by the police. Kolah Makhmali ends up in a village where he rescues the daughter of the village's mayor from a band of charlatans who intend to swindle her of her wealth. Meanwhile, the police find out the real perpetrators and realise that Kolah Makhmali is innocent. Kolah Makhmali and the peasant look-alike end up marrying their respective sweethearts and live happily ever after. Abstracted from all material and productive contexts, Kolah Makhmali thus personifies the ideals of always a *really* good man who has been falsely accused, but ultimately fate is on his side, and he emerges from the dramatic circumstances victoriously. The victory of Kolah Makhmali, however, is the victory of goodness in the most abstract, de-socialised and amorphous sense – and above all the victory of his manly manners. By now Kolah Makhmali has become a character type, a persona, with full potential for an allegorical register.

Iranian cinematic lumpenism is also evident in its active denunciation of wealth but the equally active coveting of good but un-earned luxury. Consider Majid Mohseni's *Qorbun-e Khodam* (*Thanks Be to Myself*, 1962) as a good example. Here we encounter a menial worker of sorts who earns a meagre living by doing odd jobs. He dreams of a luxurious life in which all his dreams are fulfilled. He runs into a wealthy man, as fate and the concocted script would have it, who desperately seeks a simple and modest life. The wealthy man's dream of a happy and fulfilling life is sharply contrasted by the trappings of the luxurious life he leads. The opposing characters end up living with each other for a while, leading to the poor man's conviction that wealth is evil and the source of all malice in life. He happily returns to his modest life, thanking himself for the 'choice' he has made. The active denunciation of wealth here is predicated on a tacit celebration of the meagre and simple living which the lumpen earns – not by choice but by lack of skill. The point of *Thanks Be to Myself* is that, even if the lumpen is given a choice, he prefers the meagre, or what he considers to be 'simple and sincere', life to a life of luxury. Wealth is considered to be a source of evil. Wealthy people are devoid of all humanity, sincerity, noble ideals. They have invariably earned their wealth via illicit means. It is thus not just the wealth that is demonised but a productive and fulfilling life. What is labelled 'simplicity and sincerity' is in effect an idle and useless life in which mere inaction and fatalism are celebrated. Akbari's detection of an active element of fatalism and populist conceptions of Sufism among the lumpens is very much corroborated here in this cinematic genre. The masculinist figure of the cinematic genre of the lumpen thus constitutes an ideal humanity, an ideal Man, at once superior in his qualities and outside the parameters of a productive life. We soon however realise we are not in the presence of any serious or realistic character, but engaged in the allegorical construction of a type, cast inside a fable.

Nasser Malak Moti'i's *Mardha va Jaddeh-ha* (*The Men and the Roads*, 1963) personified the character of 'Luti', yet another major variation on the theme of the lumpen. Who is a 'Luti'?[36] The word 'Luti' is one of those impossible expressions that cannot be translated into any other language. Its most immediate reference, according to Dehkhoda's encyclopaedic dictionary of the Persian language, *Loghat-nameh*,[37] is to a paedophile, an adult with a sexual fixation on young boys. Here, the etymology of the word may be traced back to the Qur'anic reference to the people of 'Lut' who were reportedly thus sexually identified. Beginning with that negative attribute, the word 'Luti' has grown to include any number of other connotations, including an idle person, or even an alcoholic. It also means a person who is not afraid of any consequence to his actions. Historically, the 'Lutis' are reported to have been among the retinues of monarchs and princes. 'Lutis' were also known as entertainers, particularly those singing vulgar songs and having a goat, a monkey, or a bear dance to their vulgarities. But, and here is the rub, the adverb of '*lutianeh*' means 'in earnest, with honesty'. '*Luti-khor-shodan*', however, means to swindle someone of their belongings, whereas '*luti-gari*', again paradoxically, means chivalrous and generous acts. The evident tension in the word 'Luti' and all its other derivatives points to the obvious opposition between the two diametrically adverse sentiments about the pervasive lumpenism of the type that the word identifies. The initially negative connotations have to do with the presence of a group of wavering mercenaries who could easily be employed by monarchs and princes to perform their violent acts of intimidation terrorising their subjects. Gradually, the group begins to be identified with a corrupted version of Sufi asceticism, and thus identified with 'simplicity and sincerity'. The occasional positive connotations associated with the group have to do with this mis-identification.

The persistently negative attitude, however, represents the general understanding of the productive forces of society against the hebetudinous existence of the 'Lutis'. The 'Lutis' lived off the productive forces of society at large, and thus their lethargic existence was offensive to people around them. In more recent times, it has been principally the function of inorganic intellectuals, because of a misidentification with the Lutis as 'the working class', that has persistently given them a positive attribute. It is not surprising that the script for *The Men and the Roads* is written by one of the most distinguished poets of the period, Ahmad Shamlou. It may come as a surprise to many Iranians to find out that the script of one of the most arcane films in the melodramatic genre of *Film Farsi*, as they were derogatorily known, was written by Ahmad Shamlou, by far the most celebrated intellectual of his generation. The fact that Shamlou did write this script, however, points to nothing but the sheer power of intellectuals' identification with the lumpen entails. The banality of the story of *The Men and the Roads* points also to the endemic misogynistic traits of this genre. 'The Luti' in this case has married a 'misguided woman' – that is, a woman who has been tricked into having sexual relations with a man other than her husband, who is in turn suspicious of her fidelity. The woman turns out to have an illegitimate child that the Luti ever so magnanimously adopts as his own, and thus they all live happily ever after. Any woman who comes near the Luti is either a chaste and asexual being (usually his mother), or else a prostitute, a whore, a loose and amoral creature who is then forgiven and led to a morally upright life in the shadow of the great lumpen. In short, the Lat or the Luti is a mixed metaphor, a floating signifier, a paradoxical persona, inspiring the most gifted poets, while a parasitical member of the society, as well as an object of derision and contempt by critical thinkers committed to revolutionary causes.

An equally important character in the lexicon of Iranian lumpenism is 'Jahel',[38] and a typical film representing the type is Sardar Sager's *Jahel-e Mahal* (*The Tough Man of the Neighbourhood*, 1964). '*Jahel*' literally means 'ignorant', or 'stupid'. It is the opposite of '*Aqel*' ('Wise') or '*Alem*' ('Man of Knowledge'.) The expression *javan ast va jahel* ('He is young and stupid') indicates that the term '*jahel*' can be used synonymously with 'the young person'.[39] The Persian word '*jahel*' is also at the etymological root of the Arabic word *Jahiliyyah*, meaning 'ignorance', a derogatory word used in the early Islamic period to refer to pre-Islamic Arabia. Beyond these etymological and standard meanings, however, the word refers to a character type among the Iranian lumpens. A typical 'Jahel' is young, innocent of any formal education, usually engaged in one kind of menial work or another, if he ever deigns to work at all. He is a social parasite, living off others – and yet he is an affectionate character, soliciting the sympathy of others for some illusory virtues. He would not hesitate to commit petty crimes to get by, or else work as a bodyguard or a tough man to shove and intimidate people around for a more powerful person. He is the tough guy of his neighbourhood. He is known to live off extortion from the local businesses. He walks, talks and behaves in a certain concocted and leisurely manner. In *The Tough Man of the Neighbourhood* we see a typical glorification of the Jahel who is first accused of some misdeed and then exonerated at the end of the story. He is never seen in any healthy and fulfilling relationship with any woman. Association with women denigrates him. His moustache is the supreme sign of his manliness. He will 'shave his moustache and put lipstick on', as their favourite expression goes, if he is not a man of his word.

By knowing who the enemy of the Jahel is, we can get closer to his character and what he is up against. The enemy of the Jahel is usually personified in such characters as drug dealers, smugglers, thieves and the like. More often than not, drug dealers in particular are plotting one thing or another against the Jahel. Upon closer examination, though, it is not just the drug dealers who are the demons of the Jahel's world. While in *The Velvety Hat* it is the drug dealers who are plotting against the lumpen protagonist, in Abbas Shabaviz's *Mo-Tala'i-ye Shahr-e Ma* (*The Blondie of Our City*, 1965), it is a blond woman who is the chief villain. What do drug dealers and blond women have in common?[40] Let's add a third element to them: the 'gigolos'. In Hossein Madani's *Jahel-ha va Gigoloha* (*The Tough Guys and the Gigolos*, 1964), we see the most vivid confrontation of the Jahels with a caricature of modern men. The word 'gigolos' in the title refers to the exact opposite of the Jahel: soft-spoken, gentle, urbane, polite, clean, clean-shaven – all of which for the Jahels, and for the filmmakers who celebrated them, amounts to the effeminate gentility that is unmanly and suspect. By identifying young and urban (to them effeminate) youth as 'gigolos', the ideologues of the culture of lumpenism reveal yet another source of anxiety for the Jahels. It is important to keep in mind that in this context the word 'gigolo' does not mean a young and handsome man who has a continuing sexual relationship with an older and wealthier woman, or is hired as an escort for a woman, or else simply as a male prostitute. Here, 'gigolo' means the opposite of Jahel: polite, gentle, effeminate, thus suspect.

What drug dealers, women with blond hair, and young middle-class men ('gigolos') represent, in the imagination of lumpenism, is the 'modernity' of their presumed appearance, which is the target of the Jahel's (fear and) loathing. Here, 'gigolo' stands as the archetypal nemesis of the Jahel, his *bête noir* – and as such the gigolo stands for modernity, which is here at once sexualised, feminised, ridiculed and dismissed (and feared at the same time). *Modernity* is here represented by certain evil (drug), foreign (women with blond hair), or co-opted natives' (young men with a polished appearance – the gigolo) characteristics. In reverse, the Jahels now come to represent a character of authenticity, of 'real' Iranians, of 'traditional values'. The foreign names of the drugs – heroin, morphine and so on – identify the source of the evil modernity with foreigners and simultaneously demonise it. 'Modernity' (taken at face value and without any critical encounter in its colonial context) is something foreign, something dangerous, corrupting, making young men sick and useless. The blond woman, always juxtaposed against a black-haired woman who is poor but chaste and noble and who finally wins the affections of the Jahel, also represents this foreign-ness of this presumed modernity. So are the young men, who are not really 'men' and next to the machismo of the lumpens are made to look effeminate and woman-like, because they are clean-shaven and dress neatly. In Reza Safa'i's *Luti-ye Qarn-e Bistom* (*The Twentieth-Century Luti*, 1968), we see even more vividly how the lumpen driver of a wealthy but uptight man has a catalytic effect on him, by having him fall in love with a 'real' woman – in this case a young woman from the provincial city of Isfahan and thus not 'corrupted' like the Tehrani girls – and consequently turning him into a 'real' human being, namely a lumpen look-alike. This is no critique of Eurocentric modernity, this is ressentiment against aspects of colonial modernity that Iranian cinema had failed to understand or stage or criticise. The function of Jaheli cinema was to sustain hostility towards a chimeric conception of modernity and conversely fetishise a fictious idea of tradition. Nevertheless, the very practice had opened up the traumatic disposition of how a cinematic persona was to face a society he was unable to read.

The anti-modernity of the Jahels, representing the fear of modernity endemic to all patriarchal cultures that thus fetishise themselves under the epithet 'traditional', obviously had to be expressed in a more direct confrontation with 'the West', the vacuous bugbear of this modernity. Esma'il Kushan's *Ebram dar Paris* (*Abe in Paris*, 1965) finally took the Iranian lumpen right to a heartland of 'the West'. The central theme of *Abe in Paris* is that the Iranian lumpen falls in love with a French woman, and she with him, but he ultimately decides there are 'cultural differences' between the two and, thus, he opts to go back to Iran and marry a native Iranian. Again, what is established in the story is that the Jahel of the local neighbourhood represents the 'traditional values' of Iranian society and that marriage with a foreigner will corrupt that authentic representation. A reversal of the lumpen going to 'the West' is equally conducive to the authentication of him as representing 'traditional Iranian values'. In Nosratollah Vahdat's *Arus Farangi* (*The European Bride*, 1964), the lumpen who is now a cab driver is afflicted by Maria, a European woman living in Iran. Maria is quite willing to marry the Iranian cab driver, but he prefers to marry his own Iranian sweetheart from the good land of flower and nightingale. The symptoms of this cinematic authentication of the Jahel as representing 'Iranian Tradition' permeates the cinema of the 1960s and 1970s. The end result of all such fetishised constitutions of 'the West' and the demonisation of an unexamined modernity is the active resuscitation of the basest and most retrograde patriarchal traits as now representing a 'true' and 'authentic' Iran, which is to be protected against both foreigners and foreign ideas. By now the figure of the Jahel has become a thoroughly mythic persona, roaming freely in the dark and shadow of a colonial modernity he could scarcely see and decipher, let alone fathom or navigate.

Siamak Yasami's *Ganj-e Qarun* (*The Qarun's Treasure*, 1965) took Iranian lumpenism in cinema to a popular height never achieved before. The legendary actors Mohammad Ali Fardin as Ali Bigham and Foruzan as Shirin, with Ali's sidekick Hassan portrayed by the prominent comedian Taghi Zohuri, along with the famous Armenian actor Arman, came together and turned the melodramatic story of a lost father and son into a historic success. The extraordinary commercial success of the film was concurrent with the two crucial decades of the 1960s and 1970s, which were mostly dominated by the genre of *Film Jaheli*, at once reactionary, misogynistic, anti-modern and altogether retrograde to the most elementary achievements constitutional to the location of a society on the premise of colonial modernity. Be that as it may, the genre was so vastly popular that it achieved an iconic status – which was never matched by the most spectacular achievements of arthouse New Wave cinema as represented by Forough Farrokhzad, Ebrahim Golestan, Amir Naderi, Bahram Beiza'i, Daryoush Mehrju'i, or Abbas Kiarostami. The tumultuous decades of the 1980s and 1990s gone by, a revolution and a war into history, and still the most enduring aspects of Iranian lumpenism survived well into one of the most popular films of the post-revolutionary cinema: Davud Mir-Baqeri's *Adam Barfi* (*The Snow Man*, 1994). The two leading lumpens had now migrated to Turkey, learned a little English and engaged in human trafficking between 'The East' and 'The West'. Thus, as both the Pahlavi monarchy and the clerical Islamism that succeeded it had sought and received active support from the genre and the social type it celebrated, some leading intellectuals had lent their support while others denounced it. In the figure of Sha'ban the Brainless, the Pahlavi regime was the historic beneficiary of the character type, and by the time we reach the dawn of the Islamic Republic, the chief nemesis of Sha'ban the Brainless, another Luti named Tayyeb Haj Reza'i (1911–63), was attracted to Khomeini's June 1963 uprising and was subsequently arrested and executed by the Pahlavi regime. The figure of Jahel, Luti, or at times Mashti (all synonymous) thus navigated between history and mythology, on both sides of the ideological divide.

With Mas'ud Kimia'i's *Qeysar* (1969), the genre of *Film Jaheli* received by far its most iconoclastic cinematic expression – a bravura crescendo that suddenly recast the entire genre of *Film Jaheli* into an entirely different allegorical register. A revenge story of a rebellious young man avenging the murder of his older brother and the dishonouring of his younger sister, Qeysar singularly reversed the genre of *Film Jaheli*, for by now the intellectual support or damnation of what was derogatorily dismissed as *Film Farsi* had opened the genre into an immaterial world, from narrative logos and moral ethos into cinematic mythos – as the lead character Qeysar (played admirably by the legendary Iranian actor Behrouz Vossoughi) became the heroic representation of a type we had never seen before. Here and now, in this film, the clash of class origin and class consciousness of the lumpen resulted in overriding creative impulses where an ordinary narrative plot had sublimated into mythic proportions. But this was not the end of it. In three consecutive films – *Qeysar* (1969), *Reza Motori* (1970) and *Dash Akol* (1971) – Kimia'i had crafted the lead characters of his stories as tragic heroes, iconic in their wider representations, entirely fabular in their doomed fate, allegorical unto themselves and therefore parabolic in what they meant. With *Qeysar*, we stepped

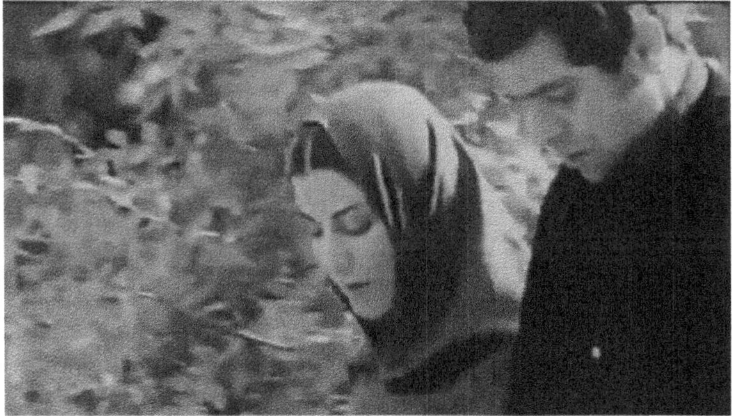

Figure 1.1 *Behrouz Vossoughi and Pouri Banayi in an iconic sequence in Masoud Kimia'i's* Qeysar *(1969). (Photo: Public domain, fair use)*

fully into the realm of cinematic myth. Nothing like that had ever happened in Iranian cinema – popular or arthouse productions. The very genre of Luti and Jahel thus opened the Fourth Wall into history and mythology, carrying the audience with them, as the three tragic heroes – Qeysar, Reza Motori and Dash Akol – became larger than life. The fact that these three protagonists were all killed at the end of their stories radically altered the perfunctory good endings of melodramas and transformed the heroes into the pantheon of Shi'i martyrology. We were now all in the presence of modern, palpable, cinematic mythology. Meanwhile, the revolutionary music of Esfandiar Monfaredzadeh, the power of the vocalists Farhad Mehrad and Pari Zangeneh, as well as the lyrics of Shahyar Qanbari had given these three films astonishing political power. Soon Kimia'i followed with the final twist to this iconic sliver of his filmmaking, *The Deer* (1974), where a useless drug addict and a committed revolutionary are placed next to each other – from then on, the history of Iranian cinema would never be the same. The final crescendo of the film where the two friends, a committed guerrilla fighter and a useless lumpen, die together closes the gap that *Film Jaheli* had created between serious cinema and critical thinking. These four films will remain a breed apart, not just in Kimia'i's own career, but in the entire history of Iranian cinema. Kimia'i, to be sure, continued to make terrible films that would yield severe criticism by Iranian feminists, and rightly so, but the genre of *Film Jaheli* (and with it the character of the lumpen) had by now flowered into something farthest removed from where it had started.

The Mythic Gap of a Gender Imbalance

Emblematic of a deeply rooted paradox of gender and sexuality, the history of lumpenism in Iranian cinema began with a sustained dose of misogyny and homoerotism. The two traits were not contradictory. They were illustrative traits of a colonially conditioned biopower whereby conflating the terms of gender and sexuality were instrumental in both the subjection and subjugation of the colonial subjects within the framework of a postcolonial nation-state. This was concomitant with the genre and the character type of the lumpen being put to effective political use by opposing ideological camps – the monarchy on one side and clerical Islamism on the other. The deeper historical roots of the character of Jahel in the literary traditions of *ayyari* and *javanmardi*, as well as the opposing critical attention that the genre of *Film Jaheli* had received eventually opened it up to a more allegorical and mythic reading, effectively reversing the power of the biopolitics that had generated and sustained it. For the longest time, the genre was staged as a profoundly reactionary gesture against 'modernity', replacing or camouflaging a principled critique of colonial modernity – and this is how the genre was squarely at the service of the prolonged trajectory of the coloniality that had conditioned it. But soon, at the peak of the cinematic genre, Masoud Kimia'i with his iconic *Qeysar* and three other consecutive films took the genre into a new direction – and radically reversed its colonising causes and consequences by (among other narrative tropes) giving his lead characters a tragically doomed ending. When he was done, it was quite clear that in the figure of the Jahel we were witness to a deeply colonised toxic masculinity, full of painful contradictions, noble yet corrupt, heroic yet tragic, fascistic yet iconoclastic, retrograde yet liberating, misogynistic and homoerotic at one and the same time. All of this suddenly transformed the trope into an archaic character with varied contemporary resonances. In the figure of Qeysar and Dash Akol, in particular, the character of the Javanmard had caught up with the iconic Jahel, the hero with the villain. Now we could read Forough Farrokhzad's poem differently and understand what she means where she refers to '*Jani-ha-ye Kuchak*' ('the Little Criminals') gazing at a fountain.

> But always in the vicinity of city squares
> You could spot these little criminals
> Standing idly by and staring
> At the overflowing of the fountains –
> Perhaps still
> Behind the crumpled eyes and in the depth of coldness
> Something half alive but confused had remained intact ...[41]

Through her iconic poetry, Forough Farrokhzad had mapped out and lived the details of an emancipated woman as the insignia of a liberated human being delivered from the condition of coloniality and patriarchy alike. The effective constitution of masculinity at the roots of Iranian colonial modernity was not just predicated on men in a generic sense, which had become definitive of a cultural anti-modernity – devoid of the slightest critique of modernity. It was a very specific kind of 'man' that was fabricated as the *modus operandi* of anti-modernity. From the lowest and most useless substratum of society, the figure of the Jahel/Lumpen was reconfigured by an inorganic caste of alienated intellectuals who mistook them for 'the labour class', or else for 'real' or 'traditional' Iran, for 'authentic Iranian culture'. The genre of *Film Jaheli* celebrated lumpen masculinity and defined manliness in specifically and decidedly xenophobic and misogynist terms, whereby women (thus fixated) became, *ipso facto*, foreign and dangerous at one and the same time. These Jahels were the archetypal degeneration of the medieval literary trope of the Ayyar, as subsequently coloured and coded in the figment of inorganic intellectuals' bewildered and alienated imagination, falsely identifying with a labour class that did not exist to its revolutionary potentials and mistakenly celebrating the misogynist lumpenism that masqueraded for it. It was a comedy of errors, the byproduct of a simulacrum of nationalist modernity, the formation of rootless new classes, the institutional collapse of the *ancien regime*, with the simultaneous rise of a weak economy, weak class formations, delusional intellectual elites and the concomitant fabrication of a masculinist lumpenism, at the heavy cost of women's healthy and wholesome social presence.

The formation of toxic masculinity bordering on the patriarchal foregrounding of fascism was and remains the byproduct of colonial biopower. The critical question of gender is at the heart of the tension that agitates cultures between their forgotten or repressed roots and their manifest and self-conscious protestations. Through a critical re-examination of the institution of Ayyari/Chivalry, we can clearly trace the idea of patriarchal and misogynistic masculinity as the cornerstone of a politics of despair and a fundamental fear of and attraction to fascism. Our understanding of the pivotal issues of gender and sexuality at the anxiety-ridden centre of postcolonial cultures must begin with that interface between literary memory and colonial conditions of forgetting them. In the course of colonial modernity, the anxiety of foreign domination eventually translates into exaggerated disciplining of the feminised body, giving momentum to the other paradox of a colonially truncated encounter with Islamic law that now rises as the cornerstone of masculinist domination and definition of the 'traditional' resistance to colonial modernity – and thus the jurisprudence and the politics of mandatory veiling.

Against this background, the vast and variegated universe of classical Persian literary, poetic, mystical and philosophical imagination leads to potent visual allegories and creates a world of pure and palpably visual verisimilitude – from which repertoire stories are made beyond the mandates of logical or reasonable truth-claims, such as the visual recitals of Avicenna and Suhrawardi. That tradition proceeds apace, until we get to the contemporary manners of storytelling we see in in contemporary Iranian cinema where their realism is in fact surreal, for the cinematic universe actively partakes in this world of pure verisimilitude, and while telling plausible stories, they are in fact tapping into these invisible worlds. The semblance of realism that results hides its surreal verisimilitude, as indeed the potent and exaggerated manliness and womanliness they exude alludes to the mythic and allegorical world from which they are drawn. These cinematic worlds are better understood as modern mythologies and potent allegories, rather than being subjected to harsh positivistic criticism of one sort or another, all perhaps necessary but all inevitably leading to a conceptual *cul de sac*. The characters we see on the screen are not real people – they are patently unreal, their melodramatic disposition akin to their mythical and allegorical wellspring. We are therefore better off abandoning their melodramatic pretences and seeing and reading them as an unreal surrealism that emerges from the world of pure verisimilitude where the mythic memories of a culture can only access such memories metonymically.

2

Women without Men

Salam Mahi ha, Salam Mahi ha ...

Greetings to you fish, greetings to you all!
Greetings to you the red, the green, the golden –
Tell me please:
Have you in your crystal room –
Cold as the pupil of dead people's eyes –
And closed and empty
Just like the late evening hours of the city –
Have you heard the sound of a flute—
Coming from the land of the fairies
Of fear and loneliness
That could be heard
At the brick-laden confidence of dormitories
And through the mechanical lullaby of clocks,
And at the glass cells of light?[1]

Forough Farrokhzad, '*Porsesh*/Question' (1962)

In 1997, Nastaran Moussavi and a number of her colleagues collected and translated into Persian a few of highly influential essays written by leading American, European and Australian feminist film and media critics and scholars. The leading feminist publishing house in Iran, Roshangaran, run by a prominent women's rights activist, Shahla Lahiji, sponsored and published their volume. 'Over the last three decades', Ms Musavi wrote in her preface to this collectively edited volume, 'countless changes have occurred around the world, including the widespread manifestation of the social presence of women in every domain. As a result of these developments, many perceptions regarding women have changed and thus made it inevitable that women's issues now need to be addressed anew'.[2] These changes, Ms Musavi insists, are not only in quantitative terms, but of such qualitative nature that they have required a serious reconsideration of the relationship between men and women, and the necessity of re-thinking their social interactions in more just and equitable terms. She then emphasises the extraordinary influence of visual media in communicating the dominant ideologies, and along with them the mutation of the figure of women either into sexual objects, or else the asexual chastity of their mother figures.

Nastaran Musavi and her colleagues consider a major film festival (gathering some fifty women filmmakers) that took place in London in April and May 1973 as a turning point at which women filmmakers began to have a visible and palpable presence in the world of cinema. Soon after that event, Ms Musavi points out, another gathering of women filmmakers in Italy in July 1975 brought home the necessity of addressing the visual registers of women in the public eye. These events, Ms Musavi believes, gradually resulted in direct feminist confrontations with the dominant masculinist visions of women in world cinema. The presence of women among filmmakers, she stipulates, does not, of course, mean that all these women have feminist sensitivities, or that men filmmakers are indifferent to the plight of women. There are also male filmmakers like Ridley Scott whose *Thelma and Louise* (1991) has been particularly influential in alerting to gender imbalances in American society. These groundbreaking developments have also led to the rise of a new feminist perspective in film criticism, among which she and her colleagues have thus selected some of the most recent and most influential sources to translate into Persian and make accessible to Iranian readers.

The first article Nastaran Musavi and her colleagues translate for their volume is Wendy Kozol's 'Fracturing Domesticity: Media, Nationalism, and the Question of Feminist Influence' (1994), which was occasioned by the brutal murder of Nicole Brown Simpson and Ronald Goldman during the O. J. Simpson trial. In this essay, Wendy Kozol, a prominent professor of Comparative American Studies at Oberlin College in Ohio, addresses the link between the visual images of women in public and domestic violence. The second essay is translated from German and is a section of the book *Sündiger Genuss? Filmerfahrungen von Frauen/Sinful Pleasures? Cinematic Experiences of Women* (1994) by the prominent German Marxist feminist Frigga Haug and her colleague Brigitte Hipfel. The section is a critical inroad into asking: 'Why do we like bad films?' The third essay, 'On Real Women', is by the distinguished British feminist film critic Annette Kuhn, and constitutes part of her book *Women's Pictures: Feminism and Cinema* (1994). The next essay is on the French writer and filmmaker Marguerite Duras and is written by Michelle Roher, an Australian feminist film theorist who had contributed this essay to a book called *Feminine/Masculine and Representation*, edited by Terry Threadgold and published in 1990. The next piece consists of an interview with the German filmmaker Margarethe von Trotta conducted in 1996; and the final piece is on feminist film theories, again translated from German, by the prominent German feminist film scholar Gertrude Koch.

The Creative Constitution of a Public Persona

The publication of this volume on feminist film criticism in 1997 coincides with the height of the global reception and popularity of Iranian cinema, in which the image of women figured prominently – both in front and behind the camera. The thematic range and topical significance of the essays collected in this volume go a long way in explaining the richness of the issues that Iranian film critics and scholars considered central to their collective endeavour to match what was happening in Iranian cinema with a critical apparatus that could address their implications for their own society.

Nastaran Musavi and her colleagues had many reasons to believe that their collective efforts in introducing some new perspectives in film criticism would much benefit the extraordinary presence of women filmmakers in the globally celebrated Iranian cinema. As Ms Musavi and her colleagues were busy collecting, translating and publishing this critical volume, another Iranian woman scholar, Shahnaz Moradi Kuchi, was equally busy preparing a detailed encyclopaedia of Iranian women filmmakers. Her achievement, *Zanan-e Sinama-gar-e Iran/Iranian Women Filmmakers* (2000), is an impressive volume cataloguing in detail the professional achievements of some 500 women film producers, directors, actors, directors of photography, editors, set designers, costume designers, make-up artists, composers, sound engineers, sound designers and so on.[3] The staggering number of so many accomplished women in a national cinema is a testimonial to the role that Iranian women have played in revisiting and radically revising their cinematic representations in a massively popular art form with a wide range of audiences in and out of their own country.

The collective works of Shahnaz Moradi Kuchi, Nastaran Musavi and their colleagues are among the multiple and varied indices of a sustained preoccupation with the *public representation* of women in an Islamic Republic. Two diametrically opposed facts define and animate this public representation: first, a massive participation in the course of revolutionary uprising, a clear indication of the demographic increase and sustained process of urbanisation, which in turn has resulted in the visible social presence of women in public space and the public sphere in general and the work force in particular; and second, the all too crucial issue of mandatory veiling of those women who were no longer observing it, as the most evident indication of a denial or limitation of their public space and social presence. In the visual and performing arts, these indices were reflective of more seismic changes in social and economic terms. For example, more than 60 per cent of university entrants by the late 1990s were women, while women constituted only 12 per cent of the workforce. Be that as it may, the publication of these two volumes, among scores of others, was a clear indication of a sustained and serious concern with how women were being represented in the public eye, in cinema in particular, as by far the most popular art form in Iran and many other surrounding countries.

The concern with the public presence, social function and visual representation of women was of course not limited to the post-Islamic Revolution era, nor limited to Iranian Muslim women. In facilitating the rise of Iranian women filmmakers, mostly from Shi'i families with varied degrees of piety and observance, the role of Armenian Iranians can hardly be exaggerated and must be particularly emphasised and singled out. The role of such pioneering Armenian photographers and filmmakers as Antoin Sevrugin (1840–1920), Ardashes Badmagrian (aka Ardeshir Khan, 1863–1928), or above all Ovaness Ohanians (1901–61) is coterminous with the earliest history of Iranian cinema. But among these, Armenian women have had a particularly significant role to play as owners and managers of movie theatres, actresses and directors – at a time when Muslim women had mountains of obstacles to overcome in order to make it to such hitherto unusual and prohibitive professions. Satopari Aghababov (fl. 1920s), who studied art in Berlin and Moscow, and thrived on Iranian stage around the 1920s, established a movie theatre in Tehran in 1929 – one of the first of its kind. Such pioneering Armenian-Iranian actresses as Annik Shefrazian (1910–96), Loretta Hairapedian Tabrizi (1911–98), Irene Zaziantz (1927–2012), Victoria Nerssisian (1937–2018) and Lorik Minassian (1944–2004) were highly successful movie actresses and as such widely influential for making Muslim Iranian women able to think of an acting or directing career. Digranohi Hovakimian (born 1952) is also a pioneering Armenian-Iranian woman documentary filmmaker, producer and director, starting at a time when such professions were almost exclusively in the male domain.[4] This was not a mere issue of 'minority' women. These were Iranian woman with prolonged history in their one and only homeland, and they had a profoundly catalytic impact on the rest of their society. These professional filmmakers were pioneers, doing something for their homeland and especially their Muslim sisters when others were still not ready to do so. The point of women's public presence was not and should never be reduced to the choice between veiling or not veiling. Muslim women had opted to veil or not to veil to the point of questioning the very dividing factor of what exactly 'veiling' meant. The question of the public presence of women therefore was a matter of choice in manners of public dressing when the ruling regimes form the Pahlavis to the Islamists either demanded forced unveiling (Reza Shah) or forced veiling (Ayatollah Khomeini) – both violently compromising women's own choice.

The presence of Armenian women at the threshold of Iranian national cinema early in the twentieth century defines the public domain they were thus helping carve out as something no longer exclusively 'Islamic', but in fact more in the direction of a civic (multicultural and cosmopolitan) space in which Iranian women were now representing themselves no longer as Armenian, Jewish, Zoroastrian, or Muslim – but in fact as citizens of a nation-state. The gradual movement towards this new status in that new space dates back to early in the nineteenth century and the rise of Iranian struggles against (Russian and British) colonialism, in which women were very much implicated and present. In such massive social revolutions as the Babi uprising (1844–52), the Tobacco Revolt (1891–92) and ultimately the Constitutional Revolution (1906–11), women were present, active and highly influential in shaping the direction of these groundbreaking events. The revolutionary leadership of Fatemeh Zarrin Taj Baraghani (1814–52), known as Qorrat al-Ayn, an important Babi leader, and the publication of *Ma'ayeb al-Rejal/The Vices of Men* by Bibi Khanom Astarabadi (1858–1921), a pioneering women's rights activist and a leading satirist of her time, should be considered as hallmarks of this collective concern with the *public persona* of women in the emerging expansion of the social space they now sought to occupy. Qorrat al-Ayn was chiefly responsible for the revolutionary expansion of the Babi movement in more radical directions, while after her Bibi Khanom Astarabadi wrote her *Ma'ayeb al-Rejal* in response to the misogynist pamphlet *Ta'dib al-Neswan/The Admonition of Women* (1895), penned by a Qajar prince, denying women that space.[5] The *Memoir* of Taj al-Saltaneh (1884–1936), a politically conscious Qajar princess, shows how the range of these rising concerns reached the very heart of the Qajar court,[6] while the poetry of Parvin E'tesami (1907–41) marks the wider literary and public domains of that very preoccupation.[7] As indicated by these major hallmarks, Iranian women were entering the *public domain* in both their masses and also amongst the leading intellectual elite – with bourgeois liberal or revolutionary radical ideologies. What was common and constant among them was a steadfast concern with how the public persona of women was to be reconfigured in this new public domain. Muslim or Armenian, Zoroastrian or Jew, Iranian women were redefining the contours of their homeland and the terms of its citizenship – and thus the particularities of their own agencies and subjections.

From these early developments in the nineteenth century to the time that Nastaran Musavi, Shahnaz Moradi Kuchi and their colleagues were active in charting the vision of women in Iranian (and world) cinema late in the twentieth century,[8] we are witness to a sustained and prolonged concern with the *public image* of women in a battle for their *public perception* and their *public persona*, as it was being nationally negotiated, legislated and, above all, visualised and imagined. Because the *public space*, at a massive social plane, was now being shaped anew (whether after the Constitutional Revolution of 1906–11, or after the Islamic Revolution of 1977–79), and the *public persona* of a modern Iranian woman was being personified, these women's rights activists were rightly concerned with the *female public persona* that was to inhabit this space. Who and what were (in plural) the modern Iranian women, and how were they to be represented?

At least since the cataclysmic moment when in the course of a revolutionary convention in Northern Iran, in Badasht in 1848, Tahereh Qorrat al-Ayn threw away her scarf in a gesture of public defiance, the question of veiling has been at the heart of the Iranian women's rights movement.[9] At the heart of this concern is the fact that the mandatory imposition of veiling conceals the body and prohibits/inhibits the *public persona* by pre-empting the formation of a sustained course of bodily memory and thereby public presence, because the forcibly veiled female body is visually concealed and juridically codified. This codification – not just under the Islamic Republic, but even before then – had mandated certain stated or implicit rules to which the body was condemned. The visual representation of women had to comply with the normative regime of a gender apartheid culture that was defined, as all other matriarchal cultures are, by exclusively masculinist terms. Again: forced unveiling that had preceded the forced veiling was as much epistemically violent on the body of a human being as the one that had preceded it, for both moves turned women's bodies into a battlefield of ideological contestation between two patently masculinist political cultures.

While in the Iranian visual and performing arts women had to formally comply with that codified body in order to creatively defy that circumscribed persona, in the Persian literary and poetic arts they had no such tropic limitations and in fact thrived, matured and flourished in incessant literary acts of self-revelation. The creative constitution of that *public persona* has been a consistent and paramount concern of poetic and literary acts over the past two centuries. Iranian women's writings of the last two centuries are not coterminous with veiling, or a literary variation on multilayered shades of veiling, as Farzaneh Milani, an émigré Iranian literary historian, has argued,[10] but in fact entirely countervailing to it. Women's writings are active occasions of narrative unveiling, not of re-enacting veiling – as she has proposed. Words are not veils. Words are revelations.

Women's writings of the last two centuries in Iran are the singularly significant sites of their self-revelation and thus unveiling – whether they have veiled or unveiled! This verbal unveiling is (as it has always been) constitutional to the formation of women's public persona, and Iranian cinema is the extended visual playground of actively imagining this very public persona for Iranian women. The simple acid test of that is to compare the pathbreaking and agential works done by Iranian feminists inside Iran as well as those who have, for perfectly legitimate reasons, opted to leave their homeland and now look at it from the vantage point of a bourgeois liberal American feminism.

Farzaneh Milani projects her own feeling of alienation, estrangement and disconnected exile, and for the right reason as a brown woman in a white supremacist country, as she describes them upon her arrival in the US in the mid-1960s, back to the writings of Iranian women. 'Iranian women writers', she writes, 'gave eloquent voice to my feelings of marginality, of not belonging, of homelessness. They, too, were in exile, even though in their homeland'.[11] They were no such things – when they live and write in their own homeland, fully in charge of what they wanted, what they demanded, and what they wrote. This is the delusional self-projection of a self-alienated racialised émigré back to a worldly culture and the women who inhabited it. 'There are no walls here', Milani says she wrote in her diary 'in an entry dated December 24, 1967. This was a few days after my arrival in America'. There are no walls in America? Those environmentally calamitous lawns of suburban America she refers to were of course barbed-wired and walled against brown and black people like her, even as she tried to pass for white. There are plenty of walls in America – only a mismatched comparison of the suburban or rural America with urban Iran can posit such a categorically flawed idea. Urban America, as anywhere else in the world, is perfectly walled – tall and towering. As I write these words, this very America has built a wall around itself, beginning with the Mexican border. But the problem with Milani's misreading of modern Persian literature lies elsewhere. 'A product of two cultures', she says, 'I felt outside the circle of both, dislodged, dislocated. I was immersed in discontinuities; engulfed in geographical, cultural, and temporal exile'.[12] This is Farzaneh Milani in America, with whom we can certainly sympathise, but it is not the fate of myriads of courageous and assertive women demanding and exacting a pride of place in their own homeland – whether their disenfranchised own in Iran or African American women in the US. Women writers have been part and parcel of a worldly culture giving birth to itself. Milani's reading of veiling is positively metaphysical, casting the entirety of Iranian culture from one essentialised end of it to another, in a thick and multilayered act of deception and veiling. 'In a veiled society', by which she means Iran in the entirety of its history, 'walls surround houses. Religious *Taqiyeh* [deliberate dissimulation] protects faith. *Ta'arof* [a ritualistic mode of discourse] disguises some thought and emotions and plunges both parties, the addressee and the addresser, into a kind of factual suspense. Houses become compartmentalised into their *Daruni* [inner] and *Biruni* [outer] areas. Feelings become disjointed in *Zaheri* [external] and *Bateni* [internal] spheres. Abstractions supplant concreteness. Autobiographies become a rare commodity in the literary arena. Generalities replace the specifics. Indirection becomes a common practice. Concealing, keeping what is private private – veiling – is not just a woman's problem [...]'.[13] These self-ethnising tropes are all, without a single exception, the psychosomatic signs of a sad and solitary soul in exile – not the description of a worldly, changing, rambunctious, unpredictable and living culture – including the United States when observed by a superior critical intelligence. The acid test: compare the extraordinary work of an Indian Marxist feminist like Chandra Mohanty with those of Farzaneh Milani. Compare Milani's truly sad self-pity with Mohanty's bold, brilliant and pathbreaking essay 'Under Western Eyes: Feminist Scholarship and Colonial Discourses' (1988)![14]

Bypassing these émigré melancholies, truly sad but misguided, we are witness to Iranian women poets and novelists instrumental in positing and crafting a public persona in their writings that would have been otherwise conceptually impossible to fathom and explore in the Iranian visual and performing arts. In their creative writings, Iranian women have run ahead of their filmmaking sisters by decades and bounds, imagining in their minds' eyes what future filmmakers will see through their cameras – and still not see as far as their literary counterparts did. In other words, in the visual and performing arts we are yet to produce anything near Forough Farrokhzad's poetry or Shahrnoush Parsipour's prose – except perhaps in the early (not the vastly commercialised later) photography and video installations of Shirin Neshat.[15] The poetic and literary arts are far more self-revealing long before we reach the domain of filmmaking. In their works of fiction, Iranian women have narrated themselves into the powerhouse of their collective national consciousness and posited their *public persona* in *the public domain* of their homeland. But how, and in what particular ways?

Knowledge of the Unknown

On Saturday, 11 May 1996, Ghazaleh Alizadeh, a young and accomplished Iranian writer, got into a car in Tehran, drove north to the Caspian shore in Ramsar, went into the deep of a jungle, and hanged herself. She left behind a note, holding no one in particular responsible for her act. Some believed that note and thought she had committed suicide. Others thought she had been murdered by the agents of the Islamic Republic because she was among the signatories of a famous public letter protesting the tyranny of the ruling regime. Some thought she had committed suicide because she had become tired of fighting an incurable and terminal cancer. Others thought she had committed suicide as a symbolic protest and out of frustration with the status of women in Iran. Conflicting speculations about Ghazaleh Alizadeh's death continue. Today, a veil of ambiguity, mystery, misery and frustration is cast on the memory of the dead body of Ghazaleh Alizadeh (1946–96).[16]

Towards the end of her groundbreaking essay 'Can the Subaltern Speak?' (1988), Gayatri Chakravorty Spivak invokes the image of 'a young woman of sixteen or seventeen, Bhuvaneswari Bhaduri, [who] hanged herself in her father's modest apartment in North Calcutta in 1926'. By way of explanation, Spivak adds: 'The suicide was a puzzle since, as Bhuvaneswari was menstruating at the time, it was clearly not a case of illicit pregnancy. Nearly a decade later, it was discovered that she was a member of one of the many groups involved in the armed struggle for Indian independence. Unable to confront the task and yet aware of the practical need for trust, she killed herself'.[17]

Though committed in the privacy of her father's apartment, there is an evident publicity, a pointed purpose, in the sense and significance of Bhuvaneswari Bhaduri's suicide in 1926, a political pronouncement, a social register, a cultural consequence to her heroic defiance of violence by diverting it towards her own body. Though committed in the open (yet secluded) space of a jungle, Ghazaleh Alizadeh's suicide in comparison, some seventy years later in 1996, lacks that public consequence, pre-empts a communal corollary and hides behind a veil of anonymity, mystery and inarticulate obscurity. Once discovered to have been committed out of a normative conflict between a political commitment to fighting colonialism and a moral conviction in non-violence, Bhuvaneswari Bhaduri's suicide assumes a universal significance beyond the domesticity of its occurrence, thus lifting the limited domains of a particular event to the much wider space of an ethical principle. This is not the case with the tragic suicide of Ghazaleh Alizadeh, the secrecy and mystery of whose evident commitment veils and shrouds it in too mysterious of an act to make it publicly relevant, politically significant, socially consequential. The Islamic Republic has an atrocious record of official abuse of power (against women in particular); Iranian women have suffered much the consequences of a brutally misogynistic theocracy; human, civil and women's rights are systematically violated in the Islamic Republic; writers, artists, journalists and other public intellectuals are systematically harassed, persecuted and even murdered by the official organs of the Islamic Republic, or else by gangs of hoodlums recruited by them. There is nothing about these atrocities that needed verification or symbolic affirmation in the tragic suicide of a young, accomplished and brilliant novelist. Literally a waste of life, Ghazaleh Alizadeh's suicide is too symbolically loaded to mean anything in particular – it has too many acts of signification entailed in it to signify anything specific. It is allegorically jammed. Bhuvaneswari Bhaduri's suicide was heroically meaningful, Ghazaleh Alizadeh's tragically meaningless.

Bhuvaneswari Bhaduri's suicide in 1926 and Ghazaleh Alizadeh's suicide in 1996 do not complement, but contradict, each other. They are at two opposing ends of a public performance staged in private and a private act committed in public. Some sixty years after its occurrence, Gayatri Spivak invokes the memory of Bhuvaneswari Bhaduri's suicide in 1926 in her now legendary essay 'Can the Subaltern Speak?' (1998) and makes a theoretical note of it in her critique of the European sovereign subject. Almost a decade after its occurrence, Ghazaleh Alizadeh's suicide is the subject of nothing more than useless and bitter conspiratorial speculations by disgruntled expatriate Iranians. Decades after her suicide, Bhuvaneswari Bhaduri thrives in the creative memory of the public act she performed in private, while her sister in death, Ghazaleh Alizadeh, increasingly recedes into the anonymity of the private act she committed in the publicity of her nation's conspiratorial politics. Decades after the fact, Bhuvaneswari Bhaduri's death is now politically potent, Ghazaleh Alizadeh's utterly futile.

The honoured publicity that Bhuvaneswari Bhaduri now enjoys and the inscrutable anonymity that Ghazaleh Alizadeh now suffers, decades after their respective suicide, are not rooted in the specificity of the tragic act they both committed but located in the immediate context of their memorial reception – of how they are now remembered. The way Bhuvaneswari Bhaduri's and Ghazaleh Alizadeh's respective suicides symbolically contradict each other ought to be seen in the context of two apparently unrelated events that structurally complement each other. The anonymity of Alizadeh's suicide can only be made visible and meaningful by placing her literary legacy in the company of other female writers who had created, crafted and framed the light in which she can now be remembered. By being primarily concerned with the cinematic representation of women, Nastaran Musavi and her colleagues' work inevitably marks the pre-cinematic moment of a creative constitution of the figure of woman as a narrative trope, where in specifically literary terms women writers were actively engaged in positing their *public persona* in the revelations of their unveiling words. Modern Persian literature in general and the extraordinary role of women in its creation predates and actively informs the role of women in one way or another in Iranian cinema. To fathom their varied social persona, that body of literature is yet to be navigated, for it is still a *terra incognita* when it comes to a global audience, now falsely distracted by more immediate, urgent, violent and false premises. On one hand, we have the flawed and self-alienated literary historiography that Farzaneh Milani represents, and on the other, the world is distracted by a literary memoir like Azar Nafisi's infamous *Reading Lolita in Tehran* (2003), written in English and put squarely at the service of US imperial projects at the height of its Neocon chicaneries in the Muslim world. Nafisi's volume is now known and celebrated around the globe by people who remain woefully ignorant of the literary heritage of her homeland, which is now overshadowed by the imperial hubris that has opted to celebrate Nafisi's memoir and sanction the ignorance of the monumental body of literature in Persian that her memoir deliberately conceals and camouflages. The enduring memory of Ghazaleh Alizadeh and the literary tradition she represents in diametrical opposition to Azar Nafisi's nefarious infamy both salvages her literary memory and opens an inroad into remembering how the public persona of a whole constellation of Iranian women has been the subject of their own literary and filmic craftsmanship. While the language barrier has limited global access to this Persian literary tradition and facilitated an English space for the likes of Farzaneh Milani and Azar Nafisi, the global celebration of Iranian cinema, on the other hand, offers a space where we can bring to world attention the literary reservoir that informs and animates that cinematic momentum.

Seven Shades of Memory

Let us opt for the symbolic number seven and bring to light seven women who over the last century have mapped out a thriving literary tradition, constitutional to the moral imaginary of a nation. Instead of fictive anonymities gathered in a self-serving memoir of young women reading Lolita in Tehran, sponsored and promoted by the Neocon chicaneries of a dysfunctional empire, the world needs to know about towering literary figures such as Zahra Kia Khanlari, Simin Daneshvar, Shahrnoush Parsipour, Mahshid Amirshahi, Goli Taraghi, Moniru Ravanipour and Ghazaleh Alizadeh – all real human beings, no figment of any careerist imagination, authors of their own lives and the life of their nation. At the time of her untimely death, Ghazaleh Alizadeh had seven shades of memory clouding her imagination. Were the conflated clouds to clear, she would have seen openly generations of her sisters parading – harbingers of hope that would have given her reasons to live, even beyond her mortal life.

She would have seen Zahra Kia Khanlari (1912–89) – the very alphabet of reading and writing of generations of Iranian students entirely indebted to her tireless work. Born in 1912 and raised in Tehran, Zahra Khanlari was initially educated in a teacher's college and began teaching by the time she was seventeen. She had to obtain special permission from the Ministry of Culture of the time to be allowed to take the college entrance examination with male students. She entered Tehran University's Faculty of Literature in 1934, the very first year that this venerable institution had opened its doors to female students. By 1937, she received her BA and by 1942 her doctoral degree in Persian literature. In collaboration with her husband Parviz Natel Khanlari, Zahra Kia Khanlari was instrumental in establishing *Sokhan*, one of the most influential literary journals of its time, to which she contributed essays and works of fiction regularly. In 1960, she travelled to Europe where she studied textbooks for elementary school. Generations of Iranian students (I am one of them) grew up learning how to read and write on the basis of textbooks for which Zahra Kia Khanlari was chiefly responsible in terms of their elegance, grace, simplicity and joy of their diction and prose. Zahra Kia Khanlari became a towering figure in adopting the masterpieces of Persian literary prose for high school education. It is impossible to exaggerate the significance of her *Dastan-ha-ye Del-Angiz-e Adabiyat-e Farsi/Lovely Stories of Persian Literature* (1958) that for generations introduced young Iranian students to a beautiful, simple and elegant Persian prose and a sea of fantastic stories otherwise hidden and buried in the heart of the masterpieces of Persian literature.[18] Although she did not produce a major literary work of her own, the simplicity, beauty and grace of the Persian prose and narrative diction that Zahra Khanlari crafted became the cornerstone of much that would happen in modern Persian fiction.

Next to Zahra Kia Khanlari, Ghazaleh Alizadeh would have noted Simin Daneshvar (1921–2012) – the most distinguished woman novelist of Iran, and one of the most critically influential literary figures of her generation. Simin Daneshvar was born in Shiraz in 1921 in a highly accomplished and deeply cultivated family in Shiraz. Her father was a prominent physician and her mother a painter and the director of an art school. In 1949, she left her hometown and went to Tehran to attend college, and in the following year she married Jalal Al-e Ahmad (1923–69), one of the most influential public intellectuals of twentieth-century Iran. In the Iran of the 1950s and 1960s, Daneshvar and Al-e Ahmad were the most famous and influential literary couple of their time, integral to the political and literary education of generations of Iranian youth. In 1948, Simin Daneshvar published her first work of fiction, *The Extinguished Fire*, chief among the very first fruitions of a feminine voice in modern Persian fiction in the twentieth century. A year later, she received her doctoral degree in Persian literature from Tehran University and in 1952, having written her doctoral dissertation with Fatemeh Sayyah, became the first professor of Comparative Literature in Iran. Daneshvar travelled to the US to attended Stanford University, where she studied creative writing and wrote and published a few of her stories in English. Upon her return, she began teaching at Tehran University. In addition to her own highly influential works of fiction, Daneshvar translated extensively from the works of Anton Chekhov, Nathaniel Hawthorne and Bernard Shaw (among others). In 1962, her second collection of short stories, *A City Like Paradise*, was published. Her principal work of fiction is *Savashun* (1969), one of the most popular novels in the history of Persian fiction. Set during the British colonial occupation of Shiraz, and written from a decidedly provincial angle, Simin Daneshvar's *Savashun* became a cornerstone of modern Persian literary prose, with its principal protagonist, Zari, one of the most memorable literary creations of modern Persian fiction.[19]

Behind Simin Daneshvar, Ghazaleh Alizadeh would have seen Goli Taraghi. Born in 1939 and raised in Tehran, Goli Taraghi was educated in Iran and the United States, with degrees in philosophy and literature. Her first collection of short stories, *I am Che Guevara* (1969), established her significance as a leading literary figure of her generation. Her *Great Lady of My Soul* (1979) was widely received and translated. Before the atrocities of the Islamic Republic forced her into exile in Paris (where she continues to write and publish), she taught philosophy at Tehran University and published highly influential works of fiction. Goli Taraghi's *Khab-e Zemestani/Hibernation* (1973) is a masterpiece of Iranian urban anomie in the 1960s.[20] To generations of Iranians, Goli Taraghi's literary prose is the exemplary model of an exquisitely urbane diction. She commands that distinctively cosmopolitan elegance of Tehrani inflection of Persian language that seems to have been forever lost under the overburdened scholasticism of the clerical diction now serving the ruling clergy. Whereas Simin Daneshvar brought to Persian prose her unrivalled command of the language from the heart of its Fars province, Taraghi's prose was a graceful elocution that spoke of centuries of cultivated urbanism in the Iranian capital.

Standing next to Goli Taraghi, Ghazaleh Alizadeh would have then seen Shahrnoush Parsipour, her kindred soul, closest to her literary imagination, and one of the most gifted Iranian novelists alive – bold, courageous, defiant, phantasmagoric, with a barely tamed command over her innermost subversive volcano of suppressed sentiments, emotions, thoughts and ideas. Shahrnoush Parsipour was born in 1946 and attended college at Tehran University, before going to France to study Indian languages and cultures. Beginning in the mid-1970s, Parsipour rapidly rose as one of the most gifted novelists and short story writers of her time. *The Dog and the Long Winter* (1976) immediately established her reputation as a major contender in the literary imagination of the late Pahlavi period; as did soon thereafter her *Crystal Pendants* (1977) and *Free Experiments* (1978). Her literary masterpiece, *Tuba and the Meaning of Night* (1988), was an overnight success, while her *Women without Men* (1989) landed her in the dungeons of the Islamic Republic. Soon after her incarceration and before her exile to the United States, where she now lives, she was diagnosed with chronic manic depression.[21] A masterpiece of narrative neurosis, fictive flamboyance and creative psychosis all in one, Shahrnoush Parsipour's *Tuba va Ma'na-ye Shab/Tuba and the Meaning of Night* (1988) is one of the greatest achievements of modern Persian literature. At the centre of Parsipour's works of fiction is a creative implosion that is introverted and explosive. In *Women without Men*, she weaves together the scattered lives of a number of women emerging from various walks of life and converging in a garden – at once real and paradisial – where they begin to plant themselves and come to flower, seed and fruition. Parsipour's stories begin innocently, inconspicuously and with perfect realistic cadence, and then gradually mutate into a surreal disposition borne entirely out of their own innate emotive universe – where she can discretely tease out aspects of women's lives otherwise hidden behind the banalities of their daily chores.

Next to Shahrnoush Parsipour, Ghazaleh Alizadeh would have seen standing Mahshid Amirshahi – wise, worldly, witty, political, with an urbane, cosmopolitan, sense of humour the very texture of her defiant diction. She was born in Kermanshah, educated in England and now lives in Paris. The publication of her *The Blind Alley* (1966), soon followed by *Bibi Khanom's Starling* (1968) and *After the Last Day* (1969), commenced her prolific writing career. Before the Islamic Revolution of 1979, she published one more collection of short stories – *First Person Singular* (1970) – and a selection of others. The publication of her first novel, *Dar Hazar/At Home* (1987), a masterpiece of post-revolutionary literature, brought to perfection her simple, elegant and deceptively straightforward narrative disposition. With a radical flamboyance so close and comfortable in her cosmopolitan confidence that, combined with her self-effacing character, projects a false sense of simplicity, Amirshahi became the creative voice of millions of Iranians living outside their homeland. She soon complemented her *At Home* with *Dar Safar/Traveling* (1995) – the two are now a set of classics about the course of the revolutionary uprising and its exilic aftermath for a major segment of the Iranian intelligentsia. More recently, Amirshahi has embarked on the publication of a quartet that she calls *Mothers and Daughters*, of which three volumes have appeared so far.[22] Amirshahi represents a breed of urban intellectuals with an unflinching cosmopolitan disposition definitive to the bone marrow of their creative character. Urbane, multilingual, deeply cultivated and widely read, Amirshahi's prose is crystal clear, a deeply moving chronicle of the generation of Iranian cosmopolitan intellectuals that she now best represents.

Closest to her in age and time, Ghazaleh Alizadeh would have also seen and noted standing Moniru Ravanipour (born 1952), her sister from the south – witty, wild, a magician of words and visions, a storyteller from the dark nights of the Persian Gulf, the forlorn soul of drowned fishermen and the sea monsters that swallowed them in the elemental force of her surreal fiction. A phantasmagoric native neurosis, combined with an inbred magic realism, brought Moniru Ravanipour's peripheral psychosis to perfection in her astonishing achievement *Ahl-e Gharq/People of Gharq* (1989). A year before that, Ravanipour had burst onto the Iranian literary scene with her *With Kanizu* (1989), and two years after that her *Satan's Stone* (1991) consolidated her reputation as a major post-revolutionary novelist and short story writer – a reputation consolidated with her other works of fiction that appeared after the Islamic Revolution.[23] Despite all difficulties, Ravanipour weathered the storms and remained inside Iran, travelled back to her native south and each time brought back ever more fantastic stories for her readers to read. She and her family eventually migrated to the United States. Ravanipour is the dark-skinned, bright-eyed, wide-chested outburst of the southern stories of her homeland, like nothing ever seen or heard before. Her prose is salty and dry, her wisdom climactic, her stories full of sea-ghosts and mermaids – shades and shadows of frightened, frightful hopes.

And then in the eyes of her six sisters Ghazaleh Alizadeh would have seen herself – the crowning achievement of generations of women novelist, one after the other the clear conscience of their nation, registering shades of hope, shadows of fears, colours of frustration and always a dogged conviction in the primacy of the promise they were about to discover. Before her untimely death, Ghazaleh Alizadeh's masterpiece, *Khaneh-ye Idrissi-ha/The Idrissis' House* (1991–92) became the iconic text of the first generation of Iranian novelists after the cataclysmic events of the 1979 revolution. In *The Idrissis' House*, Ghazaleh Alizadeh narrated the story of her nation through the macabre aristocratic mansion of an old family, presided over by an olden maid and her fruitless children, suddenly invaded by a band of coarse and crude revolutionaries. Alizadeh's prose is introverted, archaic, musty and meandered. She writes as if with a searchlight navigating the hidden corners of an attic full of antique and useless possessions. By the time *The Idrissis' House* begins to emerge as a parable of the Islamic Revolution of 1979, Alizadeh's prose has already sublated itself into a trans-historic reflection on the inner terrors of revolutionary violence and the hidden horrors of aristocratic elegance – at one and the same time.

The Idrissis' House is the story of a haunted house, inhabited by the dead and dying remnants of an outdated gentry, invaded by the crude banality of an intrusive band of revolutionaries – narrated by an omniscient narrator who seems to hover around the haunted house like the ghost of the young daughter of the family who was dead before this story began – a kind of self-projection of Ghazaleh Alizadeh right before she finished her story and hanged herself, her opening sentence the chronicle of a death foretold:

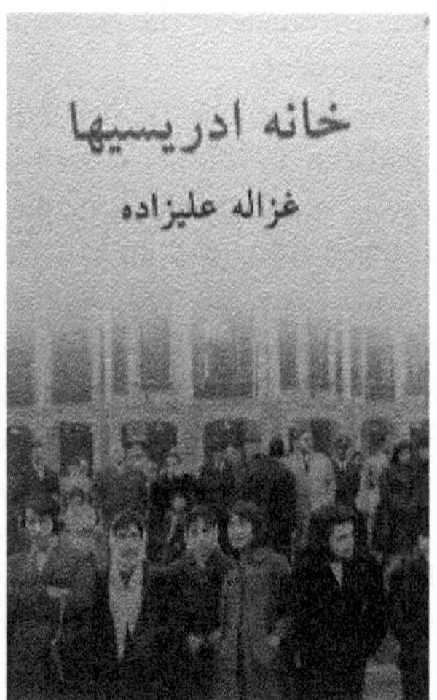

Figure 2.1 *Ghazaleh Alizadeh,* The Idrissis' House *(1991–92). (Photo: Public domain, fair use)*

> Chaos and confusion do not happen in a house quite suddenly. In the gaps of wooden boards, flanked by the creases of sheets, in between the cracks of windows, and hidden in the folds of curtains first sets a very gentle dust – all waiting for a wind to blow through the house from an opened door and let loose all the scattered pieces from their hideouts.[24]

Rethinking the Human in Literary Humanism

These women, authors of a literary modernity they invented from the debris of their patriarchal and colonial histories as they assigned themselves the *public persona* that best personified them, were not strangers in their own homeland, as later expatriate scholars would make them out to be. They were the architects of what and who and why and whence that homeland was. Nothing in their writing speaks of being outside any circle. Quite to the contrary: they were in the very middle of every emotive universe that continues to define their nation at large. They have never been dislodged, dislocated, or immersed in discontinuities. They are not in exile. They are at home – defining it, and with it their own *public persona* – thus made definitive to the gendered disposition of their national culture. Even when they are forced into exile (and only a handful of them have been), they are still at home in their writings, in their work, which is read in and out of their homeland as the continued saga of a nationhood. Still the authors of their national destiny, these women, as authors of their own *public persona*, embracing the very textured specificities of women in Iranian colonial modernity, have defined that condition of coloniality smack from the very heart of it. The heart of that colonial modernity is not at some fictive point in Tehran. It is where they are. Unveiled by the forced veiling of their expatriate misrepresentation, they reveal the heart of a homeland they have claimed in their writing. Writing them out of that forced oblivion and back into the national destiny they have authored will have them present at the moveable feast of a literary humanism that now must be saved from its European parochialism.

Retrieving the agential autonomy and narrative agency of women writers such as Ghazaleh Alizadeh, and scores of others like her, is not just to cultivate the site of resistance to a globalised capital that produces its own vacuous cultures of domination, but to map out the contour of the anticolonial literary modernity that foregrounds that resistance. Opposing the systemic and globalised eradication of individual characters and sovereign cultures are the local and regional movements that are categorically covered and narratively blinded by the native informers who sell themselves to the closest buyer by pretending to be the real thing – betraying their home cultures, while fooling their host countries.

As we retrieve the record of nations' anticolonial modernity, and the central role of women in defining it, the task of engaging the dominant terms of Eurocentric literary humanism is now particularly daunting because, as Edward Said noted, the political canonisation of its constituent texts has now become systematically integrated into denying and denigrating alternative (other and othered) sites of anticolonial modernity. Active support and detailed attention to local and regional cultures, as well as mapping out their literary and artistic defiance of cultural globalisation is the only way that the sinister eradication of historical characters and autonomous cultures can be opposed. In this respect, the whole derogatory assumptions and attitude towards so-called 'nativism' will, in fact, need to be seriously revisited.[25] What is identified and dismissed as 'nativist' is always from the hegemonic vantage point of Euro-universalism at the heavy expense of other historical evidence of alternative universalism.

In his last and most wholehearted attempt at rescuing European literary humanism from its endemic (power-basing) provincialism, Edward Said, in his first posthumously published book, *Humanism and Democratic Criticism* (2004), seeks to subject the field of literary studies to a more global reconfiguration of aesthetic taste and cultural agency. Here, Said puts forward a valiant effort at saving a continued validity for literary humanism by reviving its democratic and critical spirits, forces he sought to mobilise in order to combat the increasing domesticity of European humanism at the service of particular political interests. 'If a nationalistic or Eurocentric humanism served well enough in the past', Said observed, 'it is of no use now [...]. Ours is a society whose historical and cultural identity cannot be confined to one tradition or race or religion'.[26] There is already a variety of worlds in every 'tradition', and the task of identifying and retrieving its cosmopolitan modernity is what is at stake in mapping and navigating the *public persona* that women (or men) have narrated in diverse national and regional contexts that are embedded in their own repressed and colonised universalities.

As a founding figure of the radical critique of colonialism and its cultural foregrounding, Edward Said was acutely aware of the pitfalls of constituting a knowing and sovereign subject in his valiant struggles against the slanted relations of power embedded in manufacturing modes and manners of knowledge production that privileged one group of people over a multitude of others; as a committed humanist, he was thoroughly cognizant of (and indeed deeply concerned about) the political implications of his effort to save European literary humanism from its own recorded and effective history of disregarding the humanities of others. He noted, for example, with evident trepidation, the remarkable study of Frances Stoner Saunders' *Who Paid the Piper? The CIA and the Cultural Cold War* (1999), documenting in some incontrovertible detail the hundreds of millions of dollars that the CIA spent during the Cold War organising international academic conferences, art exhibitions, musical concerts, literary prizes and the like, spreading the uncontested premises of liberal (capitalist) democracies 'in the name of freedom and humanistic activity'.[27] These uses (and abuses) of literary humanism for blatantly imperial purposes notwithstanding, Said remained convinced that 'we must in some perhaps almost instinctual way continue to hold on to a wonderfully stable order of great works of art whose sustaining power means a great deal to each of us in his or her own way'.[28] Those works of art are limited neither to their Western European and North American domains, nor, *a fortiori*, to a masculinist imagination. Rethinking the human in literary humanism is therefore inclusive of the works of art written from a decidedly non-European, race-, gender- and class-conscious vantage point – multifarious and variegated as those vantage points are.

The steadfast conviction in European literary humanism was no mere sign of a cultural predisposition to a certain canonised set of aesthetic or literary principles, tastes, texts, or proclivities. Something far more critical was and is at stake here. As a revolutionary thinker and political activist, Said needed the primacy and principality of the knowing (and thus sovereign) subject at the centre of his humanistic project in order to make a progressive and emancipatory politics possible and meaningful. We must keep in mind that Said continued to believe in a canonical conception of literary humanism as a theorist who in the literary theory of the latter part of the twentieth century was chiefly responsible for exposing the political context embedded in the aesthetic force of the European (and by extension American) literary works of art. In his magnum opus, *Culture and Imperialism* (1993), among his other works, he was the principal force behind theorising the structural implication of literary works of art in what he called their 'worldliness'. It was in terms of such 'worldliness' of literary works of art that Said believed that 'the humanities and humanism are constitutively in need of revision, rethinking and revitalization' and that he warned, 'once they mummify into tradition, they cease to be what they really are and become instruments of veneration and repression'. He proposed what he called 'a philological-interpretive model'[29] for a radical reconstitution of literary humanism, one that takes other (and Othered) literary traditions – such as the Islamic, Indian, Chinese and so on (thus Orientally designated) – into more serious considerations and engages them in such critical manners of conversation with each other that it breaks through all their essentialising presumptions and brings them down to a worldly interlocution with the material (not just political) forces of their history. In the same vein, there is no more othered than the gendered alterity that Said's revised notion of literary humanism allows for opening up and incorporating. The key to expanded humanism is to make sure to note that, as the canon is culturally multiplied, emancipated and altered, the gendered embeddedness of the literary work of art is also registered. In other words, and as I have been arguing, the feminine public persona is always already embedded in the literary modernity they have helped shape.

The challenge that faces Said's ambitious, life-long project was not a mean task – and he was fully aware of it. In response to some of his critics who objected to his relentless conviction in the project of (literary) humanism, he once said: 'Among American and British academics of a decidedly rigorous and unyielding stripe, *Orientalism*, and indeed all of my other work, has come in for disapproving attacks because of its "residual" humanism, its theoretical inconsistencies, its insufficient, perhaps even sentimental, treatment of agency. I am glad that it has! *Orientalism* is a partisan book, not a theoretical machine'.[30]

What Said's critics do not take into consideration is the fact that his defence of (literary) humanism is not despite but because of its historical abuses by colonial and imperial powers. In her *Masks of Conquest*, Said's own student and later colleague at Columbia University, Gauri Viswanathan, has excavated the origin of English literary studies directly in the colonial rule of the British in India. It is, in fact, the startling discovery of Viswanathan that English literature as an academic subject was first established in India, long before it emerged even in England. What, alas, she entirely disregards is the manner in which the constitution of English literature as the *modus operandi* of British rule in India had deliberately posited itself against the prolonged and variegated institutional presence of Persian literary humanism on the subcontinent.[31] Viswanathan also demonstrates that the rise of British literary humanism as a disciplinary project was integral to the varied strategies of colonial domination in India. The ideological tension within the British imperial imagination, Viswanathan has argued, had pitted its patently 'secular' and Christian ideologues against each other. British literary humanism thus emerged as a potent ideological paradigm marking the archetypal project of manufacturing an ideal colonial subject, white-identified with the hegemonic ideals of British superiority. The canonisation of British literature, Viswanathan claims, is inseparable from the imperial project that had systematically institutionalised it in India. The East India Company and Christian missionaries introduced English study in India by way of 'the creation of a blueprint for social control in the guise of a humanistic program of enlightenment'.[32] The South Asian subjects of the British Empire were thus cast as 'Indians' in terms alien to their own collective identities (in plural) and domestic to the creation of a comprador class that, in the words of the British colonial officer Thomas B. Macaulay, would be 'Indian in blood and colour, but English in taste, in opinions, in morals, and in intellect'.

Precisely for these reasons, and all his commitment to literary humanism (and the creative and critical agency that it entailed) notwithstanding, Said was fully conscious that 'the schemata, tradition, and continuities proposed by Arnold, Eliot, and Frye, and by their various followers, had many features in common: all were almost entirely Eurocentric, masculine, and driven by genres, or archetypes as Frye called them'.[33] But instead of abandoning that project altogether, Said thought it could still be rescued:

> It is a fact universally acknowledged that, whereas the humanities used to be the study of classic texts informed by ancient Greek and Roman and Hebrew cultures, a now much more variegated audience of truly multicultural provenance is demanding, and getting, attention paid to a whole slew of formerly neglected or unheard of peoples and cultures that have encroached on the uncontested space formerly occupied by European cultures.[34]

He thus concluded that, 'looking back at most of the twentieth-century history of American humanism, one is obliged to say that it has been seriously afflicted with the kind of Eurocentricism that can no longer be allowed to remain unquestioned [...] all of these must be jettisoned or at the very least submitted to a radical humanistic critique'.[35] It is right here that we need to insert the central role of (non-European) women writers and their literary works of art in crafting the *public persona* that is definitive to their decidedly anti-patriarchal and anti-colonial literary modernity – upon which the emotive universe of 'the nation' is then actively imagined. The principal point of Said in expanding the cultural domains of literary humanism is of course agential autonomy for the postcolonial person – and that person, I propose, is at once *identified* and *altered* by the presence of a feminine voice in it. This is by far the most egregious negligence of contemporary literary historiography in Iran and its environs, particularly by expatriate Iranian scholars who project their own sense of loneliness and exilic marginality back to the Iranian writers they examine.

The parting gift of Edward Said to those who have inherited his revolutionary legacy was a creative wedding between a sustained critique of the colonial construction of de-humanising knowledge (predicated on an exclusively European knowing subject that had turned the world it conquered into a knowable colony) and a mode of literary humanism that opens up the space of creative agency in human affairs to a much wider feast of nations and cultures, races, classes and genders. Robbed of their humanity, the colonial people, Fanon and Said both knew well, were *object* of observations, and as such they lacked historical agency, except by picking up arms to fight for their liberties. Said's final resolution of the crisis of the European subject was to enable a postcolonial agency that was emancipated from under the colonial gaze, by participating in a democratically expanded literary humanism that crossed borders and dismantled false binary oppositions. The project of 'comparative literature' for Said, one may conclude, was this cross-cultural democratic authorisation of a literary humanism that enabled a postcolonial agential autonomy through creative interlocution with the literary text. In that project and his lifetime achievement, Said wedded the armed resistance to tyranny and conquest to the premise of a postcolonial humanism that would never take the barbarity of a loaded gun for the power of a liberated reason.

Gleichschaltung

Quintessential to the democratic criticism that Edward Said thought necessary to save the continued validity of (literary) humanism, thus to sustain the indispensable legitimacy for a knowing subject who can speak truth to power, is the defiant presence of subaltern persons and subversive cultures otherwise erased and denigrated by the aggressive cultural globalisation fully at the service of the predatory Empire that during the George W. Bush presidency Paul Wolfowitz and his Doctrine had dreamt for the world. If characters are denied their identity, if cultures are denigrated in their specific claims and locations in history, if the identity of young Iranians who are reading a newspaper to follow the fragile fate of democracy in their country are stolen and inconspicuously given to be infantilised and eroticised by presenting them as reading the most notorious literary masterpiece on paedophilia,[36] if young Iraqis fighting the colonial occupation of their homeland are stripped of their identity, insulted for their religious belief and cultural practices, and then violently eroticised and tortured, then the creative and critical agency to say no to the banality of a cultural globalisation and the barbaric cruelties of a predatory Empire that seeks to sustain it are sought to be eradicated. What in military terms is called 'Psychological Operations' (PSYOP) has a cultural connotation far beyond destroying and looting the historical records of a people's culture and civilisation, such as we witnessed after the US invasion of Iraq in the Baghdad Museum of Antiquity and other national treasures. The knowing subject of a literary tradition Said had envisioned had far-reaching political implications. But the challenge sill remained constant to the active cultivation of a moral agency for a social persona when the systematic atomisation of the individual at the service of globalised empires camouflaged and concealed such public persona.

What we witness today in such systematic eradication of individual characters and their collective cultures at the service of the US imperial design is nothing new and has its epistemic and normative origins in the history of European fascism and totalitarianism. In his classical study of the systematic failure of liberal (capitalist) democracies in Germany,

Society and Democracy in Germany (1965), the German sociologist Ralf Dahrendorf demonstrated how, through a process that they called *Gleichschaltung* ('co-ordination'), the Nazis had systematically sought to eradicate any communal and/or voluntary association that stood between the naked, 'atomised' individual and the totalitarian state. What this massive process of the 'atomisation of individuals' entailed was an aggressive plucking of people, embedded as they were emotively, and organically integrated as they stood socially, from their varied communal membership. Dahrendorf specified:

> The notion of 'co-ordination', which – like that of the 'total state' – is not an invention of interpreting scholarship, but was introduced by the National Socialists themselves in the early years of their rule, was meant politically. But inevitably it had a social dimension as well. 'Co-ordination' always means the abolition of uncontrolled autonomy. Whatever relatively self-sufficient institutions or organizations exist, they have to yield to organizations directed to the one purpose of the state and its personification in the Leader. In this process people are removed from traditional, personal, often especially close and intimate ties, and made equal in kind, if not in rank.[37]

Thus extracted and atomised, individuals were then sought to become the blank site of comprehensive ideological reconfiguration, where they were stripped of their organic links to varieties of social, cultural and emotive institutions and symbolics, and then mechanically manufactured as the ideological site of political legitimacy for the Nazi ideology and their fascist state. What the Bush/Wolfowitz Doctrine and The Project for the New American Century had designed to achieve early in the twenty-first century was no less ominous. The fate of national and regional cultures, as well as the central role of women in defining it, is always at the mercy of such global trends beyond the control of any national or even civilisational boundary. The central role of the expatriate experts effectively employed at the royal court of the imperial imagination is precisely to conflate and confuse that public persona women have curated and represented through a sustained course of literary and political cultivation.

The insights of Dahrendorf about the nature and disposition of fascism and its active atomisation of individual citizens and their social embeddedness are not limited to the social transformations under Nazi Germany. Such atomisation is in fact integral to what William Kornhauser in his 1959 classic called 'the politics of mass society'.

> Mass society [which Kornhauser also called 'atomised society'] is a situation in which an aggregate of individuals are related to one another only by way of their relation to a common authority, especially the state. That is, individuals are not directly related to one another in a variety of independent groups. A population in this condition is not insulated in any way from the ruling group, nor yet from elements within itself. For insulation requires a multiplicity of independent and often conflicting forms of association, each of which is strong enough to ward off threats to the autonomy of the individual.[38]

The principal insight of Kornhauser in this study is to navigate between an elitist critique of democracy and a democratic criticism of totalitarianism and to come up with the superior insight that there is, in fact, an affinity between democracy and totalitarianism which is conditioned by the common circumstances of a mass society – namely, a society in which individuals have become atomised, stripped of their identifiable web of affiliations and communal and cultural memberships, and thus subjected to what Kornhauser aptly called 'isolation and amorphous social relations'. In the current condition of atomised globalisation, propaganda and PR machines manufacture bestselling authors, donning a name like Hirsi, Azar, or Irshad, who in promoting their person cover up the public persona of women who have been definitive to their national, regional, communal, cultural and civilisational destiny.

While at the time of writing *The Politics of Mass Society* Kornhauser had in mind the principal examples of German and Italian fascism, on one hand, and of Soviet totalitarianism, on the other, his insights into the social formation of mass societies and the concomitant atomisation of individuals (the stripping of their varied, multiple and enriching communal and cultural identities) at the very heart of liberal democracies have made his observations particularly powerful at the dawn of the twenty-first century and the emergence of the United States as a globalised and amorphous Empire. In too much of a haste to discredit the Marxist (equally hasty) association of fascism with capitalism, Kornhauser categorically abandoned the important task of investigating the economic forces at the root of the social formation of mass societies. But long before William Kornhauser, Alexis de Tocqueville (who could not be accused of Marxism) diligently detected the roots of the atomised individuals and the formation of mass societies in the bourgeois revolution and its contingent constitution of liberal democracies:

> I believe that it is easier to establish an absolute and despotic government among a people in which the conditions of society are equal than among any other; and I think that if such a government were once established among such a people, it not only would oppress men, but would eventually strip each of them of several of the highest qualities of humanity. Despotism, therefore, appears to me peculiarly to be dreaded in democratic times. I should have loved freedom, I believe, at all times, but in the time in which we live I am ready to worship it.[39]

Tocqueville thought it the genius of American political culture to have devised the prevailing idea and the social practice of an infinite number of voluntary associations in which individuals come together and protect each other from the systematic atomisation in mass democratic societies. 'Americans', Tocqueville believed, 'have combated by free institutions the tendency of equality to keep men asunder, and they have subdued it'.[40] Voluntary associations in effect manufacture and maintain a myriad of communal and cultural identities and attachments that both give dimension and disposition to individual characters and protect them from the onslaught of totalitarian domination of all and every aspect of their social life. In pre-democratic (capitalist) and colonial societies, such communal identities have been integral to varied forms of social formations. The democratic aspirations that accompanied capitalist revolutions systematically did away with those communal (or *Gemeinschaft*, as Ferdinand Tönnies would later call them) and generated and sustained mass democratic (or what Tönnies called *Gesellschaft*) societies.[41] Today, in the communal context of such postcolonial, *Gemeinschaft*, configurations, varied forms of cultural resistance to a globalised civil society and the predatory Empire that seeks to sustain it abound – and yet they remain epistemically mute and hegemonically blinded, veiled and repressed. The task at hand is to simply mark the fact that the systematic function of expatriate comprador intellectuals has been to eradicate narratively the sites of such resistances and enable and expand the ideological hegemony of the ruling imperial regimes, and thus to conceal the organic formation of the defiant social persona of the postcolonial persons.

Tocqueville and all the subsequent theorists who have benefited from his extraordinary insights about the nature of American society have stopped short of taking the investigation one step further and carrying it into the domain of the material conditions that have occasioned such cultural traits. There is nothing in the water that Americans drink or in the air they breathe that has conditioned them to demand and exact equality and thus be exposed to tyranny. As Tocqueville himself repeatedly noted in *Democracy in America*, Europeans were not too far from getting where the Americans were. The paradoxical link between equality and tyranny is rooted precisely in what Tocqueville cherished most – freedom. That absolute and unconditional political necessity, which Tocqueville wisely recognized as the principal mechanism of resisting the tyrannical proclivities of liberal democracies, is not limited to freedom of association. It also entails and is, in fact, predicated on freedom of trade and private property, and as such it is the principal cornerstone of capitalist democracies. The reason why individuals are prone to atomisation in the social domains of capital is that, following the logic of capital, they have in their mind and soul become systematically privatised – and thus commodified. The atomisation of individuals is predicated on their privatisation and commodification. Their ownership of private properties has also mutated them – body and soul – into an instrumental locus in the chain and logic of the economic production of private properties.

From the proclivities and tendencies domestic to the privatised individuals constitutional to capitalist economies, societies, polities and cultures, and from the same propensities that the terrorising history of fascism and totalitarianism were written the world over, today we witness the organic emergence of a globalised persona – rootless and spaceless – blinding the sight and site of historically located, geographically anchored and culturally defined people. The transmutation of liberal (capitalist) democracies, the way we witness it realised from the depth of its innate proclivities in the United States today, into planetary imperial designs corresponds to a global eradication of the socially embedded individual characters and cultures as the potential sites of resistance to that amorphous Empire; thus, it extends the logic of the privatised mind, atomised individuals and mass societies, *ad infinitum*, to manufacture the recipe of a faceless, graceless, amorphous and globalised world.

The atomised individuals, once thus systematically cut off from the communal and cultural contexts of their normative behaviour, become susceptible to universal indoctrination and mass symbolic movements. 'People', under these circumstances, 'lack the resources to restrain their own behavior as well as that of others. Social atomisation engenders strong feelings of alienation and anxiety, and therefore the disposition to engage in extreme behavior to escape from these tensions. In a mass society there is a heightened readiness to form hyper-attachments to symbols and leaders'.[42] In the words of Hannah Arendt, in her seminal study of totalitarianism, 'the completely isolated human being [...] derives his sense of having a place in the world only from his belonging to a movement'.[43] Thus are structurally linked the mass frenzy of Islamist revolutionary movements and the Christian, Jewish and Hindu fundamentalism of identical fury and horror. The domain of this mass frenzy is no longer limited to identifiable, institutional religions. In the aftermath of 9/11, the entire United States corporate media metamorphosed into the singular site of a mass frenzy, where atomised and privatised individuals were systematically manipulated and mobilised for a millenarian, divinely inspired, religiously passionate, missionary zeal to 'fight terrorism' with a terror that will end all terrors. During the presidency of Donald Trump (2017–21), the zeal of his right-wing reactionary followers intimately culminated in the 6 January mob invasion and temporary occupation of the US Capitol Hill.

Robbing socially embedded individual characters and cultures of their innate and historical forces to define and resist the predatory powers that seek to dominate them, denying varied political cultures their own ability to defy tyranny and colonialism in terms domestic to their own communal language and lived experiences is one such mechanism, while the attribution of quintessential and unchanging dispositions to native cultures is another. Quintessential to a radical dispossession of people of their innate ability to make and break their own cultural habits and social practices is to assign to them ahistorical and everlasting attributes. Abstract Islamic (or any other religious) doctrines become the concrete and quintessential attributes of living and breathing human beings. Much of the cultural speculations about 'the nature of veiling' and its presumed prevalence throughout the varied aspects of the Islamic cultures (in plural) are of this nature – and yet entirely fallacious. The presumption that there is something endemic about Iranian (or Islamic) culture that has opted to veil its women is one such potent fallacy.[44] What is called 'veiling' is a social practice – and all cultures in one way or another have it. All such habits have a varied history and multiple social functions. Change those social conditions that have occasioned its historical uses and abuses, and it will disappear – if that is the problem that will solve all our other problems. The white-identified, bourgeois hostility towards veiling talks more about the anxiety of their ethnographic analysts than about the changing nature and function of veiling in Islamic (or Hindu) societies. In and of itself, veiling is neither good nor bad. What is troubling is the systematic exclusion of women from social participation, whether it is done by veiling or via any number of other repressive mechanisms – gender discrimination and/or apartheid, denial of voting rights, unequal employment opportunities, legal discrimination, social taboos, denial of their rights to their own bodies and their reproductive organs, racialised or cultural stereotypes. No culture in the world has an exclusive claim to such atrocities. Women throughout the world and across many cultures have been excluded from social participation without being veiled, and veiled women of all sorts – including Muslim women – have demanded and exacted social participation in all cultures. A captive, bourgeois imagination that is frightened out of its wits by a poor people's revolution, replete with the perils and promises of poor people, spins off baseless theories with no social foregrounding or cultural consequence, except for robbing local cultures of forces and facts domestic to their manners of resisting domestic tyranny and a globalised empire.

Books such as *Reading Lolita in Tehran* are the blueprint of manufacturing a globalised il/literacy, denial of local cultures, eradication of national and regional traditions, the wiping out of historical memories and cultural habitats that have and continue to pose – *ipso facto* – enduring resistance to a predatory globalisation and the Empire that seeks to sustain it, and above all to deny and denigrate the *public persona* for which Iranian (as all other) women in particular have fought for generations and centuries. The global function of books like *Reading Lolita in Tehran* points to a radical attempt at the erasure of the map of human agency to resist domestic tyranny and predatory imperialism at one and the same time – and thus to constitute and manufacture for the global domination of capital a vacant and vacuous void via the hegemonic reach for total power of a shapeless Empire. With the same logic that the piling of human bodies on top of each other into a shapeless mass, as we saw in those notorious pictures of Abu Ghraib, coupled with a systematic denigration of signs and symbols people hold sacred, seeks to eradicate the site of their human soul, the writing of *Reading Lolita in Tehran* is the un-writing of historical cultures and of their literary and artistic masterpieces – the sight and site of resistance to globalised cultures and amorphous empires. Under the gaze of globalised capital and the amorphous empire it has enabled, a transhistorical process of *Gleichschaltung* assimilates and camouflages prolonged literary traditions that precisely in their linguistic and historical specificities have universal claims on alternative worlds. There is nothing wrong and there is nothing particular about reading Vladimir Nabokov's *Lolita* (1955), or any other literary work in Tehran, Cairo, or Delhi, so far as the specifics of those loci are allowed to remain universal in their legitimate claims to their worldly histories.

Writing Women into Humanism

If we were to heed Edward Said's call for subjecting literary humanism to a democratic criticism, then the emerging function of cultural critique seems to navigate between two complementary poles: (1) to map out and propagate the local and regional sites of cultural resistance to the global domination of an amorphous empire and its falsely globalising culture, while (2) exposing the comprador function of *native informers* who have now joined force with old-fashioned Orientalism to become instrumental in mis/representing those local cultures, by way of eradicating their terms of revolutionary defiance of both domestic tyranny and global imperialism. It is equally imperative to articulate and theorise the *universal* terms of such local cultures that have been epistemically violated and exoticised. Very much on the model of voluntary associations that Tocqueville thought instrumental in safeguarding individuals from the tyrannies of total state domination, the recognition and active exposition of local cultures and the strength of character they *ipso facto* generate and sustain is today the single most important site of resistance to this combined banality of cultural globalism and military imperialism. Particularly notorious in this context is the comprador function of *native informers* who, by virtue of writing in English and having sided with power, have a disproportionately powerful role in mis/representing the local cultures and thus facilitating their eradication and repression. Necessary for Edward Said's call for a critical engagement with European literary humanism is the human agency, literary creativity and public persona of those who have been systematically denied such calls for conversations – and by extension their creative and artistic output that cultural globalisation (and the military imperialism it serves) seek to eradicate, deny and denigrate.

The purpose of this exercise is to turn the power of cultural hegemony which the US or any other imperial design poses to decolonial liberation against itself – and through the dialectic of that force to expose and enable the sight of a gendered women's rights discourse that is in communion with the mythic and metonymic powerhouses of historic cultures. A critique of the deeply distorting bourgeois feminism susceptible to US imperial abuse should only be done through a detailed and grounded advocacy for women's rights that is evident in classical and contemporary literary cultures. The point here is to clear the crowded field of women's rights tropes of 'white men rescuing brown women from brown men' syndrome (as Spivak puts it) and to reach for a more empowering trajectory of gendered imagination. Mapping out a wider horizon of women's voices in the Persian literary imagination paves the way towards a critical rethinking of the idea of the *human* in literary humanism. This is how the metonymic disposition of the literary imagination takes a fuller account of the moral and material presence of the dialogical disposition of the feminine voice and vision.

Metonymic allusions are like the sounds of that distant flute in Forough Farrokhzad's poem – they allude; they do not prove.

> Have you in your crystal room –
> [...] heard the sound of a flute –
> Coming from the land of the fairies [...][45]

That is how metonymic allusions coming to the world of pure verisimilitude work. An edited volume on feminist film theory is a shot in the dark and does nothing but inevitably seek to change the discourse and thus perforce clear a space for the emergence of the public persona of a repressed and denied voice and vision. In the light of that public persona, people's religious affinities – Armenian, Muslim and so on – disappear into the light of a different purpose, a fact otherwise concealed behind the rise of comprador expatriate voices that project their own anxieties and interests onto social facts they wish to read abusively for the imperial readership that recruits them. There is an inevitable dialectic at work here. These expatriate voices so deeply white-identify (for they wish to pass as white) that their interlocutors are only imagined white people. The task at hand is therefore to painstakingly detail the literary lives of real human beings who in their short or long lives craft a memorial assemblage the world cannot ignore. The challenge this assemblage faces is the hegemonic power of empires and the service of native informers they recruit to manufacture ideological consent for their war-mongering around the globe. The legacy of Edward Said on literary humanism is a crucial blueprint for incorporating the repressed and denied voices of women, in particular, into the global formation of a culture of resistance to craft literary agency which in turn becomes the groundwork for postcolonial subjection beyond the Eurocentricity of the received bourgeois feminism that the expat inorganic intellectuals represent. As evident in the services of these expats, the public persona that the globalised capitalist modernity procures is predicated on the commodification of individuals as the triumphant persona at the service of a politics of mass society that can best be resisted and overcome from the specificity of a place such as Tehran or Cairo or Delhi, where *Lolita* or any other literary text can be read to offer it an interpretation otherwise denied at the imperial offices of a bourgeois feminism. The result is a compelling semiotic proximity between the world of pure verisimilitude that these exercises implicate and the metonymic allusions where works of art mean with a non-committal aesthetic reason.

PART II

MASCULINE AND FEMININE

3

Masculine/Feminine

Aknun dobareh dar shab-e khamush ...

Now again in the silent dark night
Grow like plants
Separation walls, border walls,
To guard
The plantation of my love.[1]

Forough Farrokhzad, '*Divar-ha ye Marz*/Border Walls' (1962)

'The unchecked domination of ideology', observes Mas'ud Zavvarzadeh in his *Seeing Film Politically*,[2] 'limits historical possibilities and produces a world in response to the needs of the dominant class, the privileged gender and the hegemonic race in a society; consequently, it subjugates all other needs'. Visual and performing arts are the active occasions of questioning any dominant ideology, in both political and gendered terms. Zavvarzadeh 's generic observation assumes a particularly acute disposition on the colonial site where the dominant class, the privileged gender, indeed the very gendering of the human nature, and the hegemonic take are all a mixture of foreign and familiar products superimposed on an unruly people to sustain the colonial course. But hidden on this battlefield between the dominant and the embattled forces of a culture are its mythic underpinnings. We have to both recognize the battlefield and transcend it in order to see farther afield.

In an essay on the image of women in Mas'ud Kimia'i's cinema, Partov Nuri Ala, a distinguished feminist and literary critic, has posed precisely that challenge to the assumptions of the privileged gender and eloquently objected that, with few notable exceptions, 'women lack a positive, legal, or even human character' in Iranian cinema. The world of women, she observes, is either completely static or at best contingent on the world of the men in their lives.[3] In this pioneering essay, Nuri Ala proceeds to give a scathing critique of Kimia'i's cinema and his portrayal of women in his entire oeuvre. 'Contrary to all other intellectual elements evident in Kimia'i's cinema', she points out, 'the role of women is in fact the same as in other cheap Iranian films: Women with no assertive character, with no identity, creatures devoid of human characteristics and completely at the service of men's desires'.[4] Nuri Ala notes that the presence of women in Kimia'i's films is merely cosmetic. 'With unchanging fates, women appear on the margin of [Kimia'i's] films, without having the slightest effect on the major theme of the story'.[5]

> In his films, Kimia'i is caught between the two cultures of tradition and modernity. He tries to have a contemporary realistic perspective. But ultimately his positions are derived from the traditional culture. On one hand, he has become familiar with contemporary realism, which is in vogue among the intellectuals. On the other hand, he still defends the culture of 'honour' (gheyrat) which is favored by the masses. He appears to be intellectual, while endorsing the traditional morality. The burden of this indecision is ultimately on the shoulder of the women in his films.[6]

As Partov Nuri Ala sees it, as in all other rhetoric of anti-modernity, Kimia'i's is successful in constituting and legitimising a regressive morality which she calls 'traditional'. The trap is so successful that Nuri Ala, an otherwise exceptionally sharp critic, falls for it and keeps referring to a figment of imagination called 'tradition'. What is 'tradition', other than an invention/inversion of modernity? In Kimia'i's case, again as Partov Nuri Ala sees it, what we have is a deeply-rooted anti-modernity, in which also dwells his misogyny, against which he invents something that now even Nuri Ala can call 'tradition'. What is constituted here as 'tradition' is in fact the appositional accumulation of a negative morality which Kimia'i, as all other anti-moderns subject to Partov Nuri Ala's criticism, constructs from his deeply-rooted anxieties against a project that, by definition, dwarfs and emasculates him. We must, as a result, read Kimia'i's evident anti-modernity and misogyny simultaneously, one against and for the other. Kimia'i is anti-modern, Partov Nuri Ala tells us, because he is misogynistic; he is misogynistic because he is anti-modern; and he is both because women and modernity, at one and the same time, dwarf and emasculate him. The battlelines between the filmmaker and his critic, between Kimia'i and Nuri Ala, are thickly drawn.

Men of Honour and Fear of Castration

The principal issue in Kimia'i's cinema, as Nuri Ala sees it, is precisely the notion of *gheyrat* which needs critical attention. The word '*gheyrat*' and its immediate roots in the contemporary Iranian cultural lumpenism is almost impossible to translate. It literally and etymologically means 'honour'. However, the location of this honour is not in the character and behaviour of a man who claims to have it but grafted on the body of his female relations. A few critical points ought to be noted about the term. It is an exclusively male characteristic. Woman do not have *gheyrat*. Only men have it. If it is attributed to women, it is strictly as a male virtue that it is bestowed upon women. But men have it not in the body of their own physical presence. Their *gheyrat is* to be demonstrated by the way they 'protect' their female relations. A man is considered to be *bi-gheyrat* – that is, lacking in *gheyrat* – if his sisters or mother or particularly his wife behaves in what the cultural lumpenism considers to be indecent. The cognate of having *gheyrat* is in fact to be a *mard*, a man. One is not a 'man' if one does not have *gheyrat*. Masculinity, as a result, is not defined in any characteristic constitutional to the male body or character, but vicariously in the body and behaviour of a woman related to him. The cultural lumpenism at the root of this notion marks precisely where the endemic masculine anxiety is effectively cornered if a man's female relations do not act properly according to this norm of propriety. Man, therefore, is always a contingent being, inimically anxiety-ridden, worried and sitting on the edge of the sexual chastity of his female relations.

So far, as the image of women in the Iranian cinema is concerned, Nuri Ala believes, Kimia'i's cinema represents the most calamitous celebration of this notion of *gheyrat*. In his most celebrated film, *Qeysar/Qeysar* (1969), as Nuri Ala sees it, the entire drama in fact revolves around this female-centred conception of the male honour. Qeysar's sister is raped. She commits suicide. Her older brother Farman is killed while trying to retrieve his *gheyrat*. But her younger brother Qeysar comes and kills all the responsible parties and restores his own *gheyrat*. To start with, Fati, the doomed sister, commits suicide not because of the violence perpetrated on her own body, but, far more significantly, because by the violation of her body her brothers' manhood has been violated. She commits suicide because that is exactly what the *gheyrat* of cultural lumpenism requires. She thus exonerates both herself and her brothers by punishing her body for having 'allowed' itself to be violated. Her body here is in fact not her body. It is the location of her brothers' *gheyrat*. She is *ipso facto* the custodian of her brothers' 'honour' by simply possessing a body. Not her entire body as much as her vagina in particular is where her brothers' *gheyrat is* located. That location of *gheyrat* will have to be protected at all costs, until such time that the patriarchal culture at the root of this lumpenism allows and tolerates its religiously-sanctioned puncturing. Having been violated, punctured, before its culturally-mandated time and circumstances, Fati's vagina is the site where her brothers' *gheyrat* has been dismantled. But it is not just Fati's brothers whose 'honour' has been violated. It is society at large that expects Fati's brothers to retrieve their honour. Thus, by logical extension, the culture of lumpenism renders the moral stability of the whole society contingent on Fati's vagina. This is the full spectrum of criticism of a leading Iranian feminist against the culture of *gheyrat* evident in the film *Qeysar*.

The self-inflicted punishment of Fati's body, however, is not the end of the story. In fact, it further complicates the work of the two surviving brothers. Farman, the older brother, is now put in an extremely difficult position. Not only has his sister been violated and thus his *gheyrat* injured, but his sister, 'a mere woman', has demonstrated the superiority of her character by committing suicide. Now, what is *he* willing to do? Of course, he has to go and kill everyone in sight who is remotely responsible for this atrocity. But he is a middle-aged man and is killed in the process of trying to protect his own *gheyrat*. Enters now Qeysar, the chief protagonist, or lumpen *par excellence* as Nuri Ala sees him, with the monumental task of restoring his own *gheyrat* which has now been doubly injured by being both damaged and un-revenged.

What is completely lost in this tale of cultural lumpenism, if we were to follow Nuri Ala's line of argument, is the principal violence perpetrated against the figure of a woman. Her violated body, both by rape and by suicide, is in effect nowhere to figure in the tale of revenge. It is, conversely, the presumed dishonouring of her brother's *gheyrat* which is at stake here. What the distinguished Iranian feminist doggedly pursuing her critique of patriarchy completely misses in her reading of *Qeysar* is, of course, the classic genre of revenge fantasy that we see around world cinema, the most recent examples of which in revenging the murder of a wife are Ridley Scott's *Gladiator* (2000) and

Christopher Nolan's *Memento* (2001) – neither of which might be accused of Persian patriarchy or cultural lumpenism. Nuri Ala's critique, poignant as it is, is devoid of any awareness of this cinematic genre. But that is not the point here. If we place *Qeysar* in the same cinematic genre of revenge fantasy, the idea of *gheyrat* of course immediately transforms into the debilitating fear of castration on the part of the two brothers. Unless they restore their violated *gheyrat*, which is also to revenge the violence perpetrated against their sister, they cannot even appear in public for fear of ridicule. The repeated recurrence of a dagger in *Qeysar*, the instrument with which the lead character kills the violators of his sister and brother's bodies and therefore his own *gheyrat*, is the metaphorically evident restoration of the phallic, whereby the surviving brother has to overcome his fear of castration and reclaim his manhood. The presence of, on one hand, Qeysar's would-be wife, his ever-awaiting, ever-patient fiancé, and of, on the other hand, the figure of a prostitute he frequents both contribute to this arresting masculinity which is completely paralysed until the *gheyrat* is restored. Yes, as Partov Nuri Ala put it, '*Qeysar* is the emphatic confirmation of a culture in which women are nothing but a play-thing'.[7] But what she misses is how in the genre of revenge fantasy in cinema the dynamic fear of castration deeply informs the desire for revenge. It is that dynamic that borders the iconic significance of *Qeysar* on its mythic dimensions.

Arrested at an infantile phallic stage, the cinema that Kimia'i represents (and precisely because of its inordinate success in Iran) is a key diagnostic angle on his society and culture at large. All of Kimia'i's heroes are sexually arrested by virtue of this infantile seizure at the moment of castration anxiety. The fear of castration in Kimia'i's representation of his heroes inevitably expresses itself in deeply misogynistic traits – which finds a new momentum in his *Reza Motori/Reza, the Cyclist* (1970). Here, misogyny also assumes the posture of cliché-ridden anti-modernity. The figure of Farangis, a young woman from an opulent family, who mistakes Reza for her fiancé Farrokh because of their remarkable resemblance is the conflation of classical misogyny with rabid anti-modernism, again as seen through the eyes of a leading Iranian feminist. Farangis is staged as at once blatantly 'modern', by being different from the modest female characters in Reza's immediate retinue, and yet portrayed as deeply corrupt by virtue of being wealthy. Playing on the classical theme of Iranian cinematic lumpenism, with the rich girl falling for the poor lumpen, Kimia'i constructs the image of Farangis in such a way that not one particular, and perhaps particularly corrupt, family is condemned, but the entire ethic of 'modernity' (whose condition of coloniality he fails to detect) affiliated with it is put on trial. As Nuri Ala has rightly noted, the figure of Farangis becomes particularly maligned when she is compared to Reza Motori's mother who is celebrated not as a potentially decent human being by virtue of her character but by the mere accident of being of poor, uneducated and modest origin.[8] The juxtaposition of a young attractive and wealthy woman against the backdrop of an aging and poor mother is a particular fixation of the kind of cinema that Kimia'i best represents. The absence or the irrelevance of father figures in this cinema accentuates the latent incestuous apprehensions constitutional to an arrested sexual development when the castration anxiety has not been successfully overcome. On course of a head-on collision with Kimia'i's cinema, Nuri Ala, and the sort of feminism she represents, remain entirely oblivious to this psychological underpinning of the encounter. The patriarchal trait and the feminist response therefore remain the mirror image of each other.

The notion of *gheyrat*, precisely because of the fully exposed castration anxiety, assumes a particularly nasty twist in *Reza, the Cyclist*. Here, the lead character takes full advantage of his physical resemblance to Farangis' fiancé and in effect fools her to sleep with her and deceives her in any number of other ways. In this context, taking advantage of a rich and modern woman does not in any noticeable way interfere with Reza Motori's conception of *gheyrat*. By conflating liberation, modernity and suggested corruption altogether, Kimia'i declares open season on Farangis; thus, it is not only perfectly acceptable for Reza Motori to take advantage of her, but she in fact enjoys being so taken advantage of. 'Showing women in this image', Partov Nuri Ala points out, 'has no other consequence but give further ammunition to those who oppose the freedom of a modern women?'[9] Again, there is much more here than meets Nuri Ala's eyes. Here is where the sexual and the political coalesce. Farangis is the figure of feminine sexuality that Reza as Reza cannot have. By masking as Farrokh, Reza has the double pleasure of not only violating Farangis, but also metaphorically violating her real fiancé – two targets with one arrow. The fear of castration is thus doubly compensated, and all of that far from the anxiety of incestuous proximity to Reza's mother and the open season of 'modernity'. Here, Kimia'i represents the colonially castrated masculinity of the Iranian (as all other colonial or semi-colonial) males who are incapable of confronting the colonial officer face to face, opt to fight their surreptitious battle on the site of the 'Europeanised'[10] (white skin, blonde hair, no veiling) body of the middle-class Iranian women.

Declaring open season on Farangis, Kimia'i embodies his flagellated, colonially constituted conception of modernity in the figure of her character. Farangis in *Reza, The Cyclist* mirrors Fati in *Qeysar*. Fati is chaste, Farangis is corrupt. Fati is to kill herself if the honour of her brothers is to be safeguarded. Farangis must be violated for the masculinist culture of 'honour' to be saved. In both cases, the feminine body is the site of cultural contestation of the masculine 'honour'. But whereas Fati represents 'tradition', Farangis embodies 'modernity' – two flawed colonially constituted binaries corroborating each other. Castrated by the colonial domination, the figure of the colonised masculinity occasions the killing of the domestic women in order to hide his shame of defeat and fear of castration, and then 'Europeanises' and violates the native women as a surreptitious way of getting back at the colonial officer. This particular brand of misogyny is therefore colonially conditioned – a fact that escapes both Kimia'i's cinema and Nuri Ala's critique of it. All of this conflation of body and politics (as body politic) is predicated on a conception of the corporeal body far more symbolic than functional, far more mythic than historical. The transmutation of the body functional into the body symbolic has a rooted mechanism far beyond the immediate consciousness of a filmmaker like Kimia'i or a critic like Nuri Ala. As to why should the site of the feminine body be conceived as the location of the culture of 'honour', which itself constitutes a whole implicit theory of the body, we need to look elsewhere, far beyond Kimia'i's cinema or a bourgeois feminist critique of it.

The Metaphoric Body

Despite its immediate colonial conditioning, this metaphoric expansion of the feminine body to accommodate and locate the masculine honour, as a patriarchal trope, is predicated on, or can be traced back to, the deep-rooted Shi'i speculative theology, which is itself centred around the binary opposition between the 'createdness' (*huduth*) or 'pre-eternality' (*qidam*) of the corporeal body.[11] The Shi'i theological position on the corporeal body is one critical point where we can begin to theorise the body in a specifically Iranian context. According to Shi'i theology, the 'createdness' of the corporeal body is its most common denominator. Like 'events', 'corporeal bodies' (*'ajsam*) are created in time. Because corporeal bodies exist now but did not exist in pre-eternity, or even more simply, did not exist before, or even more specifically, because they are subject to generation, corruption and decay, then they must have been created in time. Sheikh al-Ta'ifah Muhammad ibn al-Hasan al-Tusi (995–1067), the eleventh-century founder of Shi'i speculative theology, in his *Tamhid al-'Usul*, argues that, to prove the 'createdness' of all corporeal bodies', one first has to prove that all their 'essentially-real attributes' (*Sifat Haqiqi-yi Dhati)* are different from them.[12] Then one has to demonstrate that these attributes are created. After that, one needs to show that corporeal bodies cannot be separated from their 'essentially-real attributes', and thus they too are created in time. The theoretical speculation of the corporeal bodies as contingent beings and created in time postulates the individual body within a metaphysics of corporeality that at once temporalises and sanctifies it. The constellation of corporeal bodies, as a result, constitutes the topography of a sacred landscape on which *history* must now narrate its specific events.[13] The masculine agent, in a masculinist history, we can now speculate, is principally in charge of safeguarding the feminine body as the sacred ground of this very *history*. The masculinist history is predicated on masculinist theology, which remains deeply embedded in the colonial encounter with European modernity. The assumption of 'tradition' aggravates the fact of colonial modernity. The besieged Islamic aspects of the conquered and colonised cultures inform and agitate those masculinist anxieties of the encounter.

Because of its European (Christian) disposition, the project of 'Modernity' is the most anxiety-provoking moment in the contemporaneity of that sacred history that defines Islam in general and Shi'ism in particular. Now consider the fact that, as Nuri Ala suggests, in both *Qeysar* and *Reza, the Cyclist*, Kimia'i equates opulence with corruption, and corruption with modernity.[14] Women, as Nuri Ala again proposes, are the principal victims of this equation. Farangis personifies at once modernity and corruption. Reza is there to save her. Now consider the site of Farangis' body as the cultural location of this contestation. The timely-createdness of the body temporalises its corporeality into the world. The body, in its Shi'i conception, is thus at once metaphysical, by being implicated into a sanctity beyond its control, and it is worldly, by being created-in-time. By implication, then, and via a metaphysics of which Kimia'i or Nuri Ala has no knowledge or control, and yet into which they and their creative and critical imagination are trapped, Farangis' body is where the malignancy of colonial modernity needs to be grafted. Farangis is modern, and Farangis is corrupt. Reza is heroic, and Reza is 'traditional'. Kimia'i celebrates and Nuri Ala bemoans this sight. The entire creative and critical apparatus of both the filmmaker and his feminist critic lifts the site of the encounter into mythic and metaphysical planes.

Here is how the very notion of 'tradition' is concocted from the depth of a *ressentiment* against colonial modernity. The notion of *ressentiment*, which is far more precise than 'resentment',[15] as discovered and theorised by Fredrich Nietzsche and then by Max Scheler, identifies and theorises the slavish revolt in morality. 'While every noble morality develops from a triumphant affirmation of itself', Nietzsche pointed out, 'slave morality from the outset says No to what is "outside", what is "different", what is "not itself", and *this* No is its creative deed'.[16] This is the very texture of a passive colonised response to the colonial project. Inept and emasculated, the colonised masculinity develops a *ressentiment* against the very project of modernity whose colonial disposition he fails to detect, and thus it begins to concoct a 'tradition' out of the most retrograde and reactionary traces of its native passivity. This slavish morality, as Nietzsche points out, is a *reaction* rather than an *action*. It reacts against a force, as Christianity did against the Roman Empire, by de-valuing its values. In the originary projection of European modernity, the colonised were not a party, nor were they even in a position of resistance to its extended arm of conquest and domination. *Ressentiment* is thus the inward de-valuation of the force of European modernity whereby its force is passively negated. The site of the feminine body becomes the location of this de-valuation because it is precisely on that site that the bruised masculine ego is both politically and sexually emasculated. By categorically disregarding the crucial factor of the bruised masculinity of the morally colonised men, Nuri Ala's bourgeois feminism laser beams at Kimia'i's cinema with evident insight and yet irredeemable blindness.

The feminine body is the site of this masculinist *ressentiment*, this malignancy, precisely because, for the bruised ego of the colonised masculinity, as the cinematically constituted representative of 'authentic' Iranian male, it is the most anxiety-provoking location of the anxiety-ridden culture. This is the reason why the culture of Iranian lumpenism, now constitutional to the very fabric of the Islamic republic, is so wholeheartedly for the violent imposition of veiling on the body and face of Iranian women. But the so-called Iranian secular intellectuals are far from being immune to this endemic anxiety. Because their modernity, too, is constitutionally mitigated via the colonial project, their anxiety of castration is far from being assimilated into a stable character.[17] Nuri Ala is deeply wrong if she were to believe that the 'modern' men that the Iranian lumpenism resented were in any substantial, conscious, or articulated way different from their lumpen counterparts. The rabid *ressentiment* against the encroaching culture of Europeanised modernity is rooted in the anxiety-provoking fact that, as colonial subjects, we (except in the best emancipatory art we have produced) have never had any control over the contemporaneity of our presence in the world. Here, out of his repressed colonial anxieties, Kimia'i represents the basest lumpenist denominator that actively invents a 'traditional' culture and invests it in in protagonists such as Reza. Reza's violating the body of Farangis with impunity is what Kimia'i needs to do in order to control two profoundly anxiety-provoking disturbances: first, as the embodiment of a bruised ego he is constitutionally fearful of the feminine body, and second, as a colonial subject he has a deep-rooted *ressentiment* against the colonially constituted modernity which at once 'traditionalises' and subjugates him – and that frightful fate is the site of his 'modernity'. Whereas, in his art, Kimia'i could have narrated a mode of modernity beyond that colonially constituted subjectivity, as I will soon argue that Bahram Beiza'i did so in his cinema, as he deeply resented that modernity and through his celebration of lumpenism sought to conceal, but managed to reveal, his political/sexual impotence in the violation of the feminine body. But out of the face-to-face *cul de sac* of Kimia'i's cinema and Nuri Ala's bourgeois feminism emerge the debris and fragments of a mythic domain over which neither of them had any command, control, or even consciousness. Kimia'i's cinema was metonymic in its consistent allusions to that mythic moment. Nuri Ala's bourgeois feminism buried that metonymic universe deeply in her powerful but still cliché critique.

The Colonised Masculinity

Here we reach a crucial juncture where the political impotence of the colonially constituted masculinity meets the patriarchally constituted anxiety of sexual impotence – marking the body of women as the principal site of its desperate contestations. Colonialism rapes the colonised masculinity, but – and there is the rub – via the body of the colonised feminine. The colonial masculine is rendered both politically inept and sexually impotent by the fact that his homeland, as a metaphor of his female relations, is invaded, violated, conquered and raped. Farangis in Kimia'i's *Reza, the Cyclist*, representing scores of similar characters in many other Iranian films in the genre of *Film Jaheli*, constitutes precisely the same site of contestation. The postcolonial diagnosis will have to have a rooted theological dimension. The distinction that Sheikh al-Tusi makes between the 'corporeal.bodies' and their 'essentially-real attributes' is quite crucial here. By first separating these attributes from their bodies and then arguing that no body can exist without its attributes, Sheikh al-Tusi in effect universalises a kind of ontology which is at once speculatively metaphysical and epistemologically physical – everlasting, palpable. The strategy is proto-typical in Islamic speculative theology. No mode of being is outside al-Tusi's ontology, as no mode of knowing is outside his epistemology. The result is the active constitution of the physical body upon which is cast the entirety of Shi'i metaphysics. The body is thus consecrated, or more accurately, metaphysically predicated. The individual body is no longer entitled or enabled to a private definition, so far as it is located within the Shi'i body-politic. The postcolonial body-politics of a Shi'i polity is always over-conscious of its theological roots.

What I am suggesting here is that in the Shi'i speculative theology we have a communal substitution for what Ernst H. Kantorowicz has argued for the royal body in medieval Europe – predicated on an entirely Christian theology.[18] The obvious case of the Persian theory of kingship, which is equally predicated on the body of the king,[19] is also contested in this Shi'i theory of the communal body. The site of the feminine body is therefore substitutional for the land, as its protective custody was always entrusted, or self-entrusted, to be more exact, to the masculine. The passage from contemporary

Iranian cinema over Shi'i speculative theology to Kantorowicz's theorisation of the royal body is a theoretical spectrum that exudes the classical antiquity of the mythic disposition of contemporary visual and performing arts, the metonymic playground of a distant mythic past. The more recent colonised masculinity evident in the *Film Jaheli* genre of Iranian cinema rests on these more subterranean forces – revealing and concealing them at one and the same time.

Dash Akol: The Mythic Man Idolised

In *Dash Akol* (1971), Kimia'i turns his attention to a famous short story of Sadeq Hedayat (1903–51) by the same title, which is itself based on a true story. As portrayed in this iconic film, Dash Akol is the allegorical sublimation of a Luti *par excellence* cast into a mythic persona. Predicated on the character of a trusted and valiant man of the neighbourhood, Dash Akol resonates with the characteristics of a social persona who has no evident presence in a productive life. He does not work, has no evident profession. He is just an icon. The character-type is that of a man completely alienated from society at large – standing there like a living statue. This alienation, however, is celebrated with an aura of respectability by both Hedayat and Kimia'i, representing a whole spectrum of mythic identification of the intellectuals with the Luti. The mystic of Dash Akol, and the whole ideal-type he represents, shimmers with a nostalgia for the idea of a 'Real Man'. This 'Real Man' has to be tested by a trial. Someone dies in the neighbourhood and names him in his will as the custodian of his estate and his family. The family of the diseased includes a young and beautiful girl, with whom Dash Akol falls madly in love. But he is middle-aged, his face and body full of battle scars, while she is very young, innocent and beautiful. The 'beast', as it were, cannot claim 'the beauty'. It is beneath his dignity to betray the will and the trust of the deceased man and marry his daughter. He marries the young girl off to another young man and seeks solace in the arm of a prostitute, Aqdas. But the pain of his loss finally breaks him and allows his arch-enemy, Kaka Rostam, to stab him to death. He dies immediately after he kills his murderer. While feminist critics like Nuri Ala categorically denounce Dash Akol as the epitome of masculinist vice, distinguished film historians like Hamid Naficy enthusiastically celebrate him as a hero.[20]

The 'real' story told in Shiraz, on which Hedayat reportedly based his version, is far more intriguing.[21] In that 'original' version, it is not Dash Akol who falls in love with the young daughter of a trusting friend, but his young boy-lover (*bachcheh khoshgel*), because Dash Akol is in fact homosexual. What is happening in both Hedayat's and Kimia'i's *Dash Akol* is therefore both a prevarication and a celebration of an entirely fabricated 'manhood' – bypassing the far more powerful conflation of the homo- and heteroerotics of the original story. But nevertheless: shot impeccably in black and white, located in old parts of town, with a remarkably precise lighting that gave an atmospheric nostalgia to the tenor of the narration, an exquisitely beautiful score by Esfandiar Monfaredzadeh that drew on all heroic and romantic memories of the culture, and acted magnificently by Behrouz Vossoughi as the lead character, *Dash Akol* became a cinematic legend, a carefully orchestrated staging of tragic heteronormativity. The two women of this film are either absolutely chaste, like Marjan,

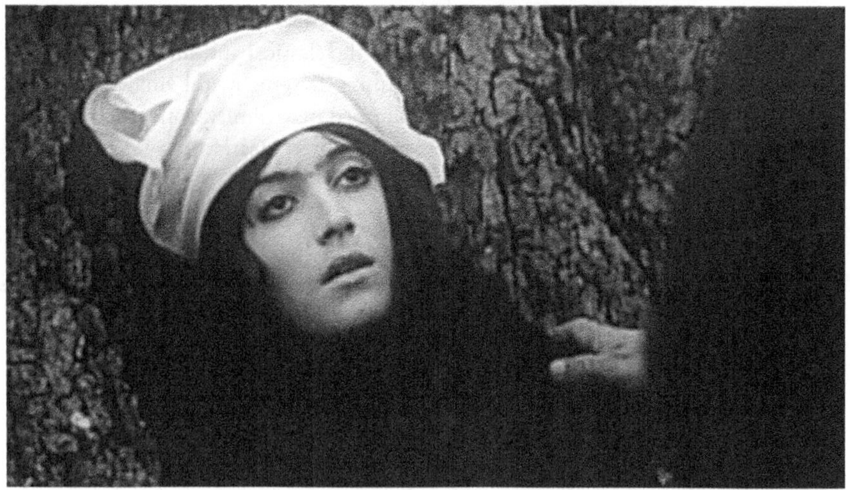

Figure 3.1 *Mary Apick in Mas'ud Kimia'i's* Dash Akol *(1971). (Photo: Public domain, fair use)*

the young daughter of Dash Akol's deceased friend, or they are prostitutes, like Aqdas, to whom Dash Akol turns for solace. The homoerotic atmosphere of *Dash Akol* survives the narrative alteration of the story and reveals a repressed truth in Iranian masculinity. What we see here, in the wide and vivid precision of Kimia'i's cinema, is the analytical evidence of a deeply repressed homoeroticism that animates the story. Kimia'i's cinema stages a frustrated psychological trauma, of inability to face reality, of ineptitude to resolve conflict or manage anxiety. There is a fear of even being born into the world in this nostalgic memory of a distant past. There is no evidence in this world of a modicum of ability to form healthy identification, enabling sublimation, purposeful displacement, creative fusion, necessary compromise, empowering renunciation, strategic compensation, or mobilising defence mechanisms. Demonstrating no ability to sublimate object-cathexes, a pathological fixation with instinctual object-choices, a constitutionalised failure to form anti-cathexes with which to oppose and overcome the instinctual cathexes, this dreamy world is the nutshell of the inability of a colonised 'Iranian' presence in the world. The worst elements of a colonised masculinity and a Shi'i theological fixation with the heteronormativity of body and soul come together to inform a gifted filmmaker as he manages to uproot the bitter fruits of an ancient tree to see its long-repressed and forgotten roots.

Contingency of the Body

The ability of Kimia'i's cinema visualising this trait endemic in Iranian culture can only point to deeper roots of the phenomenon. Issues to which contemporary Iranian culture can only indirectly point are the historically aggravated indices of far more distant memories that the contemporaneity of Iranian culture has per force both agitated and repressed. The recent resuscitation of Iranian Shi'i memories is particularly to be noted if we are to reach for a critical understanding of the culturally manufactured body of the feminine as the site of masculine anxieties. In the context of Shi'i speculative theology, Sheikh al-Tusi calls the 'essentially-real attributes' also the 'species attributes' (*Sifat-i Nu'iyyah*). The 'species attributes' are those attributes by virtue of which a corporeal body becomes what it is. A human body is differentiated from an animal body or a vegetal body precisely by virtue of these 'species attributes'. According to Sheikh al-Tusi, these attributes are not permanent; they are constantly shifting from motion to immobility and from immobility to motion, from configurational to individual and from individual to configurational, and from attachment to isolation and from isolation to attachment. The Shi'i theologian also believes that changes in a corporeal body are constitutional and not accidental to it. Because unless there is a change in the constitution of a corporeal body, there cannot be any change in its species attributes. Having then proven this, Sheikh al-Tusi proceeds to argue that corporeal bodies are in a permanent state of creation, de-creation and re-creation, as they subsist in their being.[22] This transmutational motion from vegetal over animal to human defines and designates the corporeality of the human body.

This dialectic of cross-corporeality al-Tusi has to demonstrate in order to prove the existence of an Agent outside the cycle (that is, God) who necessitates and sustains the cycle. But there is another consequence to Sheikh al-Tusi's argument to which he pays no attention. The metaphysical predicate of this Shi'i conception of the corporeal body necessitates as much a Creator who sustains its contingency as it implicates the physical body, precisely in its corporeality, into that metaphysics. The *physical body* regulated within Shi'i theology is thus no longer subject to generation, corruption and decay *before* its subjugation to a metaphysics that permanently requires its creation, de-creation and re-creation. The *physical body* is rendered the metaphysical site of a theological verification of the faith. But since that faith is a communal proposition, then the *physical body*, thus incorporated into Shi'i metaphysics, is in the public domain. The *feminine body* in particular, precisely in its femininity – that is, in its, in the masculine gaze, uncontrollable sexuality that *ipso facto* reminds the *masculine body* of its physical contingency – must be permanently controlled: thus, the juridical fixation with veiling in Islamic/Shi'i culture. The site of Iranian cinema, as one poignant example, is where the evident contingency of the masculinist history of the body implicates the feminine body into a metaphysics of uncertainty, from which premise its metonymic disposition points to a much deeper mythic history.

In Search of 'Authenticity'

The anxiety-provoking traces of cultural memory create the nostalgic prerequisites of a subconscious predisposition to an active fabrication of 'traditional' authenticity in order to oppose the paralysing effects of facing colonial modernity. In *Baluch* (1972), Kimia'i turned particularly to this search for 'authenticity'. Two antique-dealers swindle their two customers, kill them and then rape a Baluchi woman who witnesses their crime. The woman's husband, a Baluchi from the south-eastern province of Baluchistan, near the Pakistani border, chases the murderers, discovers the two dead bodies and falsely believes he has killed them. He is arrested and taken to prison in

Tehran. His wife follows him to Tehran, does not find him and ends up in a bordello. The Baluch comes out of jail and kills one of the two antique-dealers. Meanwhile, he befriends a wealthy Tehrani woman who begins to turn him into a tamed urban businessman. While he is turned into a sexual object of fantasy by the Tehrani woman and her friends, the Baluch discovers that she is actually working for the second antique-dealer murderer. An encounter ensues, in which the Tehrani woman is wounded, the antique-dealer is killed and the Baluch takes his wife and returns to his village in Baluchistan. The End.

The drama of *Baluch* rests on the close examination of a couple – a husband and wife. The Baluch and his wife are the Adam and Eve of innocence, remote in their Garden of Baluchistan Eden. Tehran is the capital is the epicentre of hellish corruption. The Baluch and his wife come from the depth of Iranian 'authenticity' – village, desert, remote lands, burning sun. Tehran is the gate to hell, with what but a 'Europeanised' woman – white, blonde, vivacious, aware of her sexuality – representing the doorway to hell, to Europe and to the centre of all evil: 'The West'.

In *Khak/The Earth* (1973), Kimia'i makes the coalescence of the colonising and the feminine even more palpable, by making the chief villain a European woman. Based on Mahmoud Dolatabadi's *Awsaney Baba Sobhan/The Legend of Baba Sobhan*, but against the very grain of the earthly worldliness of that gem of a novel, *The Earth* is the story of the two sons of Baba Sobhan who are fighting for their rights against their landlord who is a European woman. One of them is killed in the process, and the other revenges the death of his brother. The question that Nuri Ala raises about why Kimia'i abandons a realistic local woman, named Adeleh, as the landlord is important enough.[23] But a far more important question that Nuri Ala should have asked is why substitute a European woman as the landlord. The idea, Nuri Ala notes, is so outlandish that it makes absolutely no narrative sense as to what exactly a European woman is doing in a village smack in the middle of the Iranian desert, presumably as the widow of the original landlord. Nuri Ala's speculation that 'perhaps by choosing a European woman, Kimia'i is searching for a meaning beyond that of one individual'[24] is a good beginning but does not suffice. We need to dig a bit further.

The choice of the chief villain as a European woman could be read as one of the strongest misogynistic traits in Kimia'i's cinema, but at the same time it visibly identifies the colonial source of masculinist anxiety. What happens here is a contraction of two anxiety-provoking tropes, one patriarchal and the other colonial. The ultimate sign of danger for Kimia'i, operating instinctively within his libidinal fixation with domesticity as he is, is the overwhelming power of a European woman – representing race, gender, and here even class all at one and the same time. In his 1917 essay titled 'One of the Difficulties of Psycho-Analysis', Freud proposes:

> ... when we come to try to comprehend neurotic disorders, by far the most significance attaches to the sexual instincts; in fact neurosis are the specific disorders, so to speak, of the sexual function, that in general whether or not a person develops a neurosis depends upon the strength of his libido, and upon the possibility of gratifying it and of discharging it through gratification; that the form taken by

> the disease is determined by the path which the sexual function of the person in question takes in its development, or, as we put it, by the fixations his libido has undergone in the course of its development ...[25]

The cinema of Kimia'i is by, for and about men with identifiable neurotic disorders immediately traceable to a strong but arrested libidinal fixation. No culturally sanctioned, socially acceptable, or psychologically enabling gratification of the libidinal instincts are possible for these traumatised men to pan out on Kimia'i's screens. Freud's decided word is libidinal 'fixations' in plural, which points to a multiplicity of available possibilities for the growth of a fully functioning adult. But, in this particular case, no such plurality of life-affirming distribution of libidinal fixations is possible. Sexually arrested, Kimia'i's cinema verifies a whole culture of colonially conditioned masculinity – in a perpetual state of bewilderment as to what exactly is a real man, a true masculinity, or a verifiable manhood. His women folks are entirely cliché, more tropes than real, there to attest to the arrested masculinity of their menfolk. There is a subterranean state of manhood to which this cinema constantly alludes but which it cannot quite grasp. It is caught between a *modernity* it cannot quite detect in its colonial disposition and a *tradition* it has crudely invented to locate itself. The result is a cinematic conception of the body that is flat on the surface, agitated at its roots.

The Dialectics of the Body's Being-in-the-World

Even in Shi'i speculative theology we have a far more dynamic conception of the body's presence in the world. What Sheikh al-Tusi calls 'species attributes' (*Sifat-i Nu'iyyah*), he also calls the 'essentially-species attributes' (*Sifat-ha-yi Dhati-yi Nu'i*). The reason that these attributes of the corporeal body are 'created' and not 'pre-eternal' is that, had they been 'pre-eternal', they would not have been subject to not-being. The state of not-being cannot be attributed to a pre-eternal being. The reason that the state of not-being can be attributed to the 'essentially-species attributes' of the corporeal body is that when a body (*jism*) is located in a space and then moved to another space, then its attributes have either completely disappeared or have gone into another location.[26] Sheikh al-Tusi's staggering proposition is that, when a corporeal body is located in a space and when it is evident in that space by virtue of such attributes that are essential to its being the species that it is – the shape, the colour and the aroma of an apple, for example – then when that body is moved to another space, its constitutive attributes have been dissolved in and of themselves, or de-created, and then re-created in the second space. This is so, Sheikh al-Tusi suggests, because the same essentially-species attributes that constitute and locate the body cannot exist in two places simultaneously. They must be de-created in one place and re-created in another. The fact that they are de-created in one place indicates that they are constitutionally created and not pre-eternal. And the fact that they are re-created in another space necessitates a permanently, perennially creative Creator – namely, God. Sheikh al-Tusi's theological concerns as a devout Shi'i Muslim set aside for a moment, what remains is a theory of the body in which a dialectic of corporeality constitutes the body in a perennially re-constitutive mood. This state of bodily being animates the body in such a way that one moment of rest is tantamount to its final destruction. The body is thus implicated in a dialectic of sacred corporeality, *sacred* by virtue of an Omnipotent Creator in charge of its corporeality, over which the body itself has no control and to which it is perennially subjected.

Sheikh al-Tusi's conception of the body is thus necessarily contingent on its constantly re-creative attributes. A body does not, in fact, come into being except through its essentially-species attributes. This is how he formulates it:

> It is perfectly evident that all corporeal bodies, as long as they are in existence, ought to be placed in a location among the locations in the world. It is not logically acceptable for a body to exist and have measurements and proportions, and yet not be located in a location among the locations. That is exactly the reason why when we think of two bodies, they are inevitably imagined either close to or far from each other. And that precisely indicates that bodies are located in a location. Now that we have established that a corporeal body must be located in a location, and we demonstrated that no corporeal body is located in a location except by virtue of the essentially-species attributes specific to it, then we can conclude that without its essentially-species attributes no corporeal being comes into existence.[27]

If it be so, and if the very existence of the body is contingent on its constitutive attributes, and if its constitutive attributes are implicated in a dialectic of corporeality, then the sanctity of the body is perennially caught in a nexus that coagulates its attributes and its very existence. That proposition permanently consecrates the body, incorporates it into a *metaphysical body*, subjects it to a narrative of sanctity and thus renders it impure and desecrated the instance it has violated that sanctity. The *physical body* is thus anointed, made into something beyond its ephemerality. The more the *physical body* is narrated into the *metaphysical body*, the more it loses its immediate and palpable corporeality. The more the body is venerated, the more it is ritualised to obedience. In Shi'i metaphysics, then, the body is theologically antiquated, made into something prior to its corporeality, to its domesticity, to its inner logic of generation, corruption and decay. The consecration of the body is its simultaneous imprisonment in the gridlock of theological culture. Without reducing the vast body of Shi'i scholastic theology to any pre-Islamic mythology, the metaphysical corporality of the physical body becomes the site of some very distant, some very ancient mythological habitat that in Shi'ism assumes decidedly Islamic character. What the oscillation between Shi'i speculative theology and contemporary Iranian cinema frames is a reading of the physical body's being-in-the-world that makes it at once deeply rooted in ancient mythologies, scholastic speculations and cinematic gestations. This, in a nutshell, is the metonymic corridor of pure verisimilitudes that animates the contemporary visual and performing arts.

Sexual Thralldom

A body thus consecrated/imprisoned is the embodiment of the culture, with all the anxieties and the vicissitudes of its history written all over it. The character of Fati in Kimia'i's *Gavaznha/The Deer* (1975) is a typical example of his curious attachment to prostitutes. Seyyed and his friend Qodrat define the chief narrative thrust of *The Deer* as a story of friendship between two men. Seyyed and Qodrat are two long-time friends. Seyyed has turned into a miserable drug-addict who lives with an actress-*cum*-prostitute. Qodrat is a political activist who has been chased and wounded by the police. The two engage in an arduous dialogue about their respective lives when Qodrat seeks refuge in Seyyed's dilapidated room. The film is the story of these two masculine protagonists until their death by the police. Fati is of no consequence whatsoever to anything beyond a mere pathetic backdrop to make the miserable life of Seyyed look even more pitiful. But the constitution of her character as an actor/prostitute needs some critical attention. We see a similar character in Aqdas in *Dash Akol*. But the samples are representative of a much more endemic pathology in Iranian cinema, in general, and in Kimia'i's, in particular. Fati in *The Deer* and Aqdas in *Dash Akol*, as indeed scores of other similar characters, do absolutely nothing but provide solace to the misery of their male companions. But what exactly is the nature of this 'solace'?

Fati and Aqdas, as the iconic prostitutes, are easy, accessible, tolerant, even 'loyal' in their own code of conduct. They are always 'really good girls' who for one reason or another have been 'misled'. They love their male companions, Seyyed and Dash Akol, respectively. Their love is pure, simple, undiluted, uncomplicated, always available. Kimia'i's attraction to the character of prostitutes, however, is not that simple. He is a bit too cozy with these characters. So cozy, in fact, that he uses them formulaically, almost subconsciously, and in doing so he leaves behind himself a trace for us to pick up.

In his 1918 essay 'The Taboo of Virginity', Freud has a splendid little theory which he picks up from the 1892 essay of Von Krafft-Ebing, 'Bemerkungen über "Geschlechtliche Hörigkeit" und Masochismus' and which he calls 'sexual thralldom'.[28] The principal concern of Freud in this essay is the taboo of virginity and its communal designation as socially significant. He considers virginity as a particular case of the monopoly of the man over not just the woman's sexuality but, more importantly, a monopoly over her past.[29] From here, Freud proceeds to theorise the sustained denial of a woman's sexuality until such time that it is socially sanctioned and released by the loss of her virginity to a man, and he argues for the generation of something called 'sexual thralldom' in woman, because of her prolonged and exclusive dependency on this particular man. Referring to this prolonged expectation and singular release of woman's sexuality, Freud suggests that 'this experience brings about a state of "thralldom" in the woman that assures the man lasting and undisturbed possession of her and makes her able to withstand new impressions and temptations from without'.[30] Freud further suggests that for obvious reasons 'sexual thralldom is incomparably more frequent and more intense in women than in men, though it is nowadays much commoner in the latter than it was in antiquity'.[31]

What we witness in Kimia'i's libidinal fixation with prostitutes is a kind of negational sexual thralldom which points to something rather frightening in the masculinist culture he so capably represents. Prostitutes provide a safe, protective, easy and easily manipulatable haven from an otherwise complicated sexual territory that requires a whole lot of moral and psychological maturity. Kimia'i's cinema represents men who are intellectually infantile and sexually thwarted. They are, as such, constitutionally incapable of cultivating a lasting, loving and caring relationship with any other human being, particularly with women. The libidinal fixation is so brutish, and so blatantly elemental in its foregrounding of power, that the slightest suggestion of a sublimated transformation requiring the most elementary forms of moral, social, cultural, or sensual articulation is beyond their means. As a result, they are much more comfortable, and thus develop a negational sexual thralldom, with prostitutes. The incestuous element is so strong in this sexual thralldom, precisely because the prostitute functions as the lover-mother of the infantilised masculine and mothers him as she sleeps with him. Seeking haven in the mother-lover, in a sexual thralldom that helps to shut the world up and immunise the infantilised masculinity to any moral maturity, Kimia'i's men can then easily launch their misogynistic vengeance with impunity. The same sexual thralldom can also account for the prevalence of paedophilia in Iranian lumpenism, so visually glorified in Kimia'i's cinema. In either of these sexual engagements in Kimia'i's cinema, we are in the presence of almost mythical forces of human vulnerabilities.

Aggression against young and attractive women is libidinally accentuated by sexual thralldom to prostitutes as mother-lovers, with the same logic that molesting children in paedophilia is equally mirrored in the projection of violent masculinity. Deeply misogynistic, while infantilised in an incestuous engagement with the mother-lover in sexual thralldom with prostitutes, a homosexual paedophile, while violently machismo – the picture that emerges from Kimia'i's cinema is deeply troubled. This is not a pretty picture to behold, with forces of juridical patriarchy and psychotic side-effects of colonialism joining force to define a culture in at once frightful and yet revelatory insights. In a career that has spanned over half a century, Masoud Kimia'i has been a consistent force, giving ample space to the subterranean forces of an ancient culture of patriarchy, dealing with the sustained consequences of a deeply colonised masculinity. Through the thicket of this deadly mixture, we are excavating some very distant echoes of the mythic meandering of deeply repressed memories.

Mutilating the Feminine Body

In *Ghazal/Gazelle* (1976), Kimia'i's exposure of the disturbing debilities of the patriarchal culture hits an absolute rock bottom, when on the basis of a short story by Jorge Louis Borges he makes a film about two brothers who live in a hut in the middle of a jungle and whose serenity and homosociality are suddenly shattered by a prostitute whom they finally murder in order to return to that perennial stage. If Borges' short story is cynical enough, what Kimia'i does to Borges is even more troubling. The way Nuri Ala sees it,[32] if in Borges' story the prostitute is a mythical test of the two brothers' loneliness, in Kimia'i's *Gazelle* she is reduced to a non-entity, to a point that her murder at the end of the film looks almost mundane. But the murder of the prostitute in Kimia'i's film is anything but mundane – and there is no reason why we should not read the entire story in a mythical register. *Gazelle* reveals a frightfully eremitic fear of woman; it registers the very constitution of the feminine as evil, disruptive, flagitious, baneful. In *Gazelle*, Kimia'i retreats his two brothers, just like Cain and Abel, back to the pre-eternity of a non-moment in being, when there were only two men and no women. They are deep in the heart of a jungle, fully bounded by a brotherly love, in the Philadelphia of their masculinity. They leave this paradisiacal abode and enter the realm of war, the corrupt and corrupting city, where they pick up a prostitute and bring her into their inner sanctum. There, she becomes the tempting source of evil, the tempting Eve, their servant-sorcerer, the very evil incarnate, leading the two brothers to distrust each other. Murdering that woman and restoring peace and harmony among them is no mere narrative resolution here. It plunges the whole story into its mythic resonances, in Biblical and Qur'anic terms – recasting Mashya and Mashyana in a decidedly patriarchal and colonial shadow.

What is happening here in Kimia'i's cinema is a narrative and visual updating of a whole genre of literary imagination in Persian, given exclusively to an active demonisation of women. From the story of Joseph in the Bible and the Qur'an to the story of Sudabeh and Seyavash in the *Shahnameh*, traces of this phenomenon are quite evident. But the prosaic fluidity with which Kimia'i attends to his rendition of the genre is remarkably reminiscent of al-Zahiri al-Samarqandi's *Sandbad-nameh*, a literary classic of the seventh/thirteenth century devoted completely to the characterisation of women as pernicious evil-doers. *Sandbad-nameh* has a literary genealogy that is traced back to the Sassanid period in pre-Islamic Iran, to the reign of King Anushirvan (531–79), in particular.[33] The framing story of *Sandbad-nameh* is the familiar love of the King's young wife for her step-son. The young Prince refuses his step-mother's advances. Frustrated, she accuses him of dishonourable intentions, leading the King to issue him the death sentence. The young prince has a close vizier, Sandbad his name, who has seen it in the stars that his young patron should not utter a word for seven days. The young Prince cannot therefore defend himself against his step-mother's false accusations. Sandbad summons seven viziers to tell the King one story a day, on the evils of women. They do so and thus 'filibuster' the King's command. On the eighth day, the young Prince speaks in his own defence, and the King is satisfied and orders his young and treacherous wife executed.

What Kimia'i's cinema shares with the *Sandbad-nameh* is the atmospheric masculinity that animates them both – and thus roots his entire cinema in much deeper mythic traumas of gendering history.[34] *Sandbad-nameh* is not only written by men and for the entertainment of men but, more importantly, its very narrative energy has a homosocial, harem-like festivity to it. The prose is flirtatious, the diction saucy, full of poetic interruptions, with Arabic poetry interlacing Persian prose, Persian poetry embellishing Arabic phrases. Al-Samarqandi, in fact, in his own introductory remarks refers to an earlier Persian translation of the original Pahlavi text in the fourth/tenth century which in his judgment was not pretty enough. 'It was devoid of ornamentation and sweetness', he says and even suggests metaphorically that 'this bride was not made up by any beautician'.[35] The stories that are then told within this framing story are equally tantalising, suggestive, full of strong sexual innuendoes, all centred around the presumed insatiable sexual appetite of women, their cunning ways of getting the object of their desire, while fooling their husbands, lovers and even lovers that they take over their lovers. At the end of the story, when the young concubine of the royal harem is brought to face the King's justice, he turns to his courtiers and asks them what he should do with the impertinent concubine. Someone says to gouge out her eyes so that she can no longer see a young man, desire him and cause mischief. Others suggest that her tongue should be cut off so that she cannot accuse innocent men of evil deeds. Still others suggest that her legs should be cut off so that she cannot walk in avaricious ways. Someone says that her heart has to be pulled out of her chest so that she can no longer desire another man. Finally, the King turns to the young Prince himself and asks him what to do with the treacherous woman. 'Shave off her hair, blacken her face, mount her on a black mule, and take her around the capital, and have someone say out loud that this is the punishment of a person who betrays her master'.[36] Al-Samarqandi had mutilated the woman's body hundreds of years before Borges and Kimia'i together.

The metaphoric mutilation of the young concubine in narrative public is as central to al-Samarqandi's text (and in the long genealogy it carries from ancient and classical memories) as is the visually mutilated body of the young prostitute in Kimia'i's *Gazelle*. What matters here is how, from Samarqandi to Kimia'i, long before the former and long after the latter, the site of a woman's body and the very sight of her soul are so pathologically anxiety-provoking.

Where Men are Men ...

The manly cinema of Kimia'i may still be investigated further, in such films as *Safar-e Sang/The Journey in Search of Stone* (1978), where he is deeply plunged into a mythical well, nowhere to be found except in a metaphysical celebration of an accolade of masculinity, manly honour, primeval machismo and phallic-centred anxiety. *The Journey in Search of Stone* is the story of a group of men who leave their abode in search of a millstone. The only two women who chase these men in their quest do so because the men have to protect their honour while on their search. Some critics read the film as anticipation of the Iranian Revolution, while others pointed to its script and plot flaws. Central to the film, however, remains the homosocial plotting of a group of men in search of a millstone to save their village.

By far the strangest, and yet the most logical conclusion of Kimia'i's masculinist eremitism is his *Khat-e Qermez/The Red Line* (1982). Based on a script by Bahram Beiza'i, *Shab-e Samur/The Night of the Sable* (1981), Kimia'i's *Red Line* is a complete metamorphosis of the central protagonist of the story – where a female protagonist is replaced with her male counterpart. In her short paragraph on this film, Nuri Ala wonders: 'The question is why in order to make a film about a man, Kimia'i has turned to a script whose central character is a woman and her physical and emotional changes'.[37] The answer to Nuri Ala's poignant question should by now be rather evident. In his boldly masculinist cinema, Kimia'i has no realistic or imaginative place for a woman in the homo-cinematic universe where he is most at home. The potently homosocial space of his cinema does not quite know what to do with a woman except as a prostitute, an old and kind mother, or else a chaste and untouchable fiancée. Whereas in Beiza'i's story the central character is Laleh, a newly wedded woman entrenched in a psychological journey of self-discovery, in Kimia'i's film, the chief protagonist is Amani, a member of the Shah's notorious SAVAK organisation, pathetically entrapped in a whirlwind of self-hatred. For Beiza'i, Laleh is a simple, straightforward woman who meets a man, Amani, and very soon marries him. For Kimia'i, Laleh is a pre-revolutionary rich woman who is now working as a nurse and who succumbs to marrying Amani, a poor man who joins SAVAK in pursuit of power and wealth. In Beiza'i's story, Amani is part of the same psychological drama in which Laleh has to discover herself. In Kimia'i's film, Amani is a self-loathing parasite who savagely enjoys hunting, is frightened by the revolutionary outpour of the late 1970s and has escaped his poverty-stricken misery by working in a brutally suppressive security organisation. Beiza'i in his script surrounds Laleh with tangential characters – family members and friends – who contribute to her sense of anxiety as the principal force behind her own self-discovery. Kimia'i in his film isolates Laleh in an oscillation between her concerns for her husband Amani and her seeking refuge with a former friend, Jamal. In both cases, the revolutionary background of the story fades into the psychological traumas of individuals, but in one it is the emotional fate of a woman and in the other the psychotic disposition of her husband that is the main force of the narrative.

By the time Kimia'i made his *Dandan-e Mar/Snake Fang* (1989), he was ready to explore homosexuality – however subtly and by innuendo. In the emotional universe of his men, women were now made completely redundant.[38] The relationship between Reza and Ahmad, the two chief protagonists, very much sums up the homoerotic disposition of Kimia'i's entire cinema. Most of the Iranian critical reactions to the film dwell on its realistic depiction of the social circumstance of the post-war era and marking the manner in which the world around his characters was changing. But equally crucial is the location of these two protagonists in that very era – two lonely and isolated men from two ends of the country finding solace and consolation in each other's company.

... And Women are Not Men

Luce Irigaray, in her 1977 book *Ce sexe qui n'en est pas un/This Sex which is not One,* takes to task the whole metaphysical underpinning of sexing and gendering in the Platonic (what she as well as other Europeans call 'Western') philosophy.[39] What becomes evident in reading Irigaray is the unexamined metaphysical premise that underlies the groundbreaking theorisation of sex and sexuality by Freud. While Freud had thought that he had achieved access to the laboratory of human emotions through his clinical observations, beyond their mutated forms of socialisation, culturation and religious sanctification, Irigaray has demonstrated the enduring assumption of binary oppositions that Freud had inherited from Platonic metaphysics and never examined. The very Oedipal take on the formation of human sexuality, Irigaray has demonstrated, is predicated on a set of binary oppositions constitutional to Platonic metaphysics. Central in the successive generation of theorisation of the human subject has been the male subjectivity, to which there has then been attached the peripheral status of feminine objectivity. This primarily European re-examination of the masculinist subjectivity has some limited heuristic benefits for a more comparative assessment of such subjectivities. But critical thinking about sex and gender cannot remain thematically or theoretically limited to these European citations – although European philosophers have always assumed that what they are thinking is universal and in fact not very particular.

In the domain of art proper, the aesthetic imagination can as much subserve the dominant metaphysics and the privileged gender as it can challenge and subvert it. Pointing to alternative modes of being, creating substitutional possibilities of subjection, is one principal way that the creative imagination has constituted itself in critical circumstances. But forces of cultural epistemics are no ordinary trappings, not easy to evade, supplant, or transmute. The cinema of Mas'ud Kimia'i is a perfect example of how an extraordinarily talented and imaginative artist can not only fall into the trap of the most retrograde dimensions of his cultural parameters, but in fact serve and sustain them. The sum total of Kimia'i's achievement has been a cinematic celebration of the most reactionary forces in Iranian culture, particularly by show-casing the domineering force of manly power and masculine 'honour', without pausing for a minute to question their legitimacy, or the centrality of their function in disenfranchising generations of Iranian women from their most inalienable rights. But at the same time, this very cinema, by its sustained course of narrative creativity, has also tapped into the subterranean forces of a mythic culture at the fateful moment of its encounter with colonial modernity. Bourgeois feminists such as Nuri Ala were of course rightly angry with this cinema, but that anger, legitimate as it was, pre-empted any more serious reading of those mythic forces that had surfaced under colonial duress. What they missed was the creative dynamics of subject formation in both compliant and defiant terms.

Kimia'i's cinema is deeply rooted in a masculinist history where the active agency of masculine power is principally in charge of safeguarding the feminine body as the sacred ground of history. This is what the masculinist agency has inherited from its self-written history. With the dawn of colonial modernity and its extended arm of de-subjection a whole new angle on masculinist anxiety has come into full view. In this context, the feminine body is the site of a masculinist *ressentiment* that occasions the creation of an 'authentic' Iranian male, a proposition that *ipso facto* has made the feminine body the most anxiety-provoking location of the culture. The *physical* body having already been rendered the metaphysical site of a theological verification of faith, and that faith being a communal proposition, the body is then incorporated into Shi'i metaphysics as public property. The *feminine* body in particular is subjected to a permanently controlling gaze. Having been implicated in a dialectic of sacred corporeality, the body is then *ipso facto* the site of all cultural contestations, including pathological cases where a culture cannot control its own anxieties. The sacerdotal disposition of the corporeal body is precisely where the mythic memories of the homoerotic body surface. Detecting and articulating those mythic moments is the principal task guiding towards decoding the metonymic allusions to those repressed but still active memories.

What first and foremost emerges from Kimia'i's cinema is a particularly troublesome vision of toxic masculinity: pathologically misogynistic, while infantilised in an incestuous engagement with the mother-lover in sexual thralldom with prostitutes, reversed in homoerotic undertones, while violently machismo. Central to this pathological picture is an innate, inarticulate, fearsome and perturbed hatred of women as a site of anxiety. The metaphoric mutilation of the young concubine in the narrative domains of *Sandbad-nameh* as one particularly disturbing example in classical Persian literature, is as central to al-Samarqandi's text as is the visually mutilated body of the young prostitute in Kimia'i's *Gazelle*. Having maligned and mutilated the body of women in her films for such a long time, Kimia'i has completely erased the place of woman in his masculinist cinema. The trouble with this erasure, however, is not just the pathology of a particularly acute case of misogyny. The picture it reveals about the men who watch, publicly celebrate and uncritically praise this cinema is even more troubling. The site of that trouble is the location of perhaps the most potent engagement with the deep-rooted mythic dispositions of the culture. Not everything that surfaces in this cinema is pretty or life-affirming. The worst consequences of those mythic memories exacerbate the worst elements of a colonised masculinity to produce an entirely toxic environment. But transcending the creative urge of the filmmaker and the critical apparatus of a bourgeois feminist sits the task of far more serious reflections on the metonymic disposition of the unknowing subject, which results from this fateful encounter.

We are sitting on a minefield of recent and distant layers. But from the battlefield of contesting contemporary ideologies, we must transcend to read the mythic moments that they mark and measure. As we watch Kimia'i's films and read Nuri Ala's feminist criticism, we are witness to two sides of the same coin, having drawn the battlefields where men of honour face the fear of their castration and liberated women demand their rightful places. As evident in Nuri Ala's criticism of *Qeysar*, she categorically disregards the genre of revenge fantasy, or the colonially constituted fear of castration. The kind of misogyny we witness in Kimia'i's cinema is colonially conditioned, while the metaphoric body it implicates points to Shi'i theologians like al-Tusi writing on the corporeal body, which the condition of coloniality has exacerbated. We are therefore faced with a colonially bruised masculinity that can only identify itself with its power over his feminine alterity. As Kimia'i's colonised masculinity solicits Nuri Ala's bourgeois feminism, from their battle emerges the mythic moments that are metonymically mapped out, where the contingency of the corporeal body has become transmutational – albeit entirely unbeknownst to them both. As the masculine gaze makes the female body contingent, a rhetoric of 'authenticity' emerges that resurrects in the anxiety of colonial modernity, which inevitably creates nostalgic traditions, such as in the movie *Baluch*, where a new innocent Adam and Eve are placed at the centre of the story. We witness in *Khak/The Earth* how the European woman personifies the actively repressed colonial power. The sex and neurosis of a European woman (thus portrayed) exposes both the fake modernity and its contingent fake tradition. The pure verisimilitude that results marks the sexual thralldom that, in turn, reveals itself with the fixation on the figure of the prostitutes as mother/lover. The mutilation of the body of the prostitutes as we see in *Gazelle* revives the thematic of *Sandbad-nameh* and from there tapping into far more distant mythologies. In *Safar-e Sang*, the homosocial space shows us a different way of gendering the subject, which becomes aesthetically creative.

Two major themes are evident in Kimia'i's cinema: (1) tapping into distant literary and mythic origins of homosocial masculinity, and (2) its seamless fusions with the toxic masculinity occasioned by the condition of coloniality. Embedded in that background, the negative dialectics (Adorno) of gendered violence that is scripted onto the feminine body by a colonially contingent masculinity cannot in and of itself mark any gender specificity. Mapping the disposition of the masculine in specifically symbolic terms, we see how the body becomes metaphoric – a fertile ground for cinematically remembering its otherwise repressed mythic past. The metaphoric body is the fertile ground for its metamorphic disposition oscillating between a mythic memory it cannot completely remember or forget and a metonymic remembrance it cannot but exude. Both sides of this nexus are colonially mitigated. The pioneering work of French Islamist scholar Henry Corbin on the premise of *Spiritual Body and Celestial Earth* (1960) in the Mazdaian and Shi'i sacred geographies frames the theoretical thrust of this conception of the body, which pivots towards the articulation of an amorphous unknowing subject that dialectically unframes the knowable world. This creative dynamic takes the scene back to the myth of origin. Much older and far more deeply rooted than the Qur'an, or even the Bible, in the Zoroastrian traditions Ahura Mazda's sixth creation, Kayumars, was neither male nor female. The Evil Spirit or Ahriman (Angra Mainyu) sought to destroy all that Ahura Mazda had created. It therefore sent the demoness Jeh to kill Kayumars, from whose remains eventually grew Mashya and Mashyana. How has that myth of origin survived, thrived, transmutated, sublated and finally reached us in concealed and enabling terms? Corbin's groundbreaking work is a solid premise in mythic terms of that continuity. But more specifically when it comes to Kimia'i's cinema, this is where and how the politics of masculinity overrides the status of women.

According to the leading scholars of the field, the character of Jeh is crucial in this assessment. This is what one leading scholar tells us about Jeh:

> A largely parallel story [to Zoroastrian sources] has been preserved by the Syrian theologian Theodore Bar Koni [...] with one dramatic difference: in his version of the story, it is not a demoness who is rewarded by Ahriman, but it is women themselves, who were created by Ohrmazd, but defected to the Evil Spirit. By combining these two passages, from the *Bundahišn* and from Bar Koni, Zaehner believed he could prove that in Zurvanism (a purported 'heretical' variety of Zoroastrianism), women were seen as creatures of Ahriman. He attempted to support this striking idea by collecting various Zoroastrian passages which spoke about women in negative terms and then simply claiming them to be Zurvanite. These suggestions were picked up and elaborated upon by Geo Widengren and others, but they have since been shown to be unsoundly based.[40]

That scholarly debate can continue apace for generations. What is paramount for us here is the metonymic function of the works of contemporary visual and performing arts that unseal those ancient mythologies in terms immediately accessible to our lived realities. No visionary poet other than Forough Farrokhzad has tapped into those ancient mythologies to understand and explain where we stand in the world. Her conception of love was cosmic, material, moral and imaginative, beyond anything seen or heard before. She was the resurrection of Jeh in the most liberating way of reading that persona to recast the historical terms we had always dreamt but never dared to see:

> Come nearer now
> And listen carefully
> To the anxious palpitations of my love
> Spreading
> Like the rumble of African drums
> In the tribal ululation of my body.[41]

4

Feminine/Masculine

Man khusheh-ha ye na-ras-e gandom ra ...

I hold clusters of young wheat
Under my breast
And nurse them ...[1]

Forough Farrokhzad, '*Tanha Sedast keh mimanad*/
Only the Sound will Last' (1973)

As the Ma'arefi family is getting ready in Tehran for the wedding of their young daughter Mahrokh, the bride's elder sister Mahtab Ma'arefi, her husband Heshmat Davaran and her two children get into a rented car in the northern part of the country to drive south for the occasion.[2] Before getting into the car, Mahtab looks straight into the camera and with a disarmingly blank face says: 'We are going to Tehran to participate in my younger sister's wedding. We will not reach Tehran. We will all die'.

With those simple opening lines in Beiza'i's *Mosaferan/Travelers* (1991), something extraordinary happens, not only in the creative career of by far the most widely loved and admired Iranian filmmaker, but also in the very vast and variegated spectrum of Iranian cinema. Beiza'i never achieved the global fame of his counterpart Abbas Kiarostami. His cinema therefore remained very much limited in its global spectatorship. This limitation has seriously compromised the critical attention paid to his cinema. But, by the same token, Beiza'i's cinema remains the fertile ground of an untapped reservoir of Iranian memorial and modern mythologies. In addition to being a towering filmmaker, Beiza'i is also a playwright, a theatre director and a scholar of Iranian performing arts. Because he could not bear the pressure of official censorship and harassment in his homeland, he finally left Iran and opted to live and work in California. His work after he left his homeland has been seriously compromised by the politics of despair in and about the Iranian expatriate community in California. To this day, the golden years of Beiza'i's career are still those from the time he was active in Iran – and those are the works that have attracted the interest of scholars and critical thinkers the most.

How did Mahtab Ma'arefi know what would happen on their way to Tehran to attend her sister's wedding? If she was sure this would happen, why did she join her family to travel to their own death? What kind of premonition is this – basking in a richly symbolic, mythical prose in the midst of a patently modern world?

Daybreak

There is a scene early in Bahram Beiza'i's iconic film *Bashu, Gharibeh-ye Kuchak/ Bashu: The Little Stranger* (1986), when Bashu opens up the thick cloth cover he has held over his head in the back of the truck that has driven him on a nocturnal journey from the war-torn southern Iran to the northern Caspian regions. He has had a hellish night, in complete darkness and deadly solitude, and carries even deadlier memories of the war in his homeland and the death and disappearance of his entire family. From death, destruction and frightful solitude under a thick garment, and on a nocturnal journey from hell, in the course of which he has been as good as dead, he now throws off the cover of his protection, like being born from a dark womb, and gets up and rises like a resurrection right in the middle of a paradise. The truck has stopped, the truck-driver is having breakfast. Bashu does not know where in the world he is. But there is a green serenity to the world, a quiet splendour, a reassurance in the air. The nightmare is over. The day has broken.

Coming to Beiza'i's cinema after the overbearing masculinist world of Kimia'i's, one feels like Bashu on that gloriously re-assuring dawn of a new day. Bahram Beiza'i's cinema is the absolute opposite of Mas'ud Kimia'i's. Beiza'i stands precisely for everything against which Kimia'i has worked. It simply boggles the mind how two filmmakers, from the same culture and the same confluence of time and space, and precisely in the matter of the constitution of gender and sexuality, could stand so sharply against each other. While Kimia'i makes his films from the most troubled masculinist elements of his received and resurrected culture, Beiza'i reverses that culture from the highest hopes of that self-same constellation of communal sensibilities. From beneath and from beyond their evident differences, however, and from how they see the world from the vantage point of their female characters, there emerges a third space where hidden myths and meandering facts revisit.

Women at Work

Whereas Kimia'i's idea of women consists of by and large prostitutes, idle women waiting to get married, devoted mothers with no will of their own, or else good-for-nothing rich women who are bored to death and are waiting desperately for a lumpen ('real men') to come their way and show them 'the real meaning of life', all women in Beiza'i's cinema work. They work, and they are located right in the middle of a material constellation of suggestive realities. As early as *Thunder Shower/Ragbar* (1971), Beiza'i places women on the dignity ground of working. Atefeh, the lead character, works in a tailor's workshop. Her mother, despite her old age, weaves hand-made sweaters to help out with the expenses, and the owner of the tailor-shop is also a working woman. These three women are not defined by their contingency on any masculine bread-giver. They are they bread-givers, autonomous, earthly, real, tangible, their being-in-the-world conditioned by the dignity of their labour.

Rooted and confident in their working-place, Beiza'i's women have an active, even aggressive, role to play in their own destiny. In the central event of *Thunder Shower*, an emerging affection between Atefeh and the new schoolteacher, Mr Hekmati, Atefeh is a major actor. Atefeh has another suitor, the local butcher, who is wealthy, powerful, determined and influential. By marrying him, Atefeh would have made it home, she and her mother and young brother together. Her attraction to Mr Hekmati is gradual, logical and yet palpably affectionate. Even more importantly, she is an equal partner in making that affection possible, real and trustworthy. The reality of Atefeh is embraced by the realism of her mother and her employer, both of them women, both of them straight from the streets and alleys of Iranian reality. Even the neighbourhood's butcher contributes to the realisation of Atefeh as an active moral agency in her own life. Even if we agree with Shahla Lahiji's brilliant phrasing that 'these three women [that is, Atefeh, her mother and her employer] are caught in the cul-de-sac of enduring social traditions, personal emotions, fear of unknown environment, and the world outside',[3] still they are active moral agents, alert and aware, in their worldly affairs. The pragmatism of Atefeh collides with the idealism of her suitor, Mr Hekmati, and leaves the protagonist of the film in the moral position of making fateful decisions for her life – and thus the simple story assumes allegorical power.

Labouring women are equally central to *The Crow/Kalagh* (1976). The old, stately Mother used to be a nurse; her daughter-in-law Asiyeh is now a teacher to deaf children. Again, the dignity of working, the social location of a full membership in the world, is the bracing grace of these women. It is crucial to keep in mind that Beiza'i does not concoct the working status for women of his films. He is extraordinarily realistic in these depictions. His 'realism', in fact, is not only rooted in the immediate historical experiences of his society, but also in his mythological reconstitution of a pre-historical nuclear family where women have been at the epicentre of the community of labour. Throughout his cinematic career, Beiza'i has always operated on the borderline of myth and reality. Even in his most visibly modern and urban films, such as *Thunder Shower* and *The Crow*, Beiza'i sees life as the site of a 'ritual' in which collapses myth and reality, where myth animates actions and actions are mythological charged. From these earliest works, the cross-fusion of *mythos* and *logos* in the work of Beiza'i has been evident. As forms of cognitive categories, myths for Beiza'i have a constitutionally material, historical and evolving character.[4] In the presence of his cinema, myth is not something of the past. It is being revealed and recast in the daily lives of his characters.

The most significant aspect of *The Crow*, however, is Beiza'i's constitution of the figure of women in multi-dimensional, multi-temporal ways – a strategy that breaks the apparent but false solidity of the subject in any patriarchal constitution of it. The Mother in *The Crow* is narrating her memoir to her daughter-in-law Asiyeh, while a picture of her youth has mysteriously appeared in the 'Lost' section of the daily paper. Meanwhile, Asiyeh is expecting a child, which could very well be a girl. Among the Mother, her daughter-in-law Asiyeh, the picture of the Mother's youth, the narration of her memoir and the expected child there thus emerges a composite picture of one single woman: at once old (the Mother), young (Asiyeh), un-born (Asiyeh's fetus), past (the Mother's memoir), present (Asiyeh's writing that memoir), visual (the Mother's youthful picture) and verbal (the Mother's narration of her memoir). If myth is the symbolic structuring of the world, Beiza'i has a Lego-like, dismantling attitude towards myths that have been constitutional in the social formations of a culture. In *The Crow* in particular, he dismantles the fixated subjectivity of the feminine via a de-sedimentation of it in temporal and narrative terms. The break-down of the feminine subject and its cinematic reconstitution is one particularly effective way of not only screening their historical formations but, equally important, negotiating a new composition for that subjectivity. This oscillation between the factual and the mythic properties of realities thus emerges as the veritable forte of Beiza'i's cinema.

The Mythically Pregnant Reality

Beginning with an historically disenfranchised segment of his society, namely women, Beiza'i's access to what he perceives as the mythological roots of contemporary social ills thematically expands to include far more universal implications of the problem. His art, as Adorno would call it, would thus strategically start to dwell on reality in a way that can begin to manipulate and change it. 'Art's autonomous realm', Adorno suggests, 'has nothing in common with the external world other than borrowed elements that have entered into a fully changed context'.[5] The aesthetic context within which Beiza'i ritually choreographs and orchestrates myth and reality has an emancipatory angle on the self-same reality, it is not formed in pure artistic isolation, because, again as Adorno put it, 'the development of artistic process [...] corresponds to social development',[6] in such a way that the two will have authoritative correspondences with each other. Beiza'i is acutely alerted to the external world in which he lives and works. The elements of that world that he borrows and infuses into his art are there to enter a fateful negotiation with their own (hidden or manifest) mythological underpinnings. In his art, Beiza'i is ambassadorial, frequenting in between the realm of the real and the domain of the mythical. But Beiza'i is not just an ambassador from these two realms. He is also a mythmaker, his cinema is a cinema of mythmaking, both from the scattered elements of distant myths we may have forgotten and from the fragmented forms of realities we may have thought we knew too well.

By the time Beiza'i makes *The Stranger and the Fog/Gharibeh va Meh* (1973), he is completely at home with his richly implicative and pregnant mythological language, a language that despite its ascending allegorical suggestiveness has a profoundly earthly quality to it. The emerging affection in *The Stranger and the Fog* between Ra'na, the coastal woman of permanence, and Ayat, the maritime man of migration, is rooted in the twilight zone of land and sea, life and death, reality and myth. The village of Ra'na, the young widow, is ethereal, somewhere in the north of Iran, or perhaps nowhere at all. The village, on the edge of a maritime abyss, is as foggy as real, as imaginary as material. On that borderland of living and death, Ayat has to fight against the demons that have chased him from the sea into the security of the village, with the same ferocity that Ra'na has to fight the ghosts of her dead husband's ancestors that haunt the villagers with the same intensity as does the fear of an invading army of sea monsters. The crucial aspect of this dual, circular warfare is that Ra'na and Ayat fight it together, like Adam and Eve, like Mashya and Mashyana, on two simultaneous fronts, from the land and the sea. Ayat is haunted by his fatal attraction to the sea, Ra'na by the ancestral gaze of a dead husband. The invading sea monsters, apparitions from Ayat's own perturbed fears of the unknown and the insinuating, have nothing less scary about them than the invisible ghosts that roam the village in the form of 'traditions', 'customs', 'habits' and 'manners'. At the end, Ayat, Ra'na and the entire village fight as much against the invading sea monsters as they do against the monstrous apparition, a whole genealogy of fear, they themselves have invented. The unknowing subject that emerges from this foggy environment is the first palpable progeny of Ayat and Ra'na now posing as the mythically resurrected Mashya and Mashyana.

The chief protagonist of *The Stranger and the Fog*, however, is neither Ayat nor Ra'na. It is the fog. It is the furiously foggy subjugation of the real, where the real can yield alternative visions of itself. The foggy disposition of *The Stranger and the Fog* renders translucent all the received cognitive categories with which a culture constitutes itself. The symbolic structuring of the universe of imagination called culture is actively mutated under this hazy vision of the real. As a visual projection of the subconscious, Beiza'i uses the fog to melt away the presumed rigidity of the evident – and with it the knowing subject. The result is a spectacular loosening of the obvious. After watching the atmospheric mistiness of *The Stranger and the Fog*, we no longer look at reality with the same submissive matter-of-factness that there is nothing one can do about it. With the vaporising effusions of the visible, the authority of sight itself is reconstituted, negotiated anew, implicated in a whole new hermeneutics of subjectivity. Hereby the presumably knowing subject becomes the evidently unknowing subject.

'If by abolishing the mythic universe we have lost the universe', in Georges Bataille's words in his seminal work *The Absence of Myth* (1994), 'the action of a revealing loss is itself connected to the death of myth. And today, because a myth is dead or dying, we see through it more easily than if it were alive: it is the need that perfects the transparency, the suffering which makes the suffering joyful'.[7] Bataille here speaks of what Weber, earlier in the twentieth century, had termed the universal disenchantment of the world.[8] Both Bataille and Weber are responding to the predicament of instrumental rationalism as the greatest achievement of the dual projects of the European Enlightenment and Modernity – which much of the world received through the debilitating project of European colonialism. But still what they say has a profoundly implicative resonance for the world outside the enchantment of the dual European project and yet ravished by its colonial consequences. Our mythic universe, the terms of our enchantment, as the subjects of Beiza'i's visual reflections, were either actively forgotten or ferociously remembered under the dire consequences of colonialism. The culture of 'authenticity' that was created for us under these circumstances were conducive to our servile status *vis-à-vis* the colonial consequences of those projects. Beiza'i, among other visionaries of our freedom from that predicament, has been at work, not to abolish our mythic universe, but to remember and to re-invent it. In his cinema, we do not watch a 'revealing loss', because we cannot remember our own dreams, let alone lose them. For us, there is no 'revealing loss'. For us, and as we can see ourselves in our active re-imagination by Beiza'i, the world needs to be invented anew, this time with us in it. We were invented out of the world of the European Enlightenment by the very inventors of the Enlightenment and Modernity, the author of *Was ist Aufklärung/What is Enlightenment* (1784) chief among them.

In Beiza'i, among a handful of other visionary theorists of our liberation, we are being re-invented back into something we can call our own 'history', but this time with no Hegelian teleological illusion that would actively exclude us from History. The metonymic instrumentalities of his cinema take us into his mythic world in a sustained act of liberation.

In Beiza'i, we see not through the dead or dying myth but through the resuscitated re-inventions of our distant and recent myths. Bataille is correct that through a dying myth one can see the world even more profoundly mythical. But that is only if one has first benefitted from the fruits, and not merely suffered the dire consequences, of the illusion of the dying myths. In the colonial outposts of the European Enlightenment, we have an entirely different stand *vis-à-vis* our received or resurrected myths. We need, as Beiza'i intends, to re-invent them in a way that is affirming us in our place in the world, not denying us, distorting, or demeaning our historical inflections. And ultimately, because our moral and material needs are of an entirely different sort, the need of being born into the world, we cannot have any conception of a 'joyful suffering'. We have had too much of that paradoxical proposition of 'joyful suffering' in our neck of the woods. It is called 'colonial modernity'. In master mythmakers like Bahram Beiza'i, we have discovered how to be born into a mythically reimagined world of our own.

Re-Mythologising the Real

By the time he made *The Ballad of Tara/Cherikeh-ye Tara* (1978), Beiza'i had thoroughly mastered the active re-mythologisation of the specifically Iranian reality in order to negotiate a new aesthetic angle on that reality. Without a full command over the inner working of the Iranian mythological memories, it is impossible to do

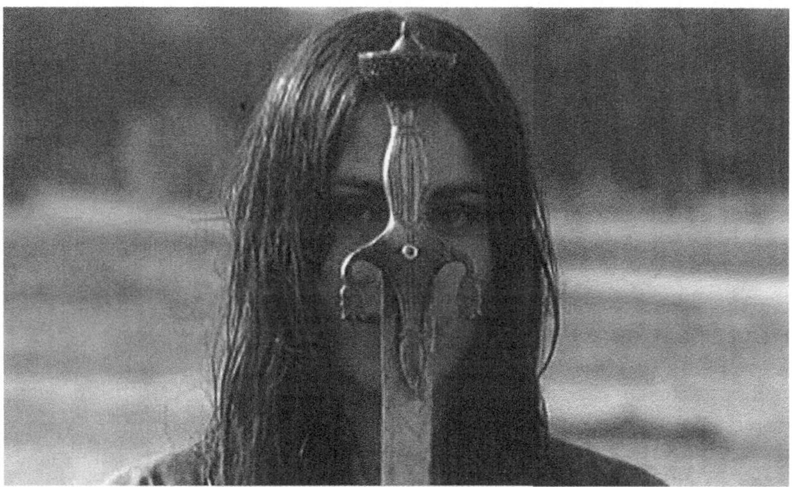

Figure 4.1 *Susan Taslimi as Tara in Bahram Beiza'i's* The Ballad of Tara/Cherikeh-ye Tara *(1978). (Photo: Courtesy of Bahram Beiza'i)*

what Beiza'i has done in his long and illustrious career, at once resuscitating them and manipulating them, to force them to yield to alternative modes of meaning, being, activating – of subjection. No one in the history of Iranian visual and performing arts comes anywhere near Beiza'i in his phenomenal command of Persian mythological culture and his ability to force it into a creative convulsion. The reason why Beiza'i has become proverbial among his Iranian critics for the 'incomprehensibility' of his cinema is precisely the deep-rootedness of these mythological referents in the mind of his Iranian audience. Beiza'i's attempt has invariably been to de-familiarise these myths in order to shake his audience into a renewed pact with them. Watching Beiza'i for the first time is like reading Ferdowsi's *Shahnameh* for the first time, and from there like being present at the dawn of history, of our humanity.

With a gaze fixated on contemporary realities, particularly the fate of Iranian women, but through women the entire crooked timbre of trying to be an 'Iranian' in the grip of a colonial modernity, Beiza'i shakes and rattles the most forgotten ancient mythologies into speaking their reason, breaking their conspiratorial silence, effacing the banality of their claim to sacred certitude, to authorial authenticity. Beiza'i opts for the archaic word '*cherikeh*', not in a vain search for authenticity, but in order to shock the familiar with the unknown, the comfortable with the mysterious, the overtly remembered with the actively forgotten. These are all effective strategies of alienating the world from its familiar habits of cozying itself up to the habitual. Any number of other words – *afsaneh*, *ostureh*, *hekayat*, *qesseh* and so on – would have been equally conveying the sense of a ballad. What '*cherikeh*' does here is to force the lazy audience to pause and ponder, to dwell on the unknown, to distance itself from the habitual, even to distrust the received definitions and locations of our place-in-the-language we call home. 'The main function of the myth', in the judicious words of Åke Hultkrantz, the distinguished myth scholar who conducted extensive fieldwork among the Wind River Shoshoni Indians, 'is to sanction the establishment and condition of the world and its institutions, thereby safeguarding the existence of people and society. In many cases, the very recitation of the myth is so filled with power that it influences – or is thought to influence – the course of actual events'.[9] But myths as such have a habit of not just making the world possible, but making it possible at the heavy price of a tyrannical subjugation of one race or one gender to another. Beiza'i's cinema is the visual access to that mythical universe to re-negotiate newer, more just and equitable myths for the world. As a learned scholar of Iranian mythologies with a gift for storytelling and filmmaking, Beiza'i has been in a very unique position to turn the metonymic power of his art into inroads accessing the mythic subconscious of his people.

In *The Ballad of Tara*, which immediately after *The Stranger and the Fog* is Beiza'i's most mythically-narrated film, he opts for a cinematic redaction of the creation-myth. Here, he draws on any number of distant Iranian mythological narratives in order to generate and render operative his own. He can do that by the virtue of the quantitatively reducible variations on the theme of a given myth.[10] In this narrative, Tara is a woman, earthly, seasonal, in tune with the land, fertile in her attendance on the real. Tara is part of nature, constitutional to and constituent of its fertile celebration of life, with two children, ready for any new season, with no sign of self-consciousness about her.[11] The description of Susan Taslimi as Tara by Shahla Lahiji is extraordinarily accurate:

> The impeccable acting of Susan Taslimi as Tara is the indication of a perfect choice and of the remarkable capability of the actor in the cultivation and performance of her role. This capability is evident not only in her acting but also in her physiognomy. Susan Taslimi – with her Wheat-like complexion, elongated nose, set-back but penetrating, open and intimidating eyes, and then at times, with that affectionate look, bony and sculpted cheeks, the wrinkle of power at the side of her mouth, the thin line of thought on her long forehead, the tall stature, and then that authority in her demeanor and speech – is the very epiphany of the Mother-Earth: That very mythological vision of woman that can very well belong to yesterday, today, or tomorrow, and all the time remain thoroughly woman.[12]

Mashyana incarnate, Tara as earth, nature and fertility appears at a moment when she has lost two of her men: a husband and a father. Meanwhile she is being suited by four men: by a half-crazed boy; by the brother of her murdered husband who is probably the murderer and who loves her sickly, his name being Ashub, meaning 'chaos'; by Qelich who like her is earthly and digs water from the depth of the earth; and then by the Historical Man who is there to get The Sword yet falls in love with her. We are already deep into the thicket of a mythic world. Located between these two manly brackets of dead and living attendants, whatever Tara has inherited from her masculine ancestry she distributes to everybody in the village, much to their delight, even The Sword which is brought back to her immediately because of the fear of its being haunted. She is given back The Sword, but she does not know quite what to do with it. She tries to cut wood, chop vegetables, or hold the door open with it. She throws it out into the sea, much to the anger of the Historical Man, but the sea returns The Sword back, much to her surprise. She discovers the use of The Sword when a wild dog attacks her and her children; she kills the wild dog and thus finds out, much to her awe, the use of The Sword. Among awe, delight, surprise and anger, Tara defines the world, locates herself and mythically locates the reality of the earthly life in which she lives. She is the original point of departure for whatever that exists, whatever that should, and does, matter. We are at the inaugural moment of creation.

In *The Ballad of Tara*, as in all other films of Beiza'i, the lead woman protagonist has the dignity of place by the ennobling grace of the work she does. Tara is a farmer. Her children, her domestic animals, her farm, her cart and the retinue that holds these together are at the centre of a universe over which she presides. In this pre-moment of History where we encounter her, only work matters. The Sword has no use in this pre-moment. Tara tries to put The Sword to work. But it is a useless, work-less instrument. History having not yet begun, there is no use for The Sword and the violence it implicates. When Tara and the Historical Man meet, he can only speak death, destruction and honour, while she tries to see if the man has any talent she can put to work.

The Historical Man is out to get her sword back to defend his honour, but while here on this earth and in the pre-moment of History he falls in love with Tara and cannot leave to go back to History, until such time as he is assured that Qelich is in love with Tara and will actually take care of her children in her absence. At such time will the Historical Man go back to History, having found a cause to re-enter it again. Beiza'i in effect holds History hostage to a mythological re-negotiation of it in the pre-moment of History. For the Historical Man, as he enters this pre-moment, masculinist honour precedes life, whereas Tara places life, in which dwells her love for the Historical Man, before any Historical constitution of manly 'Honour'. She has no use for such cultural abstracts, particularly when defined by useless men. Tara is noble in the pre-cultural materiality of the term. He speaks of honour in History. She speaks of love in the material context of a life that is too real to collapse into any abstraction of History. Central to this distinction is the function of The Sword. She first tries to use it practically, or to sell it, throw it away, or go harvesting with it. The Sword, however, belongs to the lost honour of a tribe. But the people of the village have no use for The Sword, either. She kills a dog with The Sword to protect herself and her children and thus learns the use of the sword and is petrified by it. She gives The Sword back to the Historical Man to leave, but by then she is told that he cannot go back because he has fallen in love with her: history taken hostage of its own pre-moment – between love and violence.

Far more important than defining myth as 'sacred tale' or 'traditional tale',[13] it is important to see the act of mythmaking as a sustained form of communal signification – not something of a distant past but something always in the making. Outside such sustained forms of significations, the world atrophies into confusion and chaos. Beiza'i's cinema in general, and his *The Ballad of Tara* in particular, is a singularly successful negotiation with the enduring parameters of the Persian mythologising imagination – both past and present. One of the crucial achievements of Beiza'i in *The Ballad of Tara* is to subvert and recast time and narrative in a way that enables his story to find and demonstrate its own internal 'logic'. Consider the narrative elements of this ballad. The Historical Man has exited history and entered its pre-moment in order to retrieve his sword, and yet he is held back by a love affair. The Grandfather is dead and yet he speaks in person beyond his grave, as the solitary sound of an authority that defies death and timing. Equally paramount in this pre-moment of History is a sword that always mysteriously reappears, against all logic, despite all resistance, in tune with a narrative logic that only a myth – or perhaps more accurately in Beizai's case, a 'counter-myth' – can generate and sustain. Dialogues in *The Ballad of Tara* vary in accent and intonation, implying no particular time or location, implying all times and all locations. Costumes are not all from Tavalish, the region where the film was made, but the visual regalia of a pre-moment in the world. The sights and sounds here do more than just express ideas; they actually define the terms, as they constitute the parameters, of a different world, the world of the story, the realm of the un-real, to which the real must yield. The stylised gestures are pantomime invitations into the sight of the un-seen, the place of the pre-moment of being-in-the-world. In *The Ballad of Tara*, Beiza'i enters the world of the myth in order to force his audience to exit the routinised world, alerted to a whole different consciousness of reality. This is precisely what I mean by 'pre-moment', when Beiza'i leads us back to a pre-historical instantiation of reality through myth.

To achieve that reconstitution of the real cinematically, visuality becomes the central mechanism of Beiza'i's narrative, which must begin to teach its otherwise primarily audile and literate audience how to see. Foregrounding the visual possibility of colours and shapes as the constituent forces of the narrative results in an active stylisation of colours and shapes, which in turn results in a 'theoretical' stylisation of the visual. Stylising the movements comes next, aided admirably by an almost self-conscious stylisation of the camera movement and angles. All of these are leading to the constitution of a visual world, legitimately operative on its own terms, irreducible to the outside world, giving palpable reality to film as the visual substitution of the real, from which to re-constitute the real by contesting the received and canonised reality. No other Iranian filmmaker has this kind of command over the function of the visual and is so richly rooted in the Iranian visual memories, to pull this off without collapsing into the museumisation of culture. To understand the remarkable ability of Beiza'i, all one has to do is to see Shahram Asadi's *The Fateful Day/Ruz-e Vaqe'eh* (1995) which is based on Beiza'i's script and yet visually collapses into a museum-piece of tourist attraction. Beiza'i is no museum curator. He is a puppeteer of our forgotten memories – a master mythmaker.

By re-narrating the myth, Beiza'i in effect creates the visual site of a ritual, a sign of his life-long dedication to and fascination with the Persian Passion Play, or *Ta'ziyeh*. Bringing the 'ritual' to climactic closure is the scene where Tara picks up The Sword and attacks the Historical Man receding into the sea. In the stunningly shot and acted last scene, Tara, sword in hand, attacks the sea and launches her futile blows against wave after wave. The sheer futility of Tara's act and the visual beauty of this scene is where Beiza'i rests her camera for the longest time, allowing for the ritual to sink its effect. But Beiza'i opts to end on a different note. When the Historical Man leaves, Tara tells Qelich they should get married, as soon as the next harvest.

Mythologies

In a short staccato against Joseph L. Mankiewicz's *Julius Caesar* (1953), Roland Barthes catches the fabricated spontaneity of trying to pass the fake as the real. In a brilliant reading of the connotation of sweating as a sign of oral exertion, Barthes formulates a short-cut into what he calls 'an ethic of signs':[14]

> Signs ought to present themselves only in two extreme forms: either openly intellectual and so remote that they are reduced to algebra, as in Chinese theatre […] or deeply rooted, invented, so to speak, on each occasion, revealing an internal, a hidden facet, and indicative of a moment in time, no longer of a concept (as in the art of Stanislavsky, for instance). But the intermediate sign […] reveals a degraded spectacle, which is equally afraid of simple reality and of total artifice. For although it is a good thing if a spectacle is created to make the world more explicit, it is both reprehensible and deceitful to confuse the sign with what is signified. And it is a duplicity which is peculiar to bourgeois art: between the intellectual and the visceral sign is hypocritically inserted a hybrid, at once elliptical and pretentious, which is pompously christened 'nature'.[15]

The ethics of signs that Barthes proposes here opens a whole new window on the workings of the mythic memories of a culture. Beiza'i's cinema is somewhere between the Chinese theatre and that of Stanislavsky, as Barthes typologises them here. His cinema is at once archetypal, or, as Barthes calls it, openly intellectual and algebraic, and yet squarely rooted in the moment. In fact, Beiza'i makes a cinematic virtue out of mythically impregnating the present moment. 'Simple reality' and 'total artifice' collapse in Beiza'i's cinema on the site of a 'ritualistic' constitution of an angle on the real. Barthes is here rightly disgusted with the duplicity of the pretension of Julius Caesar too 'naturally'. But in his anger, he issues a manifesto in his ethics of sign which is theoretically limited. Barthes is correct that between 'the intellectual and the visceral' Hollywood has 'hypocritically inserted a hybrid, at once elliptical and pretentious'. But he completely loses sight of the possibility of collapsing 'the intellectual and the visceral', as Beiza'i does it systematically and in almost all his films, on the site of a mythic-ritual reconstitution of the real. The reason that Barthes is theoretically blinded here is that the context of bourgeois art in which he launches his pathbreaking collection of essays in the late 1950s was, as it indeed still is in much of European theorisation of the aesthetic, oblivious to the functioning of the aesthetic in the colonial outposts of the Enlightenment project, where no autonomous national bourgeoisie could have existed and where, as a result, in the face of an entirely contingent social formation of classes and their creative and critical consciousness art has had an entirely different kind of creative disposition. In this particular case, the phenomenal cross-fusion of 'the intellectual and the visceral', far from feigning 'nature', cultivates an extraordinarily revolutionary angle on the real, forcing it into alternative meanings.

To see that proposition in practice, we can do no better than turn to *Bashu: The Little Stranger/Bashu: Gharibeh-ye Kuchak* (1985), where Beiza'i brings Tara to History – as it were. Na'i is the de-mythologised Tara in the heart of History – our history, our lived experiences. By bringing Tara from the pre-moment of History into History, Beiza'i mythologises the *now* of the moment, or in Barthes' terms faces 'the intellectual and the visceral'. There is a dialectical reciprocity at work here: the *now* of the moment is mythologised, the *then* of the myth is historicised. This confluence of time and narrative is crucial in our reading of Beiza'i's cinema. It is deadly to separate Beiza'i's cinema into historical and mythological.[16] He is one filmmaker with no sign of visual schizophrenia about his cinema. By historicising mythology and mythologising history, Beiza'i visually crosses the received borders of both and takes us into a third territory, at once historical and yet radically alerted to its self-inflicted wounds of perhaps inevitable mythologising urges. The site of the confluence between the *mythos* and the *logos* in Beiza'i is his fascination with 'ritual'. 'Ritual' for Beiza'i is the performative microcosm of a universe in which collide both the *logos* of history and the *mythos* of making it comprehensible. He is mythologising our lived experiences today, but he might as well be theorising our lasting memories of Mashya and Mashyana.

In his *Absence of Myth*, Georges Bataille seeks to strike the chord that captures the moment of the un-myth as itself mythical: 'Night is also a sun, and the absence of myth is also a myth: The coldest, the purest, the only *true* myth'.[17] 'The world' itself being mythical and 'The Myth' worldly, as someone almost condemned to realism, Beiza'i cannot but underline that cross-fusion. What is thus evident in Beiza'i is the fictive transparency of the real, the therapeutics of mythmaking in the face of the fear of the real. That fear is defiant, the rebellious disposition of a postcolonial person, a post-patriarchal filmmaker. The monumental project of Bahram Beiza'i in his cinema has been to recast the mythic character of his received culture in ever newer and more palpable registers.

Bashu is the critical evidence that the binary opposition between 'History' and 'Myth' does not hold for Beiza'i. For in his cinematic cosmovision he has collided both and construed a third world, a tertiary space, in which we become radically conscious of the *mythos* in the operative energy of the *logos.*

Despite her extraordinary critical intelligence in her reading of Beiza'i for women, Lahiji, regrettably, falls squarely into the trap of a patriarchal definition of 'motherhood', without pausing for a second to question whether or not that power-basing definition is remotely something called 'instinctual'. There is nothing 'instinctual' about a definition of 'motherhood' which is historically constituted. In a haste to celebrate Na'i as the ideal-typical 'Mother',[18] Lahiji disregards the fact that on more than one occasion Na'i's attitude towards Bashu is inexcusably racist. In their first encounter, Na'i makes a nasty reference to the dark complexion of Bashu (he is from southern Iran) and says: 'Are you an animal or a human being?' She is at first very protective of her own biological children and treats Bashu as if he were a dangerous animal in her rice paddy. The leitmotif of racism stays quite constant in *Bashu*, resulting in one of the most glorious scenes in which Na'i ritually gives birth to Bashu, but not before buying an extra bar of soap to wash his dark skin and make him white. Having failed to make him white, she says: 'No way, he will not become white'. None of these racist comments, however, have the slightest effect on the earthly majesty of Na'i's character. In the absolute self-confidence of his characterisation of Na'i, Beiza'i knows only too well that she must share the racist presupposition of her village, the universe of her physical location and material imagination before she is liberated from them.

Na'i is no 'mother' in a servile, patriarchally constituted sense, to which Lahiji unfortunately falls victim. Na'i is earth incarnate. To her, Bashu, her own two children, the animals to which she attends, the shooting stems in the rice paddy are one and the same. Beiza'i could not possibly constitute the most serious challenge in Iranian performing arts to the very mythological foundations of Persian patriarchy and yet accept and celebrate its flawed constitution of motherhood in it.

Ritual Birth

To understand Na'i better, and what Beiza'i does in his characterisation of her, we need to see her in the context of the mythological motif and against the two opposing myth-types of the world-parents.[19] In the most familiar world-parents myth-type, which is A 625 in Thompson's motif-index, we have sky-father and earth-mother as parents of the universe. This myth-type is found in a vast geographical expansion that ranges from ancient Greece to India, Eastern Indonesia, Tahiti, Africa and native

North and South America. The less widely known world-parents myth-type, which is motif-index A 625.1 in Thompson's motif-index is exactly the reverse of A 625 – that is, we have the mother as sky and the father as earth.[20] Na'i is, of course, immediately identifiable as the mother-earth motif of A 625. However, Beiza'i does not leave the matter at that simple level. The Iranian myth of Mashya and Mashyana as the vegetal/animal couple of creation foregrounds a more critical framing here.

Throughout *Bashu*, Na'i's husband is completely absent, and when he does appear in the very last sequence of the film, his most visible and symbolic phallic symbol, his right hand, is cut off, presumably in a war- or work-related accident. The plot leaves it unclear. We are never told. Bashu as a result is 'born' to Na'i by Beiza'i having her ritually give birth to him. Visually, this ritual birth-giving has a number of references. One is when Na'i washes Bashu on the bank of a river, and in Beizai's extremely accurate *mise-en-scène* the head of Bashu is precisely located next to Na'i's vagina and womb, when she is sitting and washing Bashu who is submerged in the river. A second visual effect is when Na'i fishes Bashu out of a small brook, by means of a net that she casts towards him. Bashu does not know how to swim and has just fallen off a branch on which he was playfully frolicking. While all the village men are standing by, completely paralysed and impotent to do anything, Na'i grabs her fishing net and casts it towards the drowning Bashu. Inside the pool-like brook, Bashu appears as if in Na'i's womb, and more specifically in the plasmatic meconium of the foetus. The grey-greenish colour of the water is particularly reminiscent of the meconium, which is a dark greenish mass that accumulates in the bowel of the foetus during foetal life and is then discharged shortly after birth. Na'i pulls Bashu out, in a gesture that is remarkably similar to a labour that a mother experiences to 'fish her child out of her womb'. She saves him and thus 'gives birth to him', because otherwise he would have died with all those impotent men around, and then she holds him in her bosom exactly as if he were a newborn baby, fresh out of her womb. Having been saved by the net that Na'i had cast into the small brook, Bashu is inside the net, like a newly-born baby bursting out of the plasmatic foetus. There are many more such birth-giving rituals, such as the hallucinatory, ritualistic dance of Na'i to Bashu's magically therapeutic drum-beats that appear like the twisting and turning of the body during the final stages of labour. It is exactly after this scene that we see Na'i washing her clothes that she wore while she was sick (pregnant), as women do after child-birth, while dictating a letter to Bashu to be sent to her husband. 'My son Bashu writes this letter', Na'i says proudly. 'Like all other children, he is the offspring of the earth and the sun'. Bashu is conceived immaculately, with no need for any 'husband'. The only remote 'contact' with the husband via this letter comes *after* the ritual birth of Bashu to Na'i.

The ritual birth of Bashu to Na'i in the conspicuous absence of her husband leads us to the precise site of re-mythologisation in which Beiza'i has narrated his version of the world-parenting, central to his cosmovision. To see the place of Na'i as mother-earth in that cosmovision, and the revolutionary re-imagination of the world through a re-invention of the world-parent myth, we need to look at the originary myth itself prior to Beizai's re-constitution of it.

Let me begin by drawing attention to the extraordinary work of Professor K. Numazawa of Nanzan University of Nagoya, Japan, on the related motif of creation-myth, Thompson index-motif A 625.2, concerning the specifics of 'the Raising of the Sky'.[21] Written by a Japanese scholar in German, published in Paris in 1946 and predicated on material from Japanese mythology, this study could not be farther removed from Beiza'i's *Bashu*, Beizai's knowledge of Asian performing arts and his admiration for the late Akira Kurosawa notwithstanding. Precisely in this obvious unrelatedness dwells the universal claim that 'Bashu' has over a range of mythological parameters at the heart of Beiza'i's cosmovision. The parameters of that cosmovision work through and for a specifically mythological reconstitution of the culture – any culture but, in this specific case, Iranian culture.

To achieve that objective, Beiza'i reaches for the most elemental and mythological parameters of the culture. In Numazawa's observations about the 'Raising of the Sky' motif of the creation-myth is already evident a theory of the link between agricultural communities and their mythologising proclivities. The significance of agricultural communities, into which the setting of *Bashu* falls, is in their physical approximation to the earliest forms of human society. Myths that have to do with the origin of the universe, in which a mother-earth and a father-sky play the central role, takes us directly to the communal context of patriarchal and matriarchal patterns of social formation. The myth of world-parenting usually begins at a pre-moment of the world, a moment which is also central to both *The Ballad of Tara* and *Bashu*. How does the world look like at this pre-moment? 'There is, common to nearly all the myths I have spoken of', Numazawa observes, ...

> ...the idea that darkness filled the universe before the separation of the sky and earth, and that light appeared for the first time in the universe when the sky and earth had been separated. And with the coming of the light, everything on earth which had been hidden in the darkness appeared for the first time.[22]

Now, consider the fact that, until the very last sequence of the film, we do not see Na'i with her husband. He is present by virtue of Na'i's speaking of him; her neighbours, some of whom are her husband's relatives, remind her of him, and of course her two children are presumably the result of marriage to that man. The husband arrives *after* the ritual birth of Bashu to Na'i. Hence, the narrative moment of Bashu is an un-time of the world – namely, the father-sky has left but his marks on the mother-earth, and thus the world is evident. And yet, there are many nights and days – that is, the death and resurrection of the world, without the father-sky ever being around. Numazawa again:

> This is precisely what we see every morning at the break of dawn. The breaking of dawn starts with the union of the sky and earth in the darkness of the night. This union is the union of father sky and mother earth, and all things that appear with the rising of the sun are born of these two.[23]

But we never see Na'i sleeping with any man. No sign of the father-sky in sight. The repeated emphasis on Na'i's sleeping patterns, in which she has to keep an eye on the rice paddy, are visually emphatic. She sleeps alone, in the dark. Now consider the fact that Beiza'i's intuitive grasp of this myth, at once critically intelligent and creatively subversive, leads him to have a wholesome son being born to Na'i *in the absence of a husband.* Now, again consider Numazawa:

> The myths in which father sky leaves mother earth in the morning show clearly traces of the custom of visit marriage (*Besuchsehe*). When morning comes, the man, like Uranos, must leave the woman. Therefore the myths have merely transferred what happens every morning to the first morning of the beginning of the universe – in other words, to the morning of the creation of all things.[24]

The Japanese practice of 'the visit marriage', which we see in its patriarchally reversed mode in the Shi'i practice of '*mut'ah*' or 'temporary marriage', is far closer, as Numazawa suggests, to the original matriarchal practice where the husband is only there to occasion the birth of the child and then goes away. But in Beiza'i's case, what is remarkable is the ritual elimination of the father altogether. By Bashu being born to Na'i through an 'immaculate conception', as it were, and being ritually staged, even the 'temporary marriage' is rendered 'ritually' superfluous. But Na'i and Bashu become parent and child not simply through a cinematically staged ritual, but far more effectively by 'working' together. 'Work' is constitutional to the emerging parental relationship between Na'i and her son Bashu. First Bashu does not work, and the neighbours reprimand her for giving shelter to a useless boy. Then she makes him work, which results in her neighbours equally harassing her for turning the boy into a slave. From this bit of social satire, Na'i and Bashu emerge into a parental relation which is occasioned by work. When, after her illness, Na'i habitually gets up one night and sees Bashu already awake and in charge of protecting the rice paddy against wild animals, the young boy is already born into work and into her womb. Now get ready for a startling revelation from a Japanese scholar who could not possibly have seen *Bashu* in 1946 when he wrote his *Die Weltanfänge in der Japanischen Mythologie*, or its shorter version, in 1953:

> A principal feature in so many myths, particularly those whose motif is the banishment of heaven, is agriculture, specifically agriculture whose chief product is rice. The central figure in these myths is a woman, and the principal animals are cows and pigs. In the social system one may see the prevalence of visit marriage (*Besuchsehe*), the earliest form of marriage in the matriarchal cultural sphere that developed out of the status that women had acquired economically in the course of social development. From such facts one may conclude that the myths we have been discussing are products of the matriarchal cultural sphere.[25]

The location of an agricultural community, the pivotal importance of a rice paddy, the centrality of a woman in the story, subtracting the pigs from domestic animals for obvious reasons, but adding the economic autonomy of Na'i – all these are the startling evidence of a conscious constitution of *Bashu* on a universal mythological motif that anchors its narration in the centrality of the idea of mother-earth, before launching its cosmovision towards a radical reconstitution of the myth in liberating

Na'i and the entire gender she represents from mental, moral, mythological, cultural, historical and political bondage. Nobody comes even close to Beiza'i in his ambitious thrust into a radical reconstitution of Iranian culture – on a universal, mythic and yet still historical plane.

Alan Dundes has suggested an Oedipal explanation for the myth-type that Numazawa has examined, the myth in which a male offspring of world-parents would want to separate his parents by pushing the sky-father up off the earth-mother.[26] This is quite suggestive in the case of *Bashu*, particularly in light of the last sequence when the father returns with his right hand, the most visible phallic symbol, cut off. The first time we see the father is when Beiza'i masterfully draws his figure from a scarecrow that Bashu has made. The father comes and stands in front of the sun, blocks the sun-rays, creates a momentary night and asks Bashu who has made that scarecrow. While sitting, Bashu has a conversation with the father, not knowing that he is the father, while he is in his shadow, as an extension of the scarecrow. After this conversation, during which Bashu gives a cup of water to the father to drink, Bashu hears from his friends that Na'i's husband has returned. On his way to Na'i, for some inexplicable reason nervous and even frightened, he picks up a stick and runs towards the rice paddy where Na'i resides. When Bashu gets there, Na'i is already engaged in a quarrel with her husband, objecting to his objection that Bashu must leave. Bashu comes hurriedly, stands between Na'i and the father, and automatically raises the stick to attack him and protect the mother. The angle of Beiza'i's camera here is simply astounding. From the corner of the father's right side, we see his amputated right hand, the raised stick of Bashu and then Na'i safely behind her son. The scene is too powerful and too clear to need any further elaboration. Beiza'i has by then rendered the scarecrow-figure of the father phallically castrated, visibly redundant and socially irrelevant. This is the beginning of a whole new definition of family, father, mother and son, as well as the relation of power which is to hold them together.

In this reading of *Bashu*, I have opted to work through the world-parents myth-type of A 625 in Thompson's motif-index, where we have sky-father and earth-mother as parents of the universe, rather than the specific case of the Iranian myth of Mashya and Mashyana, for the simple reason that the working of these mythic moments is at once local and global, specific and universal. We could alternatively work through the myth-type of A 1255, 'Man made from plant', or A1225.1, 'First couple originally united like Siamese twins', or A 1234.1.1. 'Primeval human pair spring from womb of mother earth' – which is closer to the myth of Mashya and Mashyana.[27] In that case, the character of Na'i would have been closer to her mythic disposition as the intertwined father and mother, rendering the father figure entirely redundant. But in either case, the centrality of Beiza'i's mythic filmmaking would stay the same. The metonymic power of his cinema is categorically cast towards a radical recasting of the gendered relations of power, and from there to the constitution of a yet unknowing subject.

Urban Legends

'The fact that a universe without myth is the ruin of the universe', Bataille suggests, 'reduced to the nothingness of things – in the process of depriving us equates depravation with the revelation of the universe'.[28] In the colonial frontiers apparently myths die harder, perhaps because we keep re-inventing them, sometime for the right reasons. What Beiza'i has done in his long and illustrious career is precisely keeping all of us at bay for a collapse into a universe without myth. In our case, it is the old myths that, by refusing to die, continue to haunt us. We are of course all and always at the mercy of falling into the abyss of the nothingness of things. Beiza'i's career, however, has been to have the nothingness of things signified or mythologised into a breaking loose from the old, lazy, overbearing and domineering myths we have passively received. His cinema has always been at work for the working of a new revelation of the universe in which we, as Iranians, as colonials, as having been written out of the history of our own history, can be born again. To be born again, in terms that will finally enable us in our own destiny, Beiza'i has always gone for the juggernaut. Here is another example.

Under the calm, even prosaic veneer of *Perhaps Some Other Time/Shayad Vaqti Digar* (1988), Beiza'i has a far more ambitious agenda, even more ambitious, I venture to say, than anything attained in *The Stranger and the Fog*, *The Ballad of Tara* and *Bashu* put together. *Perhaps Some Other Time* is predicated on a suspicion. Modabber suspects his wife Kian of having an illicit love affair, while Kian is trying to conceal a succession of inexplicable nightmarish memories, perhaps even symptomatic of schizophrenic paranoia. While pregnant and fighting to conceal her psychological predicament, Kian finds out that she is not the natural child of her parents and that they have adopted her. Meanwhile, Modabber is going mad with his suspicion. He finally locates Mr Ranjbar, the antique dealer whom he suspects of having an affair with his wife. Kian is desperate to conceal her psychological problems from her husband. Modabber is equally desperate to find out the truth about his wife's fidelity. They give each other wrong signals, add to each other's confusion, lead each other to false conclusions. Finally, Modabber finds out that Ranjbar is married to a woman who looks remarkably similar to his wife. She turns out to be the lost twin sister of his wife, and Kian finds out that her recurring nightmarish images are all from her early childhood, when her mother, out of destitution and desperation, abandoned her on a street corner to be picked up by a caring couple.

In *Perhaps Some Other Time*, and through a very simple narrative, Beiza'i examines the function of 'evidence', and the mechanism of gathering it in the constitution of Truth and Falsehood. The place of women in this film is of an entirely different sort and has nothing to do with Beiza'i's concern about the fate of women in Iranian society. Here, he is after something far more universal, far more significant, and he achieves that end in a far more ingenious way which implicates the question of femininity/masculinity in an entirely different way. To me, *Perhaps Some Other Time* is infinitely more mythical than *The Ballad of Tara* and *The Stranger and the Fog* put together. The urbanity of its simple appearance is too deceptive for those who are accustomed to see the workings of the mythical in rural settings, archaic clothing, or antiquated dialogues – and precisely for that reason the contemporaneity of Beiza'i's mythmaking through metonymic aesthetics becomes far more evident.

Both Modabber and his wife Kian begin with a visual representation: Modabber with a video shot of his wife, Kian with the nightmarish images the meaning of which she cannot fathom. But, and here is the rub, Modabber is watching something that he is not watching, while Kian is watching something that she does not know she is watching. He watches a complete stranger to him, the lost twin sister of his wife, but he thinks he is watching his wife. She sees in her dreams the real images of her infancy, but she does not have the complete data and the interpretative framework to realise what it is she is watching. Modabber begins to interpret the video images he watches on the false exegetical premise of marital infidelity. Kian begins to accumulate data, piece by piece, from her dreams and from her husband's suspicious behaviour, and yet does not have that exegetical premise to interpret them. Hermeneutically, he is deductive. Hermeneutically, she is inductive. Logically, he operates *a priori*. Logically, she operates *a posteriori*. He collects indubitable data just to end up proving himself wrong. She collects dubious data just to prove herself right. It is only here that we can see the absolutely ingenious way in which Beiza'i has passed historical judgment on the masculine proclivity to abstraction and metaphysics, and conversely, the feminine proclivity to material fact and always contingent propositions.

The two character-types, mythical images that Beiza'i construes and examines here, is that of woman as 'food-gatherer' and of man as 'animal-hunter'. Kian gathers the data of her early childhood with the sedentary patience of an archaic Woman. Modabber hunts for Absolutist Abstractions, caring very little for the facts. Kian is after no Absolutist Abstraction. She just wants to accumulate/gather enough data/food to make sense of/feed her perturbed imagination/household. Modabber cares very little for facts. He just wants to hunt/Abstract for a final explanation/Absolute Certainty that will determine his wife's infidelity/establish the Truth. Kian lives in and by reality. Modabber is a metaphysician *par excellence*. As a result, *Perhaps Some Other Time* is Beiza'i's manifesto against a whole history of Phallogocentricism.

By the brilliance of one cinematic strike seeking to alter, or at least visibly and narratively challenge, the age-old authority of a phallogocentricism – that for millennia has managed to conceal itself behind a metaphysical culture to which veiling is second nature – requires not only a comfortable command of, but a critical intimacy with the mythological working of a culture. That 'changeability is one of the specific characteristics of myth'[29] is an insight that can indeed be achieved after a long and arduous examination of myths in their cross-cultural and trans-historical settings – in the case of this particular assertion by Professor Th. P. Van Barren, an Egyptologist from the University of Groningen, via examples of mythological behaviour in as diverse a setting as in Tahiti, among the Anuak (a Nilotic tribe on the Upper Nile), among the Papuans of the Wantoat region in Northeast New Guinea, and in Tikopia. But to initiate mythical changes that are as much rooted in the contemporaneity of our problems as they are launched towards an emancipation of our future requires a critical intelligence of an entirely different sort. Here, what is gathered in Beiza'i is an unusual combination of a scholar and an artist. His exceptionally detailed knowledge of both Iranian mythology and of the Persian performing arts is squarely at the service of his creative imagination, and then all of this is geared towards a radical, surgical, breakthrough from the historical bondage to myths that have so far occasioned our slavery to the gathered and ossified symbolics and institutions of power.

Meanwhile, the Ma'arefi Family ...

After the opening sequence of *Travelers*, Mahtab Ma'arefi, her husband Heshmat Davaran and their two children all get into their car, head south towards Tehran, experience a fatal accident, and all die. Meanwhile, Mahtab Ma'arefi's sister Mahrokh and her entire family are getting ready for her wedding. The sad news of the tragic accident arrives. The wedding preparations turn into a mourning ceremony. But against all evidence, the Grandmother of the family refuses to believe that her daughter and her entire family have perished in a fatal automobile accident and insists on the wedding preparations to proceed as planned. While the whole family is stricken with sorrow, she persists in her optimism. Finally, at the crucial moment when the wedding was to happen and Mahtab was to arrive with her family to bring along the auspicious mirror for her sister's ceremonial marriage, the Grandmother insists that the bride should go and change into her wedding gown. Against all indications and her own better judgment, but unable to refuse the Grandmother's wish, she goes upstairs and changes into her wedding gown. As she descends the stairs, suddenly the door opens and ... in comes Mahtab Ma'arefi with the promised mirror in her hands and her entire family behind her.

The *Travelers* is the magnificent culmination of the work of arguably the most visually perceptive Iranian filmmaker. It is narrated with haunting precision within the double-bind of two impossibilities, two negations of the ordinary, two suspensions of the rational, two framings of the common. Thus framed and folded, *The Travelers* is visualised in a timing and a scale, a tempo and a movement, that actively suspends and transforms every shred of reality into a visual narrative of compelling power and poise. From the very first shot of a mirror laid down on the grass, and from the very first sequence of the Davaran family getting ready for their trip to Tehran, that visual narrative informs of an aesthetically transformed reality, a transformation that holds everything in suspense, from the beginning to the end of the story.

How are we to understand that suspense? All those who have written on *The Travelers* have tried in one way or another to grapple with the central tension of the narrative, which is the startling announcement in the very first sequence of the film and its precise reversal at the end.[30] How are we to understand that? Is Mahtab Ma'arefi joking with the audience? Is she mad? What sort of a film is this for a lead actor to break the Fourth Wall, face the camera and tell the audience that she (not as Homa Rusta the actor, but as Mahtab Ma'arefi the character) and her entire family are going to die in an automobile accident? Then how come that they all come back to life at the end of the film? Did we not see, in fact, that she and her family actually got into an accident and that, according to the evidence, including a police report, they all perished? The central tension of the film, then, is the fact that a whole family dies and withers away early in the film, and yet they are all somehow miraculously resurrected at the end.

The resurrection of the dead: that is at least one central creative tension of *The Travelers*. Either all the dead were resurrected back to life by some miraculous deed, or else the expecting family, the Grandmother in particular, wished them back to life. In either of these two cases, the element of 'hope' is central in a resurrection which is not into the realm of the beyond and after, but into the domain of the here and now. How are we to deal with that? Resurrection of the dead? To begin with, Muslims have a theory of resurrection in their belief, that they will all be brought back from the dead on the day of judgment to face God and be punished or rewarded for things they have done in this world. Muslims are not alone in their belief in resurrection. Christians believe that Christ was resurrected from the dead, too. To Shi'ism in particular, 'bodily resurrection' (*Ma'ad-e Jismani*), as it is called, is a central doctrinal issue. Muslim jurists have written volumes on the subject, mystics have theorised it, even philosophers, including Avicenna, have grappled with the doctrinal proposition.

One of the most recent philosophical discussions of the issue of 'bodily resurrection' in a specifically Shi'i context, but with no sectarian reason to exclude it from being equally applicable to Islam at large, is by the seventeenth-century Iranian philosopher Shaykh Ahmad Ahsa'i (1573–1626). Right from the heart of the 'School of Isfahan' and under the influence of the monumental figure of Mulla Sadra Shirazi (1572–1641), Shaykh Ahmad Ahsa'i dealt with the issue of 'bodily resurrection' in a rich philosophical language that Mulla Sadra had virtually invented in the seventeenth century, and which can very well constitute the material elements for an Islamic theory of the body. In his treatment of the issue of 'bodily resurrection', Ahsa'i makes a distinction between *jism* (the body) and *jasad* (the corpse). This distinction is not only central to Ahsa'i's own theory of 'bodily resurrection', but it is also one of the most crucial perspectives on an Islamic theory of the body. 'What seems most likely to me', Ahsa'i asserts, 'is that originally, or as time went on, the word *Jasad* in the Arabic language was taken to mean the body (*jism*) of the living being insofar as the spirit (*ruh*) is absent from it'.[31] *Jism*, as opposed to *jasad*, is that 'which is animated by the *pneuma*, the spirit (*ruh*), as when speaking of "the body of Zayd"'.[32] The domain of the existing beings that have this dual aspect to their physical body is not limited to human beings. Even metals can be 'represented as inanimate bodies without the spirit (*ajsad*), the spirit being for them the Elixir'.[33] The extension is rather comprehensive. Even 'if the astronomers [...] use the word *jism* [...] it is because the celestial spheres are in a subtle state comparable to that of the spirits, or else because astronomers regard them from the point of view of their eternal interdependence with the souls by which they are moved [...]'.[34] Ahsa'i's assumption here that celestial spheres are in the form of *jism* and not *jasad* – that is, they are living things rather than dead masses of matter, or that they have 'interdependence with the souls by which they are moved' – is a crucial astronomical observation for which the credit should really go to Aristotle. *In Generation and Corruption*, *De Caelo*, as well as in *Generation of Animals*, Aristotle believed that the sun is the efficient cause of all events, that the planetary spheres and the planets are responsible for all worldly events, and that the generation of everything, including the generation of animals are 'controlled by the movements of these heavenly bodies'.[35] From the Aristotelian sources, the idea of the planets and planetary spheres having not just a body but also a soul that animates and enlightens them and thus makes them authoritative over human affairs gradually entered Islamic astronomical beliefs. Al-Kindi, for example, as one of the greatest commentators on Greek philosophy in the earliest stages of Islamic philosophy, believed that 'the planets are rational (*natiqat*), spiritual beings capable of intelligence and speech, and [themselves] cause (*fa'ilat*) and administer (*mudabbirat*) everything in this world by the order of the prime Creator who controls all'.[36] The point here being the distinction between *jism* and *jasad*, a living body and a dead body, is definitive to Islamic (Shi'i) metaphysics.

Bodies are thus either dead (*jasad)* or alive (*jism*), and bodies have a range of multifaceted existences that extends from the stars and comes down to human beings. In their living status as *jism*, bodies move, rationalise, speak and live. *Jasad*, in particular, is used as opposed to *ruh*, or the 'soul' which animates the body. The presence of the 'soul' or its absence is the distinction between a 'corpse' and a 'body'. Then comes Ahsa'i's most startling observation:

> Now you should be informed that the human being possesses two jasads and two jisms. The first jasad is the one which is made up of elements that are a prey to time. This jasad, this flesh, is like a garment that a man puts on and later casts off again; this body in itself has neither enjoyment nor suffering; it is subject neither to fidelity nor to rebellion [...]. As for the second jasad [...], this body survives, for the 'clay' from which it was constituted survives 'in the tomb', when the earth has devoured the elementary terrestrial body of flesh [...] whereas the 'body of celestial flesh' survives and retains its perfect 'shape' [...][37]

This theory of the dual body generates an entirely new vista on the whole notion of 'bodily resurrection'. The Second (celestial) Body of which Ahsa'i speaks is not subject to timely erosion and corruption, as is the First (terrestrial) Body. We die, and we are placed in the tomb with our First Body weakened and dead but our Second Body intact. The First Body soon decomposes, and its constituent elements join their origin – fire to fire, earth to earth, and so on – but the Second Body which is celestial in nature and disposition survives even in the tomb. Here, Ahsa'i's eschatology is aided by a theory of optics which is very important for our purposes here. The obvious question is why we ordinarily do not 'see' this Second (celestial) Body when the First (terrestrial) Body has dissolved? Or, even more simply put, why do we not see dead people? Ahsa'i's answer rests on his theory of optics.

Ahsa'i's theory of optics, on the basis of which we see the terrestrial body but not the celestial body, is very simple. The reason we see Mr Zayd in his terrestrial body – when he is alive – but do not see him in his celestial body – when he is dead – is not because that body is constitutional to his being. It is only because that body 'is homologous to the opacity that exists in silica and potash'.[38] What does that exactly mean?

> When these [terrestrial bodies – namely, silica and potash] are fused together, liquefied, they turn into glass. The glass is certainly the same silica and the same potash that were completely dense and opaque. But after the fusion, the opacity

> disappeared. This means that opacity is not a property of the earth itself. The earth itself is subtle and transparent; its opacity is caused by the clash between the elements. When water is still and pure, you see everything in its depth. But if you stir it up, you can no longer distinguish anything in it so long as it is in movement, because of the collision between its parts and the rarefaction of the element of the air. What then happens when the four elemental Natures come into collision! This jasad, this body of flesh made of terrestrial elements, is comparable to the density that makes silica and potash opaque, although this is not a part of their essence, of their ipseity.[39]

If we have followed Ahsa'i so far, he is almost home free in proving why we cannot see dead people. If we agree with him that the only reason that we see the living terrestrial bodies is that the composition of elemental matters in them has caused their opacity and thus visibility, then all he has to do (and which he does) is to change the direction of the camera, as it were, and say that the reason why we do not see the celestial body is that our own bodily organs, our eyes in this case, are made of such opacity, and thus we cannot see a thing when dissolved from that opacity. The Second – subtle, celestial – Body 'is invisible to earthly beings, to the people of this world, on account of the opacity that darkens their fleshly eyes and prevents them from seeing what is not of the same kind as themselves'.[40]

This is simply brilliant! Because all Beiza'i has really done at the end of *The Travelers* is to turn his camera into an instrument of vision, which art, *ipso facto*, is supposed to be doing anyway, with which we overcome the opacity of our elementally constituted and limited organ of perception. Put very simply, with Beiza'i's camera we see things that we ordinarily cannot see, which is the very rudimentary definition of art: to see things otherwise invisible. The fusion of Beizai's cinematic cosmovision as well as Ahsa'i's dual theories of 'bodily resurrection' and its preliminary theory of optics creates a visual condition in which we can see the Ma'arefi family in their 'true', 'celestial', significant body, in the flesh and bone of their moral significance, the corporeal veracity of their very being-in-the-world. 'When God wishes to bring his creatures back to life', Ahsa'i stipulates, 'he causes a rain coming from the ocean situated below the Throne to spread out over the Earth, the water of this rain being colder than snow'.[41] For mortals with a gift to show the way out of a deadly entrapment in the real, that rain is a shower of light.

Metonymic Mythologies of the Present

Beiza'i has no antiquarian interest in myth and mythmaking. He is a radically contemporary filmmaker, with a penchant for invoking distant mythologies and reworking them for their contemporary recasting. He is a mythic filmmaker. Beginning with the opening gambit of one of his masterpieces, *The Travelers*, we see the working of both the memorial and the current juxtaposition of mythologies in the making of Beiza'i's body of work. In *Bashu*, as perhaps the best example of them all, the mythic space becomes the uncanny location of a Northern Iranian landscape where a working woman becomes the premise of active mythmaking from the torched ground of the

Iran-Iraq War. The always already mythically pregnant reality as Beiza'i sees it dissolves in *The Stranger and the Fog*, where we become the unknowing subject re-mythologising our encounter with the real. In *The Ballad of Tara*, we see the central character of Tara as a mythic persona having a dialogue with a reality we recognize and where myth has become ritualised and the two have collapsed into each other. As myth and reality collide in the metonymic power of his cinema, the contemporaneity of Beiza'i's mythmaking breaks down the phallogocentric premise of the culture, accentuated in *The Travelers* where we encounter the resurrection of the corporeal body, as Ahsa'i's optics and Beiza'i's camera coalesce.

Reversing the angle of the previous chapter on the oeuvre of Mas'ud Kimia'i, here in this chapter we witness in Beiza'i's cinema the constitution of the feminine as consciously envisioned in specifically mythic terms and farthest removed from the patriarchal masculinism of the postcolonial pathology of the fear of emasculation. In terms of the passageway from mythology to metonymy, this chapter is perhaps the most iconic epicentre of my book. In Beiza'i's masterpieces we see how the deepest layers of ancient mythologies and the metonymic power of visual culture tempt and animate the prospect of contemporary and current myths in the visual and performing arts. The symbolic 'immaculate conception' at the heart of *Bashu* completely recasts the gendered patriarchy at the epicentre of world encounter with colonial modernity. Here, the encounter between semblance and subjectivity roots deeply in mythic soils and flowers in de-gendered subjectivity.

As we have inherited it today, the constitution of gender is an interface between the colonial and patriarchal projects exacerbating each other, and as a result liberating the subject must perforce rest on the premise of the defiant disposition of art, which has in fact paradoxically been the domain of the biopower subjection of the colonial person. Therefore, the same site is to be explored to liberate the subject, redirecting it from myth to metonymy to the unknowing subject – moving towards the postcolonial premise of a de-gendered, de-racialised and unknowing subject. The path of the project is now clear: as I proposed in the Introduction, appealing to alternative particularities and marking the universalities they implicate requires a simultaneous attention to both colonial and patriarchal framings, working mostly with film, fiction and poetry, with occasional excursions into Islamic philosophy, all of which is geared to the space of pure verisimilitudes where metonymic allusions to distant myths prepare for a radical rethinking of the gendered subject.

The de-gendering of the subject is tantamount to making the unknowing subject conscious of the knowable world it now faces. The power dynamics embedded in colonial modernity was first and foremost encoded in the political formation of the nation state – but the weak bourgeois fore-structure of the postcolonial polity resulted in the disproportionate potency of the aesthetic, artistic and imaginative apparatus of subjection. The power of the state apparatus and the prolonged presence of the condition of coloniality pale in comparison to the apparatus of the imaginal artworld and its ability to instantiate subjection. As the generic condition of *governmentality* amounted to that of *coloniality* around the world, this artworld could be as much a source of agential de-subjection (Kimia'i) as indeed of radical re-subjection (Beiza'i).

Both projects have operated through the metonymic invocations of deeply buried mythologies – one in disabling and the other in enabling modes. But both have inevitably tapped into the world of pure verisimilitude that has emotively expanded the world and its lived experiences from lived realities to retrieved mythologies.

I can think of no better site to see that mythic contemporaneity of our presence in the world than in the sublime poetry of Forough Farrokhzad. In '*Tanha Sedast keh mimanad*/Only the Sound Will Last', Farrokhzad asks the supreme metaphysical question 'why should I wait', and from there where to go; with the same urgency she defies the circumstances of her existence, proclaiming defiantly and assuredly: 'I am a descendent of trees':

> Why should I wait
> I follow the command of the Four Elements, [...]
> The bloody lineage of flowers
> Has committed me to living –
> The bloody lineage of flowers –
> Do you understand?[42]

From the four elements of fire, wind, earth and water to the bloody lineage of flowers become the mythic ingredients of a life lived on the edges of reality and pure verisimilitude.

5

Liberation in Three Moves

Cheh dur bud pish az in zamin-e ma ...

How far away our earth
Used to be –
Far from these dark holes in the sky –
But now I can hear
Your voice again –
Like the sound of snowy wings of angels –
See how far I have gone –
Deep into the cosmos, the boundless, the eternal ...[1]

Forough Farrokhzad, '*Aftab Mishavad*/The Sun Rises' (1962)

Liberation movements in art are more *ex post facto* results of an accidental congregation of aesthetic events rather than a conscious decision to concoct a conspiracy of pre-meditated moves. In what must in some arguably demonstrable way be called 'the post-revolutionary Iranian cinema', three seminal filmmakers have emerged as the leading visionaries of three moments of liberation in a culture otherwise trapped in its own historical *cul-de-sac*. Abbas Kiarostami, Rakhshan Bani-Etemad and Mohsen Makhmalbaf represent three distinctly different realistic cinemas that nevertheless move in an extraordinarily emancipatory direction, liberating Iranian culture from some of its most enduring reactionary forces. If we were to think of these three distinct cinematic oeuvres in temporal terms, Kiarostami's cinema is the aesthetic vision of our *future*, free from all the received and enduring entrapments of an ancient culture. Bani-Etemad's cinema is the rich topography of a *present* at once brutal and yet pregnant with the possibility of an Otherwise. Makhmalbaf's cinema is the singular semiotics of one heroic effort to shed the thick and thickening layers of a *past* that refuses to let us go. The mode of Realism specific to these three filmmakers and their emancipatory moves I wish to typologise as *Actual* for Kiarostami, *Factual* for Bani-Etemad and *Virtual* for Makhmalbaf, in ways that I will try to specify in this chapter.

The Realism of these three cinemas always intimates a historical 'truth' but never collapses into a metaphysical ordering of reality. There precisely dwells the power of their Realism. The aesthetic expediency constituted for a concerted liberation in the work of these three filmmakers is conducive to a singular recognition of Iranian culture as an historical product of its own conceptions of good and evil. The 'truth' evident in these three cinemas, however, speaks not to a universal or atemporal objectivity but, instead, to a reality that needs re-defining for Kiarostami, re-signifying for Bani-Etemad and re-historicising for Makhmalbaf. If 'truth', as Nietzsche once said, is a 'mobile army of metaphors', to mobilise an army of aesthetic metaphors in order to liberate a culture constitutes a 'truth' at once historical and counter-metaphysical, always-already conscious of its recent visual self-Symbolisation. The 'truth' evident in these three cinemas never approximates a grandiloquent claim to a reality that transcends time and space. It breaks through all layers of cultural conditioning and reaches for those moments when a culture begins to dream in its art the terms of its own emancipation. As a result, there is an aesthetic instrumentalism about this liberation cinema, a provocative abandoning of all cultural clustering of extraneous meaning and intention. 'Reality' is re-invented, re-membered and re-signified in these three cinemas, in a newly modulated fashion, in phenomenally realistic, but significantly different, languages.

The Realism of the Real

One of the most crucial consequences of the *'fort/da' hypothesis* that Freud theorised in *Beyond the Pleasure Principle* is the active substitution of the Symbolic suggestiveness of language for reality, when the 'Gone!/There it is!' exclamation of a child playing with a cotton reel begins to substitute the reality of the fear of losing the mother. The same principle is still operative in the organic solidarity of advanced societies where the fear of the Real necessitates alternative and substitutional forms of Realism. In the Iranian case, three complementary cinematic events begin to oppose the fear that Reality in and of itself constitutes in and about the Islamic Revolution. First is the creative constitution of remedial Symbolics to alleviate the fear of the Real, as in the most recent films of Mohsen Makhmalbaf, where we can see the active constitution of a kind of *Virtual Realism*. *A Moment of Innocence* (1996), *Gabbeh* (1997) and *Silence* (1998) are counter-Symbolic parables of hope where substitutional metaphors, in the form of a *Virtual Realism* are offered to alleviate the fear of the Real. A second, complementary move has been to subvert the whole metaphysical formation of the Symbolic order. Kiarostami's *Actual Realism*, his uncanny ability to see a soothing reassurance in the total meaninglessness of being, is the cinema of that counter-Symbolic. Kiarostami's ambitious project is to rid the fear of the loss of the Symbolic altogether, so that there is no need for a metaphysics at all. In *Where is the Friend's House* (1987), *Life Goes On* (1992), *Through the Olive Trees* (1994) and *The Taste of Cherry* (1998), there is a succession of dismantling the whole authoritative grammatological ordering of the Symbolic. Bani-Etemad's *Factual Realism*, meanwhile, her exceptional ability to see the Real and yet stay away from all its culturally inherited moralising, is the third, complementary move to create a triangulated closing in on the fear of the Real. Her camera has been carefully at work, in both her documentaries and her features, foregrounding a whole inventory of social malaise which are the institutional and, far more important, Symbolic sources of the pain that a nation has endured. Although the root of her cinematic cosmovision has to be carefully grounded in her documentaries, because it is there that she has studied and cultivated her *Factual Realism*, it is in her major three features, *Nargess* (1991), *The Blue-Veiled* (1994) and *The May Lady* (1998) that her visual de-Symbolisation of the tyrannical Dominant and her simultaneous re-Symbolisation of the transgressively Possible is brought to perfection.

Fear of the Real

To understand the revolutionary nature of this triangulated cinematic vision, we must begin with the turbulent and tumultuous two decades of the 1980s and the 1990s in which this cinema is located and has been produced. Unless we remember what precisely has been the nature and disposition of the Iranian Real, we will not be able to read the un-doing of that Real in its full emancipatory force. A tyrannical authoritarian monarchy, a gut-wrenching revolution that left thousands of young men and women dead on the streets, a devastating war that took hundreds of thousands of Iranian youth to their untimely death, a collective exposure to massive propaganda and demonisation by imperialist economies whose commercial and military interests in the region were jeopardised as the result of the Islamic Revolution, and then the catastrophic inheritance of a belligerent theocracy as the ruling regime of a nation at the threshold of the twenty-first century are the principal signposts of a disastrous history of indignance, barbarity and infamy that has wreaked havoc on some eighty million people. The Iranians emerged from the brutal obscenity of being ruled by an entrenched monarchy and raised their hopes and aspiration for a fuller participation in their own moral and political affairs, only to be plunged into a religious fanaticism of an even worse totalitarian tyranny. Economically, the Islamic Revolution did not move even for an inch the logistic location of the Iranian economy in global capitalism. Iran still is a mostly single-product (oil) economy, selling its natural resources and buying finished products. Politically, the authoritarian regime of the Pahlavi monarchy is replaced by the totalitarian tyranny of a theocracy.

More than forty years into the Islamic Revolution, a government of inquisition rules with fear and intimidation. The massive vote of confidence in President Khatami in 1977 resulted in no institutional change in the organs of repression. Reform-minded members of Khatami's cabinet were constantly harassed and maligned by the clerical clique and their militant organs. Intellectually, a campaign of terror and intimidation was ferociously launched against the slightest voice of reason and protest. Intellectuals were murdered, and their murderers were brought to no justice. The leading members of the Iranian literati and artists have opted to live, even momentarily, in the indignity of exile, rather than tolerate the humiliation of constantly being harassed by ghoulish thugs acting on behalf of their clerical warlords. Socially, there is a massive and deep-rooted despair among the youth, which is unprecedented in modern history. Every year millions of high school graduates participate in national entrance examinations and compete for scarce college resources that have already been pre-allocated to ideologically compatible members of the ruling elite. The most innocent expressions of youthful behaviour are violently suppressed by an army of paid and armed thugs. In the aftermath of the rigged presidential election of 2009, a massive democratic movement emerged, dubbed the Green Movement, but it was severely crushed.[2] Millions of Iranians of all economic classes have fled their country and prefer to live abroad. Poor Iranian immigrants in adjacent countries are subjected to the most humiliating behaviour. Even such colonial outposts as the United Arab Emirates refuse single Iranian women entry visas, based on the assumption that they are going there for prostitution. A government that has little claim to legitimacy uses every means of suppression and denial to keep a massive population under the yoke of a brutish and indecent rule. Every time we see an Iranian film, we have to keep this picture in mind. This is not an art that casual film critics can claim to understand, or a handful of egocentric festival directors could be expected to grasp beyond the most superficial surface. This is an art borne out of pain and driven by the hope of an entire nation. All the petty professional rivalries among the best Iranian filmmakers aside, they are now the harbingers of hope, messengers of a possibility, fiercely intelligent visionaries of emancipation for an entire nation.

Constitutional to the recent memory of that nation has been a vicious cycle of violence, rotating between state and society. 'Every state is founded on force', Trotsky had observed in Brest-Litovsk, and in post-World War I Germany Max Weber had found it only apt to quote Trotsky and to redefine politics in terms of a 'legitimate' violence constitutional to its successful operations.[3] Decades into the successful making of an Islamic Republic, the preponderance of violence has continued to plague post-revolutionary Iran precisely, because of a fear of legitimacy of the ruling regime. Ayatollah Khomeini had personified a particular mode of charismatic authority that in violent, anti-institutional terms challenged and superseded the corrupt Pahlavi monarchy and substituted it with a theocracy with perfectly logical connections to the enduring elements in Islamic (particularly Shi'ite) political culture. From the success of the revolution in 1979 until his death in 1989, for a decade Khomeini personified the charismatic terror of one of the most violent reigns of violence in modern Iranian history. From the thousands of demonstrators being gunned down by the Shah's army, over the immediate and effective execution of the Shah's generals and the brutal elimination of political rivals (particularly, but by no means limited to, the radical Mujaheddin-e Khalq Organisation), to the colossal human sacrifice in the course of the Iran-Iraq War (1980–88), Khomeini presided over one of the most violent regimes in recent memory. There were more silent costs to Khomeini's reign of terror. Freedom of expression was perhaps the costliest. While the rest of the world was fixated on the 'Rushdie Affair', members of the Iranian literati and intelligentsia were brutally suppressed. Some were murdered (the poet Sa'id Soltanpour), some imprisoned (the novelist Shahrnoush Parsipour), some effectively silenced (the poet Ahmad Shamlou), some forced into exile (the poet Esmail Kho'i), some drank themselves to death to escape the indignity of exile (the dramatist Gholamhossein Sa'edi), and the rest were subjected to one of the most ruthless censorships in history, even more ruthless than in the notorious time of the Shah's secret police, the dreaded SAVAK. It is something of a miracle that a cinema so extraordinarily powerful could have emerged from such wanton barbarities.

Khomeini died in 1989, but Khomeinism survived beyond him. The classical crisis of successorship to a charismatic leader was resolved by the collective will of the clerical revolutionaries, determined not to let their hard-won power slip away from them either to their immediate rivals, the Mujaheddin, or to their more democratic alternatives.[4] Constitutional to the emerging political culture of the post-Khomeini period has been the ideological rationalisation of violence as the most viable political machination of power. Perhaps the greatest theorist of violence, George Sorel, combined what he took to be the logical implications of Nietzsche and the historical experience of the pioneering Americans to argue for the viability of an 'ethics of violence'.[5] Sorel's concern with a deliberate construction of an ethics of violence was primarily to provide a justification for what he considered to be legitimate violence at the service of the superior Socialist revolution, which would have to happen before a new Man was to be born from the ashes of bourgeois 'civility'. Upon the success of a major social revolution, however, the political instrumentality of violence works through the institutionalised terror with a range of power far beyond the reach of any single charismatic movement. The rising charismatic authority can only imagine and deliver a metanarrative of absolutism which includes violence. The actual implementation of that metanarrative – always based, as Sorel tried to establish, on an ethics – is an entirely different issue.

In the case of the Iranian Revolution, perhaps no other institution can better demonstrate the active routinisation of violence in the post-revolutionary period than the Revolutionary Guard Corps that was formed almost immediately upon the revolution's success in 1979.[6] The specific historicity of implementing the revolutionary metanarrative of violence reaches the farthest corners of a totalitarian absolutism, which is the necessary outcome of what Weber called the 'routinisation of charisma'. Routinised charisma became routinised violence, extending the militant implications of a political agenda over which God and its self-appointed representatives had been called to preside. The ethics that Sorel postulated for revolutionary violence became the *conditio sine qua non* of a brutal justification and use of violence. In Iran, 'the Islamic Revolutionary Guard Corps is everywhere'.[7] As a revolutionary institution, the Revolutionary Guards were recruited from a range of social and economic strata, covering the entire pyramid of the Iranian social structure. From internal security, over the upholding of the revived Islamic ethics and the waging of war against Iraq, to the export of revolutionary zeal, the Revolutionary Guards became the military arm of Khomeinism. The Revolutionary Guards actively participated in the Iran-Iraq war precisely to have an enduring claim over the political outcome of not only the war but, perhaps more importantly, the internal politics of the post-war polity and economy. The organs of violence in the Islamic Republic have had a perfectly evident ideological resiliency in the tumultuous post-revolutionary era. '[T]he Revolutionary Guard's strength as an institution in revolutionary Iran has resided in its ability to adapt to changing and difficult circumstances and to parry the challenges leveled against it since its formation in 1979'.[8] As a congregation of political interest, the Guard was not different from any other organ of the revolution, ready to take full advantage of its spills. The Guard Corps successfully aligned itself with the winning clerical faction and then exchanged its military support for political and financial power. As, in fact, Katzman documents it, the Guard took full advantage of the eight-year long war with Iraq to consolidate its power within the Islamic Republic. They indeed adopted Khomeini as their patron saint and under the extended shadow of his authority established and consolidated theirs.

The millenarian revivalism of this paramilitary apparatus consciously modelled itself for a revolutionary repetition of the first Islamic Revolution (that is, 'Islam itself'). The initial nucleus of the Revolutionary Guard was formed by devout and fervent followers of Ayatollah Khomeini. It gradually grew to include opportunist mercenaries lacking any ideological or missionary zeal, but full of political and military acumen for survival. It is in that historical range that the Iranian Revolutionary Guard was indeed a replica of the early supporters of Prophet Muhammad and his subsequent followers. From the historical confusion of that spectrum of faith and opportunism emerges the ethics of pure violence that informed the first army of Muslims as much as it does the Iranian Revolutionary Guards. Fear of the Real is real, demanding a proportionate turn to cinematic (and aesthetic) Realism.

Towards a Neo-Realism

The comparison of Iranian New Wave to Italian Neo-Realism is at once quite apt and revealing and yet substantially short of saying something specific about Iranian cinema.[9] The thematic narrative reasons for the similarities between Iranian and Italian neo-realisms are quite evident. Almost all prominent Iranian filmmakers are unanimous in their acknowledgment of the influence of the masterpieces of Italian Neo-Realism, particularly Desica's *Bicycle Thief* (1948), on their work. But the historical and material reasons for the dissimilarities are equally obvious. A cinema from the southern edges of the Western European capitalist modernity of the 1930s to the 1950s has its inherent limitations in comparison to cinema produced in the postcolonial outpost of late global capitalism. The cultural – in particular, the literary – imperatives that have at once enabled and limited the Iranian cinema of the last almost half a century are equally different from those of Italian Neo-Realism. While Italian Neo-Realism emerged in the aftermath of Italian fascism, the Iranian New Wave is equally rooted in the trauma of the Islamist revolution and its subsequent war. This simple fact also brings both of these two cinemas together, as it marks their differences.

There is a more categorical problem with the extended application of European cultural production to those of the postcolonial outposts. Here, even the most sympathetic cultural theorists fall into the trap of Eurocentrism. Fredric Jameson, for example, believes that ...

> ... film itself has never been more alive than it is globally, where in the new world system a host of local voices have found the most sophisticated technical expressions. A filmmaker in whom I have been interested was described in some local journal or other as 'the Antonioni of Taiwan': at a moment when we in the West, for all kinds of socio-economic reasons, no longer have our own Antonionis any more, or our own Hitchcocks or Ford or Godards, it is good to know that elsewhere, outside the First World, we can look forward to their reinvention, along with the culturally unforeseeable itself ...[10]

A number of caveats here: Antonioni, Hitchcock and Godard were never just 'our own'. By virtue of the global hegemony of this 'our own', they were always already global. I, in fact, met Antonioni in Tehran when I was an undergraduate student in the early 1970s. Kamran Shirdel, an Italian-educated Iranian filmmaker, had invited him to Tehran to screen his *Passenger* (1975). Furthermore, a Taiwanese, or Indian, or Iranian filmmaker are never exactly the same as any of the filmmakers whom Jameson cites. One more thing: that 'Third World' nervous tic to which Jameson is quite attached is the First World of its own history and culture. What is terribly missing here is the location of culture, the site of the fateful confrontation between a particular grammatological ordering of the Symbolic and a visual counter-narration of it. The site of the Iranian, or Arab, or Indian, or any other cultural production, by virtue of their specific location in the larger economic production of reality, is constitutionally different from that of the metropolitan centres of power. At the receiving end of the joint projects of the Enlightenment and capitalist Modernity, the whole world looks and is mirrored differently. In the phenomenally impoverished state of the under-theorisation of cultural productions in the postcolonial outposts – or what 'the First World' has decided to call 'the Third World' in order to be able to call itself 'the First' – we first need to de-theorise ourselves from the status assigned to us by Fredric Jameson, who is still among the best and most sympathetic theorists of cultural production in 'the First', before we can look at ourselves and see where in the world we stand and how we culturally produce and what we mean when we aesthetically reflect ourselves. The primary function of cultural production in Iran, or Egypt, or India, or Senegal is not to replicate a Rossellini in Kiarostami, a Fellini in Chahine, a De Sica in Satyajit Ray, or a Pasolini in Ousmane Sembène – the mastery of those Italian Neo-Realists notwithstanding. The Realism that we indeed see in contemporary Iranian cinema is palpably evident and yet in dire need of theorisation. That theorisation needs to be aware of such variations on realism as the European *Surrealism* or the Latin-American *Magic Realism* but be far more attentive to the specific circumstances of their Iranian versions. While the European Surrealism had opted for what Fredric Jameson has termed 'a certain poetic transfiguration of the object world itself', in Gabriel García Márquez, Latin American Magic Realism has fused this poetic transfiguration of the Real with a fantastic narrative.[11] Neither a 'poetic transfiguration' of the Real nor a 'fantastic narrative' of it, but a set of entirely different visual strategies have emerged in the Iranian take on an active re-modulation of the Real.

The specific circumstances of the emergence of such prominent filmmakers as Abbas Kiarostami, Rakhshan Bani-Etemad and Mohsen Makhmalbaf in contemporary Iranian cinema and their respective mode of Realism are precisely where we need to begin this theorisation – far beyond their entrapment inside any 'Third World Cinema'. Three *modes* of Realism immediately suggest themselves when the works of these three significant filmmakers of the post-revolutionary period are compared. While the cinema of Kiarostami is aesthetically narrated on the thematic thrust of an Actual Realism, stripping reality of all its *Metaphysical* orderings, Bani-Etemad's cinema testifies to a proclivity towards Factual Realism, forcing reality to de-authorise its *Symbolic* grammar, while Makhmalbaf's camera has gradually cultivated a panache for Virtual Realism, teasing out of reality its raw *Semiotic* energy. Following Julia Kristeva, I extend the use of the term *Symbolic* to denote the politically legitimated institutions of established and regulated modalities of power, and of the term *Semiotic* to point to the uncodified and disruptive energies of the libidinal outrage.[12] The *Symbolic* is the repressive carving of politically modulated authority into the rebellious effervescence of the *Semiotic*. While the *Symbolic* pulls the cultural order into its political mandates, the *Semiotic* pushes it towards its creative impulses. The *Metaphysical* is the transparent but profoundly instrumental veneer of signification of reality, which would otherwise *ipso facto* defy both its *Symbolic* codification and *metaphysical* ordering.

Abbas Kiarostami's Actual Realism is predominantly geared towards a re-reading of reality in such a way that it accentuates its irreducible *actuality*, its simply being-there, its latent potency to signify in and of itself. This kind of Realism makes of Kiarostami's cinema a quintessentially counter-metaphysical cosmovision. His cinema is counter-metaphysical, not by virtue of any aesthetic manifesto, but by the force of a *de facto* communion with the *irreducible* and *resistant* actuality of the Real. Kiarostami's camera sees that *irreducibility* to the very edge of an almost visual pointillism beyond which Reality will be atomised into nothingness. The gift of Kiarostami, however, is precisely in his ability to zoom in on the Real, precisely to that very edge and right there to hold his vision stable. At that angle, we are forced to face a vision of reality which is at once 'significant' yet not grammatologically Symbolic. At that angle, and this is equally crucial, reality is inherently *resistant* to any dictatorially assuasive and mollifying intrusion of the metaphysical. From *Bread and Alley* (1970) to *The Taste of Cherry* (1997), Kiarostami has mastered this art of zooming in and zooming out his camera and fine-tuning it precisely at that critical borderline between the *irreducibility* of reality to the edge of a visual pointillism and its *resistance* to any submission to metaphysical ordering.

Rakhshan Bani-Etemad's Factual Realism works on an entirely different level. Her cinematic vision – rooted in her early documentaries and brought to perfection in the three successive staccatos of *Nargess* (1991), *The Blue-Veiled* (1994) and *The May Lady* (1998) – is quintessentially documentational, evidentiary and corroborative, even when she is making narrative feature films. The characters in her features have just stepped out of their factual circumstances and into her narrative world. Her camera, obviously not schizophrenic, works the same way whether she is making a documentary or a feature. It is as if she has in effect condemned her camera never to blink at reality, to remain permanently and factually tied to it, and yet in the midst of that Factual Realism the gift of her vision is its uncanny ability to begin to de-Symbolise the Real, by forcing it to yield to a factually-based counter-Symbolic of the Possible. This, however, is not done by any forced manifesto, ideological pronouncement, or cultural condemnation, in the way Iranian bourgeois feminists would have liked. This is done, *almost* unnoticeably, *almost* unwittingly, by oozing out of the cultural claims and political pronouncements the facticity of the Real itself. The problem that Bani-Etemad's camera resolves is, in effect, to tease out of the matter-of-factness of reality its moral contingency. Reality is culturally conditioned to present itself as a factual and objective presence. To de-objectify that presence, via a moral dismantling of the factual – which is to say, visibly *showing it* to be intolerable – is to implicate human agency as part of that facticity. 'The concept of facticity', as Heidegger formulated it, 'implies that an "innerworldly" being has being-in-the-world in such a way that it can understand itself as bound up in its "destiny" with the being of those beings which it encounters within its own world'.[13] Bani-Etemad's camera is fully in charge of alerting her audience to their 'innerworldly' state of being. That being can understand itself *only* in relation to the factual presence of those around it. The result is a palpable implication of the spectator in the moral contingency of the Factual Realism that Bani-Etemad's camera narrates.

Mohsen Makhmalbaf's realism, too, is of a different nature. He does not have the cosmovisual patience of Kiarostami to dwell on the Actual long enough until it begins to yield its pre-Symbolic force, nor does he have the tenacity and tolerance of Bani-Etemad to stomach the Factual until the audience is implicated in its moral contingency. Makhmalbaf's Virtual Realism is born out of a constitutionally impatient agitation with the Real. The Virtual Realism of Makhmalbaf is aesthetically reductionist, abbreviated, summarised, cathartic. He cuts through the thick and the thin and to the chase. Makhmalbaf has gradually taught his camera to show things *as appearing to be things*, as the *virtual* substitutions of things. As visual phenomena, 'the possibility even exists that they can show themselves as they are *not* in themselves'.[14] Makhmalbaf's camera forces reality into a virtual *self-showing*, a phenomenal *appearance*, a cosmovisual *semblance*. Things are there and yet not there, reduced, modified, manipulated into a Neither-land of virtual signification. Makhmalbaf's Virtual Realism is *symptomatic of* the Real, but not *constituent of* it. As such, his realism is of an

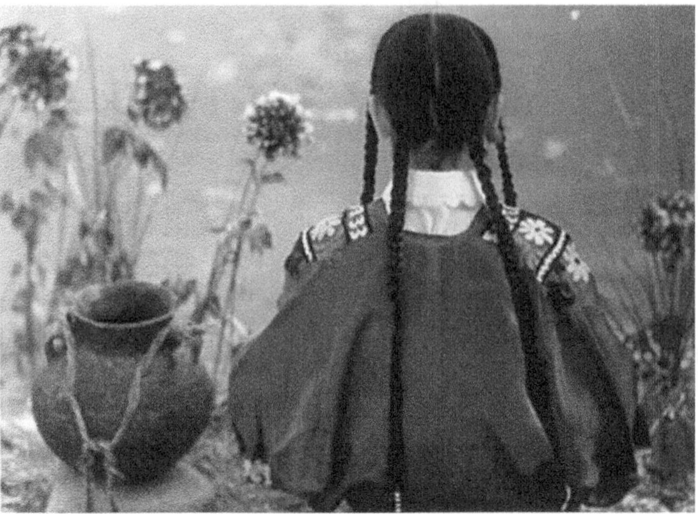

Figure 5.1 *Mohsen Makhmalbaf,* Silence *(1998). (Photo: Mahmalbaf Website: https://www.makhmalbaf.com/?q=mohsen)*

indexical nature, a manifestly *filmed* way of accessing reality. After years of training his camera, Makhmalbaf is now perfectly capable of capturing this *virtuality* of the Real precisely at the moment of its emergence from all metaphysical claims to noumenality. The *virtual presentation* of reality is such that 'appearance, as the appearance "of something" [...] precisely does *not* mean that something shows itself; rather it means that something makes itself known which does not show itself'.[15] Makhmalbaf's task is to make that which 'does not show itself' show itself, not as *actuality* bearing a testimony to a metaphysics, but as *virtuality* which could not have been there, which could have not been there. If 'appearance is a *not showing itself*',[16] then Makhmalbaf's Factual Realism is to make a virtue out of that necessity, and not collapse into a privative mourning for the absence of the actual.

Reality under Erasure

It would be entirely unfortunate if we were to think of towering filmmakers in Iran, India, China, Somalia, or anywhere else in the world as versions of Antonioni, Hitchcock, or any other European filmmakers. What a terribly arrogant and impoverished imagination to think so! That kind of epistemic violence deprives the world of its varied, actual and potential, liberating moments. There are things not dreamt in Italian Neo-Realism. Let me move on.

How can reality, always already Signified, be put *under erasure*; that is to say, its being-there acknowledged and yet its linguistically facilitated – meaning phenomenologically epistemologised and ontologically categorised – modulation questioned? If Being is the Transcendental Signified, as Heidegger took it to be, then all readings of it are always already Signified, always already subject to an overwhelming metaphysics. Through the three successive moves of Kiarostami, Bani-Etemad and Makhmalbaf – *successive* not in a chronological or teleological but only in a diachronic sense – what we witness in Iranian cinema is a visual *sous rature* in which reality is not just observed but made to yield to alternative modes of signification by seizing its pre-significatory, pre-Symbolised and abundant varied semiotic alterities. If closer to the metaphysical environment of these three filmmakers, we take Being (*Wujud*) as always-already Contingent-Being (*Mumkin al-Wujud*) and as such predicated on a Necessary-Being (*Wajib al-Wujud*), then putting reality under erasure suspends that whole metaphysical ordering of reality.

To see the radical nature of questioning the metaphysical ordering of the real, we need to keep in mind that it is not the 'ontological' or even 'epistemological' status of reality which is being challenged, but the very nature and constitution of reality – namely, its pre-ontological, pre-epistemic, pre-symbolised state which is being canvassed. Here, we need to make a distinction, made initially by Afdal al-Din Muhammad Maraqi Kashani, a twelfth-century Iranian philosopher, between a 'thing', which is pre-ontological, and an 'existent being', which is already incorporated into an ontology.[17] Arguing persuasively that a 'thing' is more universal than an 'existent' being, Kashani maintains that, since we can say that 'this thing exists' or 'that thing does not exist', then there is a difference between a 'thing' (*chiz*) and an 'existent [being]' (*hast*). Kashani's objective here is to prove that ontically a 'thing' has antecedence over the ontological supposition of an 'existent' being, because, while we can say that 'every existent being is a thing', we cannot say that 'every thing is an existent being'.[18] What Kashani is after here is nothing short of what Heidegger, some eight centuries later, calls the 'thinging of the thing'. Here is how Kashani formulates it: he wants to prove the universality of a 'thing' over the particularity of an 'existent [being]' in yet one more way. Therefore, ...

> Another reason that 'thing' is more universal than 'existent' is that if you were to say that '"the thing" cannot be outside three conditions, either its existence is necessary, or its existence is contingent, or its existence is impossible', [all] these statements are correct, and no repetitious statement is uttered in them, and none of the statements is false. But if you were to say that, '"existent" is of three kinds: either its existence is necessary, or contingent, or impossible', then the third part of the statement is false because the 'existent' cannot be in a state of impossibility.[19]

From this premise Kashani concludes that being an 'existent' being is but an attribute of a 'thing'. First comes a 'thing' – as an essent – and then it may or may not be an 'existent' being: 'Thus first comes the "thing" and then the "existent"'.[20] 'Thing', in its ontic reality, as a result, is the most irreducible limit which comes even prior to 'being', because 'being' an existent being is only an attribute of the 'thing':

> The limit of the 'thing' cannot be established, nor can it be described. In answer to [the question] 'what is it?', [we note that] the person who asks this question is [already] referring to the 'thing' as 'what is it?', because the meaning of the words 'what', and the word 'that', and the word 'it', and the word 'thing' are all one and the same. Unless the person did not know [already] what the 'thing' is he could not have asked 'what is it?', because the meaning of 'what', and 'that' are none other than the 'thing' [itself]. The word 'that' is more specific than the word 'thing', because 'that' is a specific 'thing', and a specified thing is more specific than the 'thing'. Whoever knows the specific already knows the general. Thus, whoever wants to know what is the 'thing' by asking 'what is it?', before even asking [the question] 'what is it?', he already knows what the 'thing' is. And that which has already been found cannot be given to he who wants to find it. Yes, it is possible that he would not know it in a particular language. For example, an Arabic-speaking person may not know Persian and ask ['what is a 'thing' in Persian], or a Turk about another language.[21]

What is evident in Kashani's careful distinction between the pre-ontological state of a 'thing' and its ontological assimilation into an 'existent' being is the absolute universality and ultimate irreducibility of the Real as a 'thing' – pre-ontological, pre-epistemological and pre-symbolic. This pre-ontological conception of the 'thing' is crucial in the kind of radical realism which is evident in contemporary Iranian cinema and which is geared towards a constitutional dismantling of all symbolic ordering of the Real, whether ontological, epistemological, or metaphysical.

The semiotic energy that lurks on the surface of Iranian cinema is the visual equivalent of Kashani's philosophical search for an ontic, radically anti-ontological grasp of the 'thing' itself.

Each of the three filmmakers I have identified as addressing the centrality of the Real in the trauma of colonial modernity comes close to the ontic matter in a different way. In Kiarostami's Actual Realism, the fictive transparency of the Real becomes evident under the overwhelming gaze of his camera to which there is a melting-down-laser-beaming onto the metaphysical. Bani-Etemad's camera, on the other hand, is totally oblivious to that actuality because it is incurably factual; it must always document and via that documentation produce a kind of Factual Realism in which the moral authority of the factual loses all its symbolic claims to legitimacy. Makhmalbaf's camera works in an entirely different mode. In a total absence of the Transcendental Signified, or the suspension of the Necessary Being (and this is crucial in an artist who began by seeking to put God back on the stage), Makhmalbaf reaches for a Virtual Realism in which neither *actuality* nor *factuality* can resist his manipulative abbreviation of them, cutting them down to size up to a mere *semblance of* the Real. There is a material mysticism about Makhmalbaf's camera, a corrosive lava of semiotic energy, that visibly melts both *actuality* and *facticity* to their *virtual* irreducibility. From behind these three concerted lenses, reality is de-sedimented back to its state of 'thingness', where it is made to yield not only its susceptibility to the violence of the metaphysical but also its potential access to the counter-symbolic of the possible. Right here we might note that this reduction of the Real to the Thing prepares its metonymic conduit to reach a renewed mythic moment.

What ordinarily prevents even the imagining of such a possibility is the fully operative sacred order that flaunts its metaphysical ordering of reality by in effect concealing its operation behind 'cultures' and 'traditions'. Before the introduction of the camera as a third eye, there is an explosive progression of re/signification dialectically operative between every cultural signifier and its claim to a signified that the blind spot of a Transcendental Signified or a Necessary Being conceals from the naked eye. In the absence of that blind spot, or to put it positively, once a camera is strategically located to cover it, there is a meltdown of all authoritarian claims of the conspiracy of signifiers to own their signifieds. They do not own them, as Derrida discovered in *Of Grammatology*. They claim them on loan, on credit and on IOUs. If the world is held together by the *trail* that the deferral of all the signifiers to all the un-deliverable signifieds leave behind them, then the three modes of *Realism* I identify in Iranian cinema expose that trailing in three convergent ways. Kiarostami exposes the metaphysical assumption, the Transcendental Signified, that conspiratorially conceals that *trail*. Bani-Etemad reveals the moral complacency of the observing agent in holding on to the blind spot that keeps that *trail* out of sight. Makhmalbaf unveils the moment of the emergence when that *trail* covers its footsteps. The result is a kind of collective Realism that no longer simply shows and tells it *as it is*, but that reveals the metaphysical contingency of its perception and the aesthetic possibility of how to re-imagine them.

The strategy obviously has to be specific to the visual access to the semiotic, by-passing the symbolic co-optation of the Real into one form of violent metaphysics or another. If the linguistic *sign* is always already surreptitiously burdened by the *trace* of another *sign* while ostensibly claiming the delivery of a destined 'meaning', then what about the cinematic sign? The central *moving claim* of the cinematic sign is a visual pointillism that *ipso facto* is itself always already a disclaimer. The cinematic semiotic has no claim to transmute itself to a cultural symbolic. Cinema can, of course, be forced to yield and subserve the cultural Symbolic and as such become the aesthetic agent of the political brutality of the metaphysical ordering of reality – as we saw in the case of Kimia'i's oeuvre, to which we might also add the unfortunate cinema of the later Daryoush Mehrju'i as the best examples of that collapse. But left to its own open-ended devices, the visual pointillism of cinema opens the Pandora Box of the libidinal semiotic, with no claim or ability to control its domino-effect suggestiveness. Kiarostami's Actual Realism exposes that open-endedness of the Real, without ever calling its always already metaphysical ordering to constitute a looking glass through which we symbolically see the Real as Real, actively forgetting the set of looking glasses that the metaphysical has put on our eyes. Kiarostami's camera renders inoperative our built-in cultural camera. Bani-Etemad's Factual Realism is condemned not to neglect that metaphysical ordering, but instead to de-authorise its authority, de-moralise its morality, subject to an ethic of responsibility its claim to an ethic of ultimate ends (as Max Weber would say). Makhmalbaf's Virtual Realism is corrosively abbreviative, transubstantiating, diṣtilling the Real to its bare, otherwise invisible bones. If *time* is constitutional to narrative, temporality to the metaphysical ordering of 'meaning', then Kiarostami's Actual Realism is narrated on a *dissolution* of time, Bani-Etemad's Factual Realism on an *accentuation* of time and Makhmalbaf's Virtual Realism on a *manipulation* of time. The result is that 'time' is no longer at the service of the narrative as the constitution of power or authority. Narrative, at least to the degree that it is subservient to such abuses of metaphysical power, is de-temporised and made to float on the semiotic sea of its imaginative origin.

Let us now get a bit more specific – to detect the devil in the details.

The Taste of Cherry

How is that metaphysics un-done – a life decoded of all its symbolic over-burdening with culture and compliance, with the culture of compliance?

There is a numbing stillness about the face of Mr Badi'i, the chief suicidal protagonist in Kiarostami's *Taste of Cherry* (1998). The stillness of that face, its emotive and moral immobility, gradually fills out the entire visual space of the film and stays with the audience from the very first to the very last scene. A blank look, a set of tight lips, a still demeanour, exuding long and deliberative pauses: everything about Mr Badi'i contributes to an interpretative inaccessibility to his 'soul', to the placid quietude of his presence. In effect, there is an absence of the 'soul' which is deeply counter-cultivated in the face and, through that face, in the whole atmospheric emptiness of *The Taste of Cherry*. Who is this man, and why does he want to commit suicide, or why should anyone care? He drops out of nowhere and for the duration of a cinematic life-time cultivates no sympathy, allows no empathy, bars all inroads into his character. Mr Badi'i is a counter-character, an anti-hero, a dead man driving his white Range Rover through the streets and alleys, hills and forests, coming into contact with the world but only at the very intangible surface of no meaning, no significance, no interpretation, no purpose. He is born into the moment of his death, at the moment of his decision to commit suicide. Capturing death at its very moment, Badi'i is a counter-character, a counter-culture, a semiotic un-doing of all affections, affectations, fears of death, the very terror of being made meaningful by faith. Badi'i's is a counter-faith, the emptiness of a whole divestment from the metaphysical ordering of the Real.

The claustrophobic close-ups of Badi'i's face are released against the open space of the exterior in which his car moves. Driving through the winding emptiness of a suburban whither-land, Mr Badi'i carries the hermetic seal of his own abstraction about him. There is a vague sense of utter pointlessness about Badi'i's life, which is no longer Badi'i's alone. It is everybody's. We are drawn to and repelled by Badi'i's predicament almost at the same time. But Kiarostami manages to keep us suspended on that margin for the whole narrative lifetime of his reflection, not on death but on life. On that marginality words are as much meaningless as pictures. The dialogues in *The Taste of Cherry* are entirely empty, pointless, their tight pointillism claustrophobic, mere extensions of 'sound-effects' to supplement the simple visuality of the narrative. We begin by knowing nothing about this man, and the more he talks the less we get to know about him, and the less we even care to know about him. His initially bizarre request for some unspecified thing that he needs to have done for him completely fails to arouse the slightest sense of curiosity or interest. As cultural artifacts, we have to completely let go of our interpretative machinery in order to be admitted to Kiarostami's counter-cultural aesthetics. 'None of us can ever retrieve that innocence before all theory when art knew no need to justify itself', Susan Sontag has suggested, 'when one did not ask of a work of art what it *said* because one knew (or thought one knew) what it *did*'.[22] Sontag is wrong. We *can* retrieve that moment, and it is not called 'innocence'. What we see in Kiarostami's art, in general – brought to full fruition in *The Taste of Cherry*, in particular – is precisely this pre-moment of the aesthetic when it not only refuses submission to interpretation but constitutionally collapses all culturally constituted parameters of interpretation. But the move is neither 'innocent' nor targeted against theorisation. It is targeted against the whole metaphysical ordering of the Real, all cultural constitution of the significant, all the symbolic legislation of the semiotic. *The Taste of Cherry* is against interpretation, by never allowing itself to yield any meaning and by rendering the world *ipso facto*, not via a metaphysical ordering, worth living. There is no difference between Mr Badi'i and the tree under which he wants to be buried, or the soil that he wants poured over him. Here we need not even invoke the spirit of Omar Khayyam as the quintessentially Kiarostamiesque perception of the Real – or Kiarostami's immediate foregrounding in the poetry of Sohrab Sepehri. From medieval to modern Persian poetry, we have in poetic vision what Kiarostami has achieved in visual poetry: the collapsing of the metaphysical ordering of the Real into a realistic aesthetics of materiality.

Before we know it, *The Taste of Cherry* draws us into its atmospheric seal, where we see that we are beginning to feel that we are dealing with a suicidal man who wants to find someone to come and make sure that he is completely dead and then pour twenty shovels of soil over him – he will pay 10,000 Tumans per shovel, 200,000 Tumans altogether, which he has already put in the glove compartment of his car, ready to be picked up by the person who will agree to come to this site the morning after and cover his body with the soil he has already dug out. This uncanny creeping-in of the strange inundates the entirety of the film. Mr Badi'i is strange, as his very name suggests. In perfect sanity he is pursuing an insane request. Everybody around him, the construction worker, the soldier, the seminarian and even the employee of the Natural History Museum have an orderly demeanour about them: their cause and effect are logically linked, their premise and conclusion in place. All except for him who has an inexplicable urge to find someone to come and cover his dead body. But why? When you are dead, you are dead. What difference does it make if you are covered or not, buried or not, buried or burned, eaten up by animals or venerated by the masses? Why not simply swallow the pills and sleep in your own bed and get it over with? Why pick a site on the margin of reality? In the marginal uncanny of that reality is where this entire film is narrated. In that marginality, we see one of the most overwhelming sequences of the film, when Mr Badi'i paces the walk-way around an industrial watch-tower while conducting a conversation with a security guard in charge of excavation equipment. The camera stays inside the glass-windowed cubicle with the guard and watches Mr Badi'i from behind the glass windows, unencumbered by his pointless and rambling comments. On the site of this marginality, also, we hear Badi'i refuse the security guard's invitation to share his omelette with him. 'Egg is not good for me', he says. Bad for his cholesterol, probably. Watching his cholesterol on the eve of his committing suicide is precisely the ironic mood in which his uncanny presence is narrated. The uncanny life of Mr Badi'i is to come to an end in the shadowland of this winding world. He sits on a pile of excavated soil, and over his extended shadow in the sunset of his life now crane-after-crane-loads of freshly excavated soil is poured. A premonition.

What is the function of the uncanny here? To dismantle the conservative machinery of the interpretative culture, which is the culture of conservatism. Sontag traces the genealogy of interpretation to that 'post-mythic' moment when the 'the ancient texts, in their pristine form, is no longer acceptable'.[23] But why were they no longer acceptable? Here is Sontag again:

> Interpretation thus presupposes a discrepancy between the clear meaning of the text and the demand of (later) readers. It seeks to resolve that discrepancy. The situation is that for some reason a text has become unacceptable; yet it cannot be discarded. Interpretation is a radical strategy for conserving an old text, which is thought too precious to repudiate, by revamping it.[24]

For 'what reason?' Sontag's generic insight and specific shortcoming is in her failure to see the sustained politics of interpretation. We need not go back all the way to the emergence of Biblical exegesis or post-mythical Greek hermeneutics, as Sontag does, to see the politics of 'making things understood'. The instrumental rationalism of capitalist modernity in the immediate neighbourhood of our own history is sufficient to demonstrate that the iconic force of 'the old' is constitutional to all gerontocratic urges to invoke the power of the past to legitimise the proficiency of the present. To interpret is to assimilate backward the forwarding force of the unleashed semiotics, to condemn the semiotic to the symbolic, which is always already the sublimated power of the present. The gift of Kiarostami's camera has been to defy that culture of interpretation by allowing the semiotic meaninglessness of the actually real to reveal itself. That actually real is not 'innocent', pre-significatory, or idle. It is the volcanic passage to that pre-moment of being, when reality signifies without any need for a metaphysics, makes life trustworthy without any need for a cultural constitution of meaning. Sontag is right that 'interpretation is the revenge of the intellect upon art'.[25] But it is the revenge of the metaphysically 'ordering', culturally 'dominant' and politically 'assimilative' intellect upon the aesthetically 'defiant', counter-culturally 'rebellious' and politically 'subversive' art. Missing these crucial qualifiers, Sontag's otherwise brilliant essay reads like a signature of defeat rather than a manifesto of battle. What is also beyond her purview is the ability of things stripped of meaning to become the metonymic harbingers of recast mythic truths.

Kiarostami's *Taste of Cherry* is the site of that battle. We see that Mr Badi'i has picked out the site where he wants to be buried, under a solitary tree, by the side of a winding road, overlooking a valley, far from the maddening crowd, at the outskirts of where life takes place. It is on this very site that he once gets stuck on the side of the road, one wheel of his car trapped in a hole, waiting there like a sitting duck for the construction workers in the area to come and dig him out. His attempted suicide has no (apparent) reason, waits for no explanation, results in no resolution, yields to no metaphysics of doubt or certainty. Subject to that metaphysics is, of course, the world in which this counter-cultural mobility is located. Four men come along Mr Badi'i's way. First is a construction worker who gets agitated by his weird request, takes him for a homosexual and is about to beat him up when he takes off. Second is a soldier who needs a lift to his military barracks. He is a provincial young man, boyish in his demeanour, has no will or desire to be partner to any suicide, and finally takes advantage of an opportune moment to flee from this bizarre man. Third is a seminary student, in Iran as an Afghan refuge, ready to quote the Qur'an and all other saintly sayings against suicide, finally quietly taking his leave. Fourth is the wise and talkative employee of the Natural History Museum who talks the most and tries his best to dissuade Mr Badi'i from his morbid decision. All these people have somewhere to go: the construction worker to a half-built house, the soldier to his barracks, the seminarian to his seminary, and the employee of the Natural History Museum to his work. All, except for Mr Badi'i, of whose work, life and purpose in daily awakenings we have no clue. He circles around his own grave, looking for somebody to cover it once he is 'safely' inside. Against metaphysics, against culture, against all symbolic renditions of life as meaningful and against all interpretation, on the margin of reality, Mr Badi'i reveals 'nothing', and in that revelation rests his counter-claim to a whole cosmology of meaningless living.

Mr Badi'i is searching for a man who would pour some twenty shovels of soil over his presumably dead body when ... when from the slightly extended darkness of a cut emerges a voice that for the longest time we do not associate with a face. Whose voice is this? Soothing, kind and comforting, speaking of life, at the moment of death, having just arisen from the dark, is the voice of Mr Baqeri. Mr Baqeri speaks of life, its glory, beauty, simplicity. His voice-over fills the barren landscape through which Badi'i's Range Rover rolls like a morbid apparition of a death about to happen. Through his voice, and long before we have a glimpse of his face, Baqeri's character is almost completely narrated, constructed, almost visible. The character which is thus made, out of darkness and from his voice is like 'death' himself, incarnate, personified, the angelic mercy of his comforting voice and now presence beginning to embrace Badi'i. For the first time since we saw Mr Badi'i, he is not doing the talking. Now death speaks of life, of the taste of mulberry he once tried when he was about to commit suicide and then changed his mind. Now we remember that Mr Badi'i picked up Mr Baqeri precisely from the site of his own grave, after having come to no conclusion with the man of God, with the seminarian student, the Afghan refugee who had fled the Soviet carnage and now had come to the land of Shi'i saints and Islamic faith to learn how to save people's souls. He is utterly silent, and the space of Badi'i's life is now fully covered by the accented humour of Mr Baqeri. In the presence of Mr Baqeri, Mr Badi'i is dumb-struck. He does not speak a word. In Mr Baqeri, Mr Badi'i dies the death for which he longs. But he goes through the motion. He swallows the pills (Or does he? Kiarostami's camera is scared to go to Badi'i's room. It stays outside and looks from the dark street at his slightly lit window). Mr Badi'i comes to his grave. He lays down 'dying' in his own grave. But tomorrow is another season. The autumnal season of death has given way to a spring of blossoming flowers. Kiarostami is there, filming. We see Kiarostami himself now, not through his own camera, but through the matter-of-factness of a hand-held digital-camera. Mr Badi'i, who is now Homayun Ershadi, the actor playing Mr Badi'i, is also there. Kiarostami gives directions on a walkie-talkie for the soldiers in the distance to sit down and relax and listen to the glorious trumpet, the awakening fanfare of a resurrection, of the birth of a new man. The Fourth Wall has been broken for us to see: a man with no future, no past, only a moment. A man with no history, no genealogy, no metaphysics: a man born again to the actuality of his simply being-in-the-world.

The Bread and the Flower Pot

The fate of the postcolonial artist has been cast in a poetic, performative and carnivalesque emancipation from that colonially constituted subjectivity in which individuals, the artists and their audiences are reduced to things and in which things are revealed as raw material. What is paramount in the metropolitan centres of power to capitalist modernity is peripheral to the colonial outposts. The postcolonial artist produces in the shadow of that colonial modernity, at the extended logic of an instrumental rationalism which, while at the centre, cannot be compromised in the periphery.

How did that logic assert itself at the centre? In Heidegger's reading of the post-Platonic (which he called 'Western') philosophy, the project of European modernity is perceived as the last stage of the metaphysics of representation, of dis-closure – that is to say, for something 'to be' means for something 'to be manifest'. This is predicated on the assumption that temporality, or the time-bound being-in-the-world, is the only viable range of vision within which things can manifest themselves. Predicating his phenomenological conception of 'Das Man' ['the any-person-self'] on a tradition that ranged from Hegel and Marx down to Wilhelm Dilthey, Heidegger consciously opted to root his conception of 'man' in the everyday experiences of the person's social presence. The any-person-self is thus constituted by a set of such an interrelated web of affiliations, as Georg Simmel would call them, that there is not even a conscious awareness of its full inventory of social and cultural informants. To be human, in Heidegger's critique of Enlightenment modernity, is to be constituted by a public language, a mass entity into which he is located. In the Heideggerian critique of the project of modernity, 'the any-person-self' has completely taken over and constituted the self-productionist subjectivity of the individual, facilitating the conception of things as raw material, all facilitated by an instrumental reason that was the chief product of an economic production of manifestly being-in-the-world. In Heidegger's own words:

> In utilizing public means of transport and in making use of information services such as the newspaper, every other is like the next. This being-with-one-another dissolves one's own Dasein completely into the kind of being of 'the others', in such a way, indeed, that the others, as distinguishable and explicit, vanish more and more. In this inconspicuousness and unascertainability, the real dictatorship of the 'they' is unfolded. We take pleasure and enjoy ourselves as they [man] take pleasure; we read, see and judge about literature and art as they see and judge; likewise we shrink back from the 'great mass' as they shrink back; we find 'shocking' what they find shocking. The 'they', which is nothing definite, and which all are, though not as the sum, prescribes the kind of being of everydayness.[26]

And in Michael Zimmerman's reading of this passage:

> One of the basic features of everyday life was its 'publicness' [*Öffentlichkeit*], a term often used in connection with 'civil society' [*bürgerliche Gesellschaft*], i. e., the business world. Heidegger did not emphasize the bourgeois connotation of this term, possibly to avoid revealing the extent to which his analysis of everyday life was in fact an analysis of life in degenerate commercial society. In such a society, nothing truly original can be revealed because language has degenerated to the state of idle talk [*Gerede*], the passing around of ungrounded opinions.[27]

All of this is still within the operative parameters of the theorists, practitioners and beneficiaries of the joint projects of the European Enlightenment and its corresponding capitalist modernity. The colonial extension of the modernity of subject-formation was doubly effective in the aggressive transmutation of the colonial subject into raw material. While in the metropolitan capitals the productive metaphysics of capitalist modernity was mutating individuals into instruments of production, its concomitant project of the Enlightenment was busy giving them the dignity of a place in a universal claim to victory. This was far from the case in the colonial outpost, where the mutation of the colonised persons into raw material was concomitant with their equally aggressive constitution as the colonised other of the civilising mission of the coloniser. The fate of the postcolonial artist, as a result, has been cast in poetic strategies of emancipation from that colonially constituted subjectivity in which individuals as both artists and their audiences are reduced to things and things are revealed as raw material. Colonialism is a practice of virtuality, a reductionist logic of reality to raw material, humanity to cheap labour, homelands into colonial outposts. It is but a simple reflection of this reality for the colonial artist to be equally virtual, aesthetically at work to reach for the virtually real, because as colonials they are only virtually real.

On the site of the visual, how is that poetic shattering of the Real possible? Here is where Makhmalbaf's daring imagination, his ability to reach for and cultivate a virtual realism, knows no rival. *Nun-o-Goldun/The Bread and the Flower Pot* (1996, mis-translated and mis-represented by the inane title *A Moment of Innocence*, given to the film by its French distributor, much to Makhmalbaf's chagrin), seen on the site of this poetic shattering, is the rhythmic slowing down of time, the narrative re-modulation of the living, the chronic crafting of an alternative possibility to be. Reduced to virtuality, the postcolonial artist here visually reflects himself. In *The Bread and the Flower Pot*, Makhmalbaf re-crafts his own history as the story of a people to whom he wants to, but cannot, belong; by virtue of the poetic intrusion of that possibility, the film becomes the wintry tale of a people who are not (but whom Makhmalbaf wishes to be) visually narrating them into existence. The wintry feeling of nostalgia, the snowy sensation of a hinterland, the quiet calmness of a deadly beauty: these are the visual parameters that temperamentalise this, one of the greatest achievements of Makhmalbaf. How is that possible? How did Makhmalbaf craft that calm and yet disquieting serenity of a paradisiacal coldness? Time here is no-time, space no-space, movements slowed down, frame by frame, thus to reframe the passage of an un-nerving flow of a parable that demands an unearthly attention. *The Bread and the Flower Pot* is the masterly manipulation of the Real in order to get at its virtuality. This is no simple rendition of a youthful political discretion. This is the handiwork of a master operative at the heart of the Real, the very palpitating core of how from virtuality reality is born. Makhmalbaf reverses that process, reaches for the virtual via the real, there to see what precisely tempts the agitated presence of the virtual to transcend itself and yield to a metaphysical ordering of itself. Makhmalbaf is no Kiarostami. He leaves that metaphysics alone. His is the phenomenal task of reaching for and then dwelling on the virtual irreducibility of the real, the threshold of all metaphysical intrusions, the playground of all gods, the Olympian site of the symbolic grammar of being.

The Bread and the Flower Pot is a love story. In between two young revolutionaries who want to kill for their ideals breaks through the splitting personae of a director, Mohsen Makhmalbaf/Mohsen Makhmalbaf his name. The historical Makhmalbaf, who is now a film director, directs his young version to kill. The ahistorical Makhmalbaf, who is now a director, teaches his young actor to love. The historical Makhmalbaf, who is now a director and used to be a revolutionary, directs his police officer to kill. The ahistorical Makhmalbaf, who is now a director, pleads with his victim to forgive. The seventeen-year-old actor-Makhmalbaf acts the way the forty-year-old director-Makhmalbaf wants and wishes and directs him to act. The forty-year-old actor-Makhmalbaf directs the way he wishes he had acted when he was seventeen. The result of this narrative re-crafting of the crooked timbre of a person's life is a poetics of Parousia, a parable of the pre-moment of being, accessing the virtuality which is the liberating temptation of the Real. 'The-any-person-self' of the colonial constitution is here dissolved into its productive elements, and from their ashes arises a new person, the aesthetic conclusion of a counter-colonial imaginings of the Possible. That 'person' is virtual in disposition, real in character and irreducible to the logic of the economic production of reality. That person has escaped the European Enlightenment, the capitalist production of their reality. Here the postcolonial artist is tantamount to what Deleuze and Guattari call the 'schizo': 'He has crossed over the limit, the schizo, which maintained the production of desire always at the margin of social production, tangential and always repelled'.[28] One crucial exception: the postcolonial artist did not, does not, have to cross that border. The postcolonial artist is always already outside that border. What Foucault failed to notice in *Madness and Civilization* (1961) is that the substitution of asylums for lepers' colonies in Europe occurred at almost the same time as the project of Orientalism was under way. The instrumental rationalism of capitalist modernity was too large to jail its un-reason in European mad-houses. It needed the vastness of 'the Orient' to house that un-reason. The Oriental has always already been the irrational Other of the colonial officer. The numinous energy of alterity is constitutional to the postcolonial artist who ...

> ... produces himself as a free man, irresponsible, solitary, and joyous, finally able to say and do something simple in his own name, without asking permission; a desire lacking nothing, a flux that overcomes barriers and codes, a name that no longer designates any ego whatever. He has simply ceased being afraid of becoming mad.[29]

Towards that liberating madness, there is a creative confusion about *The Bread and the Flower Pot* – a quiet erosion of dead certainties, that separates the real from the make-belief and that is precisely the trade-mark of the best of post-revolutionary Iranian cinema. The creative confusion disregards facts by subjecting them to a multi-significatory set of fantasies. When facts are constituted by a repressive reading of 'history', then they ought to be reversed by art, re-constituted, re-negotiated, let loose to hunt for their alternatives, all in a creatively multi-significatory thrust that no author or filmmaker, let alone a censor official, can control. What precisely is the nature of that 'fact' that needs to be re-negotiated via an interface with fantasy? The most foundational of all historical facts of colonial modernity for the Iranians and their neighbours in the postcolonial world is precisely their colonially mitigated subjectivity, their slanted angle on the world, and their very translucent location in their own culture. The generation that Makhmalbaf represents is at once the culmination of a whole history of colonially constituted identity and the catastrophic collapse of all hopes in political resolutions. The colonially mitigated reception of European modernity is conducive only to a specific kind of subject-formation, to a trapped trajectory of im/possibilities, that colonialism – economic or cultural, classical or reconstituted for late globalising capitalism – as the extended arm of capitalist modernity has grafted on the colonised. The specific parameters and im/possibilities available in the colonial condition obviously have their authorial roots in the project of capitalist modernity itself. Subject-formation constitutional to the project of modernity itself, even prior to its colonial extensions which stripped it of all its Enlightenment ideologies, has the epistemic and ontological proclivity of a metaphysics of dis-closure which is, and here we have no choice but see Heidegger's logic, 'reductionist' and manifests things as raw material in the economic production of reality. In the colonial outpost, in which we must also include Iran despite its semi-colonised birth into European modernity, the mutation of individuals into things and things into raw material was a matter of observational evidence and in no need of post-metaphysical theorisation and revelation. The virtuality of the postcolonial artist could not but virtually reconstitute his and their entire audience's subjectivity.

Baran and the Native

By the time she made that gem of a short film, *Baran and the Native* (1999), Rakhshan Bani-Etemad had paved her way towards a radical de-Oedipalisation of a whole culture. In *The May Lady* (1998), Forough-the-mother and Mani-the-son live together in the total absence of Mani's father and the visual absence of Forough's lover. Mani's father and Forough used to be political activists and through their mutual political concerns had been drawn together. He is disillusioned with the outcome of the revolution and leaves Iran soon after. The total absence of Forough's husband replicates the total absence of Rasul's wife in *The Blue-Veiled* (1994), while the visual absence of Forough's lover, Amir Rahbar, is replicating the visual absence of Rasul's youngest daughter, Eftekhar, who is abroad. The oral construction of Amir Rahbar in *The May Lady*, through his voice-over, then has an antecedent in Bani-Etemad's cinema in the oral construction of Rasul's younger daughter who also is characterised by telephone messages and long-distance conversations. Mani and Forough live in a palpably de-Oedipalised space, very much like Na'i and Bashu in Beiza'i's *Bashu*. The incestuous suggestions between Forough and Mani are thus narrated on a purely Semiotic plane and launched against the whole monumentality of the totally Symbolised culture of suppression that Forough and Mani both face. The struggle extends from the privacy of a sensually charged relationship between the manifestly homoerotic Mani and his mother who is his sole protector and 'both a mother and a father to him', as the saying goes in Persian. The household is sexually charged, morally provocative and socially suggestive.

Forough's attempt to make a documentary film about the 'ideal mother', while trying to raise a teenage boy in the suffocating atmosphere of an Islamic Republic, is the heavily de-symbolised and consolidated cultural context against which the raw Semiotic energy of the perennially pre-Oedipal subjection of Mani has taken place. That semiotic energy is where Bani-Etemad draws much of her cinematic vision from. Mani is palpably androgynous, and his barely hidden and visibly suggested homosexuality is the most visible sign of the arrest of the Oedipal in this father-less environment where the Oedipal moment has been kept at bay. He barely has any memory of his father. He is almost as old as the Islamic Revolution. His father left probably when Khomeini arrived. Khomeini became the abstraction of all grand/fatherly figures, there to send millions of Iranian youths to their untimely death. Mani grew up in the absence of his biological father and overshadowed by the overwhelming presence of the abstracted and generic grand/father figure. Mani is almost literally a child of the revolution. His parents were attracted to each other by virtue of their mutual political beliefs. He was born just about the time of the revolution. He grew up in Khomeini's Tehran, chanting in his school 'Death to America' and 'Long Live Khomeini'. Khomeini is now dead at the time when we encounter Mani in 1998, and Mani cannot wait to go to America. But whether he goes to America or not, which for him is the compelling illusion of freedom, Mani has grown up witnessing the physical disappearance of his biological father, the death of a monarchical father-figure in indignity and now the death of the grand/father-figure who in abstraction had substituted all fathers. Mani has witnessed something else. He has also witnessed the sacrificial death of millions of his generation in the course of the revolution of 1977–79 and the Iran-Iraq War of 1980–88. It is, in fact, a miracle that he is alive. If the war had lasted a few more years, he too would have been drafted and sent to die. The death and disappearance of fathers and father-figures and the sacrificial murder of millions of young Manis, now in the sole possession of their mothers: the site of de-Oedipalisation is almost mythic in proportion. Mani's fear of Rahbar is thus all but natural. He is going to rob him of his most prized possession, the very location of his androgynous freedom, his husband-less mother. The visual absence of Rahbar, however, allows that fear to remain at a distance, only suggesting the violence of a masculine re-possession of his maternal femininity, but never actually materialising it.

The visual absence of Forough's lover, Amir Rahbar, allows the libidinal *semiotics* of Forough-the-mother and Mani-the-son, as substitutional lovers, to remain at the explosively *suggestive* level and to never fully collapse into the abyss of raw libidinal energy. The orality of Rahbar's character, which is always exclusive to Forough's ear, makes him at once absent, so that Mani's de-Oedipalisation is intact, and yet present, so that Forough's sexuality has a potential outburst in the very last shot of the film. Bani-Etemad has prepared visually for that sexual encounter with the double voice-over of Forough and Rahbar, when his letters begin to be narrated by Rahbar's voice and then Forough's voice joins in, as in his initiating the sexual encounter and Forough responding. When *The May Lady* ends, we have no reason to believe that Forough cannot wait to go to Rahbar. All we hear is a suggestive telephone contact. It is critical to keep in mind that, from the site of the active de-Oedipalisation of her son, Forough also emerges as no longer the lacking absence of the phallocentric Oedipal. By that very last telephone contact, Forough, just like Mani, is liberated from the binary opposition of her femininity being constituted in the lacking shadow of an Oedipalised masculinity.

By far the most revolutionary achievement of Bani-Etemad in her work up to *The May Lady* is precisely this work-based emancipation from the repressive duality of masculine/feminine which, as Hélène Cixous has argued,[30] is always predicated on a privileging of the former over the latter. Forough works. Not only that. She works creatively. In her work as a documentary filmmaker, Forough is at one and the same time deeply rooted in her Factual Realism, dismantles the myth of 'man' as the-bread-winner, liberates her son from his Oedipal trap, sustains her own sexuality by aurally/orally carrying on an affair with Rahbar and ultimately breaking down the binary opposition between masculine and feminine, which is patriarchally privileging the masculine. As Cixous has demonstrated, the infamous Hegelian Master/Slave paradigm is equally applicable to Man/Woman, where masculinity is subjected on the premise, and the simultaneous negation, of femininity. Bani-Etemad breaks that repressive duality in which woman cannot appear except as lacking. Forough is exactly like Na'i in *Bashu*. They both re-constitute their subjectivity in the absence of a husband, in possession of a de-Oedipalised son, away from the phallocentricity of the patriarchal order and totally predicated on their working status. The difference between Beiza'i and Bani-Etemad, however, is that, while he narrates the patriarchal de-subjection in a blatantly mythological narrative, she opts for a Factual Realism that pushes the *semiotic* energy of subject-formation out of the heavily *symbolised* culture.

While for Cixous the space of emancipation is the 'writing' occasion, in Bani-Etemad it is the filmic (visual) manifestation of the 'working' woman. This is deeply rooted in Bani-Etemad's factual camera and her life-time dedication to documentary filmmaking. From the genealogy of that concern with documentaries have emerged character-types that are directly rooted in the factually real. Around these characters, then, realities are narrated that are constitutional to their place in the world. Forough 'works', and in the space of her working, liberation is evident, the counter-formation of a mode of subjection constitutionally challenging the dominant phallocentricity of the masculine subjectivity. The problem with Cixous, which we do not see in Bani-Etemad, is again her fixation with Greek mythological narratives, which is equally present in Julia Kristeva and Luce Irigaray. These three French feminists have collectively bought into the phallocentric assumption of the 'longevity' of the patriarchal order and are almost subconsciously drawn, as was Simone de Beauvoir, to a counter-reading of those myths. In the genealogy of European feminism, the fallacy goes all the way back to Christine de Pizan who in her *Book of the City of Ladies* also sought to counter-narrate the dominant patriarchal readings of the ancient myths.[31] Yet, like all measures of suppression, patriarchy works not in generic imposition but in specific institutionalisation. The instrumentality of phallocentrism in capitalist modernity is because of the active instrumentalisation of the masculine in the instrumental rationalism of masculinity itself. The advantage of Bani-Etemad's counter-subjection of the femininity and, with it in the figure of Mani and even Rasul, masculinity is precisely in her ability to do so in the immediate context of her social realities, with no evident need to translate this act into the realm of the *mythos*. The result is a mode of emancipation which is factually real, immediately accessible and in need of no symbolising re-codification.

Predicated on the work of Georges Bataille, Cixous has articulated a revolutionary conception of 'feminine gift' that precisely in its non-reciprocity disrupts the consumer culture of 'masculine gift-giving'.[32] Productive giving without an expectation of reciprocity is precisely the mode of being that disrupts the instrumental rationalism of capitalist modernity. The revolutionary aspect of Bani-Etemad's cinema is in its emancipatory power beyond a narrowly bourgeois 'feminist' manifesto that simply attacks the culture and thus leaves its patriarchal assumptions even more solidly enforced. What emerges through her camera is the creative constitution of a new mode of subjectivity in which both femininity and masculinity are located and defined in an entirely different relation to productivity. In *The May Lady*, in particular, her aural/oral construction of Rahbar's character goes directly to the heart of the ocularcentrism of masculinist gazing. Rahbar is, in effect, the narrative construction of Forough's own active imagination. Notice that his love letters are all begun by his voice but soon yield to hers. Forough's voice, her invocation of a poetic range, is the site of not only her own re-subjection, but, equally important, the re-subjection of a mode of masculinity which is closer to her aural/oral defiance of the literary.

Forough and Mani de-Oedipalised, *The May Lady* is the predicate of Bani-Etemad's next move which is visually to give birth to a new Adam and Eve, or Mashya and Mashyana, to be more precise – a birth that comes into view in her bold short film *Baran and the Native*. Baran is on a vacation tour of the island of Kish in the Persian Gulf, with her Mother. She meets a Native boy on the island. A raw, inarticulate, irreducibly visual, but palpably sexual attraction brings the two young 'things' together. The Native boy is a pearl-diver. He shows the island to Baran. They both end up aboard a small boat. He dives into the sea. She stays on the boat and watches in excitement. Up once he comes with a basket full of shells. Back into the sea he plunges. She waits in despair. He does not come up. She leaves in tears. The End.

Baran and the Native is the birth of a whole new fusion of femininity/masculinity, bringing to full fruition whatever Bani-Etemad has done in her active re-subjection of both gender and sexuality. Baran and the Native are barely at the threshold of their entrance to sexuality. They are at the point where they both have left their childhood almost behind and not yet fully entered their adulthood – their genders yet to be articulated. On the site of that purgatorial adolescence, Bani-Etemad narrates the emerging sexuality of these 'Adam and Eve', the Mashya and Mashyana surfacing to the site of their living histories. Baran and the Native are the freed and emancipated and, above all, remembered Mashya and Mashyana born out of the radically de-Oedipalised Forough who has no husband and Mani who has no father. On the paradisiacal island of Kish are thus born two new versions of reality, unencumbered by either the name of a father or the identity of a culture. Baran means rain, and the Native has no name. Baran pours over the Native's soil like a bountiful rain. The two are reversed in their subjectivity: Baran as in rain coming from the heavens, the

Native as in the barren soil. Baran will impregnate the soil of the Native, and in that reversal of patriarchal roles Bani-Etemad's new Mashya and Mashyana give birth to themselves. The Native has to remain in the depths of the sea, in search of yet another basket full of possible pearls. Baran is already possibly pregnant, like the oysters that the Native has already given her. As the Native says, she may get a pearl inside, but if not, she will eat the flesh.

Baran leaves the site of her encounter with the Native, the Medusa of a new life, Mashyana to a submerged Mashya, the vision of a femininity that may or may not be pregnant with a masculinity, just like a possible pearl inside an oyster. Thus, in Bani-Etemad's gem of a short film, the moral liberation in three moves comes to a sustained mythic closure. In these three moves by Abbas Kiarostami, Rakhshan Bani-Etemad and Mohsen Makhmalbaf, the most potent cases of a metonymic rapprochement between the real and the mythic moment of the culture scale multiple registers of the interface between enduring mythologies and the metonymic gestures that articulate them. Three complementary visions of the mythic and the metonymic have come together here to map out the varieties of the lived experiences of an effervescent culture of decoloniality from the heart of the colonial experience. Here we are witness to multiple registers of 'inheritance' – of cinema as an aesthetic of ocularcentrism, of genderfluidity formed across three cinematic gestations and of the constitution of a reframed knowable world at the disposal of an amorphous and unknowing subject.

These three liberating moves come in three modes of realism – Actual, Factual and Virtual – all responding to a particularly anxiety-provoking moment in the contemporary history of the filmmakers, when a total Islamist state and its pure acts of violence have defined the age. To understand this response, we cannot reduce Iranian cinema to any of the formal cinemas of European origin in which they may even partake and which they may assimilate backward to what we already know. In this cinema, as we see, Reality is put particularly under erasure, and thus predicated on a renewed encounter with the distant and recent mythologies of discontent. The result is an aesthetically reconstituted subject liberated from its colonial predicament.

That predicament, however, was propitiously met by visionaries of the unseen – from the prophetic voices of poets to the revelatory insights of filmmakers. Long before Kiarostami, Bani-Etemad, or Makhmalbaf stood behind any camera and said 'action', in 'The Sun Rises' Forough Farrokhzad had spoken of a resurrection of light over darkness, by the grace of love, and concluded with the image of her beloved dawning on the cradles of her poems, cosmic in proportion, mythic in the palpable immediacy of its imageries:

> Look how the wax of night
> Melts and drips drop by drop
> On our path –
> See how the dark cup of my eyes
> Is filled with the wine of sleep –

With your sweet lullabies!
Look how you dawn on the cradle of my poems
And the sun rises![33]

Farrokhzad was the natural-born metaphysician of an aesthetic of cosmic order that took generations of filmmakers to see and show.

6

To Be at Home in the World

Khaneh-am abri-st ...

My home is a cloud –
The earth in its entirety is cloudy with it.[1]

Nima Yushij, '*Khaneh-am Abri-ast*/My Home is a Cloud' (1952)

When Abbas Kiarostami's *Through the Olive Trees/Zir-e Derakhtan-e Zeytun* (1994) was commercially released in the United States in February 1995, one reviewer credited it with having 'complicate[d] one's view of life in Iran'.[2] After the unprecedented event of *Recent Iranian Cinema/Abbas Kiarostami Retrospective*, organised by The Film Society of Lincoln Center at the Walter Reade Theater (26 April-23 May 1996) in New York, much more than one's view of life in Iran was made complicated. The easy banality with which formulaic political assumptions, for or against the Islamic Republic that rules over Iran, tend to dictate and dull one's reading of Iran are made particularly transparent and mendacious when one is faced with a rich and diversified cultural output that makes a mockery of all such distorting clichés. Confronting these cultural artifacts and their rich and diversified inventiveness, their gentle yet quietly corrosive musings on the nature of their historical place in the world defies all ready-made formulaic grits and demands theoretical responses specific to their creativity. There is a pulsating effervescence, a thunderous urge to create, a remarkably rich, rambunctious, riveting uproar of minds and souls in a self-regenerative spin that no generic term, no meta-narrative of ideological generalisation, no master-term of any enduring validity can define or confine where the very idea of 'Iran' stands today. The diverse realities that these films represent, working their blood and bones through the creative narrative of Iranian cinema as one particularly poignant cultural artifact, defy the self-celebrating, narcissistic traits now radically transmuting the critical edge of academic readings of the so-called 'Third-World' cultural production. Iranian cinema not only deserves but effectively demands its own theorisation. That theorisation is a peculiarly simple task. That cinema must be allowed to speak for itself. But, and there is the rub, 'to speak for itself' that cinema has not just a narrative history but, far more important, an aesthetic genealogy.

'Complicating one's view of Iran' is the outcome of a discrepancy between the political production of the idea of 'Iran' by its friends and foes alike, and the cosmovisual reality that Iranian cinema now represents. That discrepancy can be bridged by a more careful reading of the aesthetic genealogy that this cinema now represents. What is precisely the nature of that 'representation'?

We enter the Walter Reade Theater at Lincoln Center in New York to watch Iranian films in a political context where not just an 'Islamic Republic' but the very idea of people's national culture has for decades been actively demonised and maligned by politicians, journalists and academics alike. On the very day that the film festival opened in New York, A. M. Rosenthal, a leading reactionary columnist for the *New York Times* at the time, took one of his habitual swings at Iran and used the politically flamboyant question of the Clinton administration's allegedly tacit approval of the Islamic Republic's aid to Bosnian Muslims, to assert that 'Iranians have trained Bosnians in an Iranian specialty – death squads created to operate on foreign soil'.[3] In large print, A. M. Rosenthal's column warns of the 'Iranian base in Europe'. But other than in Bosnia, 'Iranians' have had another sort of 'base in Europe'. In fact, it has been the unprecedented presence of this 'Iranian base' in Cannes (France), Locarno (Switzerland), Venice (Italy) and Berlin (Germany), among scores of others, which has been partially responsible for this film festival in New York. For every Ayatollah in Iran, there are ten A. M. Rosenthals in the United States. But fortunately for the rest of us, the world is not made totally of Ayatollah Rosenthals. If we were to begin from the premise that reactionary hacks like Rosenthal had already established, anything 'an Iranian' does other than plotting to maim and murder people 'complicates' one's view of Iran – let alone producing one of the most glorious chapters in world cinema.

What the politics of mis/representation demonstrates is that Iranian cinema today is being produced under one set of specific political circumstances inside Iran and then received and celebrated under an entirely different set of circumstances abroad. These divergent sets of circumstances create conflicting hermeneutic horizons against which the specifics of this cinema are received and read. The prestigious awards that the Iranian filmmakers are receiving, and that they richly deserve, has the unintended consequence of creating interpretative traps of which one has to steer very carefully clear in order to see what exactly is happening in this cinema. These filmmakers are, to make a ridiculously obvious case even more evident, Iranians. They come from and they create within a specific cultural context, historical reality, social circumstances. Their art has not just a 'presence' in, but also a 'dialogue' with all these forces. While the reality of that art as a phenomenon irreducibly *sui generis* has to be kept always and particularly in mind, so must the circumstances in which it is being created, the anxieties to which they are responding.

What the New York Film Festival of 1996 made possible was a fresh look at one of the richest cinematic traditions in the world today. Names such as Rakhshan Bani-Etemad, Bahram Beiza'i, Abbas Kiarostami, Mohsen Makhmalbaf, Daryoush Mehrju'i, Amir Naderi, or later Jafar Panahi and Asghar Farhadi are the common staples of international film festivals from Tehran to Tokyo. The global audience which has been generated for Iranian cinema has had a catalytic effect on the texture and diversity of this cinema. But underlying this global reception is the ferocious introspection of a culture much maligned by forces and fantasies domestic and foreign to its own self-perception. The nature and disposition of that 'introspection' is what ultimately animates and distinguishes this cinema. The plight of Iran in its colonially-mitigated encounter with 'modernity', the 'Islamic Tradition' that was rhetorically re/invented to confront it and ultimately the economic mis/location of Iran in the world global capitalism are the principal circumstances that have consistently occasioned the place of art and cultural production – from poetry to performing arts, from fiction to film – on the trajectory of that 'introspection'.

If from the Constitutional Revolution of 1906–11 well into the making of the Islamic Revolution of 1977–79 poetry was the principal artifact of cultural soul-searching in Iran, cinema has emerged as the single most important medium of introspection in the post-revolutionary period. Although the roots of the post-revolutionary cinema go back to the early 1960s – with such pioneering visionaries as Farrokh Ghaffari, Sohrab Shahid Sales, Daryoush Mehrju'i, Bahram Beiza'i, Parviz Kimia'i, Amir Naderi, Abbas Kiarostami and Bahman Farmanara – it is in the post-revolutionary period in which those promising seeds have come to full fruition. What is evident in this cinema, and what is crucial to note, now with the global audience that Kiarostami's cinema in particular has generated, is its active involvement with the terms of cultural negotiations for the very place of Iran in history, an enduring issue that has animated and plagued us since the dawn of the colonially mitigated project of European modernity. What that 'place' is, where in the world Iran stands today, what has been our political and moral disposition in the shadow of the project of European modernity, are all among the kinds of questions that we need to keep in mind when we watch these flickering images dancing for attention in front of a global audience.

Dis-Engaging the Metaphysical

If Reality is put cinematically under erasure, as I argued in the previous chapter, and thereby made metonymic to mythologies of discontent, and if, again as I suggested in that chapter, the aesthetically reconstituted subject is liberated from its colonial predicament, then we are in the throes of actively dis-engaging the metaphysical grip on reality. This philosophical proposition has an historical frame of reference.

The predicament of being caught in the project of capitalist modernity from the colonial end of it has sustained a relentless history for at least two-hundred years. But it is the immediate political context of the last few decades that is of immediate consequence to Iranian cinema in particular. The fact that the best of Iranian cinema came to full fruition precisely in the two decades of the 1980s and 1990s cannot be totally irrelevant to the political context in which this took place. There is no doubting the fact that both the technical and the aesthetic roots of contemporary Iranian cinema goes back to the pre-revolutionary period. But Iranian cinema became what it became, achieved its global status and produced top-notch filmmakers, right at the heart of one of the most brutal periods in modern history. The Iranian exilic community totally discredits the Islamic Republic from having anything to do with the rise of Iranian cinema, whereas officials in charge of the Ministry of Culture and Islamic Guidance, at the head of which once was none other than President Mohammad Khatami himself, claim much of the credit for themselves. Wherever the blame or the praise rests for the particulars of Iranian cinema in the Islamic Republic period, one thing is certain.

There is a correspondence, albeit negational, between the absolutist metaphysics of certainty that animated much of the revolutionary period that led to the downfall of the Pahlavi monarchy and the emergence of the Islamic theocracy, on one hand, and the aesthetic specifics of the Iranian cinema of the last two decades, on the other. In the course of the revolution, the two institutions of Persian monarchy and Shi'i patrimonialism had to mobilise their most effective rhetoric and thus perforce revealed their most pernicious patriarchal proclivities. This resulted in a period of unbridled Absolutist claims on the believers' pieties. The metaphysics of certainty at the root of both these enduring institutions thus defined the very terror under which Iranians have had to live for the last two decades. The particular predicament of a colonially mitigated capitalist modernity, as a result, has coagulated all its genealogical forces in and about the last few decades when the very 'location' of Iran in the world has had to be re/negotiated in nationalist, Islamist, or Socialist terms, which were all re/invented in the immediate atmosphere of the post/colonial context.

Iranian cultural production could not but be placed in that turbulent site where the politics of tyranny were being transmuted into the metaphysics of certainty. Much that has happened in the Iranian cinema of the revolutionary period, as a result, may be read as a visually sub/conscious response to this violent resurgence of the metaphysics of certainty, constitutional not only to Shi'i patrimonialism, but equally to Persian monarchy – the two sides of the same patriarchal coin of terror and intimidation. What seems to have happened in Iranian cinema is a strategic return to what Jacques Lacan has called the Imaginary phase in the developmental constitution of the psyche.[4] What Lacan has theorised for the psyche-personal, I think can be cautiously extended to the psyche-social. For Lacan, the Imaginary is a pre-symbolic phase in the development of the psyche-personal in which the mind still operates on a pre-verbal modulation which is *ipso facto* visual. For Lacan, the Imaginary stage is a 'mirror' stage where the ego is not yet formed.[5] By collectively resorting back to an Imaginary stage, the Iranian psyche-social has sought to disengage itself from the metaphysical ordering of its cultural identity-formation, the most violent manifestation of which has been the phenomenally brutal episodes of social upheaval, patriarchal rivalries, ideological warfare, barbaric wars and, most significantly, the violent superimposition of a government of abstractions. Reigning in the Name of God, commanding with His Words, invoking the Authority of His Emissaries and all other such frightful Absolutes have scared the Iranians away from all Capital-Letter claims to Absolutist Salvation. Between the colonial extension of capitalist modernity, on one side, and the jargon of authenticity, on the other, the Iranian psycho-social seems to have taken refuge back into the Imaginary order, where what Lacan calls the symbolic signification of reality has not yet paved the way for the violent metaphysical ordering of the Real.[6]

For Lacan, the Imaginary phase in the development of the psyche is pre-Oedipal, when a unified personality has not yet been formed.[7] In the organic life of a culture, too, it can be made, through its aesthetic re/imagining of itself, to resort back to the collective equivalent of that pre-Oedipal absence of personality-formation when that formation is psychologically conducive to debilitating fear and paralysing anxiety. But whereas in the case of the psyche-personal what we witness is an 'absence' of the personality, in the case of the psyche-social it is an active dis-engagement with the already consolidated Symbolic order. It is precisely through the culturally constituted Symbolic order that both the individual character and cultural identities are formulated and legitimised. By resorting back to a primarily visual and deliberately pre-Symbolic stage, Iranian cinema at its best has sought to find a form of signification that does not yield its soft authority to any metaphysical ordering of the Real. Seeking refuge in the Imaginary from the fear of the government of the absolutes and the reign of abstractions is constitutional to any metaphysical ordering of reality, particularly when institutionalised in a theocracy.

There is a memorable scene in Jalal Al-e Ahmad's novella *Nun va al-Qalam/By the Pen*,[8] where the revolutionary Qalandars are about to invade the City, and the citizens are about to vacate their habitat for fear of bloodshed. The scene is surreally powerful because what will remain in the City are the governmental forces facing the revolutionary Qalandars: two political claims on the obedience of the population who have all fled and vacated the scene. In the course of the Islamic Revolution in Iran, the two claimants to the land, the Persian monarchy and the Shi'i clerics, one in a repressive and the other in a revolutionary posture, were at each other's throats. Seeking refuge in their cinema, Iranians seem to have had vacated the political dominion, left it for all the violent claims on their political servitude to fight each other and settle their differences. The Imaginary dis-engagement with the Real, when the Real is so pathologically violent, is from the fear of the Real, an active de-Symbolisation of it, so that it can no longer signify terror. From the onset of the revolution over the eight years of brutal war to the cruel barbarity under theocratic rule, Iranians have experienced the most violent manifestations of their symbolically mitigated metaphysical order. By retreating to the Imaginary, to continue with a slight re-modulation of Lacan's theory, Iranians have collectively sought to de-signify the metaphysical ordering of the Real.

Identification with the Imaginary world of cinema under these circumstances is a strategically asocial move, fusional with the liminality of the pre-Symbolic subversion of the metaphysical order. Lacan considers the active identification with the father and the submission to his interdictions the opening gate into the Symbolic order. What we witness in Iranian cinema is a resorting backward from that heavily Symbolised interdiction that was brutally manifested in the course of the revolutionary period. In the cinema of Abbas Kiarostami, in particular, we see this deliberate concentration of the gaze on the visual, without ever allowing it to collapse into the Symbolic. Here, Kiarostami's *Taste of Cherry/Ta'm-e Gilas* (1997) is by far the best example of a cinematic insight in which one watches a suicidal man for the entirety of the film, without ever empathising with him. This is by far the most compelling achievement of Kiarostami in one of his masterpieces. We spend the entirety of the film in the presence of a character who is about to kill himself, but we never transmute what we visually observe into any Symbolic order of signification. The act simply does not mean or signify anything. We could not care less if he does or does not kill himself. The result is that the ultimate interdiction of all interdictions – that is, death – is emotively robbed of all its loaded metaphysical ordering of reality. There cannot be anything more liberating than this. Because the result of that concentrated visualisation is surprisingly not apathy to reality but, instead, being embraced by it. Resisting the metaphysical ordering of reality is achieved through the precision of this 'embrace'. The Real, as a result, assumes a mode of signification which is existentially counter-Symbolic – it does not symbolise. It ends all symbolism.

Cinema as visual counter-Symbolic: this is how one mode of cultural production can erode the metaphysical ordering of the Real. The collapsing movement from the Imaginary into the Symbolic, particularly in a culture of endemic proclivity to detect hidden meaning in just about everything, *ipso facto* creates an open-ended spiral that sucks in the entire fusional relationship of the psycho-social and the Imaginary, all to the detriment of the Imaginary and at the service of the Symbolic. Kiarostami, as indeed the best of Iranian cinema, keeps the Imaginary visual at arm's length from the danger of that collapse into the Symbolic. Because the Symbolic order is social, de-Symbolisation is a strategic move away from such forms of socialisation that have historically resulted in catastrophe. What happens in the psycho-social, which is the equivalent of what presumably occurs in the psycho-personal, is the transition from the Imaginary into the Symbolic through a collective re-enactment of the Oedipal crisis. In this case, it seems that we have a deliberate regression back to the pre-Oedipal, precisely because of the infanticidal tendencies of so many fathers ordering their sons to go and be murdered either on the revolutionary streets or else on the Iran-Iraq War's battlefront. Whether as soldiers to the Shah or as revolutionary guards to the ayatollahs, hundreds of thousands of young Iranians were ceremoniously (with revolution and war as 'ritual') sacrificed, while their sacrificial murder was presided over by the priestly order. What we see in Iranian cinema, particularly in its pre-Symbolic articulation of the visual, is the strategic rewinding of the psyche-social back to its pre-Oedipal stage, in an attempt to de-circulate the fear of the father from the developmental cycle. The authority of the father, his violent ability to say 'no', is thus sought to be dis-engaged. But how?

To De-Oedipalise the Oedipal

To de-Oedipalise the Oedipal, the father's ability to say 'no' is to be the primary target. Lacan believes that the active formation of the subject, via Oedipalisation, is through language.[9] This insight is central to my concern with the aesthetic strategies of de- and consequently re-subjection. The predominantly verbal disposition of Iranian culture has naturally been conducive to a language-based formation of the subject. In general, the verbality of Iranian culture is far more predominant than its visuality, which is very much secluded in Persian painting, being a constitutionally private collection of courtly sentiments. The ocularcentrism of the cinematic visual, predicated on the tradition of coffeehouse painting, as a result, is profoundly corrosive of all verbally-based subject-formations, *ipso facto* paving the ground for a de- and a subsequent re-subjection, but this time around with no willingness or desire to cross the border from the Imaginary into the Symbolic. If in the Lacanian conception of the Symbolic order we are after a transcoding of the 'libidinal' into the 'linguistic', then we can also see the Symbolic as the purgatorial passage from the absolutism of reality-as-nothingness into the metaphysical ordering of the Real. If for Lacan the Oedipal crisis is the subject's awareness of 'the Name of the Father', then what we are watching in Iranian cinema is a visual 'forgetting of the Name of the Father', so that the next move (which is the Symbolic constitution of the metaphysical ordering of the Real) does not take place.[10] But whereas Lacan thought that the alienating process of the Symbolic discovery of 'the Name of the Father' is mono-directional and, once learnt, can never be forgotten, in the case of Iranian cinema we are witnessing a massive orchestration of that cultural erosion of the memory of the father. But the amnesia is not of a classically repressive nature that can come back and haunt the forgetful children. It is of a retracting, rewinding, regressive nature, as a strategy of going back to a pre-moment of 'history' to prevent the Oedipal, by arresting its emergence on the borderline between the Imaginary and the Symbolic.

The significance of Lacan's theory here is precisely in its active rendition of the subject-formation as contingent on the 'discourse of the Other' – that is, on the social awareness of the father through language. If this be so, then the formation of the subject and the cultural constitution of meaning are concurrent. Thus, any strategic act of de-subjection via the activation of the Imaginary can radically dismantle the otherwise transparent metaphysical ordering of the Real. An equally significant aspect of Lacan's theory is that it is anthropologically predicated on Lévi-Strauss; as such, the intermediary awareness of the constellation of taboos around the figure of the father mitigates the visual access to the metaphysical ordering of the Real, an awareness which would have been otherwise inaccessible. Here, the crucial distinctions between the cinema of Beiza'i and Kiarostami present themselves as two strategically complementary forms of dismantling both the constitution of the subject and its related phallogocentricism of the metaphysical order. Whereas Beiza'i is re-activating the *modus mythologos* in order to arrest the moment of transition from the Imaginary into the Symbolic visually, Kiarostami forces his camera on a numbing concentration on the Real, until all its metaphysical and symbolic orderings have effectively dissolved into the pre-culturally, and pre-meaningfully visual. The sum total of both strategies is metonymically tapping into the mythic moment.

What happens through Kiarostami's cinema, then, is a particularly revolutionary counter-cultural movement. He has an uncanny ability to keep his cinematic gaze at the pre-Symbolically visual, and then forcing it to yield, not 'meaning' but 'visual signification', and that without ever collapsing into any metaphysical ordering of the Real. The result is not only an active de-symbolisation of the Real, but, even more important, the de-metaphysicalisation of ordering it. As a strategy of de- and subsequent re-subjection, the mutation of the verbal into the visual is critically crucial here, particularly in the context of a culture of almost pathological proclivity to over/interpretation – that is, the over/verbalisation of the visual. 'In some cultural contexts', Susan Sontag suggests in her *Against Interpretation*, 'interpretation is a liberating act. It is a means of revising, of transvaluing, of escaping the dead past. In other cultural contexts, it is reactionary, impertinent, cowardly, stifling'.[11] The problem here is not of an either/or geographical distinction between one culture and another, as Sontag seems to suggest. Within one cultural context, interpretation can subserve the dead certainties of its metaphysical order, and all cultures share in that order, or else subvert it. In the case of the pre-Symbolic visualisation of the Real that prevents the purgatorial passage of the symbolic leading to the metaphysical, the subservient interpretation is that which activates the verbalisation of the visual and thus facilitates its symbolisation, as indeed is the case with a whole history of cinematic (journalist) interpretation, in Iran as indeed in much of the rest of the world. Cinematic journalism in Iran in this crucial regard is worse than its foreign counterparts, its foreign counterparts worse than their Iranian counterpart. In Iran, the journalists tell their readers that the 'A' that they see in Beiza'i or Kiarostami's cinema is not *really* 'A'. It is *really* 'B' symbolised as 'A'. Foreign journalists, all the way from *Cahier du Cinema* down to the *New York Times*, tell their readers that the 'A' they see in Iranian cinema is really the 'B' of the 'Western Cinema' in an 'Islamic' disguise. That is the only difference between Iranian and foreign journalism *à la* 'film critique'. Interpretation, however, should not necessarily collapse into such banal subservience to the dominant metaphysics of verbalising the visual. Interpretation can equally effectively point back to the visual without 'interpreting' its visuality into verbality. By 'theorising' the visuality of the visual, interpretation can equally effectively mark its counter-symbolic irreducibility.

De-symbolising the Oedipal by resisting the verbalisation of the visual: that is one effective aesthetic strategy of re-subjection of the post/colonial persons against the government of abstractions in which they live. Against all attempts at verbalising it, the fact is that the visual resists verbalisation, not by being 'rich' in suggesting interpretation, as one hermeneutic principle would have it, but by being extraordinarily poor in any such claim to richness. The over/verbalisation of the visual is the punishment of the metaphysical against the rebellious impertinence of the visual. The more defiant the visual rebellion against the tyranny of the metaphysical, the more active the agents of symbolisation would be at work. In the case of Iranian cinema, Abbas Kiarostami has been extraordinarily successful in abstaining from being party to any outlandish over/interpretation of his own cinema. In contrast, Bahram Beiza'i has collapsed squarely into that trap and has been a willing accomplice in having his cinema over/interpreted, its visuality verbalised, its Imaginary symbolised, drawn back into the very metaphysical order he wants to subvert.[12] Partly this distinction has to do with the nature of Kiarostami's and Beiza'i's cinemas, one defying the metaphysical ordering of the Real altogether, the other trying to transmute it, respectively.

The verbalisation of the visual subserves the verbal constitution of the subject, facilitating the vocal cords to utter the 'no' of the father and the subsequent successful implementation of the Oedipal. What Sontag's brilliant dictum, 'in place of a hermeneutics we need an erotic of art', means here is the rebellious movement of the sensuality of the visual against the repressive regime of the over/interpreted Symbolic. In and of itself, the visual is sensual, and as such it resists assimilation and domination by the verbal and the interpretative. In the government of abstractions, constitutionalised in an Islamic Republic, the verbal is Oedipal, the visual the conspiracy of the rebellious bastards, whose fathers are not their fathers.

For Lacan, as indeed for Hans Blumenberg, the Real is what resists Symbolisation into the meaningful.[13] Here, there is much happening in Iranian cinema. Frederic Jameson's assertion that for Lacan the Real is simply 'History itself'[14] is conclusive but not sufficient. What we see in Kiarostami's *Taste of Cherry*, as one of the best examples, is not the resistance of the Real to the symbolic, but the divestment of the Real from all its symbolic significations. The Real that resists symbolisation is culturally irrelevant, because psychologically it does not generate anxiety, and socially it does not invoke confrontation. The Real which is radically and in fact 'historically' signified into a culture is the singular concern of Kiarostami as an aesthetician of de-signification. Throughout his films – particularly in the Rostamabad (Koker) Trilogy, but most emphatically in *The Taste of Cherry* – we see an almost surgical removal of the symbolic from the imaginary, so that in its texture it begins to become once again Real. This is by far the most significant strategy of de-signification available in any visual counter-culture of subverting the dominant metaphysics. By dwelling on the borderline of an attempted suicide, in *The Taste of Cherry* we are already on the borderline of the tension between the symbolic and the Real. The suicidal protagonist goes about arranging for his suicide without the slightest significance attached to the act. The greatest achievement of Kiarostami in *The Taste of Cherry* is precisely having us watch for about two hours close-ups and medium shots of a man who is about to commit suicide and yet for us not to cultivate the slightest sense of empathy with him.

The Real in this case, though divested of all its loaded symbolic significations, collapses neither into a Lacanian atrophy, nor into a Blumenbergian absolutism, nor indeed into what Bataille has called 'the nothingness of things'.[15] Through Kiarostami's camera, the Real remains Real, until such time that its fictive transparency, without collapsing into the symbolic or submitting to a metaphysics, begins softly to *suggest* (which I use deliberately to stay away even from 'signify') a kind of '*il pensiero debole*'[16] that makes life at once trustworthy and yet metaphysically meaningless. It takes two brutal centuries of colonialism on the fringes of capitalist modernity, a being narratively written out of the project of the European Enlightenment and a paralysing jargon of authenticity operative in one 'Tradition' or another, to produce an artist who can teach his camera to look at the Real, divest it of all its symbolics, discredit all the metaphysical ordering of it and yet have it make life look like worth living.

Re-Configuring the Body

The dis-engagement from the metaphysical through a visual resistance to the symbolic ultimately results in producing an ocular counter-ethics that can now suggest without signifying, show without symbolising, mean without submitting to a metaphysics. Dis-engaging the metaphysics, as a visual move, strategically pulls back the Symbolic to the Imaginary in order to safeguard the Real from collapsing into the Metaphysical. Re/configuring the body, through various visual strategies, is one effective way of resisting the mandate of Islamically symbolising it. In re/configuring the body of a 'Muslim woman', for example, Mehdi Fakhimzadeh's *The Spouse/Hamsar* (1994), a fairly successful comic adventure in the battle of the sexes, has a totally unintended consequence, producing a textual example of such a re-configuration of the feminine body as a visual counter-ethics.[17] Islamic metaphysics demands bodily submission to the authority of its religious symbolisation. However, the vibrant and vivacious presence of women in this film defies the Islamically imposed dress code, the submission of the body to the symbolic of obedience, and manages to give a *semblance* of normalcy to an otherwise perfectly abnormal appearance. Fatemeh Motamed Arya, as the lead character in *The Spouse*, was at the time emerging as the leading Iranian actor with a remarkable versatility in the range of the characters she portrayed, and particularly effective in having her bodily movements being at once 'normal' yet 'Islamically' tolerable, Real yet defiant of the Islamic symbolic order. Whether she portrays the sprightly and agile pharmaceutical employee in Fakhimzadeh's *The Spouse*, the poverty-stricken but remarkably noble Nobar Kordani in Rakhshan Bani-Etemad's *The Blue-Veiled*, or the flamboyantly mad Simin in Mohsen Makhmalbaf's *The Actor*, or a host of other characters, Fatemeh Motamed Arya portrays the sort of public persona that an Islamic Republic can tolerate – or, to put it perhaps more accurately, that the Iranian filmmakers have been able to weasel out of the Islamic censorship. What is emerging in the cinematic persona of Motamed Arya is a kind of reality of bodily configuration that in its very idea of the feminine body resorts to its pre-significatory Real, and yet not in a public defiance of the custodians of the sacred, all directed towards giving a new meaning to the term 'optical illusion'.

Clothing becomes one effective way of disrupting the Islamic symbolic, by eroding its de-sexualising intentions. The mandates of the Islamic censorship about women are directed almost entirely towards their effective de-sexualisation. Strategies of 'clothing' women in a surreptitiously defiant way is to restore that sexuality. The strategy is effective in two simultaneously disruptive ways: (1) the bodily memories of actors betray their Islamically symbolised dresses, and (2) variations and colour of local dress defy the dark tyranny of the mandatory *chador*. The body of the feminine that Motamed Arya, perhaps best among many others, portrays has the memory of a daily reality that she manages to sneak through the Islamic censorship. Pictures and videotapes of private parties that escape Iran, the data-base of that memory, reveal a picture of Iranian women, in their post-Islamic Revolution appearance, that empirically sustain the inventive repertoire of the body Motamed Arya represents. In these private pictures, one sees an easier continuity with a history of modernity to which both Reza Shah who ordered veils removed and Ayatollah Khomeini who ordered them put back are mere accidents. Older and more pious mothers and grandmothers may be more comfortable with more layers of clothing, while their daughters and grand-daughters are more so with less. There is a colourful combination of individual tastes and choices, personal preferences or degrees of piety and beauty. But this is all behind closed doors or else for the private viewing of members of the family abroad. The public personae that the Islamic ideologues wish to portray find their most effective characterisations in films produced or sponsored by the Ministry of Guidance. An Orwellian nightmare come true, the 'Ministry of Guidance' in effect uses the understandably uncontrollable urge of Iranian filmmakers to normalise this forced picture of an Islamic women. But what happens, then, is a victorious battle of the bodily memories of reality overcoming the Islamically exacted symbolic ordering of the Real.

The strategy of launching an avalanche of colours and designs in local clothing against the tyranny of dark and baggy mandatory *chadors* is equally effective. Some splendid attention as a result of the official imposition of the Islamic symbolic order is being paid to local variations of female dress by a number of filmmakers. These are all strategies of resisting the Islamic symbolic order through the defiant reality of the visual. Since the *chador* is an urban phenomenon, dress that is native to any number of Iranian localities is increasingly used by filmmakers as an attractive alternative to the Islamic garb.[18] The character of Na'i in Bahram Beiza'i's *Bashu: The Little Stranger* (1985) wears perhaps the most successful example of northern Iranian dress common among women actively working on rice paddies. The same is true for Tahereh Ladanian's dress in Kiarostami's *Through the Olive Trees* (1994). Southern Iranian female clothing is splendidly exhibited in the leading character of Kiumars Pour-Ahmad's *For the Sake of Hanieh* (1995). In Kamal Tabrizi's *End of Childhood* (1994), a vivacious example of Kurdish clothing is used for the leading female character. What Mehrju'i does in *Hamoun* (1990) is even more brilliant. In one of her creative urges, the turbulent Mahshid becomes a fashion designer and surrounds herself with the most fantastic collection of brave and blatant fabrics and models in bright, boisterous and colourfully turbulent dresses.

Whether through an active effusion of bodily memories that *ipso facto* subverts the Islamic symbolic order or having colourful garments rise in defiance of the tyrannical (mandatory) black *chador*, the function of the cinematic visual is to disrupt the political tyranny of the inherited and hegemonised subject. Lacan believed that it is through the 'acquisition' of language as a social product that subjectivity is formed and sustained. The 'I' of the subject is the mirror-image of the linguistically-constituted 'Thou' of the society, the culture, the collectivised Other. Under revolutionary circumstances, the collectivised Other is a distinctly political proposition. The prohibitions that the tyrannical powers impose in the name of 'public morality' are no longer the dialectical outcome of an 'I-Thou' relationship. The reign of the religious revolutionaries is *ipso facto* the reign of terror. Under these circumstances, creative and artistic strategies are all that remains to the collective will of a resistance to safeguard a modicum of space in which to sustain and negotiate a life-affirming subjectivity. That subjectivity is to be salvaged and in effect re-invented from the afflictions on which it is already grafted. In the otherwise prosaic Puran Derakhshandeh's *Connection/Rabeteh* (1986), Naser's affliction – he is hearing-impaired – is the narrative basis of an examination of how the emergence of a new dialogical relationship between him and his friends and family begin to change, not only him, but also the entire atmosphere to which the others are subjected and characterised.

What we see then in Iranian cinema is a visual re-Imagining of the body in direct defiance of an actively Islamic symbolisation of it. The body here, as indeed always, constitutes the site of cultural contestations between the sources of power and the visionaries of emancipation. The custodians of the Islamic sacred reign of terror are so obviously aware of the political power of the dead body that they create an inventory of dead soldiers, civilian militia and revolutionary guards and officially designate them as POWs and MIAs. They then systematically feed the collective guilt of the surviving society by gradually releasing these corpses from a morgue that functions like the dead-blood bank of the revolution. Two years (1977–79) of revolutionary turmoil resulted in tens of thousands dying in the streets of Iranian cities. Eight years (1980–88) of barbaric war with a neighbouring country resulted in hundreds of thousands of more dead bodies. A corrupt theocracy of terror will neither physically nor metaphorically let go of these corpses, until full advantage is taken of them in legitimising an otherwise illegitimate rule and crushing any voice of reason raised against the madness of a tyranny.

Trusting the Camera

The battle between the symbolising agencies of the metaphysical order and the visual de-symbolisation of the Real is not always won by the liberating Imaginary. Particularly under the political ascendancy of the metaphysical, the theocracy victorious, the symbolising agencies can and do find their ways into the cinematic cosmovision. The challenge here is with the visual irreducibility of cinema itself, its non-verbality, its uncompromisingly fragmented visuality. To picture the soul of a self-wondering world, cinema must trust its own fragmented and fragmentary de/constitution of the subject. If cinema forgets itself and begins to ape the Hegelian absolute and absolutist subject (and that in a postcolonial age that has philosophically overcome Hegel), then it not only betrays by forgetting itself, but it equally betrays by misguiding its audience. This, alas, is precisely what has happened to Mehrju'i's cinema in the post-revolutionary period. Mehrju'i's early cinema, up to *The Tenants/Ejareh-Neshin-ha* (1987), released a year before the end of the war with Iraq, can arguably be considered a sustained creative drive, the work of one of the most brilliant Iranian artists in living memory. Beginning with the triangulated nightmare of *Pari* (1995), *Leila* (1996) and *Sara* (1997), the road was paved for the final catastrophe of *The Pear Tree* (1998), the last *coup de grâce* to one of Iran's greatest filmmakers.

Pari is such a nightmarish specimen of an absolutist conviction that only an equally nightmarish revolution and war could have produced it. It is a haunting Bergmanesque film in that, in its extremely successful *mélange* of the beautiful central character, her Stalinist determination and her neo-mysticism, it scares the living daylights out of any rational being. *Pari* demonises the university setting and the professoriate, condemns the mundane banalities of young intellectuals and draws the world into a mystical act of self-signification that, precisely because of its nightmarish beauty, is deeply disturbing. The living world of Pari and her brother Dadashi is collapsed into the metaphoric world that Pari's neo-mysticism relentlessly dreams. The ultimate test of this film is whether Dadashi's turn from mysticism to acting can match Pari's reverse turn from acting to mysticism. Whatever the result, the cinema of Mehrju'i is here at the service of the government of abstractions, the reign of metaphysical terror.

At its best, the fragmented imagery of cinema corresponds to and reflects the fragmented reality before 'editing' into a meaningful sequence, as it were. Its 'language' being ocularcentric, cinema is visually suited to reflect its mediation and cross-fertilisation of self and society. But that is only the case if cinema does not collapse, as Mehrju'i's has, into an absolutist manifesto of essential and essentialising attributions. In the case of Mehrju'i's cinema, this aesthetic corruption is almost categorically traceable to the advent and outcome of the Islamic Revolution of 1977–79, very much on the model of the medieval Persian poetic turn to mysticism after the Mongol invasion of the thirteenth century. From a potentially critical commentary on that revolution,

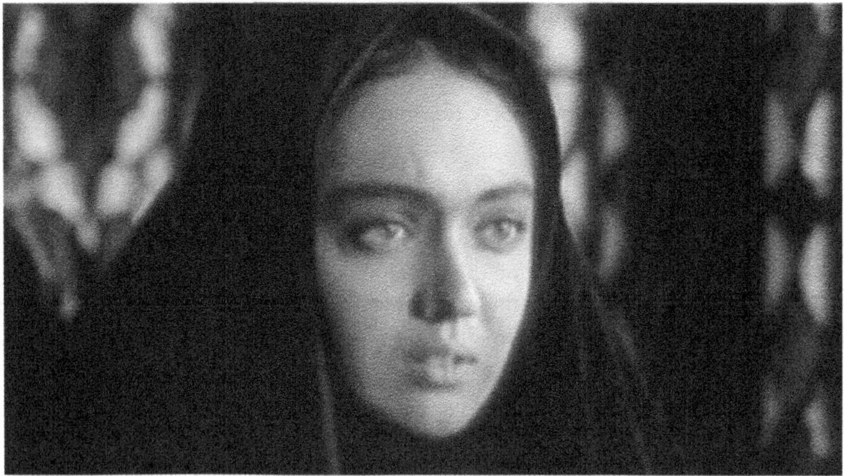

Figure 6.1 *Niki Karimi in Daryoush Mehrju'i's* Pari *(1995). (Photo: public domain, fair use)*

Mehrju'i's cinema has, alas, collapsed into corroborative evidence of it. In its absolutism of truth-telling, its symbolic totalitarianism, its narrative tyranny and, most damagingly, its mystic resignation, Mehrju'i's cinema is the mirror-image of the deadliest metaphysical elements at the heart of the Islamic Revolution and Republic. What is deeply disturbing in *Pari* in particular is this radical oscillation between a search for, and a conviction in, an Eternal and Absolute Truth for Pari and an empty dwelling in life-as-acting for Dadashi. The intellectual flirtations of the two older brothers, 'role-models' for these two younger siblings, have led one to a ceremonial suicide and the other to a pathological isolationism.

The dominant character in the narrative, by virtue of her stunning beauty, eloquence, convictions and determination, is Pari: a driven mystical visionary who has recurrent nightmares about being drowned in a small pool, who has a passionate intensity for writing with chalk on a blackboard, who storms out of the class of a pretentiously idiot professor, who sees nothing but confusion, anarchy and despair in her house which is in an absolute state of chaos for presumably being renovated, and who abandons her home in Tehran to seek solace, salvation and Truth in the Shaykh Lotfollah Mosque in Isfahan. The embodiment of her Truth manifest is a strikingly beautiful male apparition of the figure of Christ (blond, blue eyes and all) who hangs himself upside down from his ankles into a well in the middle of a ruined and abandoned dwelling and thus recites the Qur'an from the first to the last chapter. That Christly figure is there to negate everything about Pari's fiancé in Isfahan, a supercilious, pretentious pseudo-intellectual who gobbles up hearty portions of Chelow-kabab while Pari tells him of her most intimate fears, hopes, anxieties and confusions. The fact that Pari has to seek refuge in the restaurant's bathroom to find peace and tranquillity, and there and then to have a mirror-image of her 'Dearly-Beloved-Truth-Manifest-as-the-Christly-Figure' appear, would have revealed its utter banality, had it not been for the intensity and brilliance of Niki Karimi's extraordinary performance as Pari.

Thus oscillating between life as an act (*bazi*) and life as a quest (*soluk*), Pari and Dadashi act out the two gut-wrenching extremities of a life at the centre of its glorious confusion. Kiarostami's cinema has taught us how to look and simply be. Mehrju'i's superlative cinema, his admirably beautiful shots, precise *mise-en-scène*, masterful camera movements and so on help create and sustain the two extremities of 'Truth' and 'Theatricality', or 'Mysticism' and 'Make-belief', all occasioned by the radically pompous intellectuality of his lead character. Kiarostami's cinematic gift, on the contrary, has been to find a bizarre angle on the confusing-yet-enabling nature of being before and beyond its radical intellectualisation either into Acting or into Mysticism. Mehrju'i's cinema, visually far more learned and contemplative, is best suited to reveal the extremities of our cultural maladies into 'Truth-seeking' and 'Make-belief'. Kiarostami's cinema, operative on a radical modification of the very tempo of our visual encounters, pushes both these extremities aside in order to create a cleavage, as if the opening of a door onto a vastly rich and new way of looking at things. In a space thus carved the binary opposition evident in our culture and depicted in Mehrju'i's cinema collapses into an undefined, un-definable and perfectly confusing, yet ennobling vision of life. The visual 'language' of cinema, structurally contingent on its mode of narration, is central to its ability, not only to reveal the indeterminacy of the subject, but also effectively to dismantle all the presumptions of any Hegelian Absolutist assumption about the subject. It is the singular insight of the Lacanian psychoanalytic that the act of subject-formation is a Symbolic imposition of meaning by a culture over its bodily members.[19] In the world of art, Mehrju'i's cinema became an instrument of that imposition, rather than an aesthetic of resisting it, and as such he and his cinema became some of the most tragic victims of the Islamic Revolution. Those countless numbers of visual gibberish that the Islamic propaganda machinery produced *ad nauseam* all pale in comparison to the wasting of the phenomenal gift that was once Daryoush Mehrju'i to Iranian cinema.

Subjectivity, Sexuality and the Imaginary

Because sexuality posits the most disruptive threat to the Metaphysical ordering of the Real, the Symbolic constitution of gender is the most frightful manifestation of a culture. Re-subjection of the person thus ultimately has to work itself through the Symbolic labyrinth of the culturally constituted masculinity/femininity. Read dialectically and not as a consolidated state of affair, the triangulated analytics of subjectivity, sexuality and language in Lacan makes any aesthetic disengagement with the metaphysical both possible and liberating. What is effectively and radically decentred in Lacan's psychoanalytic is the presumption of an instrumentally rational, assertively self-conscious and symbolically modulated subject. Although this innate critique of the Enlightenment and its humanist constitution of absolute subjectivity is evident in Lacan, in his reading of 'woman', he might be read as collapsing into those very humanist assumptions. The idea of woman as the other, as the castrated and as lacking may be detected as surviving from the Enlightenment Humanism of Freud and finding its traceable way even into the poststructuralist psychoanalytic of Lacan. As Luce Irigaray has argued, the female subjectivity is psychoanalytically construed as a substratum of the male subjectivity.[20] Central to Lacan's psychoanalytic can thus be detected a conservative tendency in his presumption of a static consolidation of the idea of the Symbolic, among whose stabilised assumptions is that of the female as castrated and lacking. As Irigaray has argued, in her take on Heidegger, in the post/Platonic (or what she calls 'Western') metaphysics, to be 'seen' is 'to be'. The ocularcentrism of the post/Platonic metaphysics privileges 'seeing' over 'not-seeing'. Since women have 'nothing' (the absence of the phallus) to show, then they are not, except as lacking, absent and vacuous.[21] In her critique of Lacan's theory of the mirror-formation of subjectivity, Irigaray thus questions Lacan's use of the flat mirror as a self-reflective mechanism of subject-formation, because in a flat mirror woman's sexuality can only appear as a 'hole'. Irigaray proposes the use of the speculum to reflect more fully a woman's subjectivity/sexuality.[22]

If the constitution of gender in post/colonial outposts is economically contingent on the project of capitalist modernity, then the project of the Enlightenment and its subsidiary instrumental rationalism will have to bear on the specifics of subjection under such circumstances. Irigaray's critique of the Enlightenment and of instrumental reason focuses on the proposition and, conversely, the contingency of masculine subjectivity on this instrumental reason. What becomes evident in Irigaray's reading of subjectivity/sexuality is their active trans-codification. What is lost to Irigaray, however, is that the production of masculinity in the project of Enlightenment is constitutionally instrumental to – that is to say, fully at the service of – the project of capitalist modernity. The problem with Irigaray and the rest of the Heideggerian critique of what they call the 'Western Metaphysics' is that, first, they have never been able to shed the Hegelian teleological narrative from their critique and, second, they have failed to see the joint projects of the Enlightenment and capitalist modernity as a disjointed accident rather than as an anticipated consequence of the Greek conception of *techne*. The phallogocentricism which is the subject of Irigaray's critique and Lacan's psychoanalytic is a by-product of the instrumental reason and the necessity of a conception of man as tool-making and productive in the course of the project of capitalist modernity. The phallus as instrument became central in the constitution of masculine subjectivity because the masculine himself was rendered instrumental in the project of Modernity/Enlightenment. The problem with the term 'patriarchal' and with the feminist ahistorical and undifferentiated use of it is that it glosses over the historicity of the production of the phallus as an instrument of masculine subjectivity, precisely in order to make the masculine himself instrumentally useful.

Irigaray is right in seeking the generation of a whole new Symbolic in which the constitution of the feminine subjectivity is no longer contingent on, and a subsidiary of, the phallocentric production of masculinity. Whatever the merits or promises of her project in the metropolitan centres of power, she has, however, very little to say about the post/colonial outpost where the constitution of subjectivity has an entirely different disposition. In the post/colonial outpost, the situation, as always and by virtue of being on the periphery of power, is vastly different. To begin with, we need to delimit the constitution of subjectivity not only in the metropolitan centres of capitalist modernity, but equally in their extended colonial outpost, to the project of Enlightenment as the ideological modulation of the capitalist revolution. The generic term of 'patriarchy' will dilute the issues and lead to a categorical, and thus analytically shallow, condemnation of phallogocentricism without foregrounding its critique on an historical precision that can lead to an emancipatory reading of the whole predicament of power-based production of subjectivity in both masculine and feminine directions. If we identify the phallocentric constitution of masculine subjectivity in the metropolitan centres of capitalist modernity as a specifically modern phenomenon – without, of course, exempting the pre-modern from a similar possibility, but not an identical necessity of the instrumentalisation of the masculine – then the fate of the subjectivity of both men and women in the post/colonial outpost assumes an entirely different course of development. Because Enlightenment Humanism categorically bypassed the colonial, and in fact defined itself as the civilisational Other of the Oriental as the exotic, then there could not have been any ideologically constituted subjectivity of the colonial masculinity on the premise of his phallus. Quite to the contrary, the project of colonialism was *ipso facto* a process of emasculating the colonial, not just sexually but, far more importantly, politically.

The subjectivity of the colonial woman cannot be predicated on the phallocentric constitution of her masculine counterpart. She has been a witness to her father/husband/brother's effective castration by the colonial officer. The colonial masculine is in no position to define the femininity of his colonial counterpart on the basis of her absence of the phallus, while his own masculinity is effectively castrated. In the case of the colonial masculine, his entire Oedipal crisis is politically arrested. If, like Deleuze and Guattari, we are to anticipate a politics of Lacanian Imaginary predicated on an anti-Oedipus in which the cultural construction of the Symbolic has not consolidated the retardation of the culture,[23] then we have to see in what particular way the objectification of the colonial subject is to be reversed.

By being the object of the colonial officer's gun and gaze, the colonised masculine could not have been phallogocentrically subjected. He is subjected, in effect, by being objected to the colonial gaze and the gun, and as such he is effectively de-subjected as castrated. His Oedipal crisis is thus politically arrested or psychically reversed. Next to a phallically castrated masculine, the colonial feminine could not have been possibly subjected as the subsidiary of a phallogocentrically-subjected masculinity. In the colonial context, 'seeing' is not tantamount to 'being', as Irigaray has argued the case in the metropolitan centres of power, because the colonial masculine does not have much to offer by way of showing. He is effectively castrated. All the 'showing' and 'seeing' is in fact done by and for the colonial officer. The visual domination of the colonial person is by the 'Odalisque'-like visualisation of the feminine and the *ipso facto* castration of the masculine. The whole genealogy of Odalisque paintings, from Delacroix to Matisse,[24] is launched towards an active visualisation of the feminine colonial being laid-down and visually fucked, as much as it is a strategy of objecting her to the colonial gaze as that of emasculating her father/brother/husband.

In the pre/colonial context, if we were to think in such periodic terms, one can argue, it is the centrality of Work which is constitutional in the formation of the subject. The centrality of working women in Beiza'i's cinema – in *Bashu* and *The Ballad of Tara* most particularly – is concurrent with the pulling back of the image of woman into a pre-modern, rural era and thus de-Symbolising her from the colonial modernity of her objection. In the pre/modern, rural, one can argue, subjectivity is constituted neither by the 'seeing' nor by the 'showing' of the phallus. There, the subjectivity is constituted by Work. For Beiza'i, the paramount task of course always remains a re-Symbolisation of the feminine on the mythological drawing board. The process of urbanisation in the course of the colonial project, as the extended arm of capitalist modernity, removed women from their rural setting and, by forcing a hand-held veiling on them, rendered their hands inoperative and their productive force redundant. The cheap labour that the colonial project required from the newly urbanised societies only needed men and their two free hands; as a result, the superfluous labour force of women was made idle by the imposition of a kind of veiling that to this day is alien to rural settings. In the cities, men were instrumentalised into cheap labour in the extended productive machinery of capitalist modernity, while women had to abandon their working habits and stay at home to breed and raise more consumers and producers (children). In the course of the colonial project, women as a result became productively idle, socially absent and politically irrelevant. Under these circumstances, the masculine subjectivity of the colonial was consolidated by working as cheap labour, yet de/formed by their *de facto* castration, because of political subjugation to the colonial gun and their productive reduction to raw material. The female subjectivity was formed by being a non/productive partner to a politically castrated masculinity. Thus removed from their pre/modern, rural setting and cast into the newly urbanised colonial outposts, the colonial men and women now had to negotiate their subjectivity, not against each other, but simultaneously against the constitutionally emasculating presence of the colonial officer (factual or figurative) and his long gun. Under that gun, and by the logic of capitalist modernity that it represented, both men and women were reduced to raw material on the assembly line of the economic production of reality.

The constitution of the colonial subjectivity as objectivity cannot and does not go unchallenged. Men resist their effective emasculation and try to reclaim it by any number of ways. Colonised men try to reclaim their phallus by fighting in liberation movements against the extended gun of the colonial officer. This is an act of restoration. Claiming the land, raising the national flag, declaring independence, and pushing the colonial officer out are heroic acts of epic proportion that fight and narrate the masculine into the liberation of the motherland.[25] 'Mother' is both the safe and the transgressive metaphor of a masculine conquest of his own land. Whether she fights along her comrades on the battlefield or stays home to raise the next generation of fighters, the colonial woman is digging her own grave by helping to constitute the emerging subjectivity of her masculine comrades. War, by definition, is a phallocentric proposition. The constitution of phallocentric masculinity on the battlefield of liberation movements against the colonial occupation are heroic deeds and constitute a romantic pause that awaits the instrumentalisation of the phallic when the fighting men win the war and go to work and become assimilated into the instrumentalising logic of global capitalism.

Colonial men try to reclaim their phallus also by turning the colonising woman into a whore and thereafter metaphorically raping her. The image of the 'European' and 'Europeanised' women in the Iranian lumpen cinema in general and that of Mas'ud Kimia'i in particular is almost categorically at the service of this visual whoremongering. Mohamad Tavakoli-Targhi has carefully studied the image of 'European' women in Persian sources and suggested a kind of 'Euro-eroticism' as evidence of 'the fields of vision and meaning' being 'contested' by the Orientals.[26] Attempts at the whoremongering of the 'European' woman and a feeble effort at the restoration of phallocentric masculinity cannot be considered as visual contestation. The entire range of pathological whoremongering is done under a slanted relation of power. Tavakoli-Targhi's assertion that ...

> Misogyny and ethnocentrism were the shared characteristics of both Orientalist and Occidentalist narratives of otherness. European fascination with the imagined Muslim harems, 'seraglio', and 'gynaeceums' paralleled Asians' view of Europe as an eroticized 'heaven on earth' and European women and men respectively as nymphomaniacs and effeminates ...[27]

... is correct in its observation, but false in its conclusion. If we are to read the travellers he examines to have 'gone to Europe' and disregard the totalities of their itineraries, they are indeed the subject of the gaze of colonial officers – as they narratively try to reverse that gaze, not by looking at their women, but by recasting their conception of the world.[28] Their effeminisation of 'European' men is equally targeted at a counter-castration of the colonial officers. What Tavakoli-Targhi totally forgets is that most of these travellers were on ambassadorial missions to the colonising capitals, carrying their castrated subjectivity along with themselves when in Europe. They lacked the phallus with which to fantasise the fucking of the 'European' woman. Tayeb Saleh's *Season of Migration to the North* (1966) is the fictive narration of an Orientalised masculinity reclaiming his phallus by sexually conquering and then murdering his European feminine conquests. In the course of the Indian Mutiny of 1857 in India, reports of the Indians raping English women were staged precisely on the battleground of a restoration of the phallus.[29]

Colonial men try to reclaim their phallus also by producing an idealised native woman who is chaste and virgin, thus closing the gate of her being conquered by the intruding colonial officers, thus the added momentum to veiling women. While the colonising gaze, best represented by the Odalisque paintings of the Orientalist school, strips women of their clothing in order to conquer them visually, the colonised masculinity tries to reclaim his phallus by visually veiling the women and metaphorically covering her availabilities.[30] The interchangeable metaphors of the feminine body and the occupied territories intensifies this politicisation of femininity. The feminine body in effect becomes the contested field of a dual battle between the colonial officer and the colonised masculinity, one to restore his phallocentric masculinity, the other to prevent it. Because the restoration of phallocentric masculinity is constitutionally anti-colonial.

Colonial men try to reclaim their phallus also by investing the sexuality that is denied the colonised woman, for having covered her all, in a prostitute who now acts on the transgressive border of both mothering the colonial masculinity and letting him overtly own her. The result is a negational consolidation of the Oedipal by the *ex post facto*, metaphoric conquest of the mother. The conquest of the mother/lover as prostitute, best represented in most *Film Jaheli* in Iran, and particularly in Mas'ud Kimia'i's cinema, is equally conducive to the wishful political conquest of the land under occupation. By virtue of his extended gun, the colonial officer is in effect a substitutional father-conqueror-figure. The constitution of the prostitute as lover sexualises her to compensate the active de-sexualisation of the colonised feminine; her rendition into the mother/lover turns her into a metaphor of the occupied territory which can now be liberated by a plunging deep into the Oedipal. The result is *not* an overcoming of the Oedipal but a deeper entanglement with it, because the confrontation with the colonial father is only surreptitious here and not confrontational, as in the case of the liberation movement. Kimia'i's cinema is the most representative example of this mode of restoring phallocentric masculinity.

Under these circumstances, colonial women may have to negotiate their subjectivity by joining the liberation movement, which means, *ipso facto*, helping to restore the masculinity of their male comrades in precisely phallocentric directions, and as a result defining their own femininity as subsidiary and lacking. Anti-colonial national liberation movements thus can lead to a replication of the rampant misogyny in the metropolitan centres of power. Capitalist modernity here succeeds in instrumentalising the masculine colonial by having his subjectivity constituted on the instrumentality of his phallus, which results in the subjectivity of the colonial feminine being determined as lacking and absent. The key intermediary function here belongs to the homoerotic disposition of postcolonial subjects.

Colonial women could conversely enter a different sexual subjection by being physically attracted to colonial officers, or their intellectual surrogates, the colonial Orientalists. This is obviously the negational reversal of the same phenomenon, where the political powerlessness of colonial men is translated into their sexual impotence. The physical attraction of the colonial officers and their surrogate Orientalist substitutes in colonial women is equally reflective of the metaphoric substitution of the female body for the occupied territories. In Michel Khleifi's *Wedding in Galilee/Ors fil Jalil* (1987), we see a profoundly agonised version of this phenomenon, when on his wedding night, which is celebrated right under the extended gun and gaze of the occupying Israeli soldiers, Adel the groom cannot have an erection, and in order to protect his 'honour', his bride Samiah takes her virginity with her own finger. The character of Sumaya, Samiah's younger sister, is even more provocative. In her direct confrontation with an Israeli soldier – tall, handsome, with dark sunglasses – she presents an energetic effervescence which is at once sexual and political. The homo-erotic scene between Tali, the Israeli women who is a soldier, and the Palestinian women adds to the creative tension at the heart of the encounter. The assassination attempt of the young Palestinian males is all a futile attempt at the restoration of their compromised masculinity. Having translated the political powerlessness of the colonial male into his sexual impotence, the colonial woman is attracted to the colonial officer.

Alternatively, and here is where the material condition of the Symbolic production of culture has escaped both Lacan and Irigaray, the colonial woman could altogether shift the constitution of her subjectivity away from a relation of tangentiality to the phallocentric masculinity and direct it towards Work. Here, her femininity is constituted in the speculum of her organic relation to Work, to extend Irigaray's observation, as an emancipatory movement. The most significant attention to the centrality of Work in the constitution of feminine subjectivity is to be seen in Beiza'i's and Bani-Etemad's respective cinemas, in *Thunder Shower*, *The Ballad of Tara*, *Bashu*, *The Blue-Veiled* and *The May Lady*, in particular. The problem with Work as the defining instance of engendering subjectivity is that its cinematic cosmovision as imagined by Beiza'i or Bani-Etemad has its constitutional limitations and needs to be carefully modulated when it is extended to the context of the capitalist modernity in which both masculinity and femininity are instrumentalised in relation to production. Here, the constitution of feminine subjectivity can again be at a visible disadvantage because she lacks the Symbolised instrument of re/production, and as a result her subjectivity may again be defined in terms of this lack and absence. In the absence of the instrument of re/production, she can again become the receptacle of re/production. Thus, a division of labour emerges again, in which the labourer with the visible instrument of re/production assumes domination over the labourer with a hidden, absent, concave receptacle of re/production. In this case, too, capitalist modernity can triumph in its instrumentalisation of the phallus and the privileging of the phallocentric constitution of masculinity and femininity.

There is a Work which is carried out outside the fold of capitalist modernity, and which is not instrumentalised and alienating. It is a conspicuously pre/capitalist, rural and heavily mythologised version, as in *Bashu* and *The Ballad of Tara*, and as such suggestive of an active de-Symbolisation of the dominant and the re-Symbolisation of the possible. And then there is a Work which is constitutionally non/productive by being anti/productive, and which is equally directed towards a de-Symbolisation of the dominant and the re-Symbolisation of the possible, as perhaps best represented in the entire oeuvre of Rakhshan Bani-Etemad.

Towards a Counter-Symbolic

Contesting the phallocentric, Oedipally-constituted masculinity is contesting the entire cultural Symbolic of suppression constitutionally embedded in that masculinity. But how exactly is that masculinity to be counter-Symbolised? In their *Anti-Oedipus: Capitalism and Schizophrenia*, Deleuze and Guattari propose an emancipatory politics on the premise of the Lacanian Imaginary. But how exactly is that pre-Symbolic moment of the Imaginary possible? Beyond children, pre-Modernity and the schizophrenic, the evident cases to which Deleuze and Guattari pay particular attention, how is de-Oedipalisation possible? When the Symbolic has already been coagulated in the Oedipal crisis and thus invested in the culture that socialises, how is de-Symbolisation possible? How is the tyranny of the Symbolic, in the Lacanian language that Deleuze and Guattari celebrate, to be opposed?

Instrumentalisation of the phallus as the supreme Symbolic of masculinity is because of the instrumentalisation of the masculine in capitalist modernity, where the working hands represent the potent phallus. Absent in both the Lacanian psychoanalytic and Irigaray's feminist critique of it is the material condition constitutional to the formation of subject. The phallocentricity of subject-formation in capitalist modernity is a reality *sui generis*, and it cannot be assimilated backward and forward into a vacated history. That historicity of the perception of patriarchy has been to the detriment of the specificity of capitalist modernity and of the way its instrumental rationalism instrumentalises the labour force as it turns everything into raw material. The phallus is instrumentalised in the constitution of masculine subjectivity *because* man is already instrumentalised by the instrumental rationalism constitutional to capitalist modernity – particularly evident on its colonial edges.

The increasing need of global capitalism for ever cheaper labour, to match its need for ever cheaper raw material and ever more expansive markets, means the incorporation of women and children as cheap labour into the economic production of reality. The rise of feminist movements in both advanced capitalist societies and in the post/colonial outposts corresponds to the need of these societies for cheap labour. The logic of the instrumental rationalism constitutional to capitalist modernity has had nothing against the feminist movements, to the degree that such movements have provided a healthy market for cheap labour. The result of the incorporation of women into the economic production of reality is quite revolutionary. The equal instrumentalisation of the feminine in capitalist modernity de-instrumentalises the phallus as the measure of masculine subjection and domination, with the two working hands of women de-Symbolising the working hands of men as phallic Symbols. The final sequence of Beiza'i's *Bashu* is extraordinarily suggestive here when the absent father returns to Na'i and Bashu with his right hand cut off. After a sustained cultivation of Na'i's and Bashu's respective characters in relation to work, in effect we have the working constitution of an entirely different mode of subjection of both masculinity and femininity.

The liberating costume that Na'i wears in *Bashu*, which is instrumental to her relation to work, is a critical indication that the imposition of veiling as a constitutionally urban phenomenon was not to cover the faces of women, but to de-instrumentalise their two hands. The early colonial intrusion of capitalist modernity into globality needed and exacted only the cheap labour that men could provide sufficiently. The active de-instrumentalisation of women's two working hands, perfectly capable and at work in rural and pre/colonial contexts, was the predicate of the instrumentalisation of the phallus in masculine subjectivity. But when the inner logic of the selfsame capitalist modernity demanded ever cheaper labour, *chadors* were lifted. Even in an Islamic Republic which seems to be very particular about veiling women, the nature of that veiling is such that it leaves the two working hands free. In the Islamic Republic, the kind of veiling now accepted and encouraged by the custodians of 'public morality' consists of a scarf that covers the head, as well as a baggy cover-all called '*manto*' that covers the body completely but leaves the two working hands completely free to work in factories, schools, hospitals, governmental bureaucracies and so on. The two working hands of women, even from behind their Islamic garb, instrumentalises their subjectivity into the productive forces of the economic production of reality and, as such, de-instrumentalises the phallocentric constitution of masculine subjectivity.

The symbolisation of any culture and the constitution of subjectivity in its terms of legitimacy occur in the material world of production. The changing material condition in the economic production of reality changes the mode of symbolisation in a culture. Genders are cultural constructs, to the degree that cultures operate within the material forces constitutional to the economic production of Reality. Being on the post/colonial periphery of global capitalism creates and constitutes a mode of economic production of reality, which is potentially emancipatory from the outreaching forces operative at the centres of capitalist modernity. To the degree that working in the post/colonial outpost is far from the centres of capitalist modernity, there is that much distance from its instrumental rationalism. In the economic production of reality and in the creative counter-Symbolisation of the Real, the process of globalisation can be countered in matters at once material and aesthetic.

Visions of the Invisible

Between counter-Symbolising the Real and re-Symbolising the Possible, Iranian cinema has visually narrated itself by seeking to acculturate a nation's vision of itself – and with it the manner in which the unknowing subject becomes metonymically self-conscious of itself. If Kiarostami's and Makhmalbaf's cinemas are two visual modes of the de-Symbolising return to the Imaginary, each in its own way, then the cinema of Bani-Etemad is one of counter-Symbolisation of a whole culture, by means of a visual assault on its most vulnerable vista – namely, its constitution of femininity. To see her work at full throttle, we may concentrate on the three successive moves of *Nargess* (1991), *The Blue-Veiled* (1994) and *The May Lady* (1998).

In her daring narrative of a *menage-à-trois* in *Nargess* (1992), Bani-Etemad sought a radical counter-Symbolisation of the very constitution of sexuality. The love affair between the young thief, Adel, and his visibly older lover, Afagh, is narrated with such dark and passionate intensity that with this one single stroke Bani-Etemad has countered generations of two pathologically contradictory and yet thematically complementary moves in the over- and/or de-sexualisation of women in Iranian cinema. Between the paralysing chastity of the ever-virgin, would-be bride, waiting-for-the-hero and the pathological investment of promiscuous sexuality in a whore – the two common staples of *Jaheli* cinema, and that of Kimia'i, in particular – Bani-Etemad has inserted the provocative character of Afagh. She is aware and confident of her sexuality without ever collapsing into either frivolity or abstruseness. There is a quiet dignity about Afagh, a subdued self-awareness, a factual realism, about her demeanour. Next to Afagh's rugged but assertive dignity, Adel is reduced to complete emotional shambles, his sub-lumpenist sexuality contingent on Afagh's generosity. What is successfully shattered and dissolved in front of Bani-Etemad's confident camera is the presumption of the primacy of masculine sexuality. Afagh is, in fact, at the centre of both the sexual and the narrative tension of *Nargess*. This reversal of the primacy of masculine sexuality Bani-Etemad achieves even though it is Afagh who is being obviously abandoned by Adel for a younger and more 'respectable' woman. While steadfastly holding on to her Factual Realism, quintessential to her counter-Symbolising vision, Bani-Etemad both sexually and narratively holds Afagh at the centre of all events. *Nargess* is inundated with a powerful erotic tension, despite the fact that there is (for obvious censorial reasons) not a single sex scene in the film.

To see how Bani-Etemad holds Afagh at the centre of the sexual tension in *Nargess*, the most compelling moment to examine is when Afagh volunteers to go and ask for the hand of Nargess for her lover Adel. Equally rooted in Bani-Etemad's Factual Realism, this single move dismantles the patriarchally-constituted sexuality of both genders. Afagh suffers all the miserable consequences of having facilitated the marriage of the man she loves with a younger woman. But the dark entanglement of the suffering centralises even further her presence as the focal point of the narrative as the defining catalyst of sexuality. The ingenious achievement of Bani-Etemad in her characterisation of Afagh is precisely in her Factual Realism, in her camera not blinking even once at the brute reality and yet shattering all the fabricated myths of feminine passivity. Afagh is the defining moment of *Nargess*, both in character and disposition, in emotional intensity and moral authority. As such, she is the acid test of a whole Symbolising culture of repression.

To de-Symbolise the Real by holding a woman at the centre of a sexual entanglement smack in the heart of an Islamic Republic is not enough if the move ultimately is to re-Symbolise the Possible. Conspicuously absent from the love-triangle among Afagh, Adel and Nargess is any child. The *de facto* bracketing of the nuclear family, as the coagulated institution of patriarchy, is the preliminary move to dis-entangle the moment of the Oedipal crisis. The triangulation of the two women and one man is conspicuously on the margin of society, on the site of social rejects and the abjectly poor. This narrative simplicity which on the surface just creates more room for dramatic tension does something far more drastic. It traces the patriarchal Symbolic back to the state of the Imaginary in order to expose it aggressively to a counter-Symbolisation. The strategy of counter-Symbolisation, and of the conjunctive dismantling of the metaphysics that goes along with it, is directly anti-Oedipal because here all we see are a woman/mother and a man/son operating on strictly instinctual raptures. In the presence of Afagh, Adel is de-Oedipalised, conquers his absent father by having his mother, and with him the entire constructed history of gender-constitution is de-Oedipalised. What makes this rather revolutionary counter-subjection of both the masculine and the feminine possible is no work of mere cinematic vision. It is deeply rooted in Bani-Etemad's committed, almost instinctual, dedication to Factual Realism. It is as if she is condemned to see and make others see the factually real, and yet begin to flower her restoration of a radically different kind of being, directly from the site of her presence-in-the-world.

Dis-arresting the moment of entrance into the Oedipal, or culturally reversing it, *Nargess* is the site of the dismantling of what Deleuze and Guattari have called 'the Imperialism of the Oedipus'.[31] 'Oedipus restrained', as Deleuze and Guattari assert, 'is the figure of daddy-mommy-me triangle, the familial constellation in person'.[32] Bani-Etemad breaks that triangle by substituting it with a far more real coagulation, smack from the middle of her already extraordinary career as a documentary filmmaker. The *menage-à-trois*, here, substituting what Deleuze and Guattari identify as 'the Holy Family', is a thief, his older lover and his younger wife. By breaking all those possessive adjectives, 'his', by reducing the turbulent relationship to pure catharsis, and by narrating the story on the premise of a breathtakingly Factual Realism, Bani-Etemad launches her effective counter-Symbolisation of the Real from the depth of her documented reading of Iranian society and targets nothing short of a total dismantling of the Empire of the Oedipus and of the tyranny of Oedipalised psychosis. The result is the cinematic cosmovision of an Imaginary de-Oedipalisation of the whole culture by an active counter-Symbolisation of its claims on the Real. The imposing edifice of patriarchal order, from its Symbolic ordering of the culture to its Metaphysical transparency, is hereby visually de-subjected.

Dis-arresting the Oedipal by dismantling 'the Holy Family' (which here authorises a supra-denominator signifier for globalised capitalism) is done in front of Bani-Etemad's incurably factual camera. She does not *invent* that revolutionary dismantling via an ideological manifesto, a fact that many of her Iranian critics have failed to understand, and as a result they have accused her of anti-feminism.[33] She proclaims it through her incessant attachment to the Factual Realism of her camera. It is the poverty and misery of Afagh and Adel that brings them together, their being socially discharged, economically disadvantaged, culturally demonised. And it is because of Adel's pathetic attempt to be socially mobile by marrying a 'respectable' young woman that they are separated. This is not a revolutionary manifesto. This is a piece of brutal reality that Bani-Etemad confidently, with the experience of decades of deeply engaged involvement with the plight of the poor and the disenfranchised, has achieved. The kind of hope that Bani-Etemad cultivates has to emerge from the most gut-wrenching fixation with realities as they are. This is what ultimately distinguishes her realism from the realisms of Kiarostami's and Makhmalbaf's, which liberate and set loose an entirely different emotive modulation.

Bani-Etemad's Factual Realism is far from being transgressively mute. Here, she has an uncanny ability to plant the seeds of a vertiginously transgressive jolt in the soil of a perfectly realistic narrative. Central to the formative move of *Nargess* is the active de-Symbolisation of the Oedipal via a *suggestion* of the incestuous. It is extremely crucial to note, before anything else, that Afagh's and Adel's is primarily an amorous relationship between an older woman and a younger man. That Afagh had initially 'adopted' Adel is a powerful reversal of what in the language of prostitution in Iran is called '*neshandan*'. *Neshandan* literally means 'to have someone sit down', but in the bordello house lingo it means for a man to put an exclusive claim on a prostitute, to which she agrees; from then on, she will see no other man. Afagh's relationship with Adel is precisely a reversal of *neshandan* – namely, she has put an exclusive claim on him. This practice is also common and has a name. The invariably younger lover of an older woman is called a '*faseq*', which literary means 'the man with whom she commits sin'. In such cases, she is usually older, wealthier and more powerful, whereas he is younger, poorer and inexperienced. Within this doubly transgressive *suggestion*, further energised by the intensity of its contravening charge by the fact that both Adel and Afagh are thieves, the amorous liaison only *intimates* an incestuous relationship. Adel is not *really* Afagh's son, he is *like* her son. To keep the power of Bani-Etemad's vision fully charged, we need to remain constant on the borderline of that transgressive *suggestion*. If we lose sight of this suggestion, we will lose the site of Bani-Etemad's Factual Realism. The active imagination of a suggestively incestuous relationship between Afagh-the-mother and Adel-the son successfully breaks the cultural constitution of the Oedipal and forces it to atrophy back, to use Kristeva's language, to its *semiotic* stage.[34] The suggestion of the incestuous in *Nargess* dismantles the Oedipal via a conspiracy of the mother/lover and her son/lover against the inconsequential father. The thematic genealogy of such conspiracies goes all the way back to the *Shahnameh* and the story of Seyavash and Sudabeh, in which the potential alliance of Seyavash, the young Prince, and Sudabeh, his young step-mother, against Key Kavus, Seyavash's father and Sudabeh's husband ultimately fails because Seyavash sees his own succession to his father jeopardised in such a potential coalition. The Iranian/Islamic reading of Seyavash has, of course, opted to interpret his refusal to respond to Sudabeh's sexual advances as an indication of his heroic 'nobility'.[35]

Bani-Etemad's visual de-Symbolisation of the Real and the simultaneous re-Symbolisation of the Possible works through a transgressive *suggestion* that does not violently confront the Metaphysical ordering of the Real, but effectively jolts it. The strategy works precisely because it is aesthetically predicated on such a *visual* de-Symbolisation of the Real that effectively divests its Symbolic ordering of all its regulating grammar. The thematic dismantling of the Oedipal in Bani-Etemad's cinema, as an example, squarely rests on her visual cosmovision. The place of the inarticulate visual Imaginary, if we can bear with her Factual Realism, is central to her project of counter-Symbolisation. By the time of *Nargess*, some two decades into her career as a documentary filmmaker, Bani-Etemad had already traversed a long way from her earliest attempts to translate visually her preoccupation with documentaries into a rich realistic cinema. Her command of the camera, the depth of emotions she invests in every shot, her acute sense of *mise-en-scène*, motion and camera movements, and ultimately her judicious sense of light, shadow, shapes and darkness come to a rich maturity in *The Blue-Veiled*. Here, her sense of alignment in her long shots reveal her impeccable awareness of proportionality and the range of the sentiments they generate and sustain. Trains, train tracks, roads, highways and long chimneys are among the vertical and horizontal lines that Bani-Etemad uses to graft the range of rigid sentiments operative in a repressively routinised culture. To remain factually realistic to that culture and yet visually intimate, a radical counter-Symbolisation of its repressive measures is a specific gift of Bani-Etemad's cinema.

There is thus a transubstantial movement in Bani-Etemad's cinema, from the visual counter-Symbolisation of the Real towards the re-Symbolisation of the Possible via a thematic challenging of the dominant. The result is not just a jolt that questions the grammatical ordering of the Symbolic, but even more seriously the metaphysical ordering of the Real. Echoing the central theme of *Nargess*, *The Blue-Veiled* is a forbidden love story between a rich and powerful widower and a poor but dignified young woman. Far more important than what happens in front of Bani-Etemad's camera is what occurs behind it. Paramount in the telling of this story is how exactly a woman director can tell a love story in an 'Islamic Republic'. The sheer fact of a woman telling a love story on a wide and voluptuous screen in a land of veiled faces, denied sexuality, concealed bodies and distorted sensuality is perhaps the most significant part of Bani-Etemad's film. In order to tell her story, Bani-Etemad reaches deep into the most recent and distant memories of her cultural repertoire. There is detailed attention to the semiotics of naming in *The Blue-Veiled*. The name of the widower at the centre of the story is Rasul Rahmani, which means 'The Messenger of the Merciful' and thus conjures up the memory of the Prophet of Islam. Like Muhammad, Rasul Rahmani has lost his pious and dignified wife halfway through his life. The Prophetic figure of Rasul Rahmani, emphasised by his genuine care about his employees and customers, rides into the tomato field of his agricultural business in a white car, the colour of which provides Bani-Etemad with yet another visual remembrance of classical folk tales of saints and heroes riding on their white horses. She also calls the woman who functions as a messenger between the two lovers 'Kabutar' (pigeon), again reminiscing about a critical element in classical Persian story-telling. Bani-Etemad's *semiotic* sense of names, shapes, objects and colours assumes a mythical proportion when it comes to the point of visually insinuating moments of intimacy between a man and a woman. All such features are geared towards a visual assimilation of the audience into the culturally familiar where the most transgressive counter-Symbolics can be generated and sustained.

'Semiotic Chora'

How exactly is this counter-Symbolic to move from one creative occasion to another, as it equally moves from the *semiotic* to the *symbolic*, to continue with Kristeva's distinction?[36] As Kristeva has taken the Lacanian lead, the *semiotic* stage is the zone of the libidinal energy, the domain of the mother, where, following Plato's *Timaeus*, she locates a haven she calls the *semiotic chora*. The *chora* is the space of the subversion of the subject, where the libidinal energy is not yet regulated by the cultural mandates of propriety and normalcy. Beyond the *semiotic* and into the *symbolic*, the Oedipal is inaugurated and the Law of the Father imposed. The dominance of the *symbolic* over the *semiotic* is, however, precarious. For Kristeva, the triad of subversive forces – madness, holiness and the poetic – creates counter-institutional moments of rupturing the *symbolic*. Poetry as the transgressive breaching of the *symbolic* points to specific moments of the transgressive shattering of the *symbolic*. Now, if we consider the fact that sexual differences occur precisely at the moment of entry into the *symbolic*, then any aesthetic strategy of arresting the Oedipal pulls the symbolic authority of cultural institutions back to the open-endedness of their *semiotic* origins. Kristeva associates the pre-Oedipal with the polymorphous erotogenic zones when culture is not yet carved unto the body. There is always a tense relationship between the body as the repressed reservoir of the *semiotic* and culture as the (successful) *symbolisation* of its controlling mechanisms.

The tension between the *body* and the *culture*, and between the *semiotic* energy of the visual and the *symbolic* grammar of the forbidden, is nowhere more evident than in the critical corners of cultural taboos. The *suggestion* of the incestuous moves from *Nargess* (1991) to *The Blue-Veiled* (1994), but it is strategically reversed. Here, we have an older lover/father and a younger lover/daughter being entangled in a love affair.

The complete reversal of roles here is crucial. In *Nargess*, Afagh is older, wealthier and more powerful, while her lover Adel is younger, poorer and less powerful; in *The Blue-Veiled*, Rasul Rahmani is older, richer and more powerful, while the object of his affections, Nobar Kordani, is younger, poorer and less powerful. As two bookends, *Nargess* and *The Blue-Veiled* transgressively complement each other: one *suggests* an incestuous relationship of the mother-son type, the other that of the father-daughter pair. Whereas in the case of *Nargess* we have an active dismantling of the Oedipal by the son having the mother, in *The Blue-Veiled* we have a sexual seduction of the father by the daughter, which results in the patriarchal de-authorisation of the father.

The seduction of the father/lover by the daughter/lover is done in the absence of the mother, Rasul's dead wife, and equally in the absence of her substitute, the daughter whom Rasul loves most and who is abroad. The other two daughters are violently against Nobar, because she is going to have what they desire most and cannot have, a *suggestion* intensified in the full view of their two extraordinarily feeble husbands. Rasul, as a result, is completely surrounded by seductive daughters, three of his own, as well as Nobar to whom he is allowed to be attracted and Nobar's even younger sister Senobar. In what is intimated as Rasul and Nobar's wedding night, Senobar, her younger sister, has a visibly intermediary function as a sexual icon when she sleeps on Rasul's lap, while Nobar, true to her name, offers her husband fresh fruit. The complete absence of the father-figure in *Nargess*, in which the de-Oedipalisation can effectively take place, is mirrored in *The Blue-Veiled*, by de-authorising the father via a collective seduction by all his daughter-figures. The result, however, is the same. Bani-Etemad captures the moment of Oedipalisation, right before the pregnant energy of the *semiotic* is to yield to the grammatical order of the *symbolic*.

In *The May Lady*, the *suggestion* of the incestuous is extended even further and brought to a radical conclusion. Here, Forough-the-mother and Mani-the-son live together in the total absence of Mani's father and the visual absence of Forough's lover. In *The May Lady*, as a result, the total absence of Forough's husband replicates the total absence of Rasul's wife in *The Blue-Veiled*, while the visual absence of Forough's lover, Amir Rahbar, is replicating the visual absence of Rasul's youngest daughter who is abroad. The oral construction of Amir Rahbar in *The May Lady*, then, has an antecedent in Bani-Etemad's cinema in the oral construction of Rasul's younger daughter who too is characterised by telephone messages and long-distance conversations. The incestuous *suggestion* between Forough and Mani is thus narrated on a purely *semiotic* plane and launched ferociously against the whole monumentality of the totally *symbolised* culture of suppression that Forough and Mani both face. Forough's attempt to make a documentary about the 'ideal mother' while trying to raise a teenage boy in the suffocating atmosphere of an Islamic Republic is the heavily symbolised and consolidated cultural context against which the raw *semiotic* energy of the perennially pre-Oedipal subjection of Mani has taken place. Mani is palpably androgynous, and his barely hidden and visibly suggested homosexuality is the most visible sign of the arrest of the Oedipal in this father-less environment where the Oedipal moment has been kept at bay. The visual absence of Forough's lover, Amir Rahbar, allows for the libidinal *semiotic* of Forough-the-mother and Mani-the-son, as substitutional lovers, to remain at the explosively *suggestive* level and to never fully collapse into the abyss of raw libidinal energy. The orality of Rahbar's character, which is always exclusive to Forough's ears, makes him at once absent, so that Mani's pre-Oedipal stays there; yet present, so that Forough's sexuality can potentially burst onto the scene in the very last shot of the film. Bani-Etemad has prepared visually for that sexual encounter with the double voice-over of Forough and Rahbar, when his letters begin to be narrated by Rahbar's voice and then Forough's voice joins in, as in his initiating the sexual encounter and Forough responding.

In the sheer tenacity of her visual fixation with the factually real, the transgressively explosive bordercrossing that her camera perpetrates and the revolutionary counter-Symbolisation of a whole culture, no one comes even close to Bani-Etemad in Iranian cinema. One would much better understand the revolutionary character of her cinema when one sees it against the visual re-constitution of the Real sub-serving, rather than subverting, the metaphysical ordering of the Symbolic. Playing with variations on the Karbala theme, for example, has provided Iranian filmmakers with much opportunity for a dramatic re-narration of tragedy, sacrifice and redemptive suffering, all of which are put squarely at the service of the infanticidal Symbolics and an active authorisation of the Oedipal. Kiumars Pour-Ahmad's *For the Sake of Hanieh/Beh Khater-e Hanieh* (1995) is a good example of this genre. The active remembrance of the Karbala motif in *For the Sake of Hanieh* very much serves an active re-constitution of the Oedipal. When the father of a southern family in Bushehr dies while playing *dammam* (a kind of drum played on both ends while hanging from the neck), his young son's ambition becomes to take his father's place as the drummer in the Muharram ceremony. The new role of the young boy, Bashiroo, also requires that he provide for 'his' family by doing various jobs. Returning from one of these jobs, he drops the money he has earned on the ground where his mother is sitting. Offended by this disrespectful gesture, the mother slaps Bashiroo in the face and tells him that he has to come and offer his earning to his mother respectfully, 'like a man'.

Pour-Ahmad relies heavily on the visual remembrance of thirst, central to the renewed memory of the Karbala motif, and makes sure that Bashiroo's repeated attempts to drink water are thwarted by various events. Bashiroo has a handicapped sister, Hanieh, for whose sake and in the hope that she will be miraculously cured he has vowed to play his father's drum through the night of the tenth day of Muharram, the most sacrosanct night in Shi'i collective memory, when Imam Hossein was martyred. The elder of the community, the man in charge of the Muharram ceremony, refuses to allow Bashiroo to play the drum, lest the older and more eligible members of the community would be offended. Finally, the tired, thirsty, disappointed and heartbroken Bashiroo is accidentally locked in a cellar where the drums are kept. About to pass out from exhaustion and thirst, Bashiroo is bitten by a scorpion. Bashiroo kills the scorpion and, to save his life, he uses the broken piece of a glass, from which he once tried to drink water, to cut himself where the scorpion has bitten him. In despair, he tries to drink water from a well which proves to contain undrinkable water. Just before he completely passes out, he notices the drums in the cellar. In the quiet darkness of the night outside, the people of the community, including Bashiroo's mother and sister, are awakened by the muffled sounds of a drum. The elder of the community and his wife trace the muffled sound to their cellar. They open the locked door, and out comes the haunting figure of Bashiroo, moved by a spirit of inexplicable force and gravity. His visage pale, ashen and livid, his eyes emanating a mesmerising gaze, his completely white lips dried like the barren surface of land ravaged in a draught, and yet a drum hanging from his thin neck, Bashiroo walks out of the cellar, with the old man and his wife having no choice but to make way for him to come out. In this the most moving sequence of the film, Bashiroo plays his drum as he walks through the village, covered by the night and the thunderous shower of a bounteous rain.

What such films as Kiumars Pour-Ahmad's *For the Sake of Hanieh* perpetuate in the Shi'i memory of Persian patriarchy, Mohsen Makhmalbaf – Bani-Etemad's kindred soul, but her camera working at an entirely different angle – undermines in his disquieting tragi-comedy *The Actor/Honarpisheh* (1993). *The Actor* is narrated with such visual precision and balance that Makhmalbaf's Felliniesque camera always suspends the audience between the two conflicting emotions of laughter and sorrow, viewing comedy and witnessing tragedy. A comedian husband and his wife driven to 'madness' by the communal expectation of her having a (preferably male) child become the centrepiece of a deeply moving meditation on the nature of reason and madness, love and sacrifice, private anguish and public despair. In this beautifully crafted anti-tale that for eighty-six minutes carries the audience through a rollercoaster of conflicting emotions, Makhmalbaf reaches for a Virtual Realism that has been the trademark of his craft. What is particularly disturbing in this film is Makhmalbaf's almost vicious inventiveness to break loose the customary boundaries of comedy and tragedy, sanity and madness, reason and unreason, life and art, art and decadence, and – perhaps most subversively of all – masculinity and femininity. All of these are done first and foremost with a Felliniesque camera staging an uncanny ability to generate and sustain creative confusion, unresolvable tension, asphyxiating anxiety and, above all, the debilitating terror of not knowing whether one is to laugh or cry, embrace or escape, kneel down or run away.

Through Kiarostami's Actual Realism, Bani-Etemad's Factual Realism and Makhmalbaf's Virtual Realism, just to distinguish among three different takes on reality, the received Iranian culture is constitutionally triangulated by a triple act of aesthetic encounters, as done never before in its long and everlasting memory. Thus, a number of key Iranian filmmakers come together to take Jacques Lacan's psychoanalytic theories beyond their Eurocentric limitations, and through them the idea of the 'imaginary' phase in the constitution of the psyche helps us expose a link between visual arts and the subconscious tapping into the otherwise repressed mythic moments of a culture. This is where we see how cinema stages a visual counter-Symbolic – when one mode of cultural production can carve into the metaphysical ordering of the Real. The collapsing movement from the Imaginary into the Symbolic, if we follow Lacan's trajectory, creates an open-ended spiral that sucks in the entire fusional relationship of the psycho-social and the Imaginary, all to the detriment of the Imaginary and at the service of the Symbolic. This is how the best of Iranian cinema has kept the Imaginary visual alive and well and at arm's length from the danger of that collapse into the totalising Symbolic. The result is the evidence of a dynamic effervescence at the heart of the metonymic culture that facilitates an ever-renewed encounter with its mythic memories – as when, by the end of Nima's poem 'My Home is a Cloud', the cloud is about to rain:

> My home is a cloud –
> But the cloud is about to rain –
> Recalling my bright old days now lost
> I sit upon the sunshine
> Overlooking he sea ... [37]

There is no totalising Symbolics at work here – for the fresh and flowering memories of the present thus enable the recollection of all the mythic memories of the cosmic pasts.

PART III

HOME AND EXILE

7

The Cinema of Solitude

And this is I:

A solitary woman
At the threshold of a cold season –
At the beginning of grasping
The polluted existence of the earth –
And the simple sadness of the sky –
And the inability of these cemented hands ...[1]

Forough Farrokhzad, '*Iman Biavarim beh Aghaz-e Fasl-e Sard*/
Let us Believe in the Commencement of the Cold Season' (1973)

Among the masterpieces of Iranian cinema, few have achieved the status of Amir Naderi's *Davandeh/The Runner* (1984) as a landmark event that defined much that has happened after its release.[2] Although it exists halfway through Amir Naderi's film career, *The Runner* marked the height of the awareness of a global audience of extraordinary developments in Iranian cinema. Much has happened since the mid-1980s when the film took the Three Continent Film Festival by storm. Later, the names of Abbas Kiarostami, Mohsen Makhmalbaf, Jafar Panahi, Bahman Qobadi, or Asghar Farhadi overshadowed Naderi, who has long since moved to New York, Los Angeles and Tokyo, although he continues a productive cinematic career (with considerable global success). Whether or not he can even be considered an 'Iranian filmmaker' today is subject to debate. However, the importance of *The Runner* in defining much of Iranian cinema's recent history remains the same.

The most celebrated film of Amir Naderi, *The Runner* is in many ways an autobiographical film, and it is this factor that became a critical component of what has now flourished in Iranian cinema at large. When Amir Naderi was six years old, he once told me in a conversation, he was accidentally stranded on a ship and taken to a faraway land of which to this day he does not know where it was. The story of this mysterious voyage, indelibly carved into Naderi's childhood memories, is very simple. An uncle, the husband of the aunt who had adopted him after the death of his mother, used to work as a painter on a ship in Abadan, where Naderi was born and raised. Amir was assigned to bring lunch to this uncle every day. Afterwards, he would roam through the ship and play on its various decks and floors. One day, as he found his way to the lowest level, where the engines were, he fell asleep on some potato sacks. Soon after he had fallen asleep, the ship pulled anchor and left the port, carrying the six-year-old Amir to its next destination. He woke up frightened and was soon discovered by the crew. He was kept on board for about ten or eleven days during which time he remembers only the sea. At their next destination, Amir remembered seeing a traffic cop with white gloves, controlling traffic on some street off the sea front, where the ship had come ashore. The ship then returned to Abadan, and Amir returned to his aunt, now obviously terrified as to what could have become of him. Amir reported that his aunt told him that for about six months after that incident he was not able to speak a word, and the first thing that he said after he started talking again was that he wanted to leave on a ship for some faraway land.

A Nocturnal Journey

What happened to Amir Naderi during this strange, ambiguous, outlandish journey? He speaks of it in realistic terms, like another biographical detail of his life. But did it really happen, or did he dream it? All indications suggest that it really did happen. He also reminisces how, when he was eleven years old, he tried to run away to Kuwait. However, he did not make it beyond a couple of islands off the coast of Abadan. That there has always been a restless disposition about Naderi, and a desire to be somewhere else, is evident in practically all his films. But central to the story that he narrates about his accidental journey on board a cargo ship is saturated with the imageries of a lonely child, a solitary *Mosafer* (sojourner), lost on an unknown ship, leaving a familiar island for an unknown destination, of which Naderi only has a memory, seen through the small window of a cabin where he was stranded. That small window transformed into the lens of his camera. His cinema is like watching the world through a child's point of view, through a small window in that fictional or factual journey.

The abandoned ship in *The Runner*, on which Amiru lives, is the miasmatical memory of a ship on which Amir Naderi has always dreamt of living, departing for another destination. In some sense, he still lives on that ship. His small apartment in downtown Manhattan where I regularly visited him for about a decade has a remarkable similarity to a cabin aboard an abandoned ship. Central to this ship, the abode of both Amir and Amiru, is the solitary disposition of its whereabouts, a space removed from society, suspended in mid-air between his dreams and his visions as a filmmaker. What is the meaning of this beautiful solitude in and about Amir Naderi?

A poor orphaned boy growing up on the seashore of a nameless land, Amiru is fascinated with every moving object – huge ships, small boats, speeding cars, lazy bicycles, noisy motorcycles, rambunctious trucks, slumbering trains, flying airplanes – anything and everything that moves by itself and can carry him away from where he is. He is terrified when he sees a man with one leg, his other leg having been amputated, or an aging woman, or a crippled man. They are people who cannot run away. In the absence of any access to a moving vehicle that can carry him away from where he is, Amiru runs. He runs until he can barely breathe. When a man drinks a glass of water from a bucket full of ice water that Amiru carries around to make a living and then absconds on his bike and runs away, Amiru chases after him, both for the challenge of catching him and to get his money. When another man steals a piece of his ice, Amiru runs after him, grabs hold of his ice and runs away, both for the triumphant joy of out-speeding the much more muscular man and for reaching his destination before the ice melts.

Running has become essential to Amiru – definitive of who he is. What is he running from? What is he running to? Nothing and everything. Running is his state of being. He becomes mesmerised by moving objects. Anything that moves and can carry him away from where he is. Because he cannot gain access to these objects, he runs. He runs because of the indeterminacy of not being where he is not. There is a scene early in the film, as he and his friends are collecting empty bottles that foreigners have thrown into the sea. They are suddenly attacked by a shark. A fisherman alerts the kids, and they frantically run out of the sea. Amiru comes out, frightened out of his wits, not by the possibility that he could have been killed, but by the terror that the shark could have eaten his limbs, his claim to mobility, to running away. It is wrong to read Amiru as someone simply running away from poverty. Amiru is poor, but his life is not desolate or joyless. He has the company of a band of young, equally poor boys, with whom he plays soccer, rides bikes, chases after running trains and shares joyous songs on top of speeding wagons. His relationship with his friends is not free of quarrels. Poverty reigns supreme – to be sure. But there is a serenity about Amiru, a gentility about his manners, a solidity to his friendship. While trying to run away (from nothing and everything), Amiru lives a rich and fulfilling life – rich in the dimensions of his solitude that he explores, fulfilling in the company of friends he keeps. There is a scene where Amiru is washing his shirt in the abandoned ship (his home), where Amir Naderi leads his camera to come close (ever so gently) to a diverted gaze on the face of this poor, orphaned, solitary soul. That diverted gaze on the face of Amiru is the look of humanity at a loss, facing an abyss beyond recognition. At that moment, *The Runner* is no longer the story of a lonely boy, and Amiru is no longer a poor orphan. Amir Naderi pictures our entire humanity at a loss.

Naderi is capable of the cruellest insights when his camera gets so close to his character's soul. It is as if he has seen something terrorising, a nightmare perhaps, a metaphysical cruelty beyond our human measures. He has seen the absurdity at the root of a solitary being that for him is the state of humanity at large. He seems to have seen a disturbing nightmare, the solitary visage of a journey, and he has mastered a way to show and tell it – ever so softly, gently even, for the vision he wishes to reveal is no source of solace.

Amiru is illiterate. He collects pictures of airplanes and such and hangs them on the walls of his cabin/room on his ship. He goes to a magazine seller, buys more magazines to look at their pictures. His inability to read and write bothers him, so he enrols at a local school. At school, his teacher begins to teach him the letters of the Persian alphabet. The result is not that Amiru now learns how to read and write. The result is something else. Amiru does not learn the letters of the Persian alphabet. Conversely, Amir Naderi teaches the Persian alphabet's letters to un-learn themselves. Amiru, guided by Amir Naderi, takes the letters of the Persian alphabet to the seaside so that they can unlearn their repressed significance. The alphabet sequence of *The Runner* is a memorable example of literacy beyond words. Sounds of water, wind, fire and dust collect momentum to syncopate Amiru's recitations of the Persian alphabet.

Amir Naderi himself is not a very literate person. He dropped out of school early in life and has since had no formal education. To him, the letters of the alphabet are strange creatures, not just in Persian (as we see them in *The Runner*), but also in English (which appear in his *Marathon* [2003]). To him and to his visual disposition, letters of the alphabet are mere signs. What are these things, he seems to ask? Who are they? And who, by the way, gave them this authority to sound, seem and suggest one thing or another? Amiru takes the letters of the Persian alphabet to the seaside, into the heart of rocks, waves, and starts memorising them – there for Amir Naderi to teach them to behave. Amiru memorises them to the beat of the waves storming the sea rocks, to the sound of wind, water, fire and dust (the theme that Amir Naderi will pick up in his next film, *Water, Wind, Dust* [1989]). In the alphabet sequence of *The Runner*, humanity is reduced to literacy, literacy to words, words to letters, letters to alphabets, alphabets to sounds, sounds to noises, and these noises are given back to the earth. What Abbas Kiarostami would later do in his mature cinema by way of his ingenious fictive transparency of the real, Amir Naderi had already achieved in *The Runner* through his trademark visual realism.

Ice as a Floating Signifier

The final sequence of *The Runner* is one of the most memorable scenes in world cinema. Amiru and his buddies have made yet another wager as to who runs faster. A huge block of ice is placed near the inferno of a roaring fire caused by an underground gas reservoir. The object of the wager is to be the first to get to that block of ice before it melts. What do people see when they see this block of ice near that roaring fire? A universe. Those two items are insignia of a universe – ice, the soul of salvation from the ungodly heat of summer, placed next to a fire whose raging flames exude an elemental violence at once life-affirming and deadly. The visual contrast of the block of ice and

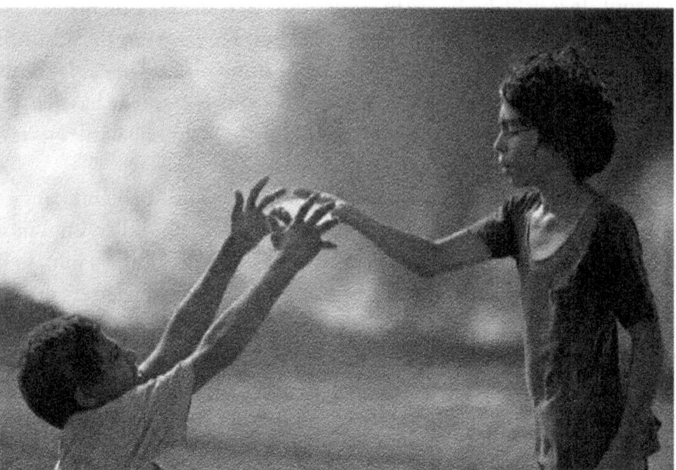

Figure 7.1 *Amir Naderi,* The Runner *(1985). (Photo: Courtesy of Amir Naderi)*

the raging fire command the camera's undivided, almost fixated attention. Again, collected here are fire, wind, water and earth, and racing towards them are boys running from a fate they cannot articulate – a useless flight, yet made meaningful temporarily, by virtue of the significance it has *ipso facto* occasioned and will soon lose, as soon as the game is over.

Gathered in the anonymity of this elemental space is a cosmic moment, when history has no longer much of a claim over reality, where reality has become evidence *sui generis*. Amir Naderi is a master of crafting these moments – where time and space vacate the site of their articulation of all signs of historicity – and thus make it ripe for a renewed mythology of its own. These are metaphysical moments, where Naderi has brought humanity at large for a quick look, a cursory visit. We are no longer in Iran, or Asia, or Africa, or planet earth, or anywhere in that vicinity. Here we have entered the miasmatical zone of what medieval Persian philosophers would call *Sarmad* – 'the everlasting'. Time is suspended here, space morphed into a cinematic site of visual contemplation. There is no sign of society – solitude is writ large. We are inside Amir Naderi's creative intelligence. All signifiers have metamorphosed into their originary signs – signs that signify in mythic terms.

The marathon begins, and Amiru and his friends rush to race towards the melting ice by the inferno. The challenge is to be the first to get there before the ice has melted. On the way, between the origin of that match and its destination, a brutal banality becomes evident. If you cannot get there, then you must also prevent others from succeeding. In that match, Amir Naderi has discovered and displayed a barbarity of unsurpassed terror in the very heart of our innocence. Amiru and his friends sabotage each other's progress, blocking each other's way, as they run towards the fire. In no other major Iranian film has a banality of such disturbing proportion been so vividly and honestly captured. The kids do everything to be the first to get to the ice, or at the very least prevent anyone else from getting there. Amiru gets there, against all odds, against all that was meant to prevent him. He gets to the ice by the fire, reaches for the barrel on which the piece of ice is (was) placed. He begins a triumphant, joyous, jubilant beat of victory on the barrel/drum. He is calling out: '*Barandeh shodom*'. I won. Beating on the drum, on the melted ice, rhythmically, splashing the water, he is ecstatic with joy. He picks up the last remaining piece of ice, lifts it above his head and begins a triumphant dance, dancing to the rhythm and the tune of his own victory. He brings the piece of ice to his lips, drinking his victory, juice of his exultant defeat of the fire. Reality finally creeps in, and Amiru comes to his senses. He turns around, looks at his fallen friends, his comrades turned rivals. They beg for a drop of water. They are passing out from thirst in the vicinity of the brutal fire. Amiru holds out the piece of ice. It is no longer a trophy. The moment of myth has passed. The first boy immediately behind Amiru drinks from the ice, then passes it on. The boys unite in the last drop of life that the melting ice can give. Life is restored. Amiru is victorious.

At the moment of his triumph, Amiru is the picture of solitude. No one is there to share his victory, his joy, his accomplishment. Amir Naderi's is a cinema of solitude – solitude as the aesthetic articulation of social alienation and cultural anomie. And yet, this sense of anomie is not ailing or fraught. It is predicated on an enabling solitude, pregnant with all of its own opposites. As an artistic space, Naderi's cinema is the site of a creative transformation of alienation and anomie, for cinema is where society comes together in solitude – we always watch a film in the company of strangers, in the social presence of all our singular solitude. The result is a creative entry into the social function of solitude, constitutional to a creative space that is no longer culture-specific, in that it smells and looks local, and yet it is global by virtue of the creative space it has cultivated in solitude, in a socially significant, communally enabling and emotively charged solitude.

Simple, Solitary and Serene

The solitude definitive of Amiru's character extends beyond *The Runner* and runs through the rest of Amir Naderi's cinema. Naderi did his haphazard apprenticeship in cinema in the 1950s and 1960s, first in southern Iran and then in Tehran, where he was exposed to the best of world cinema in the capital of a thriving cosmopolitan culture. Almost all the eleven feature films that Naderi directed between 1970 and 1986, while he was in Iran, deal with a solitary figure at the centre of their narrative. All such solitary characters, in one way or another, are narrative translations of his own solitary life, orphaned at a very young age and raised by a maternal aunt until he was old enough to leave home for good. Most of the menial work that Amiru does in *The Runner* to make a living – selling ice water, shining shoes, collecting bottles from the sea – are jobs that Naderi himself had in his childhood. His first cinema-related job was as still photographer on film sets of the most important filmmakers of his time. On those sets he did more than just taking pictures. He listened, watched and learned the minutest aspects of the craft of filmmaking. In those pictures that he took, he looked for more than just the proper angle and matching light on an actor or a scene. He framed the forms of reality the way he envisioned them in his own solitary mind. Still photography, snapshots of what there was to see, and solitary visions of reality became definitive of his cinema.

When Amir Naderi began making his first films, that sense of overwhelming solitude was already evident in his cinematic vision. In *Tangna/Deadlock* (1973), we meet Ali Khoshdast, a solitary soul roaming through the slums of Tehran, engaged in petty crimes, dreaming high, a victim of his own delusions, a paramount sense of anomie written into the very fabric of his loneliness. Tehran as a cosmopolis emerges in its full urban landscape in the background of Ali Khoshdast's soaring solitude. The same Ali Khoshdast resurfaces in Naderi's next film, *Tangsir* (1973), where we follow the legendary life of Zar Mammad, a local hero who singularly rebels against tyranny and kills the officials who have been tormenting him. Zar Mammad is the split image of Ali Khoshdast, exonerated into a more compelling political figure, both seen through the childhood memories of a solitary filmmaker. In *Saz Dahani/Harmonica* (1974), it is as if we go back to the neighbourhood of Zar Mammad or Ali Khoshdast's childhood, where we witness the absolute fixation of a young boy on a harmonica that a tyrannous friend has somehow acquired and with it rules mercilessly over his covetous playmates. That *Harmonica* soon mutated into the political allegory of a tyrannous monarchy is almost incidental to Naderi's preoccupation with solitude. In *Entezar/Waiting* (1975), that solitary boy in Amir Naderi has grown up a bit and now faces the mysterious magic of adolescence; we are witness to his coming of age and drawn to his inarticulate sexual fantasies, fixated on the extended hand of a young woman who offers him a bowl of ice water. In *Marsiyeh/Requiem* (1978), it is as if this young man has grown up, committed a petty crime as did Ali Khoshdast, gone to prison and now comes out as Nasrollah, again a lonesome and solitary soul, roaming through the streets of Tehran trying to make a meagre living against the rambunctious and indifferent background of a cruel and calamitous urban landscape. Thus, when we get to *The Runner* (1985), the lonesome figure of Amiru needs no introduction. We have known him as Ali Khoshdast, or as Zar Mammad, or as Nasrollah before. He has been changing scene from one of Naderi's films to another. But he remains the self-same solitary figure preoccupied with life and the mysteries of growing up in the miasmatical company of a soulless society. In *Ab, Bad, Khak/Water, Wind, Dust* (1989), we see Amiru again in the heart of a heartless desert, looking for the inhabitants of a long since forsaken village – just like Amir Naderi himself, lost in the wilderness of a mercilessly vast and boundless wonder.

Amir Naderi brought his solitude with him when he moved to New York and began a second cycle in his cinematic career. In *Manhattan by Numbers* (1992), we meet George Murphy, a laid-off journalist with only twenty-four hours to come up with the back rent he owes his landlord or else be thrown out of his apartment. George Murphy's journey through Manhattan in search of someone to lend him the money is identical with the journey of all the other characters of Naderi through the slums of Tehran, the landscape of southern Iran, or the desert of its heartland. The same is true of *A, B, C, ... Manhattan* (1997), this time in the form of the story of three solitary souls, three young women – Colleen, Kacey and Kate – with three autonomous but interrelated life stories, at once simple and singular, yet full of the inner violence of a cosmopolis they share as their city. The failed marriage of Colleen, the bisexual wonderings of Kacey and the incestuous relationship of Kate with her brother are examples of what happens to these solitary souls when they dare the elements and find a partner in life. The same holds true for Gretchen in Naderi's *Marathon* (2003), a young woman obsessed with solving the daily puzzles in newspapers, roaming through New York subway cars and stations, and setting one insane and obsessive goal for herself after another, her only connection to the rest of the world the answering machine of her home phone on which her distant mother keeps leaving unreturned messages. The solitary disposition of Naderi's cinema finally comes to a crescendo in his most recent masterpieces, such as *Sound Barrier* (2005), at the centre of which is Jessie, a dumb, deaf and mute boy in search of the mystery of his predicament in an audiotape that his deceased mother has left with some talk show radio station. In *Vegas: Based on a True Story* (2008), and subsequently in *Mountain* (2016), we are again witness to the obsessive disposition of Naderi's solitary protagonists plunging even deeper into their self-destructive ruins. By the time we get to his most recent films, *cut* (2011) and *Magic Lantern* (2018), Naderi indulges in deeply nostalgic views of the whole history of cinema. It has always been between him and the history of cinema, where he spent a lifetime inserting his solitary soul.

From the facts of his own solitary life, Amir Naderi has cultivated a cinematic sense of solitude as the creative space where the society, on the side-lines of which he lives, is seen more proportionately to both its cruel and caring compositions. In his small apartment in downtown Manhattan, which has an uncanny similarity to a cabin aboard an abandoned or wandering ship, dwells the solitary soul of a filmmaker wondering about the moral and normative whereabouts of a rambunctious universe he cannot but call home. A space at once removed from society and yet embraced by it, suspended in mid-air somewhere between his lifelong dreams and his recurring visions as a filmmaker, Naderi's cinema is thus solitary but not hermetic, wondering but not asocial, monadic as he makes a home out of his nomadic life. He is invested, morally and ethically, aesthetically and even politically, although in the *longue durée* too long to cut, too short to remember. He knew Tehran, as we say in Persian, like the palm of his hand, as he does New York, and yet he walks through their streets and alleys, parks and slums as if every single scene he sees were a singular shot in a film that will make the world wonder about its own strangeness – all seen and suggested from the self-assured solace of a solitary but ultimately caring filmmaker.

The Site of the Solitary Unknowing Subject

In Amir Naderi's cinema, we come to the ground zero of the formation of the solitary unknowing subject and the will to reframe the knowable world, as perhaps best evident in his masterpiece *The Runner*. The philosophical concept of *Sarmad*, or 'Time Immemorial', is the temporal space where *The Runner* stages a metonymic simulation of a mythic moment when humanity is stripped of all time-bound belongings and made into a simulacrum of itself. When we look at the protagonist, Amiru, the solitary figure of an orphaned boy, living in an abandoned ship, we are back at the mythic moment of creation. This is the first child: for here humanity at large has disappeared, the world has vanished, and Amiru is the first child of Mashya and Mashyana. Born again to a reframed world, the amorphous subject is the author and inhabitant of an interstitial space where history has reverted to its heroic and mythic moments. Amiru is the first child, and everything around him, albeit familiar, suddenly becomes the foreign insignia of a mythic Noman-land – behold the *tabula rasa* of solitude.

On the site of this solitude, the colonial disposition of the modernity of biopower descending from Europe upon the ravaged earth holds no sway – and no human being is subjected to any form of subjection. There is no sovereign power here, nor the transformation of the sovereign power into the biopolitics of the populace and control. All population has vanished here, and we are transported into a mythic moment. Amiru's body restores itself to the pre-colonial (pre-historical even) citation when his fragile humanity was yet to be subjected to discipline and punish – he is not schooled, and when he goes to school to learn how to see the pictures better, he turns it upside down by reminding the letters of the alphabet that they are just signs, and by teaching these signs a new way of the living power of the sea, rocks, salt and solitude. Beginning with this school turned upside down, all other institutions of biopower disappear – no hospital, no factory, no army – nothing. The first child ever born to the memories of Mashya and Mashyana is defiant of the biopower of his disinherited earth. Running is no sport to discipline and punish the body. Running is a defiance of the gravitational field of the world where Amiru is trapped and from which he is running away.

Just one quick epistemic or imaginative jump, and we might see Amiru as a renewed version of *Hay ibn Yaghdhan*, the mythic character at the heart of both Avicenna's and Ibn Tufail's respective allegories of that title.[3] *Hay ibn Yaghdhan* is the story of a young boy, not unlike Amiru, who grew up solitary on an island in the Indies, entirely isolated from the rest of humanity. Mothered by a doe (or antelope), who had lost her own child, Hay ibn Yaghdhan grew up with other animals far from humans, and thus he reconnects to his own animal origins and begins to study his immediate environments, from the earth under his feet to the heavens above him and everything else in between. Unschooled by any civilisation, the mythic person whose gender is indeterminate becomes a learned person, entirely on their own.

Much hermeneutic import has been given to the story of Hay ibn Yaghdhan, some reading it as a philosophical or else mystical allegory, others as a literary text on autodidactic education, still others as a precursor of the rise of European novels. There is a significant body of scholarship on its Islamic and European reception that reads and overreads its possible meanings. My allusion to it here is to see how in such stories we are reading archetypal prototypes that can pop up in all sorts of forms, including, as some have speculated, in Daniel Defoe's *Robinson Crusoe* (1719). While in the Islamic philosophical context the contested issue is the relationship between Ibn Tufail and Avicenna, and their respective sources, in the European context it is between Ibn Tufail and Daniel Defoe – and their possible connections.[4] The common denominator in both these cases is the fact that the evidence of *Hay ibn Yaghdhan* as a seminal allegorical source invites insightful or abusive over/interpretations in one direction or another. The surest way to come close to that seminal work itself is in artistic variations such as *The Runner*, where the filmmaker could not possibly be accused or even suspected of having been influenced by Avicenna, Ibn Tufail, or Defoe. If so, we are then watching an even more common denominator of placing a solitary subject at the epicentre of their material surroundings, where we might suggest how these mythic memories do not travel literally, but in fact become floating signifiers, transmutated like chameleons, assuming the colour and composition of their changing environments, and as such they become like the metonymic dreams of a distant, always already lost or fading mythic memory.

Consider the argument of Paul de Man in his *Allegories of Reading: Figural Language in Rousseau, Nietzsche, Rilke, and Proust* (1982), where he demonstrates how a literary prose made up of self-generating aporias of figuration, or the allegorical dispositions of a prose become at once definitive of and destructive to all its subsequent readings. If so, then what I refer to as the metonymic disposition of any and all acts of mythical recollections effectively taps into such systems of self-generative figurations, not in any specific rendition of it, but rather in the collective memories it has engendered and informed. There is always already a residual reading available to the text beyond its resolution by any subsequent commentators. Following Paul de Man, we might see how allegorical texts such as *Hay ibn Yaghdhan* operate between logical and rhetorical, thematic and symbolic registers, never one completely yielding to the other. Such deconstructive gestures are not *ex post facto* superimposed on the text, but in fact evident and detected in the text itself, precisely because of their outlandish disposition, of refusing to yield to the authoritative idiomaticities of the existing philosophical or mystical prose. Finding distant relatives like Amiru to the solitary figurative persona of Hay ibn Yaghdhan in contemporary Iranian cinema is one such deconstructive gesture to see the self-generative figuration both intertextually and in a transhistorical register.

Similarly archaic memories are at work in Forough Farrokhzad's iconic poem 'Let Us Believe in the Cold Season', where we read:

> *Dar Kucheh bad mi-ayad ...*
>
> The wind is blowing through the alley
> The wind is blowing through the alley
> And I am thinking
> Of the flowers secreting chemical copulations,
> Of the blossoms with their weakling stems –
> And of this tired tubercular time.
> A man passes by the wet trees –
> A man whose blue veins –
> Just like dead snakes –
> Crawl over his throat –
> As in his agitated temples
> He is repeating that bloody syllabus:
>
> *Salam!*
> *Salam!*
> And all I can think of
> Are the flowers secreting chemical copulations ...[5]

It is impossible to exaggerate the cosmic character of such powerful stanzas in Farrokhzad's poem – itself a superb specimen of a figurative aporia. 'The tired tubercular time' is here both the time and the un-time of the universe that embraces us but remains beyond our temporal grasp. From Amir Naderi to Forough Farrokhzad, the site of the solitary unknowing subject becomes the *tabula rasa* of a postcolonial subjectivity beyond the reach of the condition of coloniality.

8

The Ballad of the Occidental Exile

Dast bardar az in dar vatan-e khish gharib ...

Let me be:
An exile that I am in my own homeland![1]

Mehdi Akhavan Sales, '*Qasedak*/Dandelion' (1959)

When I traveled with my brother Assem from the region of Transoxiana to the lands of the occident in order to hunt down a flock of birds on the shore of the Green Sea, we suddenly fell into a town whose inhabitants were wicked, that is the town of Kairouan. When the people perceived that we had come amongst them unexpectedly, we being sons of the elder known as al-Hadi ibn al-Khayr al-Yamani, they surrounded us and took us bound in shackles and fetters of iron and imprisoned us at the bottom of an infinitely deep pit.[2]

This is the opening gambit of *The Ballad of the Occidental Exile*, one of the most beloved and widely read and celebrated allegorical stories of the twelfth-century Persian philosopher Shihab al-Din Yahya al-Suhrawardi (1154–91). Suhrawardi himself tells us this story he wrote as a response to Avicenna's similar allegories, which he found suggestive but not sufficiently understood. Generations of Muslim and non-Muslim philosophers have written commentaries on these stories. The allegory resembles numerous other occasions, from the poetry of Rumi to the philosophy of Avicenna, where the idea of exile as both factual and allegorical has had countless occasions to show itself in the Persian literary imagination. In contemporary Iranian cinema, the idea of *Gharib* and *Gharibeh* as *Stranger* and *Exile*, shows itself in two of Beiza'i's films, *Gharibeh and the Fog* (1976) and *Bashu: The Little Stranger* (1986). The peculiar thing about the word *Gharib* (and, by extension, *Gharibeh*) is that it means 'strange', 'stranger' and 'exile', but the idea finds its most powerful manifestation in the persona and cinema of Sohrab Shahid-Saless (1944–98) – one of the most beloved and admired Iranian filmmakers, who began his career in Iran but ended it in self-imposed exile from his homeland. The idea of cinematic exile is crucial here because the site of the exilic condition is where the normative and habitual forms of belonging are all made to look stranger and outlandish – for here the artist becomes a stranger to himself. Exile is away from home where the habitual formations of *identity* are all imperceptivity dissolved into *alterity* – and the knowing subject becomes positively and productively unknowing. Himself exiled form his Palestinian homeland by force, Edward Said (1935–2003) theorised the condition of exile as the ideal state of being an intellectual, or a critical thinker, even if one lives in one's own homeland. Questions of gender and sexuality are particularities of the larger issues of the dialectic between self and society, or home and exile – which is always mitigated through the aesthetic functions of verisimilitude and metonymic allusions otherwise impossible to register without the central role of what Russian formalist Viktor Shklovsky called *Ostranenie/Estrangement*. Being in exile is the *locus classicus* of becoming a stranger to oneself, where all one's allusions become strange, and the knowing subjects become unknowing to the world around them.

The allegory of exile that Shahab al-Din Yahaya Suhrawardi immortalised in his philosophy in the twelfth century suddenly exited the small circle of its immediate readership and resurfaced for a much larger public audience through its critical editions in the twentieth century. Before long, the idea found a historic location in some serious aspects of Iranian cinema. But how?

The Exile as the Unknowing Subject

Let me first recap what has brought me to the idea of 'exile'. In this book, I have put forward and am carrying to a conclusion a simple proposition. The 'modern' constitution of gender, I have suggested and detailed, has been under crippling colonial duress and as such coterminous with the prerequisite of colonial de-subjection – of the positioning of the colonial person as integral to the colonial persona as part of the knowable world and, as such, not fit to be a knowing subject. We have become a thing to be known, and thus deprived of the agency to be the knowing subject of any thing. I have therefore examined and excavated the site of Iranian film, fiction, poetry and drama as the veritable *loci* of a battlefield between gendering and de-gendering, subjecting and de-subjecting the colonially conditioned modern Iranian person. I have therefore argued that the creative site I have been excavating is in fact the metonymic verisimilitude of the mythic moments of the distant past and the immediate present (evident in the cosmic figures of Mashya and Mashyana), which have metaphysically collapsed into each other to form a fertile ground to achieve precisely the opposite effect of the colonially gendered and de-subjected postcolonial person. To become knowing Iranian subjects, we must unlearn the colonial condition of having already become knowable colonial objects. The result, if successful, is the emergence of a gender-fluid decolonial unknowing subject that is the *conditio sine qua none* of a liberated postcolonial persona with an intuition of self-transcendence beyond the reach of the postcolonial trauma. I have driven this point home through a galaxy of visual and performing arts gathered in Iranian cinema of the last century and more.

The winding passageway of gender fluidity at the heart of the myth of Mashya and Mashyana to subsequent epochs and generations has been consistent and unwavering. The text of the Persian epic *The Shahnameh* remains a crucial conduit, but so are the Greek, Arabic and Persian (among other) renditions of stories like *Salaman and Absal* and *Hay ibn Yaghdhan*, as detailed by Avicenna, Suhrawardi and Ibn Tufail, where gender is equally fluid in decidedly mythic and philosophical terms, and thus through successive metonymic allusions they have eventually come to our time and captured our repressed imagination. In Henry Corbin's *Spiritual Body and Celestial Earth: From Mazdean Iran to Shi'ite Iran* (1960), and even before that in Mohammad Mo'in's *Mazdayasna va Ta'sir-e an dar Adab Farsi/Mazdaism and its Influence on Persian Literature* (1947), we have a solid body of scholarship documenting such critical and creative passages from distant mythologies to a successive generation of literary and philosophical renditions. But in the more recent musings on Suhrawardi's work, such as on *The Ballad of the Occidental Exile*, this transmutation assumes the most potent mythic and philosophical character of our own time. My contention here is not just to mark the textual transmission but, more importantly, the metonymic allusions that are not merely differential or substitutional yet have, in fact, metamorphosed through entirely literary and visual gestations – and thus the power of their catalytic impact on our contemporary culture.

While gender is colonially conditioned as Foucauldian biopower, whereby we are gendered and de-subjected at one and the same time, by reading the inherited mythic heritage in metonymic aesthetic terms we decolonise and liberate the codified gender and let loose the body, thereby positing the viability of the nomadic unknowing subject. Here the metonymic apparatus is where we change particular names for open-ended attributes, and here is also where the whole aesthetic machinery becomes metonymic – and the metonymy is what thereafter stands for the metaphysical that it supplants, as does poetry for prose, visual for the verbal, semiosis for semiotics, signations for signs. For signification, the mythic dissolves into the metonymic – who watches the watcher, where the watcher is watched by that which they watch, the person who gazes is gazed back at, the beholder becomes the beheld, so we become the subject of the gaze of the things we gaze at, and thus the gender of the watcher is determined by the gendering act they watch. This reversal of the gaze becomes metonymic and repeatedly reiterated: we become that which we watch, we cross-identify, we the spectators become the Fourth Wall, as the actors and their acts exit onto and into us.

The remnants, gestations and memories of the myth of Mashya and Mashyana has moved and meandered in varied forms through the Iranian and Persianate histories. The story of the Sassanid Emperor Anushirvan's persecution of the legendary Prophet Mazdak (died circa 528) and his followers, planting them upside-down into the ground, alludes to the myth of Mashya and Mashyana as plant and human – now transformed into a potent political metaphor. By the time the version of *Salaman and Absal*, in which Salaman is conceived from his father's semen being placed inside a Mandragora plant, reaches Abd al-Rahman Jami (1414–92) in the fifteenth century and subsequently the renowned English poet and translator Edward Fitzgerald (1809–83), they anticipate the prominent French scholar Henry Corbin's (1903–73) philosophical preoccupation with the myth. Their collective revival of the allegory for the nineteenth and the twentieth century marks the sustained course of the distant myth of the androgynous plant-human into posterity. The Qur'anic allusion to the tree of Tuba meanwhile reaches Rumi, and from there trickles down and eventually reached Forough Farrokhzad's poetry, Shahrnoush Parsipour's fiction and Shirin Neshat's photography – all variations of *Salaman and Absal*'s allegory as dramaturgical metaphor. There is a direct link therefore that traces Abbas Kiarostami's photography of trees to the tree to which we see Xerxes singing (praying) early in Handel's famous aria in his *Serse*. Here real and make-believe collapse into each other, while pure verisimilitude takes over. Meanwhile, Bahram Beiza'i breaks the Fourth Wall, through the crucial philosophical space of *Hurqalya*, as theorised in the Shaykhi School in the nineteenth century and where truth and verisimilitude collide, so that in his cinema the porous space of *Hurqalya* becomes the *locus classicus* of all the visual recitals, as Corbin would say, as Abbas Kiarostami's enduring significance becomes pure verisimilitude, while outside Iran Shirin Neshat's passing fame implodes into the North American and Western European commercial industry, while farthest away from that culture industry Forough Farrokhzad continues to operate between totality and infinity. From the distant past, through the meandering intervals and down to colonial and postcolonial gestations, the mythic foregrounding of the androgynous gendering of the subject persists.

Against this deep, invisible background, gendering the post/colonial nation was a byproduct of European colonial modernity – a gendered (like coloured and classed) codification of power, while the rise and effervescence of the visual and performing arts was the most public stage and spectacle on which this gendering took place. A reverse (critical) reading of that spectacle against its own grain is the most effective strategy of exposing its forced gendering consequences, for there is no (and never will be) liberating the unknowing subject of the decolonialised postcolony, unless and until the colonially gendered subject is de-gendered – thus the point of my trajectory from myth to metonymy and from there towards the unknowing subject.

What could 'metonymy' mean here? It means two things: intertextuality and dramaturgy – and through these two forms we are witness to the internal engine of how these common themes were sustained in the course of our post/colonial history. What is the main thrust of this argument? Through myth and its sustained metonymic gestations, we are witness to the constitution of the unknowing subject, presiding over a hermeneutic of creative misunderstanding, whereby the loosened gender binaries liberate the postcolonial subject into an uncharted but knowable world. I have read the evidence of Iranian visual and performing arts through these lenses, informed by but not limited to Foucault's pioneering articulation of biopower. This is so because the presence of the postcolonial thinking subject on the site of the European critical thinking is perforce nomadic, in fact, a mere pilgrim, even a bandit. The unknowing subject is the nomadic persona venturing into a hermeneutics of creative misunderstanding, of perpetrating epistemic violence, which perforce works through a syncretic prose that comes close to 'First World Theory', only to snatch an idea or two, reverse-engineer them for our own purposes and run away to our own playing filed.

Exilic Cinema

It is right here that the idea of 'exile', of being away from one's own homeland, especially at the peak of one's creativity, becomes central to some key contemporary critical thinkers such as Theodore Adorno and Edward Said – a Jewish German philosopher and a Christian Palestinian literary critic. German philosophers and critical thinkers like Adorno and Hannah Arendt, dispossessed Palestinians like Ghassan Kanafani and Edward Said, and the whole Parisian expansion of Harlem Renaissance figures such as James Baldwin, all allude back to some earlier thinkers like Jean-Jacques Rousseau, Karl Marx, Sigmund Freud, Pablo Neruda, Bertolt Brecht, Ngũgĩ wa Thiong'o, Ivan Turgenev, Salman Rushdie – the list can expand and by every twist complicate our conception of exile. A key issue, however, remains the nature and function of the organicity of these exilic intellectuals, as Antonio Gramsci would first theorise and Edward Said later expand on the idea.[3] The same is true for the similarly rich reflections of Rosi Braidotti who has fruitfully expanded and liberated the idea of 'exile' into that of 'nomadic' subjectivity, which for my purpose here pivots towards the postcolonial unknowing subject.[4]

The question of exile, or nomadic subjectivity, however, as most of these thinkers had come to see, was more than a physical distance from one's homeland and had conditioned a metaphysical meditation of where precisely one's home might be. In Iranian and Islamic contexts proper, the iconic treatise of Shahab al-Din Yahya Suhrawardi, *Qesseh al-Ghorbat al-Gharbiyyeh/The Ballad of the Occidental Exile*, transforms the prospect of being in exile into the idea of the exilic (nomadic) subject, now actively read in a new way after exhausting the condition of coloniality. Suhrawardi's philosophical allegory opens the horizons of 'exile' to a far richer and more potent metaphor of being at home in the world. In this renewed reading of 'exile', in Iranian cinema proper, after the success of the Islamic Republic in its armed robbery of the Iranian revolution of 1977–79 for and with their militant Islamism, a significant aspect of this cinema developed outside Iran. From 1993 onwards, an entire film festival of exiled filmmakers was created in Gothenburg, Sweden. But before and after that festival, a few key Iranian filmmakers – such as Parviz Sayyad, Bahram Beiza'i and Mohsen Makhmalbaf – altogether left their homeland, joining filmmakers like Ebrahim Golestan, Sohrab Shahid-Saless and Amir Naderi, who had done so earlier.[5] Of this elite group of filmmakers, Ebrahim Golestan never made any film outside his homeland, nor did Bahram Beiza'i, while Mohsen Makhmalbaf and his family mostly made Afghanistan and Tajikistan the main domain of their filmmaking and Parviz Sayyad wasted much of his time lambasting the atrocities of the Islamic Republic. Sohrab Shahid-Saless and Amir Naderi, making Europe and the US their new filmmaking home, respectively, formed a whole breed apart – as one became a key figure of the German New Wave, and the other recast his entire Iranian cinematic legacy into an even richer and more powerful cosmic perception of the world. The condition of 'exile' as nomadic subjectivity found a whole new panorama in the works of Shahid-Saless and Naderi.

Born in 1948 in Tehran to a middle-class family, Sohrab Shahid-Saless left his homeland in the early 1960s, first for Vienna and then for Paris, to study acting and filmmaking.[6] He returned to Iran in the late 1960s and was employed at the Ministry of Culture where he began making his first documentaries; from these experiences soon emerged his two earliest masterpieces, *Yek Ettefaq-e Sadeh/A Simple Incident* (1973) and *Tabi'at-e Bijan/Still Life* (1974). In *A Simple Incident*, Shahid-Saless dwelled on the daily life of a poor boy trying to make a meagre living by smuggling fish. In *Still Life*, he portrayed an elderly couple where the aging husband works at a remote train station and

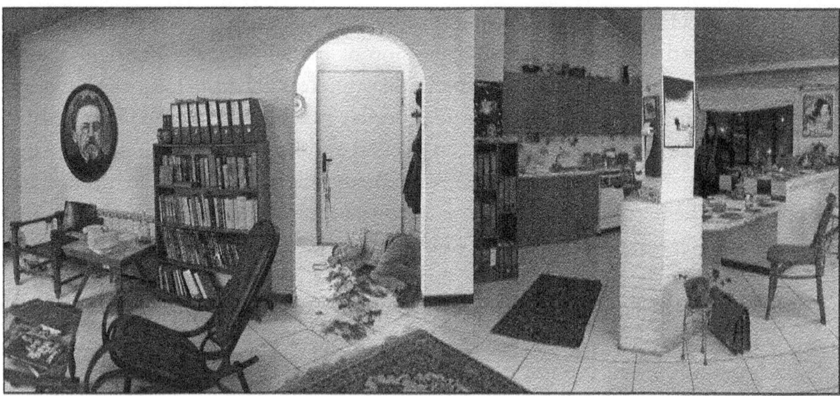

Figure 8.1 *Azadeh Akhlaghi, 'Sohrab Shahid Sales, 01 July 1998'. (Photo: Courtesy of Azadeh Akhlaghi)*

suddenly faces mandatory retirement. By the mid-1970s, Shahid-Saless found himself in Germany where he resumed making a number of widely received films for German media – including *Dar Ghorbat/Far from Home* (1975), *Reifezeit* (1976), *Tagebuch eines Liebenden* (1977) and *Rosen für Afrika* (1991). About two decades later, in the early 1990s, he moved to Chicago where he died in solitude and exile. The exquisite Iranian artist Azadeh Akhlaqi later meticulously depicted his death scene in one of her photographs.[7]

Exile on Exile: Amir Naderi on Sohrab Shahid-Saless

Soon after Shahid-Saless' death in Chicago in the summer of 1998, his kindred soul Amir Naderi and I grew much closer to each other in New York. Naderi is not a very sentimental person. There is a powerful stubbornness in and about him. But still there was a palpable gentility about him when talking with his close friend and about his fellow filmmaker Sohrab Shahid-Saless. Naderi was particularly talkative about Shahid-Saless after his death – at some point, he asked me to record his thoughts on his friend and colleague, and I did as he said. Our conversations extended over a few days and were obviously conducted in Persian. What follows is the English translation of those conversations with a minimum of editing for purposes of clarity.

'I met Sohrab Shahid-Saless for the first time in the summer of 1973', he told me while we were eating his legendary soup in his little apartment in Alphabet City, 'when I was looking for someone to edit my film *Harmonica* (1973). Mohammad Reza Aslani, another director of the emerging Iranian New Wave, who knew and was very much admired by Shahid-Saless, had introduced him to me'.

Hamid Dabashi: What sort of a person was he?

Amir Naderi: Shahid-Saless was the most sensitive man I have ever met. The volume of his thoughts was larger than his small body. He had a unique and complex character.

Despite being very sociable and charming, he was quite distant from those around him. He was exceedingly kind and generous. But he was also a difficult person. Few were spared the sharp tongue and sarcastic disposition of this bittersweet man. He didn't trust or believe people easily. He had a love-hate relationship with women and never believed in romantic love – and yet he had an over-abundance of love for people in general. His treatment of his women characters, however, was exceedingly gentle and caring.

HD: He seems to have been an introverted person – how did you relate to him?

AN: He had very little love for himself. Nothing could save him from his own inner world – not his extraordinary intelligence, not his amazing knowledge, not his international success and artistic prestige. He was his own worst enemy. His self-destructive urges were only controlled when he was busy making a film.

HD: What was the impact of his education in Europe?

AN: Shahid-Saless had spent much of his life outside Iran. His education was mostly in Vienna, Austria. Except for his early childhood and youth, he spent only a few years of his life in Iran, in the course of which he made a few short films and two long feature masterpieces. From early 1976 he went to Germany and stayed there until just about the end of his life. As a result, Shahid-Saless has a long and illustrious career as a German filmmaker, and as such ought to be considered as one of the founders of German New Cinema – along such filmmakers as Rainer Werner Fassbinder, Wim Wenders, Werner Herzog and Volker Schlöndorff. For his significance in the German New Wave, one must look at his German films – all among the most significant in German New Wave cinema. Despite his love for Iran, for his parental culture, he had direct access to a darker side of European culture in both Austria and Germany.

HD: Could we then consider him a European as much as an Iranian filmmaker?

AN: He was very much at home in Europe. He knew a few European languages. I remember, in Cannes, after the screening of his film Ordnung *(1980) he was responding to his audience questions in several languages – all very fluently. Shahid-Saless had a universal awareness of the human condition and cultures, and he was able to relate to people in many different places – Europe and Iran made no difference to him. It is important to note that his death was not because of his distance from anywhere or anything. Some people in Iran believe that being far from his homeland, from Iran, caused his decline and death. This is not true. The death of Shahid-Saless was a prolonged and self-afflicted suicide. Towards the end of his life, his sole connection with everything and everywhere was just by phone. Whatever he earned from his film distribution, he spent on his telephone bills. This was all to escape solitude and be able to tolerate himself. He rarely saw people. He would only talk to them on the phone.*

HD: How would you describe his solitude – was it always there?

AN: Shahid-Saless was quite lucky to have had an amazing stepmother who had a huge influence on his manner of thinking. But towards the end of his life, he was trying to stay away from her so he could remain within his own darkness. He had an extraordinarily dark humour. He read a lot and watched very few films. He loved Chekhov dearly. This was known among all his friends. He also very much admired Edgar Alan Poe. He did not have much patience to write, but he thought a lot – and when he reached the point where he wanted to be, he used to write his thoughts very swiftly, and he made his film very quickly, too. On these occasions, he was full of energy, turned into a young boy – humorous, full of enthusiasm and with a perfect rhythm to his life. As soon as his film was over, he would fall back into his own solitude.

HD: Who would you say had the most influence on his cinema?

AN: Shahid-Saless had something of a Kafkaesque character – both in his life and in his German films. He knew the work of Franz Kafka, Anton Chekhov, Edgar Alan Poe and Rainer Maria Rilke very well. He rarely talked about cinema. But I remember once, during a film festival in Berlin, I had a rare chance of spending a few days with him talking about filmmaking. Because of heavy snowfall after the festival, we were stranded at home, which gave us an opportunity to sit down and do nothing but talk cinema. Shahid-Saless himself was to some extent under the influence of the early Robert Bresson, as well as the work of Yasujirō Ozu. He also admired other directors such as Andrei Tarkovsky, Ermanno Olmi, John Cassavetes and Luis Buñuel – namely, filmmakers whose works were quite different from his. Cassavetes, in particular, and despite the fact that his cinema was entirely different from his, Shahid-Saless deeply admired him. Cassavetes was a passionate and totally out-of-control filmmaker who put everything on the screen, while Shahid-Saless was exceedingly minimalist and totally in control.

HD: What about Iranians?

AN: He praised the work of those of his contemporaries who had contributed to the serious artistic cinema in Iran, including the works of Mohammad Reza Aslani (whose style in filmmaking was quite close to Shahid-Saless' own), Kamran Shirdel, Ahmad Faroughi Ghajar, Bahram Beiza'i, Fereydun Rahnama, Ali Hatami, Nasser Taghva'i and Arapik Baghdasarian (who was unfortunately lost during the Iranian Revolution, for if he had remained, he would have occupied a major position in modern Iranian cinema – if there were a possibility that his film Tehran, Kilometer 100 *could be seen, this would be thoroughly demonstrated). Shahid-Saless also admired the work of Abbas Kiarostami. They were like twins, with identical style and manner of thinking, but with two entirely different characters; for this reason, they never got along with each other. Kiarostami had a great degree of self-control, while Shahid-Saless was very angry and vindictive. Many contemporary Iranian filmmakers believe that Shahid-Saless was the one who invented this style of filmmaking. But even before Shahid-Saless and*

Kiarostami, it was really Mohammad Reza Aslani who had initiated the minimalist approach. He was one of the founders of this form of cinema.

HD: How would you characterise his cinema today?

AN: What was amazing about Sohrab Shahid-Saless was his clarity and purity of vision (true about his attitude toward cinema as well as other arts). The simplicity yet powerful quality of his films come from this uncompromising commitment to his vision and a deep knowledge of his personal experiences. Although, as a person, he was incessantly restless and emotional, he controlled the emotional performance of his actors and stayed at a distance from them, in order to avoid dramatisation and sentimental treatment.

HD: How do you assess his legacy?

AN: The new style of narrative in Iranian cinema, with its minimal plot structure, was a phenomenon that emerged during the 1970s, at a time when commercial cinema was dominant in the market. Sohrab Shahid-Saless was, in fact, the true father of modern and realist cinema in Iran. He opened the possibility for a different kind of filmmaking and inspired several generations of filmmakers to come. Although Iranian cinema may go up or down in the future, Shahid-Saless' films stay at the very top. There are two things that we can say about the two films that he made in Iran and the seventeen films that he made in Germany: (1) he was a master of using sound, and (2) his extraordinary command of rhythm – something at the level of Robert Bresson and other filmmakers like him. The poetry of Shahid-Saless' cinema relies on its rhythm. Rhythm of the shots, movement of the characters or camera, spaces between dialogue, silence and the use of sound effects as character, and rhythm of colours and compositions convey the mood of the film and the emotional experiences of the characters. In short, Shahid-Saless was a master of cinematic rhythm. Cut!

Amir Naderi's New York

A few years after that interview, the Museum of Cinema in Torino, Italy, invited me to write a major essay on Amir Naderi in New York. Only the Italian translation of that essay was published. What follows is a slightly revised version of that essay.[8] The key issue in that essay, paramount on my mind when I was writing it for his Italian audience, is the condition of exile in Naderi's cinema, the significance of the city of New York in his cinematic imagination – and what could the very idea of exile mean in this city in the way we watch and understand Naderi's cosmovision. Although their cinemas were radically different from each other, Shahid-Saless' and Naderi's identical condition of exile has shed a particularly poignant light on their collective work.

In New York, Amir Naderi and I used to live on the two opposite sides of Manhattan. For much of his New York sojourn, he lived near the Lower East Side, I live on the Upper West Side – he in the East Village, to be more exact, and I on Columbia University's campus. For us to see each other, we had to change two subway lines. When I used to go down to see him (particularly in the summer of 2003, when I was helping him out with a script, almost every day, otherwise once a week when he was not shooting, and less so when he was), I used to take the 1/9 train from 116th Street down to Time Square and then change to N/Q/R/W down to Union Square. Then I walked for a few blocks south to 10th Street and then east towards 1st Street, just before Avenue A, where he used to live. When he came up to see me, he followed the same route in reverse. When the big blackout of 14 August 2003 (just the day before his birthday) hit New York, I was at Amir's apartment, working with him on the script of what later became *Sound Barrier* (2005). On that day I had to borrow a transistor radio from him to follow the news of the blackout and walk all the way from 10th Street and Avenue A to 116th Street and Broadway. It took me about five hours. He kept me company and walked with me for about fifty blocks – all the while talking about his encounters with Bernardo Bertolucci and his love of Michelangelo Antonioni's cinema. To this day, I can never have a stationary notion of Amir Naderi. I can only imagine him mobile – walking, talking, laughing, eating, drinking tea, feeding his plants, all the while telling me stories of films he wants to make. In all these years, I have never seen him resting, sitting still, napping, keeping quiet, or sleeping. In his apartment he has no bed. 'Great men', I once read somewhere, 'have small beds'. Naderi has no bed. He once told me, 'I hate sleeping'.

Although constantly mobile, Amir Naderi has scarcely left New York – except to attend a film festival. It seems as if New York had always been his final destination. One of the oldest friends of Amir Naderi in New York is the distinguished Iranian artist Nikzad ('Nicky') Nodjoumi. Nikzad lives in Brooklyn and has his own gentle manner of negotiating his way into the opening nights of art exhibitions, SoHo and Chelsea galleries that invariably find most of us together: some greying, grown and grumpy men and women bewildered at the spectacular achievements of our younger siblings – Ramin Bahrani, Kouross Esmaeli and Laleh Khorramian are the latest additions to our midst. 'Grumpy ol' lions', one of these younger siblings once affectionately called us. In the midst of the Metropolis, right here in the heart of Gotham City, Amir Naderi has assumed a stable, iconic, impermeable significance – for us as permanent and stable as the Statue of Liberty. Naderi, too, is not going anywhere (though at times he did talk about 'going West'). Others come to him, young and older Iranian artists, much like pilgrims paying their respect to a shrine. 'Is it possible to see Amir Naderi?' is the first question Iranian artists ask when they come to visit New York. More than talking to or learning from him, these pilgrims were mostly eager to touch him, kiss him on the cheeks, hug him and shake his hand. There is something visibly tactile about the evident pieties of these visitors. We Shi'is, I often think, are incurable. Naderi had become the first Shi'i shrine in New York – even though he did not know it – for his mind was always somewhere else, not in the physical world, but in the setting of his next film, including one he had always wished to make on the moon – namely set on the moon!

Like all other icons, Amir Naderi has never been quite conscious of his iconic demeanour. But his physical attachment to New York and his reluctance to travel speak otherwise. Except for his later short sojourns to Japan or Italy to make films there, Amir Naderi travels rarely – for he intensely dislikes going anywhere outside the United States, almost with the same intensity that he absolutely adores living in what he calls 'Emrika'. This seafarers' adulation for 'America' he attributes to his birth and breeding in the southern coastal town of Abadan in Iran, where he was born on 15 August 1946. Since his first journey to the United States in 1976, he has decided that 4 July, the American Independence Day, is his 'American Birthday'. The symbolism is so thick that he once made a film (which was never released) called *Made in Iran, Made in America*. Amir Naderi was in a way 'made in America', even though he was born and raised hundreds of thousands of miles away. 'There was a world', he once told me. 'Beautiful and shining in my mind, all made of movies; and then another world, ugly and boring outside, made of the real world. I always preferred to close my eyes and live in that beautiful world – of film, fiction and fantasy'. The shot in his *Runner* (1984), where Amiru is sitting by the waterfront with his back turned to the camera, facing the shimmering water and the anchored ships in the sunset, eating his watermelon, with a beautiful Louis Armstrong score in the background, is, so Naderi once told me, a visual record of that indelible memory. New York for Naderi is the ultimate destination of those ships. He has landed on this island the way persecuted Protestant pilgrims dared the tumultuous seas of yore to seek their freedom and test their fortunes in the permanently 'New World'. Among all the American authors, Naderi prefers Ernest Hemingway and Herman Melville – *The Old Man and the Sea* (1958) and *Moby Dick* (1851), in particular. It is only from his landed assurances in America that he can dream of the seas – for he has done a lifetime of dreaming the other way around, of coming to America.

What Naderi means by 'America', however, is really just New York – although his *Vegas: Based on a True Story* (2008) shows that his camera is quite at home in the Nevada desert, too. He occasionally travels to spend time with his relations in Virginia, or with friends in upstate New York. 'I hate trees, meadows, ponds, woods, jungles, rivers, mountains and such', he says on these occasions with a vengeance. All he remembers from these occasional trips is the colour green. 'He hates the colour green', says Michael Simmonds, his long-time friend and ingenious cinematographer. But Naderi has a green thumb, plants small plants in oddly shaped bottles and speaks to and of them in anthropomorphic terms. 'You see this one', he once told me, referring to a tiny plant inside a bottle. 'She always likes to turn towards the window and screw up my arrangement'. By 'arrangement' he meant a 'seating arrangement' he had put together of a group of short and tall plants, as if they were sitting for a family portrait. Simmonds' reading of these plants is that Naderi wants to know where the greens are and to have them under his control. But I believe Naderi dislikes colour, period – not just green. Once I had a tiny streak of red on a T-shirt I was wearing. He gave me a long lecture against the colour red. On the *tabula rasa* of his cinematic imagination, he wants a clean slate to remap the world as he sees fit.

Naderi has an equal aversion to Europe. 'I cannot stand these old brick pavements, fancy shops, old castles, dilapidated fortresses and such – what the hell are they for anyway'. His preference? Modern architecture, spectacular skyscrapers, 'steel, iron, copper, brass, concrete blocks – I thrive at their magnificent sights', he says, his sharp and brutal intelligence sparkling in his beady eyes. Barren desert is the only landscape of his choice. John Ford's *Monument Valley* is definitive of Naderi's notion of 'America'.

On one of my birthdays, he gave me one of his most prized possessions – a copy of a very old magazine on the cover of which is a picture of Monument Valley. He had found it off the street in SoHo. He is proverbial for finding exquisite objects in outlandish places off the streets of Manhattan. I am convinced he knows (and has walked through) the five boroughs of New York more and better than the five mayors of New York put together. His visual perception of New York is full-bodied, visceral, physical – brick, bone, steel and concrete. He has possessed New York, as New York has possessed him.

Walking with Amir Naderi in New York is bodily exercise and mental gymnastics at one and the same time. First of all, you have to walk to his left. He cannot stand anyone walking to his right. I never figured out why. Does he prefer the right profile of people or is he phobic of his own right visual angle – or maybe something entirely different. I have no clue. He walks through the streets and back alleys of New York with his attention, it seems, fully devoted to the conversation at hand, and yet with an extra set of antennas up and about gathering noises, sounds, pictures and shots from every which way around him. In his physical bearings, Amir Naderi is short, stocky, rectangular – with an astonishingly gentle and delicate set of hands that are entirely oxymoronic in their attachments to this body. Naderi's hands look like they belong to someone else. They are amazingly (and surprisingly) feminine, soft, gentle and delicate – if I did not know better, I would have suggested that they are manicured. But they are not. That is just the way they are. If you look at Amir's hands, spot-lighted and with the rest of his body hidden in darkness, you will not guess in a million years that they belong to that heavy, weighted, timber-like and bouncing body. But people scarcely notice Naderi's hands. They are usually hidden from the naked eyes of people casually glancing at him, invariably drawn to the most prominent feature of Amir's bodily presence, which is his head – bold, balding, cheeky and wide, and above all disproportionately bigger than the rest of his body and marked by two beady and always piercing (though in a bewildered kind of a way) eyes. There is an agitation about Amir Naderi that seems to reside somewhere in the centre of his head as he talks and argues, balanced in his brain, nurtured in his mind and sustained in his unrelenting intelligence. The stark contrast between his imposing head and his gentle hands, between his agitated intelligence and his scrupulous craftsmanship, finds its way into his cinema – at once exceedingly alert on its cutting edge and yet surprisingly gentle in its poetic disposition. The same combination that is most evident in his cinema is also paramount in his cooking. Naderi is a great cook – what is more important, he talks about his cooking almost in the same language as he talks about his cinema – boastful and confident. A masterful chef of cinematic craftmanship and cuisine – the two pillars between which he lives his nomadic life in New York.

I have walked with Amir Naderi, on innumerable occasions, from his home in the East Village down towards the Williamsburg Bridge, and then further down towards the Lower East Side, bypassing Little Italy, which he does not like at all ('fake and bogus', he calls it), marching resolutely towards Chinatown, which he absolutely adores. In Chinatown, in a triangular urban landscape between (1) one end of the Manhattan Bridge, (2) the Manhattan side of the Brooklyn Bridge and (3) the Eastern-most side of Canal Street, Amir Naderi is the happiest man alive, most jovial and talkative, agile and gesticulating – completely at home. Among a million restaurants that abound in Chinatown, he singularly prefers this dilapidated little Vietnamese restaurant on Baxter Street, where he always orders a huge seafood soup with a mountain of rice (he is classical vegetarian). Half a block from this Vietnamese restaurant, at the mouth of the block, there is an apartment building on the roof of which he shot the central, dramatic sequence of his *ABC, Manhattan* (1997). Of another million pastry shops that exist in Chinatown, he prefers yet another rundown place further down on Baxter Street, where he has two Chinese pastries with two cups of hot tea. Just across from the window where we sit and have our tea and pastry, there is the opening of a small foyer leading into an apartment building. Next to it, there is a public phone, at the foot of which he has sat down and written the script of his *Marathon* (2002). When I was working with him on a script, a version of which later became *Sound Barrier* (2005), we used to take my laptop and his freshly brewed tea and sit in front of a laundromat right in front of his apartment. There is a fire hydrant right next to that laundromat. On top of the fire hydrant, there is enough room for exactly one cup of tea. 'That's my table', Amir used to say, as he placed his cup of tea there, took his chocolate bar out of his pocket and sat down to work. I have marvelled at and learned Amir's sublime asceticism.

The map of New York is nailed into Amir Naderi's mind and carved in his soul, with his specific habits and aging routines, locations he likes and routes he regularly traverses, places in which he has literally sat down and written his scripts, and the shades of light he prefers to see on specific buildings at specific times of the day – his scripts having been written from these very lived experiences of peoples and sentiments, shapes and colours, looks and gazes, sounds and noises, cries and whispers of New York.

Born Again in New York

It is as if Amir Naderi was always meant to come to New York. Born and raised in the southern city of Abadan in Iran, Naderi had made a successful career as a pioneering filmmaker in his homeland. By the time he was thirty years old, he had established himself as a major filmmaker with a distinct visual vocabulary of his own, widely influenced by the best in world cinema and deeply rooted in his own poverty-stricken background. The colonial history of the oil-soaked southern Iranian provinces has given them a rare character, at once provincial and yet exposed to the colonially mitigated introduction of a highly sophisticated oil industry and a bourgeois culture meant for European expats who run it and yet vicariously available to the rest of the native society as well. The look of Abadan, as a result, is far more cosmopolitan and industrial than even that of the capital city Tehran. The industrial parts around New York City, say, the shipyards scattered along the Hudson River, look far more like Abadan than Tehran – a sprawling city at the foot of Damavand Mountain. The move of Amir Naderi from the coastal town of Abadan in southern Iran to the capital city of Tehran when he was still a teenager was no less traumatic and exhilarating than his journey from Iran to the United States. To understand Naderi's cinema in New York, it is imperative to picture him always on the move – not just from Iran to the United States, but from Abadan to Tehran, from Tehran to Paris and London, and ultimately set upon a course that seems could have come to no other destination but New York.

Naderi made much of his cinematic career in the Tehran of the 1970s, at once booming with an oil-based economy that brought a bonanza of wealth to the Pahlavi court, yet shaken to its foundation by anti-government guerrilla movements launched by both secular and Islamist militants. Between 1971 and 1976, Naderi made six major feature films in Iran, beginning with *Khodahafez Rafiq/Goodbye Friend* (1971) and ending the first phase of his career with *Marsiyeh/Requiem* (1976). His first attempt to come and settle in the United States occurred in 1977, when he travelled to New York and made a film called *Sakht-e Iran, Sakht-e Emrika/Made in Iran, Made in America* (1977), a film that he wrote and directed but never released. Unsatisfied with what at the time he considered a shallow and artificial exposure to New York, Naderi returned to his native Iran and remained there (with the exception of a short sojourn in Paris) between 1980 and 1986. At this second, post-revolutionary stage of his career in Iran, Naderi made four films – the two documentaries *Josteju I/Search I* (1981) and *Josteju II/Search II* (1982), his legendary *Davandeh/Runner* (1985) and one of his most globally celebrated masterpieces, *Ab, Bad, Khak/Water, Wind. Dust* (1988). The third phase of his cinematic career began in 1986, when he permanently moved to New York, where he made such feature films as *Manhattan by Numbers* (1992), *ABC ... Manhattan* (1997), *Marathon* (2003) and *Sound Barrier* (2005). Later, he made, in Las Vegas, *Vegas: Based on a True Story* (2008), in Japan, *Cut* (2011), in Italy, *Mountain* (2016) and, back in Los Angeles, *Magic Lantern* (2018). Throughout all these films he has remained a nomadic New Yorker.

Naderi has an allergic reaction to nostalgia, cares very little about the two Iranian phases of his cinematic career and wishes (artistic procreativity always in his mind) only to think of himself and thus be considered as an 'American filmmaker'. This deliberately cultivated sense of denial is definitive of both Amir Naderi's character and cinema. Any mention of going back to Iran (even for a visit) provokes an almost violent reaction from him. 'Never', he says, 'go back to the country from which you come, or to the woman you once loved'. This resistance to and defiance against nostalgia is constitutional to Naderi's cinema – always marching forward, as if he were running away from something, what exactly, he cannot quite tell. He attended the complete retrospectives of his films reluctantly – not because he is ashamed of what he achieved in Iran ('*Tangsir* still works, I tell you', he whispered into my ear when we saw one of his absolute masterpieces in September 2001, when Richard Peña curated a major retrospective of his work in New York) – but because his mind is always on his next project and because he thinks dwelling on his past achievements is a certain sign of decay and decline. He wishes for his New York films to have absolutely no visual resemblance to his Iranian films. He detests with a vengeance those artists, filmmakers, or literati that come to the United States or Europe and make a career out of their nostalgic reminiscences about their Iranian past – 'and this kind of bordello house charlatanism in particular', he once said, abruptly stopping as we were passing by the window of a Barnes and Noble's bookstore in the Village displaying Azar Nafisi's ignominious *Reading Lolita in Tehran* (2003). He continued: 'I intensely despise'. His mind speeds around a globe that seems figuratively revolving in his mind. 'My next film will be set on the moon', he told me recently, 'the earth no longer satisfies me'.

A Migratory and Mobile State of Mind

The New York state of mind is migratory and mobile, and there is a migratory and restless soul searching through Naderi's depiction of New York – from his very first to his most recent films. His first feature film in New York, *Manhattan by Numbers* (1992), is shot almost entirely in exterior takes, showing an unemployed journalist, George Murphy (John Wojda), navigating the streets of Manhattan, from its Northern tip in Washington Heights to its Southern climes in the Financial District, in search of money to pay his back rent, only to give Naderi an occasion to have his camera wrestle with the sculpted Charging Bull aggressively announcing the spirit of American capitalism. If *Manhattan by Numbers* maps out the exterior of the cosmopolis, at once brutal and beautiful, *ABC ... Manhattan* (1997) turns Naderi's camera into the reflection of that architecture in the interior of the humanity it inhabits, the minds and souls of its inhabitants, three young women in particular – Colleen (Lucy Knight), who is a single mother struggling to make ends meet as a photographer and who finally loses her daughter to her former husband; Kacey (Erin Norris), who has already lost her girlfriend, her boyfriend and her dog; and finally Kate (Sara Paul), who in her solitary musician soul has long kept a deeply troubling secret. Shot mostly in interior takes, medium and close-up shots, *ABC ... Manhattan* gives Naderi's camera an occasion to become psychoanalytical in its probing of the reflection of the architectonic exterior of New York in the hidden souls of its inhabitants. In his third feature film in New York, *Marathon* (2003), Naderi opts to move underground, literally, and to take a long and lasting look at the subterranean soul of the city, the labyrinth of its subway system and the sinuous spirits that move the body of a people. Shot almost entirely in the New York subway system, with the exception of its final sequence that carries the noisy soul of that subway into the interior of an apartment, *Marathon* is the story of Gretchen (Sara Paul) who is determined to break her own record of solving seventy-two crossword puzzles in a twenty-four-hour period, while addicted to the sound of noise, most evident when echoed in the serpentine sinuses of the underground world. Solitary obsession, dogged singularity and the physical embodiment of a phantasmagoric machinery that is New York, Gretchen is how Naderi sees his adopted city: introverted, self-absorbed, indifferent to the fate of the universe it projects. Finally, *Sound Barrier* (2005) moves Naderi's camera into a navigation between two singular sets – the interior of a storage room and the exterior of a bridge traffic to map out the soul of a deaf and mute eleven-year-old boy, Jesse (Charlie Wilson), in search of the suspected secret of and possible cure to his ailment. By the conclusion of his fourth New York film, Naderi has drafted *the exterior* of the cosmopolis he now calls home, searched through its traces *inside* the soul of its inhabitants, plunged deep into the subterranean spirits that sustain its exterior awe and narrowed in on a solitary soul, deaf and mute in the language of its inhabitants, yet observant of its ways in manners unheard of and unseen before. These four films are the autobiography of a city (as they are the autobiography of their maker) as seen and heard by one of its millions of immigrant and emigrated souls. His subsequent films are shot in Nevada, Japan, Italy and Los Angeles – but in all of them dwells his permanently New York state of mind.

Like his own physical presence in New York, Amir Naderi's New York films are overwhelmingly physical, embodied, corporeal in their aesthetics, evidentiary in their visual narratives. Naderi has a reputation for being primarily a photographer and then a filmmaker. While it is true that he is a gifted photographer of uncommon perception, his cinema is not photographic; it is irreducibly visual.[9] He is incurably anti-narrative. He could not make a narrative film if his life depended on it. He *sees* the world; he does not *understand* it – and that precisely is the central drama of his cinema. For that physical and evidentiary visuality to be for real and to work, Naderi has systematically cultivated an almost allergic reaction to politics. He deliberately suspends all political notions of his whereabouts. He lives in New York – and what political implications that might have (exile, immigration, colonialism, imperialism and so on) seems to be entirely irrelevant to him. At the height of the US war in Afghanistan, the invasion of Iraq and other similar exploits, his most political utterance (if he ever were to say anything) would be something along the lines of 'so the situation is really dangerous, right?' – and this would not be an affectation and asked only if it affected his travel plans for a film festival (he still travels with an Iranian passport). Sometimes I genuinely believe that he neither knows nor cares to know who the president of the United States is.

The full-bodied presence of Naderi in his adopted city is equally evident in his photography. In March 2003, I organised a major photography exhibition for Naderi at La Maison Française of Columbia University, where we exhibited some fifty of his black-and-white photographs of New York. This exhibition was in anticipation of the world premiere of his third New York film, *Marathon* (2002) in May 2003, in the course of the Tribeca Film Festival. These were mostly pictures of various street walls that Naderi had photographed over a period of ten years, between 1992 and 2002. The idea of these photographs would usually begin with a torn flyer, a ripped poster, or a washed-out announcement, sometime pasted on top of each other and then left and abandoned to ruin on street walls near where Naderi lives. Naderi would first 'work' on these traces of life in the streets of New York, 'curate' them as it were, 'treat' them with fire, smoke, water and the like, and then let them 'pickle' for a while in an open and naked exposure to the natural and urban elements – rain, wind, dust, snow, smoke, occasional hail, accidental paint, systematic pollution and so on, and then at an opportune moment, when his visceral guts and aesthetic eyes came together and concurred, he would frame them precisely the way he wanted and take a picture of them. The result is a spectacular, at times uncanny, visual evidence of the traces of the rambunctious urbanity that a cosmopolis at once generates, ignores, or hides, yet reveals to the perceptive eyes of a very few of its residents.

Throughout this decade (1992–2002), and as he was making his New York films, Naderi was also deeply involved in photographing his beloved city and exhibiting the growing body of his work in the US, Europe and Asia – with major exhibitions in Washington DC, Houston, Rome, Bologna, Milan, Bergamo and Tokyo.

These pictures reflect Naderi's vision of the unforgiving layers of urban memories that erase each other, more by repetition of overlays rather than by amnesia. The city does not forget, it just remembers too much – and in that embodied con-fusion of memories, Naderi's vision of New York dwells. He considers these pictures a form of visual documentation of his thoughts and feelings, as he has made his New York feature films – and they are, in effect, the variedly conjugated visual lexicography of his perception of New York, reflecting the same sensibilities that define his New York films. Naderi himself believes that his photography is, in fact, an extension of his cinematic vision and helps him sustain his imaginative space within which he then dreams and interprets his vision of New York. These photographs are, in fact, the pictorial record of extending the iconic universe of his cinema to the spell cast on his imaginative soul. In between his films, these photographs in effect 'tide him over', as we say, until such time that he can again stand behind a camera and shout 'Action!' and then, as he habitually and abruptly ends all his phone conversations, 'Cut!'

Amir Naderi's political detachment from his whereabouts and his material rootedness in New York – evident in both his films and photography – are interrelated. His connection to New York is corporeal – buildings and streets have a living resonance with him. He was furious after 9/11. 'What have these innocent buildings done?' He spoke of the Twin Towers of the World Trade Center in endearingly anthropomorphic terms. 'What have these beautiful, innocent, creatures done? Why take it out on them?' On the day of 9/11, he went to the rooftop of his apartment building and took magnificent, mournful pictures of the WTC. These pictures are the visions of an homage, a panegyric poem, an elegy for two fallen friends – whom (not which) he had shot so hauntingly in his first feature film in New York, *Manhattan by Numbers*.

Amir Naderi detests politics with a vengeance (and is entirely oblivious to the fact that there is already a politics to his being apolitical, especially when he protests too much) – but his cultivated distance from politics is materially connected to the architectonic weight of his New York. When I appear on national television commenting on current affairs, he calls me and says he saw me on television and liked the colour combination of my shirt and tie. When he finds out, usually from Nikzad Nodjoumi, that I have been attacked in the New York press for having said or done one thing or another to anger the powerful and nasty people of the city, he has one of three reactions. First, he does not call me for days; second, he calls me and comes up to my place with a rare and precious Ford or Kurosawa, to have dinner and watch a movie with me (never ever uttering a word about the terror that has been unleashed against me); or third, he goes on a rampage against politics. For a man who made *Tangsir* (1973), *Harmonica* (1974) and *Requiem* (1978), three of the most political and anti-Shah films of the 1970s and definitive of the political consciousness that gradually led to the 1979 revolution in Iran, Amir Naderi has a bone-deep reaction to political activism. 'Well, I learned it from you', I would tell him on these occasions. 'I am a child of your generation of filmmakers'. 'Did I not make *Tangsir*?' he would respond with a rhetorical question on these occasions. 'Yes, you did', I concur. 'Well', he concludes triumphantly, 'I tell you, fuck politics. Stick to your work'. Anything I do other than watching Ford, Kurosawa and Lane (on whose cinemas he knows I am writing a book), he disapproves. When I helped put together a Palestinian film festival in New York, he utterly disapproved. On the opening night of the festival, however, he called to wish me luck. When the political fallout of the festival began to hit me hard (every single day a nasty article against me and my colleagues appeared in the New York tabloids), there was an 'I told you so' written all over the cups of tea he offered to me in consolation. When he was a member of the jury in Chicago and saw a film by Elia Suleiman, he called me at 2:00 o'clock in the morning to tell me what a great filmmaker Elia Suleiman was – and said nothing of our Palestinian film festival. When I invited Hany Abu Assad for dinner to meet him – for Hany is a great fan of his cinema – he was his usual public persona, charming, affectionate, talkative, boastful. For Naderi, Elia Suleiman and Hany Abu Assad are filmmakers, not Palestinian filmmakers. Once in a café in Damascus (it was in July 2004), I had a chat with Osama Muhammad, one of the most gifted Syrian filmmakers I know. He told me how once, in India, he was a member of a jury, and Niki Karimi, an Iranian actress and now filmmaker, asked him the proverbial question – do you like Kiarostami better or Makhmalbaf? 'Neither of them', Osama had responded. 'Amir Naderi is the real master of your cinema – that's the filmmaker I look up to'. When I told this story to Amir in New York, he blushed.

'Suppose', he tells me when he wants to make a point of his aversion to politics, 'suppose all your political ideals of justice and fairness, democracy and equanimity are materialised tomorrow. What then? What will you do with yourself, if you get up one morning and there is no political cause that you advocate and everything you hope for has materialised – eternal justice for all mankind, food on everyone's table, all clothed and sheltered. What will you do with yourself then? If you think the world is unbearable now, wait until you don't have any political cause to espouse – then you see the real terror of this world'. He pauses for a split second and then adds, 'I am the filmmaker of that morning after, when the world no longer has a political cause to distract it from its real misery. Who cares to read Maxim Gorky today – but Chekhov, he is forever'.

On the Poetry of Concrete and Steel

One of Naderi's most perceptive American commentators is the film critic David Ng. Ng clearly grasps and admirably articulates the environmental fascination of Naderi with the cosmopolitan New York that he inhabits – and that for him represents technological postmodernity at the height of its paradoxical achievements. 'Naderi's poetry', Ng notices, 'is of a much harsher nature [... than D. A. Pennebaker's *Daybreak Express* (1953), with which he compares Naderi's *Marathon*]. A Stygian voyage shot in caustic b&w, *Marathon* inhabits its grimy environs so convincingly that the director may well have used an unwashed subway car window as his lens'.[10] Ng has also noted the creative mutation of Naderi's own person into the persona of his principal characters – but he misreads their (and with them Amir Naderi's own) location. 'For Naderi', Ng observes of Gretchen in *Marathon*, 'she's clearly an alter ego: a maniacally driven perpetual-motion machine stranded in an alien land'.[11] That 'alien land' is not New York *qua* New York, the US, or particularly that hugely empty abstraction called 'the West'. That 'alien land' is the world at large (for which New York stands in Naderi's cinema) – the technological world, the world abstracted to instrumental reason, to machine, to manufacturing, production, distribution, marketing, consumption, to men, women and children mutated into things, things into objects, objects into in/animate simulacra of reality.

The nebulous disposition of that world is what Naderi's cinema now inhabits, and New York is the cosmopolitan epicentre of the technological postmodernity that animates it. Naderi is fixated on being contemporary with his time – and that is the reason why he so succinctly detests nostalgia. But the intensity of his allergic reaction to nostalgia means that he is haunted by it. Between the goblin of a nostalgia that haunts him and his first and second names, and an obsessive fixation with being the creature of his time and place, Naderi maps out the creative contour of his art. New York is the absolutely best place for that kind of creative disposition, for New York is equally miasmatic, out of its own place. It has no time to impress its inhabitants, let alone its casual visitors, with the depth of its character. Paris and London, Tehran and Cairo, as indeed all other major cities, have already a firm and formed opinion of themselves – opinions that they nervously impose on their inhabitants and show off to their visitors. The glory of New York is that it has no time for such shallow and fragile egos of its less gifted relatives. It embraces its inhabitants and welcomes its visitors into its vast, generous, cruel and careless bosom, finds out what and who they are and then moulds them and itself in the mirror-image of each other.

Ng comes closest to what Naderi is up to in New York when he notices the non-verbality of Naderi's obsessions:

> For someone obsessed with words, she [Gretchen in Marathon] exists in an almost pre-verbal state, her only meaningful contact with other people being the messages her mother leaves on her answering machine. Her tunnel-vision existence mercifully explodes in the movie's final scene: an entire city muted by snowfall – a startling cinematic negative of our lightless, noise-polluted civilization.[12]

That civilisation for Naderi has now assumed iconic significance for the world at large. In *Marathon*, Naderi reduces that civilisation to its innermost layers and labyrinths of abstractions, not just to mere words, but beyond that deep into the frightful fury of the meaningless letters of the alphabet – long before they could mean anything, mere signs with no significance attached to them, symbols devoid of any mythic universe outside their own self-referential hubris. The most frightful scene in *Marathon* is the bathtub shot of letters, words and pages of the dictionary floating in an abstracted eternity in Gretchen's apartment. The same reduction of glorious words into meaningless letters, of confident signifiers into anxiety-ridden signs, is echoed in Naderi's obsession with noise – music reduced to the elemental noisiness of its absolutist abstractions. There is something apocalyptic in Naderi's vision of our present, pushing it forward to its logical conclusions into its (perhaps inevitable) future.

From this angle we can see how and why Naderi abandons *the politics of the present* for *the metaphysics of the presence*. The politics of the present, the systematic mendacity of our being politically positioned in the world (one way or even another), he seems to see as a camouflage fictively covering the metaphysics of our presence, our ability to see and suggest ourselves in our being-towards-the world, as Heidegger would say; or better yet, our Being-towards-death. But Naderi is far more an elegist than a coroner in this autopsy, for his careful construction of an apolitical take on reality in his cinema is categorically coterminous with an *almost metaphysical* dwelling in the physical facticity of life – a physicality that he visually sublates to a poetic take on shapes, shades, volumes and sounds (teasing out of their matter-of-fact-ness an overriding significance otherwise hidden under the guise of too much familiarity – and thus the confusion of those who believe that Naderi is primarily a photographer, for they cannot see the centrality of abstracted objects and shapes in the general thrust of his cosmovision.

Central to that physical hold on reality is an *existential solitude*, operative at the heart of all of Naderi's films. Naderi's cinema is a cinema of solitude – and that is the only feature of his vision that has remained consistently definitive of his cinema (from Iran to the United States) and, I daresay, will remain so, even if he were to go to the moon (as he plans to do, figuratively speaking, in his next film) and articulate his vision in the rugged aridity of its solitary distance from everything. At the centre of *Manhattan by Numbers* (1993) is George Murphy (John Wojda), at the centre of *ABC ... Manhattan* (1997) are three solitary and unrelated souls – Kacey (Erin Norris), Colleen (Lucy Knight) and Kate (Sara Paul); at the centre of *Marathon* (2003) is Gretchen (Sara Paul), and at the centre of *Sound Barrier* (2005) is Jesse (Charlie Wilson) – all of them solitary, driven, obsessed, self-referential, desperate, yet calm and quiet in their exteriors. We never see any one of Naderi's characters in the company of their parents (Naderi himself was orphaned at a very young age), siblings, family, or friends. It really does not matter what these characters are looking for – George Murphy is looking for some money to pay his rent, Colleen is desperate to keep her daughter, Kacey is chasing after her lost dog, Kate is seeking to break up with her brother/lover, Gretchen is after breaking her own record in solving crossword puzzles, Jesse is looking for the voice of his mother to find out why he is deaf and mute. All of these characters are lonely, lonesome, with no organic connection to anything or anybody. It is not sufficient to say that these solitary characters are reflections of Amir Naderi's own solitude, not just as an immigrant living in New York, but in fact as a stranger even or perhaps particularly in his own homeland, in Iran. In his innermost being as an artist, Naderi in fact does not have any homeland – does not feel particularly connected to anything or anybody. The solitude we witness in Naderi's cinema is existential, cosmic, universal – something in that solitude speaks to humanity at large: disconnected, anomic, free-floating in the realm of worldly connections, material belongings; thus integral to a metaphysical mutation to *things*, in/animate objects that he depicts and pictures. 'I am a rock', he might as well sing with his fellow New Yorkers, Simon and Garfunkel:

> I am an island.
> I've built walls,
> A fortress deep and mighty,
> That none may penetrate ...
> I am an island.

David Ng has admirably detected this existential angst at the heart of Naderi's cinema:

> His U.S.-set films, including 'Manhattan by Numbers', 'A, B, C ... Manhattan' and his most recent, 'Marathon', merge the anti-narrative style he pioneered in Iran with the ultramodern setting of his adopted home, New York. The results are a poetic but often jarring deconstruction of the familiar, in which mundane objects and events become almost abstract.[13]

That abstraction is purposeful, definitive of Naderi's vision of the world, the way, in fact, he de-familiarises the familiar by way of showing its inner angst, barely holding itself, and with itself the illusion of a worldly permanence, together.

To see the fragility of that elusive permanence, the way Naderi exposes it, it is crucial not just to read those who admire his cinema, but also to consider those who find it unbearable and even troubling. It is important to know why, for example, Ronnie Scheib of *Variety* considers *Sound Barrier* 'a black-and-white excursion into obsession, [which] may be the most extended mise en scene of pure frustration in cinema history',[14] and why Jared Rapfogel of *Senses of Cinema* believes, even more strongly, that *Sound Barrier* is 'almost unbearable to sit through', or why he describes it as 'manic and feverish rather than calm and contemplative'.[15] To be sure, film critics like Jared Rapfogel are not entirely oblivious to Naderi's cinematic virtuosity. Rapfogel, in fact, believes that ...

> The boldness of the film's structure is admirable, and I found myself fascinated by the first scene, with its hypnotic repetition, its almost sculptural representation of obsessiveness [*sic*] for the first 15 minutes or so, anyway. Its power has something to do with the fact that, at this point, we don't really know who this child is or what exactly he's looking for, leaving us only with this remarkable, animal immediacy, this pure spectacle of feverish physical activity.[16]

The problem for critics like Rapfogel (quite typical of others who have similar issues with Naderi's cinema but have not put it so succinctly) begins precisely with this inscrutable obsession of characters such as Jesse. Describing the storage room scene of *Sound Barrier*, Rapfogel objects:

> As the scene goes on and on (and on), as it ceases to be a scene, per se, and becomes the core of the film itself, it begins to test the patience even of those among us who love say, [James Benning's] 13 Lakes, or an ostensibly narrative but radically uneventful film like Chantal Akerman's Jeanne Dielman, 23 Quai du Commerce, 1080 Bruxelles (1975).[17]

The conclusion of this line of argument is, of course, long foregone and pretty much pre-determined, for ...

> ... when *Sound Barrier* squanders the interest inspired by its structural purity, it's in trouble, having little else to fall back on. Its derivative, melodramatic plot (the revelation of a childhood trauma miraculously curing deafness), its student-film-like direction and editing, and its crushingly obvious experiments with sound and silence (which basically consist of cutting back and forth between subjective shots

> accompanied by a low rumble and objective shots with ambient sound), fail to compel. And in the last half hour, with Jesse's prolonged freak-out occasioning a much more cacophonous passage of sound-silence counterpoint, *Sound Barrier* becomes truly excruciating – it left me longing to be deaf.[18]

The problem that Naderi has with these critics is, of course, the problem that the good Captain of Road Prison 36 had with Luke, in Stuart Rosenberg's *Cool Hand Luke* (1967): 'What we have here is a failure to communicate'. The barely visible storylines in Naderi's films are just there to suggest the mere simulacrum of a non-event. Definitive of Naderi's cinema is precisely the instance of obsessive discovery – the maniacal moment when Jesse completely forgets not just himself but the whole universe around him and has absolutely no consciousness of anything but the focal point of his discovery – which at this point happens to be a tape that may contain the voice of his mother, in which she may have revealed what happened so that he lost his ability to hear. In other words, what Rapfogel cannot wait to get over with is precisely the moment of the film – there is nothing before or after it. That is it. The narrative drama in Naderi's cinema, whatever it might be (whether a young woman tries to beat her own record in solving crossword puzzles in *Marathon*, or a young boy looks for water in the middle of the desert in *Water, Wind, Dust*), is entirely tangential, almost irrelevant to the obsessive moment of discovery itself – and that discovery dwells in a *moment* and has no claim to a *duration*, for the entire *Sound Barrier*, as indeed the entire *Marathon*, is really just a split second, the blink of an eye. Time stands still in such obsessive moments; the second hand does not move. There is an eternity in the moment of obsessive discovery that Naderi wishes to unpack.

There is a scene in *Marathon* (that unfortunately did not make it into Naderi's final cut, but I have seen it among his rushes) when Gretchen stands in Time Square, staring at a clock and waiting for the strike of the hour so that she can start her twenty-four-hour marathon. The entire film, and the rest of Gretchen's story, dwells on that very second when she is waiting to start. The rest of her day and the rest of her evening, night and midnight – until the hour strikes again and she has run out of time – and whatever number of crossword puzzles she will have solved as the final number (seventy-two and a half) stand absolutely constant. Naderi once said to me that people only see the final result of an artist's creation, when Van Gogh, for example, has painted the sunflower and gone home to sleep. 'People just look at that sunflower', Naderi said, 'and have no clue how it came about. My ambition is to enter the moment of obsessive creation, the madness that is hidden under the serene surface of the work'. Unless one is with Naderi in that equally obsessive urge to capture the moment of (almost epileptic seizure of) creation, of course his storylines appear almost ridiculous, non-existent and even blasé. The point of his entire cinema is lost if one abandons the spontaneity of the moment of creation for the consumer-oriented, quick-fix, put-it-in-my-hand, final result of where we are headed and for what purpose. There is a fundamental discrepancy between Naderi's fixation with the authenticity of the work of art and the triumphant reign of the *culture industry*, as Adorno called it,[19] an industry that needs and exacts fast, furious and dispensable results – works of art,

McDonald's hamburgers, or Starbuck's coffee cups make no difference (I have always thought that the 'Emrika' that Naderi has actively imagined and sustained in his mind since childhood is really a figment of his own imagination, and the projected epicentre of the globalised monstrosity of capital has no relation to it – for today, from Dubai over Tel Aviv and Disney Europe to New Jersey shopping malls, we have an entirely different map for 'Emrika'). A Hollywood scriptwriter once said that, if he did not threaten to blow up the entire universe in the first thirty seconds of a script, he has already lost the attention span of his American audience. That is the patience and poise that critics such as Rapfogel bring to Naderi's cinema. This is neither Rapfogel's nor Naderi's fault – this is just the mis-matched discrepancy of a kind of artistic creativity caught in the snares of a long since vacated world. What Walter Benjamin called the vanishing aura of the work of art in the age of mechanical reproduction is particularly meaningful in the light of the disease (now the *conditio sine qua non*) that Adorno diagnosed as the *culture industry* – against both of which artists like Amir Naderi have waged an entirely lost and always uphill battle.[20]

Notice Rapfogel's almost accurate description of the crucial scene of Jesse in the storage room:

> The central character is Jesse, an 11 year-old deaf-mute child who discovers that there may be a tape recording of his dead mother's voice in a locker in a Queens storage facility. In a brief and elliptical series of scenes, we witness Jesse's discovery of this knowledge and his securing of the key to the locker. The great bulk of the following 90-plus minutes consists of two scenes: for something like 45 minutes, we sit by as Jesse enters the storage locker, finds boxes and boxes full of labeled cassette tapes, and systematically searches through these boxes, growing increasingly desperate, violent and destructive, ripping open the containers, hurling the cassettes aside, and generally laying waste to the room until, finally (FINALLY!), he finds what he's looking for.[21]

The frustration that you see in the parenthetical capital letters with the added exclamation mark, (FINALLY!), is precisely where Rapfogel loses not just his patience but also the entire point of the film. That scene is not preparatory for something else. That scene IS the final and definitive scene. That scene is not going anywhere, and it is desperately trying to draw attention to itself. But the culture industry, the fast-food consumer culture, has of course no patience or poise to pause and see, note, notice, or above all care – for creativity in that culture is defined by mechanical (and now electronic) productivity, by the very speed that consumes it at the moment of its creativity, as fast as a newspaper column written and read punctiliously to the deadline of a meaningless tomorrow; a piece of news in the newspaper today, soaking wet in the litter box of a cat tomorrow. 'The fact that we know so little about Jesse', Rapfogel believes, 'becomes less a matter of mystery and more of a liability. The little we learn about him by observing his behavior – that he is desperate and hysterical – can't justify 45 minutes of endless repetition'.[22] What repetition? There are literally thousands of cuts in *Sound Barrier* – and not a single one of them is like another. '*Sound Barrier*', Rapfogel finally concludes, 'may have been awful, but it was at least memorably awful'.[23] In that memorial remembrance, even when one has spectacularly failed to understand a work of art, is precisely where an artist leaves the traces of his time and leaves.

The failure of Naderi to convey what he is up to in his cinema and to convince such film critics as Rapfogel, symptomatic of a more pervasive reaction to his New York films, casts Naderi on the exact opposite side of what is offered by the Danish filmmaker Lars von Trier, whose cinema is shot and projected from a diametrically opposite angle on the self-same 'America' that over a lifetime has fascinated and preoccupied Naderi. Beginning with his *Dancer in the Dark* (2000), and now two-thirds into his projected 'USA Trilogy', of which *Dogville* (2004) and *Manderlay* (2005) have already enthralled, bedevilled, embarrassed, angered and disturbed his American audiences, Lars von Trier has a take entirely different from Amir Naderi on 'America'. Without ever as much as setting foot in the United States (for Lars von Trier is reportedly quite phobic and does not travel), the brutally wise and unmercifully perceptive Dane has hit hard at not just the political disposition but at the a/moral underpinning of the very idea of this thing called 'America'. While the American film critic crowd is busy trying to figure out whether or not Lars von Trier is 'anti-American' (self-delusional verbosity has rarely been so confounded), Lars von Trier is busy ripping the very fabric of 'America' to pieces. While Andrew Delbanco, the distinguished American literary critic, is busy linking Melville's American myth of Ahab and his search for the white whale to President Bush's presumably dogged pursuit of Osama bin Laden halfway around the globe (an entirely delusional misconception, for Bush needed and, in fact, manufactured Bin Laden),[24] Ahab of a different sea comes to Delbanco's doorstep and tells him of the horror under his own nose. How poor is Delbanco's America in teaching the world anything; how rich is von Trier's world in teaching America everything.

Naderi's cinema is the exact anti-dote to von Trier's – if only Rapfogel had a little bit of more patience with it. From the belly of the beast, he is desperate and, perhaps purely for the salvation of his own soul (for having devoted a lifetime of believing in it), he is trying to find a redeeming light in this dark terror called 'America'. 'To me', Naderi once told me, '*Moby Dick* is everything – that dogged, obsessive, consuming search'. He then paused for a second and said: 'But I don't have the heart of that ending in the future of Ahab. I need a dram of hope'. Jesse's smile at the end of *Sound Barrier*, the snowfall over New York at the end of *Marathon* and the few dollars that an accidental acquaintance finally gives to George Murphy in *Manhattan by Numbers* are all just sparks of that grace, fragile rays of hope, that Naderi, perhaps the last hopeful immigrant to this godforsaken land, can offer.

Perhaps Naderi's New York is the salvation of von Trier's America – and yet they both may be too late.

Suspended of All Imported Meanings

Naderi's cinema is a poetic of visual *reflection* – suspended of all imported meanings, saturated by the imaginal universe of their own making – and this is at once the most exhilarating and the most frustrating aspect of his cinema. It is exhilarating, for with

Naderi you never know where he is taking you, for he does not quite know where he is going himself. It is frustrating (particularly for major film festival directors and film critics who consistently have difficulty with his lexiconic asceticism), for he is a visual physicist and not a narrative engineer. Naderi's visual reflections are anti-metaphysical in the sense that they are not predicated on any particular set of epistemic suppositions. In defiance of any received and meaningful epistemic, Naderi's cinema (as that of any other great filmmaker) in effect has created, crafted and coined its own visual vocabulary – over the course of a long and illustrious career. The specific nature of that vocabulary in the case of Naderi is his fixation with the post-industrial technological machinery. If the *cosmopolis* is the setting of Naderi's cinema – from Bushehr over Tehran to New York – the very epitome of *technological postmodernity* is the soul of his cinema. In this sense, no other Iranian filmmaker comes even close to Naderi in consistently being an urban filmmaker, a filmmaker of the technological mammoth he at once fears and adores.

In Naderi's cinema, the physical evidence of *technological machinery* – cars, airplanes, helicopters, trains, bridges, motorcycles, ships, bicycles, industrial refuse, oil refineries, city slums, gas reservoirs, traffic jams, skyscrapers, subway systems and so on – is no longer predicated on a science that he neither posits nor wishes to question. In his cinema, this machinery has assumed a reality *sui generis*, irreducible to whatever advances in various sciences may have occasioned them. The iconic manifestations of technological postmodernity in Naderi's New York cinema are the elemental forces of his visual reflections, his poetics of dwelling on that factual phenomenon rather than a politics of questioning or criticising it.

Given the radical contemporaneity of Naderi's cinematic reflection on technological postmodernity, his cinema is not reducible or assimilable to any national or regional aesthetics – his aesthetics is neither Iranian nor American, neither Eastern nor Western. In fact, his cinema radically resists national or regional aestheticisation. This resistance, in turn, prevents his cinema from becoming integrated into any metaphysics of significant meaning – as it insists on remaining visually irreducible, reflectively poetic and as such definitive of the technological postmodernity it inhabits.

Naderi's cinema equally resists cultural classification – not just in his New York films, but even in the films that he made in his native country. In other words, even his Iranian films are not Iranian in any enduring, meaningful, or markedly cultural sense. This aspect of his cinema may be traced back to the marginal coloniality from which he as a filmmaker hails, or it may be equally articulated in terms of the world cinema to which he was habitually exposed as a youngster. Abadan, Naderi's birthplace, is a peculiarly syncretic location. Like the rest of Khuzestan province, Abadan is located on the crosscurrents of four cultures – African, Arab, Indian and Iranian. People like Amir Naderi, as the rest of us who come from that region, are located on the borderline of two colonial peripheries – both European-based colonialism and Tehran-based racism. While the British colonial officers in Southern Iran considered us native Iranians in their racially profiling, the Tehranis looked at us as 'Arabs', an equally condescending and racist category in their eyes. To this day, the principal figures in Iranian cinema – Abbas Kiarostami, Mohsen Makhmalbaf, Bahram Beiza'i, Dariush

Mehrju'i, Bahman Farmanara, Rakhshan Bani-Etemad and so on—are either born-and-bred Tehranis, or else have completely assimilated and identify with a Tehran-based condescending attitude towards what they dismissively call '*shahrastani*' – or 'provincial', with a strong negative connotation. In the crosscurrents of two racist/colonial gazes, the dual marginality assumes an entirely new meaning. We in the south feel neither completely Iranian (the way in which, from Pahlavi monarchy to Islamic mullarchy, the leading Iranian public intellectuals and literati think of themselves as 'Iranian'), nor indeed do we completely see ourselves as Arab, African, or Indian. We belong to all of these colonially manufactured cultural traits and yet none of them exclusively – and thus our very factual evidence dismantles them all. 'Culture', as result, for filmmakers like Amir Naderi (or novelists like Ahmad Mahmoud and Sadeq Chubak) is an entirely fluid if not futile category. Thus, not just culture but, in fact, its inevitable mutation into the politics of cultural identity is an entirely useless and pedantic proposition in our neck of the woods.

The suspension of cultural identity in Naderi's cinema in turn leads to its deferral of all received and regurgitated god-terms – of 'Tradition versus Modernity', 'Islam faces the West', and so on. All such god-terms, unexamined meta-narratives of colonial modernity, are absolutely and entirely useless and irrelevant in the making of Naderi's cinema. This is at once the blessing and the curse of his cinematic cosmovision – *blessing* for it is a space of emancipation from all such inherited traps, *curse* for it systematically prevents his cinema to be globally celebrated, as it richly deserves, because it defies the logic of national cinema, now seemingly forever cast in the guise of the cinema that most caters to the political atrocities of the season (Iran was yesterday, Afghanistan is today, Iraq has now followed, and Iran may indeed come back again, or perhaps Korea). Cannes as a result follows Bush in his designation of what he calls 'the Axis of Evil' – for the French (and by extension Europeans) to feel superior to Americans (their perennial complex) and thus to whitewash their own colonial atrocities.

By creatively dwelling on technological postmodernity as the sight of its own peculiar (anti-)metaphysics, Naderi's cinema thrives in those counter-metaphysics, the bodily resurrection of the visual testament of a civilisational state that at once frightens and exhilarates him. Inside that machine, he is the happiest discoverer of the terror that technological postmodernity has perpetrated upon man – and, thus, Stanley Kubrick's *2001: A Space Odyssey* (1968) remains one of his absolute iconic references. New York is thus both the Alpha and the Omega of Naderi's cinema – its commencement and its conclusion, its point of origin and its visceral return. It is not just the Cosmopolis of the final world dis/order, but also the Gotham of no return.

The Troubadour of the Occidental Exile

The idea of exile, which we have received most recently through the work of (among others) Antonio Gramsci and Edward Said, has paved the way towards a new conception of organicity in the global condition of thinking, being, working and the formation of the creative subject. For Adorno, this was occasioned by his escape from his German homeland under Nazi barbarism, and for Said from his occupied Palestinian homeland. With an allusion to the iconic work of the twelfth-century philosopher

Shahab al-Din Yahya Suhrawardi's *Qesseh al-Ghorbat al-Gharbiyyeh/The Ballad of the Occidental Exile*, we might rethink the idea of the exilic (nomadic) subject after (or in the aftermath of) the exhaustion of the condition of fascism and coloniality. Anticipating Rosi Braidotti by centuries, Suhrawardi's philosophical allegory opens the horizons of 'exile' onto an exilic/nomadic consciousness as the premise of the unknowing subject.

Exile, or the condition of the mobile memory enabling the unlearning subject through suspenseful metonymy, is where the formalised gender specificity comes undone – so that mythic memories are altered and updated. The cinematic worlds of Shahid-Saless and Naderi become substitutional and mythic – as their respective cosmovision basks in its exilic being-in-the-world. As cinema becomes mythic in exile, it replaces the physical world it occupies, where Berlin or New York become the locations where myth and metonymy conflate, and where the unknowing subject now faces the renewed unfamiliarity of the knowable world. Shahid-Saless and Naderi travelled away and never returned to their homeland – there to meet Mehdi Akhavan Sales' '*Qasedak*' that even in the depth of its pessimism and despair still wonders if a floating dandelion may indeed bring good news somewhere else in the world.

> *Boro anja keh to ra montazerand ...*
> Go where they are still waiting for you![25]

With that very paradox, the poem anticipates Shahid-Saless and Naderi decades before they had left their homeland and opens onto the metonymic verisimilitude of somewhere other than one's immediate habitat being the abode of hope – where Iranian troubadours of an existential exile may have a message for the rest of the world.

PART IV

MYSTICISM AND MYTHOLOGIES

9

The World of Verisimilitude[1]

Life is perhaps
That enclosed instance
When my look
Destroys itself in the pupil of your eyes –
And there's a feeling in this
That I shall mix with understanding the moon
And grasping the darkness.[2]

Forough Farrokhzad, '*Tavallodi Digar*/Another Birth' (1962)

Years ago, perhaps in the mid-1990s, I was in Milan during a summer holiday, and in a bookstore in its famous Galleria Vittorio Emanuele I chanced upon a book by Roland Barthes, *Sul Cinema*. I picked it up and started thumbing through it with my hesitant Italian. I came across this passage:

> *Nietzsche distingue due figure, il prete e l'artista. Di preti, ne abbiamo oggi da vendere; di tutte le religioni e anche senza religione; ma di artisti? Vorrei, caro Antonioni, che tu mi prestassi per un attimo qualche tratto della tua opera per permettermi di fissare le tre forze, o se preferisci, le tre virtu che ai miei occhi costituiscono l'artista. Le dico subito: la vigilanza, la saggezza e la piu paradossale di tutte, la fragilita.*[3]

There and then I realised that Barthes' take on Nietzsche's typology, which he had addressed to Michelangelo Antonioni, has a crucial consequence for what was happening in Iranian cinema. This is what Barthes says:

> Nietzsche distinguished between two figures: The priest and the artist. Of priests we have enough to sell from all religions or non-religions. As to the artists, I would like you, my dear Antonioni, to lend me a part of your work for a while to allow me to construct the three forces, or if you like the three virtues, that in my eyes constitute an artist. Let me tell what they are: Vigilance, wisdom, and the most paradoxical of all, fragility.

Barthes' first assumption here is that we can easily distinguish between priests and artists. We usually can – if by nothing else, then at least by the way they invent things. But what happens when artists, while being artists and while in the act of creation, come dangerously close to picking up priestly habits? What do we do then? 'Fragility' is perhaps the most operative distinction that we, following Barthes, need to keep in mind.

That fragility dwells in the twilight zone located between the dead certainties of a reigning metaphysics and the daunting doubts that artists interpret from their perturbed dreams. To take you to the twilight zone of one set of such dreams, in this chapter I want to talk of Iranian 'cine-mysticism'. There is an emerging pattern of cine-mysticism in post-revolutionary Iranian cinema that is as much conducive to collapsing itself into a kind of New Age Mysticism which in a roundabout way subserves the Islamic metaphysics, as it is prone to foregrounding a visual culture in its literary antecedents and thus rescue it from that entrapment. Whether artists turn into priests and begin to preach, or else priests submit their authority to artists and let them imagine otherwise: there is the rub.

The Nature and Disposition of Creativity

The theoretically articulated ideological parameters that after the Islamic Revolution in Iran have brutally curtailed the nature and disposition of creativity in all artistic mediums have had a particularly pronounced presence in Iranian cinema. Three kinds of cinema have emerged in the post-revolutionary period: a cinema which is governmentally financed and squarely at the service of 'Islamic Ideology'; a commercial cinema which is privately funded; and a cinema of independent vision which leads a precarious life, always at the mercy of a whimsical censorship and oscillating financial resources. All these three cinemas, whether sub-serving the self-legitimising propaganda of the Islamic Republic or subverting it, are subject to modes of visual and narrative imperatives that an 'Islamic' revolution inevitably entails. The emerging patterns of 'cine-mysticism' now evident in aspects of Iranian cinema are the immediate by-products of this particular turn in the political context of their production.

The gradual, and perhaps inevitable, rise of this cine-mysticism has quite naturally taken the Iranian cinematic (visual) culture back to its immediate and distanced literary sources. Although after nearly a century of cultivation of its own visual culture Iranian cinema has a reality *sui generis*, there are still enduring links that hold this cinema and the Iranian literary past together. While Kiarostami's cinematic vision reveals an unmistakable affinity with the poetry of Sohrab Sepehri, Bahram Beiza'i's cinematic narrative consciously adopts classical Persian literary (epic) and performative (*Ta'ziyeh*) leitmotifs. Streaks of classical and modernist Persian literary aesthetics are equally evident in any number of other leading Iranian filmmakers. While the origin of this cinematic link to its literary antecedents can be traced back to the pre-revolutionary periods of the 1950s to the 1970s, the successful Islamisation of the Iranian Revolution of 1979 and the radical theocentricity of its ideological foundations have inevitably centralised a mystical core to this active visualisation of the 'Absolute Truth'.

While to the leading ideologues of the Islamic Republic this cine-mysticism is God-sent, an auspicious development that can only strengthen the metaphysical foundation of the theocracy, a closer examination of the phenomenon from within Iranian cinema demonstrates a clearly bifurcated division between a cine-mysticism that accepts, adopts, celebrates and thus subserves that metaphysics and a different kind of cinema which uses the potential powers of that cine-mysticism to subvert it. The difference has to do not just with a particular filmmaker's felicity of access to the nature and dynamics of classical Persian Sufism, but also with their ability to manipulate that legacy in life-affirming and emancipatory ways.

Towards a Culture of Bodily Denials

By far the most striking example of how uncontrolled attraction to 'Persian Mysticism' can collapse into dangerous flirtation with a metaphysical culture of bodily denial is to be seen in Dariush Mehrju'i's *Pari/Pari* (1995). One looks at this film and wonders what calamitous consequences the censorial politics of an Islamic Republic can have for the creative gift of a filmmaker who once could shatter the cinematic culture of a nation with such masterpieces as *Cow* (1969) or *The Cycle* (1977). The two central characters of *Pari*, the deliriously beautiful Pari and her brother Dadashi, stand on the two opposite sides of a deadly attraction to mysticism. Dadashi, on the one hand, had started his moral and intellectual quest with mysticism and is now an actor who sees the entire world as a big theatrical scene. Pari, on the other hand, starts as an actor and now is deeply and almost violently mystical in her demeanour. Pari and Dadashi have had two older brothers, one of whom has committed suicide by setting himself on fire, having reached the end of the rope in his futile quest for 'Absolute Truth', while the other leads a pathetically isolated and empty life in a remote village. The memory of a dead idol and the shadow of a lesser ideal now loom large over the mutually contradicting lives of Pari and Dadashi.

Mehrju'i's juxtaposition of the tetralogical narrative is set to pronounce in particular the pronounced mysticism of Pari, whose stunning beauty, acted admirably by Niki Karimi, is put squarely at the service of her steadfast determination to 'see the Light'. The 'Light' appears to her in the shape of a ghostly apparition, an equally beautiful man with long blond hair, green eyes, a mesmerising gaze, all wrapped up in a shabby cloth. The intervals between Pari's encounters with the ghostly apparition are filled with the pompous professors of literature at Tehran University, servile classmates who know nothing better than go through the motions, a dilapidated and anarchical house which in one way or another is being renovated. Mehrju'i, incidentally, is a master of creating confusing houses as a metaphor of his nation. He has done this brilliantly in *The Tenants/Ejareh Neshinan* (1987), and above all with the ghastly encounters with her gluttonous, self-absorbed, pseudo-intellectual fiancé in Isfahan. The more deeply Pari is plunged into her nightmarish fixation with 'What is the Truth', the more pathetic, pompous, empty and ridiculous appears just about everything around her.

Balancing Pari's debilitating fixation with 'Truth' is not any conception of reality that might challenge the absolutism of that quest. Balancing that quest is Dadashi's utter denial of any 'Truth' and immediate collapse into the world of acting. The whole world is an act to him, nothing beyond the mask. There was a time when Dadashi was seeking the 'Truth' and Pari was acting. Now, Pari seeks the 'Truth', while Dadashi is acting. Caught between the oscillating extremities of these two poles, Pari and Dadashi, *ipso facto*, complement each other by contradicting each other, and they thus deny any other possibility, any other occasion in which the illusion of 'Truth' and the fictive reality of 'Acting' might indeed serve the purpose of celebrating life as it is: truth-less but good, act-full but real.

The ghostly apparition of a strikingly handsome man who hangs himself upside-down in a forsaken well from dusk to dawn and recites the entire Qur'an *verbatim* is precisely the pre-condition upon which Pari's entire physical world appears ugly, dilapidated, confused, full of pompous literature professors, shallow intellectuals, mindless women numbed by a shallow religiosity and extremely opulent bourgeois life. Nothing about or around Pari is beautiful, intelligent, healthy, worth living for, and that is a frightening recognition in light of the fact that she is portrayed by a strikingly beautiful and intelligent woman roaming through some of the most beautiful parts of Isfahan. Mehrju'i is at his best in his remarkable use of colour and light, dialogue and camera movements, emplotment and narrative, in which Pari's nightmarish life is at once visualised and narrated.

Fabling the World

In his essay on 'Myth Rediscovered' in *The Transparent Society*, Gianni Vattimo observes that 'one of the most urgent problems faced by contemporary consciousness as it becomes aware of how the world is "fabled" [...] is that of redefining its own position with regard to myth'.[4] How the world is 'fabled', in Vattimo's beautiful phrase, has a lot to do with the location of a culture, not just in its own imagined history, but also in its commanding geography. What happens when a prominent filmmaker like Mehrju'i makes a film is the active re-fablisation of a culture in terms of its own self-perceptions. The re-fablisation is a social act by virtue of the publicity of the creative move. What *Pari* represents is one among many crucial turning points in the re-making of a culture of inevitable signification. The aesthetic potential of this culture can be manipulated as much in creative and emancipatory directions as in directions of entrapment, passivity and the opiated dozing off of all critical intelligence.

What precisely is the normative disposition of that re-making? Following the example of her older brother, fearful of the moral degeneration of her second-oldest brother, and equally rejecting Dadashi's refuge in the world of acting, Pari is ultimately driven to suicide, prevented at the last moment by Dadashi who now has *to act* as that ghostly apparition who comes to his sister. As Dadashi convinces Pari that the whole 'world's a stage' and thus persuades her not to commit suicide, he gets ready for a part he is to play in a film: in the film's last moment he, playing a soldier, is to die from a gunshot wound. The moment the make-up artist is done putting the finishing touches on Dadashi's face, feigning a gunshot wound, the camera of the film's director now has the dual function of becoming Mehrju'i's camera, too, confusing us in this very last shot of the film about whether this is a real or fictive death.

The direction of re-fablisation is thus very vividly evident. *Pari* emerges as a frightening example of a kind of cine-mysticism that cannot but subserve an anaemic presence in the world, a submissive and dismissive attendance to reality, and thus serve obediently the reconstituted metaphysics of the 'Islamic Ideology' which perforce frames and controls it. Manipulating classical Persian mystical leitmotifs is an extremely dangerous enterprise. The seduction of its metaphoric/metonymic parameters can easily collapse the objectives of even a highly alert and articulate filmmaker into a tacit or active celebration of that foregrounded metaphysics that sustains and animates it.

What is lacking in Iranian cine-mysticism is precisely a critical awareness of what is categorically labelled and thus jaundiced as 'Persian Sufism'. What we generically identify as 'Persian Mysticism', however, has a range of uncontrollable metonymic implications whose logistics can only signify within specific historical and textual contexts. The 'mystical' discourse is constitutionally an oppositional ecstatic discourse, always there to confront the *status quo*, the inevitable seriousness and sobriety of tyranny, the established truth, the normative behaviour. Consider, for example, this passage from *Tadhkirat al-Awlia*, a canonised text of the seventh/thirteenth century in Sufism:

> After the Qur'an and the Prophetic Traditions, there is no other words more sublime than those of the Masters of the Path, May God Have Mercy on Them, because their words are the fruits of action and passion and not the consequence of education and scholarship, of observation and not of expression, of [discovering] the secrets and not repeating [the already evident], of Divine Wisdom and not of acquired knowledge, of effervescence and not of perseverance, of the world of 'my God admonished me', and not of the world of 'my father taught me'. Because they are the successors of the Prophets, May the Benedictions of the Merciful be upon them all.[5]

What Farid al-Din Attar (died 1230), the author of *Tadhkirat al-Awlia*, is doing here, early in his collection of the miraculous deeds of Sufi Masters, is postulating a counter-intelligibility for every established form of normative knowledge – 'fruits of action and passion', as opposed to 'the consequence of education and scholarship'; or 'effervescence', as opposed to 'perseverance'; 'the world of "my God admonished me"', as opposed to 'the world of "my father taught me"'. What occurs here in Attar's passage, reminiscent of many similar narrative manoeuvres, is the meticulous break-up of all metaphysically constituted and politically sustained correspondences between the constellation of signifiers that a culture needs and thus the links to their constellation of signifieds. Far more frightened of the challenge to their political authority that this theo-erotic language constitutes, philosophers, theologians and jurists, the custodians of the sacred, were scared witless of the epistemic shattering of their world by such counter-intelligibilities that the mystics generated and sustained. The mystical narrative shocks the order of things, shatters the serenity of tropic orders, exposes the violence of the metaphysical terror that disciplines the world. The mystical counter-narrative disturbs the peace and quiet of the metaphysical by issuing the knowing signifier and then suspending all the expected signifieds. What crumbles in this untelling of the Truth is the structural correspondence between the *real* and the *realised*, between *being* and *knowing*, between the *facticity* of being-there and the *epistemics* of its fabled moderation. The post-metaphysical mystic person becomes the unknowing subject.

The Metaphysics of the Absolutes

Under the phenomenally repressive circumstances in which Iranian filmmakers live and work, the reigning metaphysics of the Absolutes can at times completely collapse all creative instincts into subservience. If this is evident in a serious filmmaker like Mehrju'i, younger and far less experienced artists are in double jeopardy. Consider the celebration of the 'spirit' in Alireza Raissian's *The Journey/Safar* (1995). Although based on a script by Kiarostami, the execution of this film yields squarely to a mode of cine-mysticism that subjects matters of physical reality to a docile celebration of 'spiritual emancipation'. *The Journey* narrates the story of Farhad and Pari, husband and wife, who along with their son Arash and his grandfather escape the Iraqi bombing of the south and seek refuge in the north. An accident on the road, for which Farhad's reckless driving in the rain is partially responsible, is the only potential event in the film. While in a remote village with which Farhad has some distant history, we get to know his disposition as a disillusioned intellectual, angry at the son of his host, a former friend, for having left Iran and migrated to England. While Farhad roams the garden, takes naps by the brook, speaks to a cow and shares an apple with it, Pari attends to the needs of her son and father-in-law. When the young boy, Arash, is accidentally lost one morning, we witness the utter desperation of Pari and the abuse that she has to endure from Farhad. The story then seeks for some sort of conclusion, when one early morning Pari gets up and traces the path of their elderly hostess who has taken her domestic animals to the mountain. A mist-ical dance in the early morning fog is the final sequence of *The Journey*.

What can be the consequence of such active mystifications of characters and their locations in the world? In the same essay of 'Myth Rediscovered', Vattimo identifies a typological reading of myth as 'archaism' or 'apocalyptic view', which constitutes the practice as a form of cultural resistance to the imperialist imposition of scientific categories on the rest of the world.[6] The problem with this typology, as with many similar philosophical confusions of the particulars of capitalist modernity with the universals of something called 'the West', is that it imagines the presence of myth in various parts of the world as some kind of 'authentic relation to ourselves',[7] denying its dynamics the same kind of dialectics operative in any other form of human construct. Whether we are in the so-called 'First World' or in the rest, myths (such as that of Mashya and Mashyana) are human constructs subject to the dialectics of historical re-modulation. Cinematic visions of reality, as a particularly poignant form of myth-making, are visible examples of the unpredictability of mythological constructs once they are placed in the location of their culture. The turn to mysticism in Iranian cinema, precisely because of the un-legislated and un-legislatable relationship between the signifiers that Persian Sufism issues and the signifieds it does not deliver or deliver in carnivalesque, is a particularly powerful locus of investigation for how a culture can remember or forget itself. The self-forgetful constitution of character is the most significant consequence of this mode of remembering/forgetting. While the character of Pari in *The Journey* has the personality of a lamp-shade throughout this story (even though she is portrayed by one of the most talented Iranian actors, Fatemeh Motamed Aria), Bibi, the elderly hostess, is a wise, worldly, but submissive-to-fate personality who nonetheless dispenses with her wisdom while remaining at the centre of nothing. One can only imagine what, in the hands of Kiarostami himself, could have happened to this story. As it is, the narrative builds sluggishly towards a jaundiced cine-mysticism at the conclusion of which one could not possibly care for any of its characters or their doomed fate. What in effect takes place in this film is a passive submission to fate, to an absolute stillness of events and realities, from which there is no escape, in which there is no hope, upon which presides no redeeming force. Whereas in Mehrju'i's *Pari* there is a violent mysticism that animates his heroine, in Raissian's *The Journey* even that radical mysticism has collapsed into a passive submission to the overwhelming stillness of fate, to the bland irreducibility of shapes, colours, events, to the very matter-of-factness of being in the world.

Between the aggressive mysticism of Mehrju'i's *Pari* and the submissive mysticism of Raissian's *The Journey* stands Daryush Shokof's *Seven Servants* (1996). Although a joint German-American production, and despite the fact that the story of this film has scarcely anything to do with Iran, the fact that its director, Daryush Shokof, and its executive producer, Bahaman Maqsudlu, are both Iranian qualifies *Seven Servants* as a variation on the theme of cine-mysticism evident in Iranian cinema. Shokof's *Seven Servants* carries the implication of this cine-mysticism to even deeper and more dangerous consequences. *Seven Servants* visually modulates the story of an old and dying man who begins to hire young and robust servants for the sole purpose of inserting their fingers into every hole in his body. Gradually he and his physical addenda turn into a grotesque shape moving up and down in his mansion. From these fingers he receives new energy that sustains his life. His physical capabilities increase. With his newly-found strength and the multiple arms and legs at his disposal, he can now knock out three burglars who come to his house and is even ready to marry again.

Subjection and Re-Subjection

In *The Seven Servants*, we thus begin to cross the very act of individuation into the realm of communitarian fascism: All for One and One for Himself. Patriarchal and absolutist figures, a category that embraces Mohammad Reza Shah Pahlavi and Ayatollah Khomeini with equal justification, have always thrived precisely on the mythological sub-plot of One Great Father subsuming the energies of all His male offspring. In the *Shahnameh*, the figure of King Zahhak is even more emphatic in having two serpents growing out of his shoulders and being fed with the brains of young men. But the assimilation backwards of the modernity of such figures into a 'tradition' in Iranian culture is a particularly scandalous fabrication that needs to be emphatically discredited. Patriarchal traits in all cultures are always coagulated in particular political circumstances and under specific historical conditions. To see how such 'traditions' were invented in recent memory, we need to consider the specific location of colonial outposts like Iran in the European project of capitalist modernity.

It was not only in the heart of capitalist modernity, as Foucault extensively demonstrated in *Discipline and Punish* (1975), that the industrialist bourgeoisie began to transform the productive forces of feudalism into the political order of the economic production of reality. In the colonial outposts, this un-compromisable logic of capitalist modernity was stripped even of its Enlightenment sugar-coating. The social technologies of the disciplinary constitution of the subject were even more naked and brutally evident in the colonial outpost. The constitution of the myth of 'authenticity', far from Vattimo's Eurocentric theorisation of the phenomenon for 'the so-called third world',[8] as he calls it, in the colonial outposts in the form of 'traditions' of one sort or another was the mirror-image of precisely that colonially mitigated subjectivity. As Stephen Vlastos' edited volume has brilliantly documented for the case of Japan,[9] a host of such 'traditions' were in fact the invention of the project of capitalist modernity. In colonial outposts such as the so-called 'Islamic Societies', similar circumstances have resulted in the invention of 'traditions' of patriarchal, monarchical and Islamic nature. In the case of 'Persian Sufism' proper, the Orientalist project and the colonial condition of these societies at large have had an elective affinity with a peculiar kind of 'mysticism' which has been conducive to these circumstances. The calamitous consequence of the kind of cine-mysticism that Mehrju'i, Raissian and Shokof represent is precisely in their visualisation of the most troubling aspects of 'The Tradition of Persian Sufism', invented in and by virtue of the colonially mitigated project of Orientalist modernity. The metonymic allusions to embedded mythologies of a culture work in precisely the opposite direction of these Orientalist scenarios.

More often than not, these 'traditions' to which Iranian filmmakers fall victim stand in sharp contrast to what is otherwise present and evident in the textual evidence of those very 'traditions'. Consider, for example, the fact that the idea of forming an integral whole from otherwise scattered energy of opposing units is at least as old as Farid al-Din Attar's *Conference of the Birds* (1177), a treatise in which 'thirty birds' (*si-morgh*) get together to look for Simorgh, a mythological bird who would become their king.[10] In Shokof's version of the quest, the idea of an old and dying man using the strength of young men to attain power and become more robust in his activities has a frighteningly metaphoric allusion to recent Iranian history and its patriarchal underpinnings of either an absolutist monarchy or an Islamic republic. The notion of conformity, of bringing together diverse and divergent forces into a Supreme Metaphysical Whole, a kind of cine-mysticism which falls victim to the idea of *Wahdat al-Wujud* ('the Unity of Being'), precisely negates the modes of subjective individuation with which the project of capitalist modernity, even in its extended colonial outposts, has been concerned. Shokof's tale is narrated in a paradise-like garden, an opulent mansion and a festive celebration of colours, shapes and forms. (Shokof is an accomplished and theoretically perceptive painter.) Against this background, his cine-mysticism has a doubly powerful proclivity to abstract life from being, humanity from the world, subject from the object, meaning from the form. The result is a visually rich, politically naive and ideologically dangerous cine-mysticism that consciously or otherwise can only subserve a frightening fall into metaphysical absolutism.

The attraction to cine-mysticism of this sort is thus in part rooted in a reading of Persian Sufism which is historically modulated by a pessimistic, morbid and life-rejecting inflection. All such perceptions are, however, far more reflective of the Iranian history of the past two centuries than constitutional to Persian Sufism itself, even if we accept the very appellation as a legitimate category. In its long, arduous and multifaceted history, a 'history' that radically modifies the very categorical appellation of 'Persian Sufism' as a generic term, a vastly divergent body of texts, social institutions, revolutionary movements and even dynastic formations have been identified with the term Sufism. In fact, if we carefully consider the very text of Attar's *The Conference of the Birds*, which is a seminal source in the iconoclastic narrative we call 'Sufism', an entirely different critical intelligence will surface. *The Conference of the Birds* is the story of a group of birds who come together and decide that they want to find a king, a leader, for themselves. They are an unhappy group of birds who think that every other community of animals has its own king, so why should they live their lives in the absence of such great glory? Thus, they decide to set out on a journey to find a king for themselves. There are many procrastinators and lazy birds who are not really up to the task, and they drop out. Finally, a group of 'thirty birds' get to the top of a mountain where they are to meet their king. Here the term 'thirty birds', which in Persian is '*si morgh*', becomes the key operative term in Attar's point. '*Si morgh*' means both 'Thirty Birds' and 'Simorgh', as it also denotes a famous mythological bird. If we pronounce it with a pause, '*si morgh*', it means 'Thirty Birds', but if we pronounce it as one word, 'Simorgh', it is the name of the mythological bird. The thirty birds are now on the top of the mountain, and then this is what happens:

> There in the Simorgh's radiant face they saw
> Themselves, the Si Morgh of the world – with awe
> They gazed, and dared at last to comprehend
> They were the Simorgh and the journey's end.
> They see the Si Morgh – at themselves they stare,
> And see a second Simorgh standing there;
> They look at both and see the two are one,
> That this is that, that this, the goal is won […].
> And silently their shining Lord replies:
> 'I am a mirror set before your eyes,
> And all who come before my splendor see
> Themselves, their own unique reality;
> You came as thirty birds and therefore saw
> These selfsame thirty birds, not less nor more;
> If you had come as forty, fifty – here
> An answering forty, fifty, would appear;
> Though you have struggled, wandered, traveled far,
> It is yourselves you see and what you are.[11]

This is by far the most daring counter-imagination of the sacred certitude of One Absolutist Truth at the centre of Islamic metaphysics. A mirror put in front of thirty birds (standing for all our humanity) and showing nothing more than Thirtybirds: that is the final truth, the individuation of reality, the particles of beings amounting to nothing but their own aggregate, the journey that has occasioned them and the will that they are to truth. Against the nomocentricism of Islamic law and the logocentricism of Islamic theology and philosophy, Attar's allegorical realism promises and delivers nothing but the earthly reality of being-there. This is a vastly different kind of 'mysticism', if we can even call it that, than the one promoted by the troubled disposition and resignation-unto-death that we see in certain aspects of Iranian cinema.

Against Dead Certainties

Standing exactly on the opposite side of the kind of cine-mysticism evident and operative in Mehrju'i, Raissian and Shokof's cinema is one of the boldest and most imaginative films to come out of Iran in recent memory, Bahram Beiza'i's *Travelers/ Mosaferan* (1992), which I introduced briefly in Chapter 5. Demonstrating a potent adaptation of mystical leitmotifs to work against their metaphysical certainties and for the construction of a rich visual poetry, *Travelers* is the representative achievement of a filmmaker relentlessly at work to rescue a culture from its own demons by re-charging its liberating forces. *Travelers* finds a visually compelling narrative to tell the simple story of a potential wedding momentarily turned into a funeral before it is miraculously restored back to a joyous occasion via a particularly beautiful Persian version of a *deus-ex-machina* resolution.[12]

As Mahrokh Ma'arefi is getting ready to marry Rahi Burhani in Tehran, her sister Mahtab Ma'arefi and her husband Heshmat Davaran are packing their luggage into a car to drive from a resort near the Caspian Sea to come to the wedding. Safar Molavi, the driver, is very particular about an antique mirror which he secures to the top of the car. When everything and everybody is ready, when the driver, Mahtab's husband and her two sons are sitting in the car, Mahtab pauses for a moment before entering the car, faces the camera and quietly, calmly and with an utterly expressionless face says: 'We are going to Tehran to participate in my younger sister's wedding. We will not reach Tehran. We will all die'. Then she gets into the car, and they drive away.[13]

Upon that simple premise, and from the very first shot, there is an unrelenting tension in the film, which does not let go until the very last sequence. The camera movements, *mise-en-scène*, points of view and the whole choreography of gestures and shapes of the first sequence in the resort house near the Caspian Sea, where Mahtab and her family are getting ready to come to the wedding, are nothing short of a cinematic feast. Every move of the camera, every gesture of the actors, every angle of vision is so precisely measured, so impeccably executed, so matter-of-factly flat that one is inescapably caught between the two opposing emotions of the ballet-like gestures of the actors and the startling pronouncement of Mahtab. From this to the very last sequence of the film, Beiza'i masterfully adopts for his cinematic vision a whole repertoire of Persian theatrical and performative possibilities. From *Naqqali*, over *Arusak-bazi* and *Kheymah-shab-bazi* and *Ru-Hozi*, to *Pardeh-Khani*, of course ultimately a whole range of *Ta'ziyeh-khani* tropes are adopted and choreographed here into a cinema at once magically real and profoundly liberating. Those who have read *Travelers* as a dark version of a Khayyamesque puzzle[14] have done so with a total disregard for the very narrative fabric of the story, in which the Grandmother's refusal to believe in the death of her daughter Mahtab and her family on their way to the wedding becomes the principal charge and energy from which the tragedy *must* absolve itself. While everybody else accepts the *reality* of the tragedy and re-arranges their lives accordingly, there is an unreal (cine-mystical) resistance on part of the Grandmother to do so. Not the police officer who was at the scene of the accident, not the truck-driver's participation in the funeral, not even the overwhelming transformation of Mahrokh's wedding into a wake can convince the Grandmother. There is an unshakable conviction on her part, an inexplicable trust in her expectation that her older daughter must come and bring their family mirror which has always served, generation after generation, on such auspicious occasions, so that her younger daughter's wedding can proceed as planned.

Opposing the Grandmother's optimism is mounting evidence that Mahtab and her family, as well as a peasant girl, Zarrinkola Sobhani, who had joined them on their way to Tehran, have indeed been killed in an automobile accident. We physically see the scene of the accident, we hear a police officer filing a report with his headquarters, we sympathise with the anxiety and sorrow of the members of the family as they begin to receive the news of the accident. A funeral follows. Everybody comes to the Grandmother's house, not to participate in the promised wedding but to express their condolences for the tragedy that has occurred. The Grandmother is resistant. The truck-driver and his assistant join the wake and, in one of the most moving adaptations of the Persian *Naqqali* tradition, join in the sad remembrance of what had happened. The house is now a complete picture of mourning, just like a mosque, like a *tekyeh*, where a Persian Passion Play, the *Ta'ziyeh*, is performed. The lights are dim; everybody wears black; the movements are slow, deliberate, hesitant; the faces are dawn, countenances sad, expressions sombre, rueful, grieving. The Grandmother is resistant. She does not understand why everybody is sad. She admonishes Mahrokh for not having yet put on her wedding gown. Her sister is about to come to her wedding, the Grandmother reminds the bride, and she is not ready yet. Suddenly Mahrokh stands up and goes upstairs to change into her wedding gown. Amidst a confused crowd, sad about the tragedy they think has happened, concerned about the Grandmother's mental health, baffled by Mahrokh's intention to put on her wedding gown despite these circumstances, downstairs comes Mahrokh, her beautifully lit face and her white dress shining like a star against the deep darkness of this firmament of sadness and

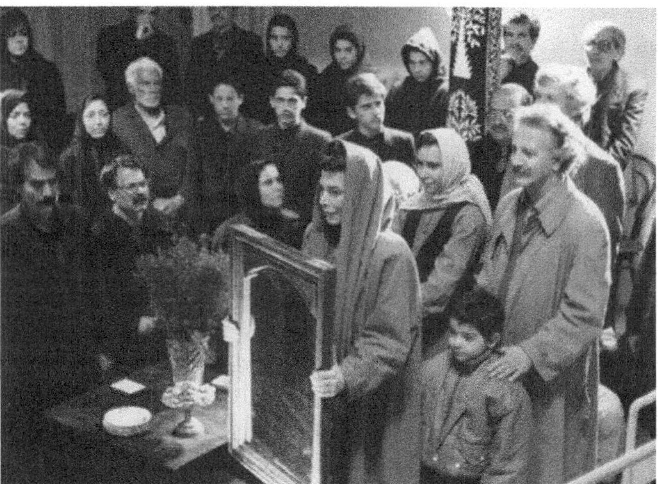

Figure 9.1 *Bahram Beiza'i,* Travelers *(1992). (Photo: Courtesy of Bahram Beiza'i)*

confusion. A soothing silence begins to prevail as everybody's attention is raised and focused on this descending grace. As the Grandmother throws petals of fresh flowers over her daughter, the entire gathering rises in awe, in respect, in an un-articulated, inexplicable attraction to a centre of gravity, and then ...

... and then in comes through the front door, *deus-ex-machina*, the joyous chorus of a gathering, the sunshine of an entire galaxy of lights, hope, happiness, bliss, the expected delivery of not just one Grandmother, of one bride, of one family, of one nation, but of the whole world. As Mahtab, the mirror in her hand, with her husband and children, and the peasant woman, too, enter through the front door, Beiza'i pours a whole cascade of love, hope, liberation, forgiveness, absolution over everything that is ugly, sad, tragic, melancholic, destructive. The ensemble of Mahtab and her family is not the aggregate of individual faces and bodies. In a *mise-en-scène* that is on a par with Titian's majestic construction of dignity, Beiza'i brings in the entourage as one singular epiphany of earthly truth, of everything that a culture is promised but never delivered, of the hope that all metaphysics of certainty turn into fear. *Travelers* is thus a story of salvation, a tale of absolution, a fable of hope. At the centre of the fable is a constellation of women, all of them harbingers of life, joy, happiness, the happy occasions of birth, from the Grandmother who is the very picture of hope, to Mahrokh on her wedding night, Mahtab the mother of two sons, Hamdam the mother of two daughters, Mastan the mother of an invalid child, Zarrinkola who hopes to become a mother.

It is not accidental that one of the best readings of *Travelers* approximates its narrative to Zen Buddhism and Haiku.[15] Nor is it accidental that women have such a central role in Beiza'i's cinema in general.[16] Beiza'i's cinema is a poetic cosmovision that puts a particularly poignant twist on the Nietzschean-Bakhtinian idea of 'the carnival',[17] whereby the inherent properties of a culture are used against its own destructive forces. As such, Beiza'i is the last metaphysician of a sacred culture that has already dreamt itself beyond all metaphysics; or alternatively, the first counter-metaphysician of a culture that has already absolved itself of all the terms of its fearful reading of the world. That *Travelers* is read inside Iran as a complicated tale of the dead coming back to life[18] is itself the sign of how a pervasive fear of the sacred – institutionalised in the patriarchal order of a monarchy, the patricidal anxiety of 'killing' a king, the making of an 'Islamic' revolution, and ultimately in the very idea of a theocracy – continues to haunt a captive imagination. In *Travelers* itself, however, are evident the visual terms of a liberation, the narrative occasion of a moving beyond the metaphysics of fear.[19] Living people having a premonition of their approaching death, actors facing the camera and informing their audience of their narrative fate, a Grandmother defying all terms of reason and logic and refusing to believe the death of her loved ones, and ultimately the triumph of an old woman's wish against fate are all the fictive terms of an earthly truth whose veracity does not lie in its being believed, but in its being beautiful.

A Material Celebration of Life

Although in his cinematic cosmovision Beiza'i has far greater affinity with Akira Kurosawa, on one hand, and with his knowledge of Persian performing arts, on the other, his immediate poetic antecedent of elevating mystical proclivities to a material celebration of life is to be found in the modernist Persian poet Sohrab Sepehri (1928–80) and his orchestration of a radically physical aesthetics. But by far the most successful cinematic version of Sepehri's poetic vision is to be found in Kiarostami's cinema in general and in his *Where is the Friend's House?/Khaneh-ye Dust Kojast?* (1987) in particular. First in a trilogy that would later include *And Life Goes On/Va Zendegi Edameh Darad* (1992) and *Through the Olive Trees/Zir-e Derakhtan-e Zeytun* (1994), *Where is the Friend's House?* is the commencement of a cinematic vision of reality entirely unprecedented in Iranian cinema. Kiarostami took the first line of a famous poem of Sepehri and turned it into a visual narrative beyond anything achieved in the Persian aesthetic imagination. The poem begins as follows:

> 'Where is the friend's house?'
> It was in the dawn when the rider asked this question.
> The sky paused.
> The passenger presented the branch of light he held with his lips to the darkness of sand
> And pointed to a white poplar and said:
>
> 'Before you reach that tree
> There is a tree-road, greener than God's dream.
> On it, love is as blue as the feathers of honesty.
> You go to the end of that road,
> Which takes you to the other side of puberty.
> Then you turn to the flower of solitude.
> Just two steps before that flower,
> You pause at the foot of the eternal fountain of earthly myths.
> A transparent fear overcomes you there.
> Then you hear a hissing sound in the fluid sincerity of the air
> And you will see a small child
> Who has climbed a tall cypress to catch a bird in the nest of light
> And right there you will ask him:
> 'Where is the friend's house?'[20]

Evident already in this poem, brought to full fruition in other poems by Sepehri and then successfully visualised in Kiarostami's *Where is the Friend's House?* is a radical transformation of all metaphysics of 'the beneath' and 'the beyond' animating Islamic metaphysics. In that metaphysics of the unseen, there is a metaphoric transmutation of here and now into there and then. The world is an epiphany of something more beautiful, our temporality a mere anticipation of an eternity, to come. Neither here nor now can be trusted or should be dwelled on. There (*Rozeh-ye Rezvan = the Divine Garden*) and then (*Azal* leading to *abad = Pre-Eternity* linked to *Post-Eternity*), not here (the mundane world) and now (our limited life) ought to be believed, wished for, celebrated, glorified. At its best, what we call Persian Sufism thus emerged as a festive transformation of the metaphysics of fear into an ecstatic of love. God, and by extension His dominion in the afterlife, was not to be feared but loved. In the poetry of Sohrab Sepehri, we see a radical reversal of both that metaphysics and that aesthetics into an aesthetics of materiality, a carnival of life, a festive re-enchantment of the world, a loving remembrance of the here and now. It is precisely this strand of Sepehri's poetry that Kiarostami takes and visualises into its rhetorical conclusions. The advantage of Kiarostami over Sepehri is that his cinema need not be read against an entire history of Persian literary mysticism. He can, and does, take Sepehri's poetic transformation of there and then into here and now and tells simple stories with it.

The simplicity of *Where is the Friend's House?* defies any possibility of complicating its reading. Mohammed Reza Ne'matzadeh, a third-grader, always forgets to write his homework in the proper notebook. The teacher admonishes him and threatens him with severe punishment should he forget to do his homework properly. Ahmad Ahmadpour, Ne'matzadeh's friend and classmate, is particularly attentive to his friend's unfortunate fate. The class is over, and the students pour into the courtyard to play. The school over, Ahmadpour comes home and sits down to do his homework, just to discover to his horror that by mistake he has put Ne'matzadeh's notebook in his bag. Catastrophe looms large over Ne'matzadeh's head, and Ahmadpour must take his notebook to him or else. From these bare bones of a plot there emerges an odyssey of the most astonishing simplicity. Ahmadpour does not know where Ne'matzadeh lives. He has to go through a myriad of troubles, and an endless labyrinth of turns and twists in his young but inventive imagination, to get to his friend's house. After what seems like an infinity of hurdles and disappointments – all lifting one layer of metaphysics after another from the sheer innocence of wonder, the very fact of being – he returns home with his mission not accomplished. What else can he do but to stay awake into the middle of the night and write his homework, and the homework of his friend in his notebook, using a dried yellow flower as a bookmark?

Kiarostami's cinema operates on a carefully constructed borderline between the sheer narrativity of non-events and the fictive transparency of the real. In effect, his cinema is a celebratory aesthetics in which things can mean beyond their narrativity and yet never succumb to metaphysics. In this respect, he is a direct descendent of modern Persian poetry, while successfully sublimating it into visual terms. How to signify without succumbing to metaphysics, how to celebrate without theorising happiness, how to hope without collapsing into a culture of fear: these are among the principal parameters of Kiarostami's cinema. To achieve this, Kiarostami opts for a cinema of radical contemporaneity, of relentless presence. In this respect, he is a filmmaker constitutionally different from Beiza'i. Beiza'i subverts the fearful culture by going for the juggernaut. Kiarostami does the same but by depleting the real of all its cultural pretences, by detecting and revealing not how an ancient culture operates but by how the fictive transparency of the real is still visible. Beiza'i tackles the culture of denial by reaching for its Achilles Heel, Kiarostami by de-signifying it, by making it forget itself via an active remembrance of the real, the now, the here, by letting the fictive transparency of the real signify itself with no need for a logocentric agency.

Revolting against the logocentric agency was also the principal charge of that branch of classical Persian poetry categorically called 'mystical'. If we bracket that term momentarily, we will see that the dual tension in which the physical reality of the world pulls against the relentless pushes of the Islamic metaphysics is already evident in the poetry of the most celebrated Persian poet of the 'mystical' turn, Mawlana Jalal al-Din Rumi (d. 1273). Here is an example from his *Mathnawi*:

> Whoever has an open gate in his heart
> Can see the sun in every town.
> Truth is always evident among things otherwise
> Just like a moon among the stars.
> You put your two fingers upon your eyes,
> Now you be the judge, can you see anything in any size?
> If you don't see it, the world is not naught,
> But for your fingers who is to blame or what?
> You pick your fingers from thine eyes,
> Then you can see everything in any size.
> [...]
> You have covered your faces and eyes in layers of clothing
> Thus perforce you have eyes but you can see nothing.
> Man is nothing but his sight and the rest is an excuse,
> The eye is but the countenance of a friend to muse.
> If not to see a friend, then the eyes should better be blind,
> If not faithful, better not to have a friend at all.[21]

Even before Rumi, Attar could and did re-signify the real beyond and prior to its metaphysical signification. In his *Tadhkirat al-Awlia*, he has a passage in which he maps out in iconic strokes the path of individuation, the act of becoming a critical subject:

> And one might even say that this is a book [referring to *Tadhkirat al-Awlia*] that will turn impotent men into men, men into lion-hearted men, lion-hearted men into individuals, individuals into pain. And how could it not turn them into the very essence of pain, when if they read and understand this book the way it must be read and understood, they would discover what pain it has been to have afflicted their soul [that is, the soul of mystic masters that Attar narrates in his book] that such deeds and such words could have come forth from them.[22]

This is no escaping from the world, no dismissive denial of the real, no seeking haven in the unreal fantasies of sickly imagination. This is written and read from the very centre of a life that must always, as Adorno thought, act as the other of art in order to make it art.

The Sound of Gabriel's Wing

Central to a work of art is its ability to take the world and make it point to something beyond itself. 'Nature is beautiful', Adorno thought, 'in that it appears to say more than it is'.[23] Iranian cinema, especially when it goes cine-mystical, can learn much from its own literary antecedents, particularly when it has been able to use the literary devices at its comfortable disposal to achieve a metempsychosis of the real. It is precisely in that metempsychosis that reality can begin to palpitate with possibilities beyond itself. In *The Sound of Gabriel's Wing*, one of the most brilliantly imagined and construed Persian allegorical narratives, Shahab al-Din Yahya Suhrawardi (1154–91) achieves a metempsychosis of reality, by a constellation of successive narrative moves, as if the medieval mystic had Federico Fellini's camera in mind, Gabriel Garcia Marquez's pen in hand, and yet a critical intelligence of an entirely uncharted disposition.

First and foremost, Suhrawardi opts to narrate the story of *The Sound of Gabriel's Wing*, which is about how everything that exists in the world is because of the fluttering of those wings, on the transgressive landscape of Persian language. This needs an explanation. The question is rarely asked by intellectual historians as to why perfectly bilingual philosophers like Suhrawardi opt to write some of their treatises in Persian and use Arabic for others. At least one potential explanation is the fact that things written in Persian in Suhrawardi's time and milieu have a far less, and more select, audience than things written in Arabic. When Suhrawardi wants to write something 'serious' to establish his scholarly and philosophical authority, like his seminal work *Hikmat al-Ishraq*, he obviously opts for Arabic, the *lingua franca* of the Islamic world of his time and location in Aleppo. But when he opts for Persian, he clearly has something more discrete in mind, and thus the signal he gives is that of opting to operate on the transgressive landscape of Persian language. Persian, or any other non-Arabic language, is transgressive by virtue of its non-canonical, non-Qur'anic status. Arabic is the language of the Qur'an, the language of the angels, the language with which archangel Gabriel spoke God's Words to His Last Prophet. It was hence the language of the Sacred, of power and of conquest. Persian, however, was the language of a defeated civilisation, a culture condemned to the periphery of a universal empire – until its triumphant resurrection in the Eastern imperial domains from the Samanids to the Safavids. When Suhrawardi, or any number of other bilingual philosophers, mystics, poets and the like opted to narrate their stories in Persian, then the very act of writing and reading that narrative, *ipso facto*, was a transgressive act. Transgression, the atmosphere of the forbidden, is thus constitutional to the very act of writing *The Sound of Gabriel's Wing* in Persian, even before one reads one line into this allegory. The use of language as a strategic move in the context of medieval intellectual parameters points to an alert awareness of the political and hermeneutic consequences of the very acts of writing and reading.

Suhrawardi's next move is in his opening invocation, where he praises God in the counter-conventional language of He-ness and Being-ness, an epistemically remarkable twist that brings to full philosophical resonance all that Persian language, far on the periphery of the philosophically rich Arabic, can offer. Here is how he does it:

> Praise be to that Sacred-ness that the he-ness [*u'i*] of whoever who can call Him He is the result of the He-ness of Him, and the being-ness [*budeh*] of whatever that deserves the status of being-ness is because of the Being-ness of His Being-ness.[24]

It is impossible to translate the poetic impact of the way in which Suhrawardi plays with the Persian words '*u*' (he, she, it) and '*u'i*' (he-ness, she-ness, it-ness), or with '*bud*' (being) and '*budeh*' (being-ness). Thackston, the translator of this treatise into

English, is right that '*u'i*' here is the Persian equivalent of the Arabic '*huwiyya*'. But he is wrong in identifying it with 'ipseity' and 'is'-ness.[25] '*U*' is referential, not ontological, and there precisely is the rub. '*U*', which in Persian is gender-neutral, neither feminine nor masculine, both feminine and masculine, is indexical, significatory, but most significantly absential: '*U*' as 'he', 'she' and 'it', and precisely in the ambiguity of its inevitable referentiality is always-already absent, not here, somewhere else, where, no-one knows exactly. The metempsychosis of reality thus begins right here in the *bira'at-e istihlal* section of the treatise, where Suhrawardi is to give the conventional clue as to the nature and function of his story. Reality as ontic here gives its soul and authority to reality as merely referential. The whole authority of Islamic metaphysics may be argued to collapse unto itself with this simple narrative move.

Now is the time for Suhrawardi to run the whole story through the shock of the unexpected. The unexpected-ness of the narrative commences on a spatial axle. Here is the story in brief: Suhrawardi says that one day he witnesses a rather crude and illiterate vulgar man attacking the old mystic masters for having said that '[m]ost of the things your senses perceive come from the sound of Gabriel's wing'.[26] He sets upon himself the task of proving this statement correct and thus admonishing the vulgar man for having dared to attack or question it. How does he do that? He proceeds to prove this statement by telling a story, an autobiographical, allegorically realistic story. This is how he begins his story:

> During the days when I had just emerged from the women's quarter and some of the restrictions of infants had been lifted from me, one night as a jet-black gloom settled over the concave of the cobalt sphere and a darkness that was like a brother to non-existence spread over the lower world, I was spared from the onslaught of sleep. Distressed, I took a candle and headed for the men's part of our house, and there I wandered until the break of dawn. Then I had a desire to enter my father's quarters. It had two doors, one onto the city and the other onto the field and the orchard. I went and I shut tightly the door to the city. After closing it, I went and opened the door to the field. When I looked I saw ten old men of beautiful countenance seated on a bench. I was so amazed by their magnificence and splendor and so staggered by the sight of their presiding presence, by their majesty, their royal regalia and panoply, that I could not speak.[27]

Suhrawardi then proceeds to overcome his awe and strike up a conversation with the first of these ten men. They turn out to be ten ethereal characters from Utopia. Nine of them never utter a word to mortals like Suhrawardi, but the tenth does. He is their logos. Suhrawardi begins to ask this Tenth Man a series of questions, to which he answers politely, concisely and to Suhrawardi's full satisfaction. Finally, Suhrawardi asks him about the sound of Gabriel's wings, to which the Tenth Man also answers with patience:

> 'Gabriel has two wings', he replied. 'The right wing is pure light, all of which constitutes the abstract entirety of his attachment to God-the-Truth. Then he has a left wing, upon which are partial signs of darkness, similar to the dark spots on

> the face of the moon, not dissimilar to peacock's feet, and that is an indication of that part of his existence which faces the non-existence. Now, if you consider the attachment of Gabriel's existence to the Existence of God-the-Truth, that existence has the attribute of His Existence. However, if you consider the capacity of Gabriel to acquire Truth, then he has the capacity of non-existence, and that incapacity is constitutional to his being.[28]

The shock of the unexpected, beginning with an autobiographical simplicity and then plunging into a phantasmagoric allegory, bewilders the reader/spectator as to where the story began and where it is to lead. The discrepancy is arresting, shocking, destabilising. The metempsychosis of reality that results from the backlash effect of this narrative begins to pull in all that is here and visible, precisely in their locational and visible realism, into the allegorical world and thus creates an allegorical realism, where one is both here and not here. The result is a visual mutation of the fantastic into the real and then the retrieval of the real into the fantastic. This is how reality can be made pregnant with modes of signification otherwise absent in its flat immutability.

Suhrawardi's next move, all of these moves being spontaneously momentous to his mind, is to contemporise the unexpected. Notice the various narrative strategies of contemporising the very commencement of the story: 'A few days ago', Suhrawardi says, he witnessed a vulgar person bad-mouthing the mystic masters. 'When I was a child', he says, he had this nocturnal experience. 'One night', he emphasises, when it was particularly dark and nothing was visible, he has insomnia.[29] Contemporising the unexpected familiarises the unfamiliar premise of the allegory, impregnates reality with otherwise absent possibilities, expands the signifying horizons of the world, palpitates the visible with the invisible. Suhrawardi is remarkably visual in his depiction of the world beyond his father's quarters. By closing the door to the city and opening the door to the field, he begins to surpass the urbanity of the always-already attained and to cultivate the virgin soil of an entirely different mode of signification. This results in a visual metempsychosis of the real.

Equally conducive to this active metempsychosis of the real is Suhrawardi's next move in narrativising the person of the narrator. We have no way of knowing who in fact the narrator opening the treatise is; or who is the person who is incensed by a vulgar man who doubts that everything that exists is by virtue of the sound of Gabriel's wings, or ultimately the person who gives an account of his early youth and his nocturnal adventure in his father's quarters? Who is it that begins with the opening philosophical invocation? Is he the same person who witnesses a disrespecting utterance against the mystic masters? And is he the same as the person who once had insomnia in his childhood? Are these three persons one and the same? Are they all Suhrawardi? All we know is the narrative constitution of these three personae. The person of the narrator is thus completely at the mercy of 'its' narrative constitution. The three narrative shifts – from the opening paragraph's philosophical persona, over the intermediary personal intervention, to the final, autobiographically modulated, allegorical realism – more than anything else make the narrative constitution of the narrator palpable. There remains no (nor can there be any) narrator, no Suhrawardi the author, outside its/his narrative constitution. The result is a resounding proposition of the contingency of truth on narrative. Thus made contingent on narrative, the nature of all truth-claims becomes conducive to the active metempsychosis of the real, its almost uncontrollable melt-down into progressive pregnancies with the possible.

There is also a reversal effect of the narrativisation of the person, as a subsequent move, towards the personification of the narrative. All the narrative devices that are operative in this tale – the philosophical invocation, the personal outrage against anti-Sufis, the autobiographical reminiscences of childhood, the dialogical conversation between the young narrator and the ethereal old man – are centred around a person, told from his vantage point, narrated via his/her/its particular inflection of the events, fully palpitating with the emotional anxieties of narrating the self. The effect of this is complementary to the narrativisation of the person. What is achieved in the personification of the narrative is to strip it of all its epistemic presumptions. Truth-claims become personal, reality contingent on the horizon of its perception, being on time, interpretation on history.

All of the preceding elements ultimately lead to the constitution of a realism which is richly suggestive, fully iconoclastic and totally uncontrollable. We may call this narratively constituted angle on reality 'allegorical realism', by virtue of its active metempsychosis of the real, of its personification of narrative, the narrativisation of the person, contemporising the unexpected, the constitution of the shock of the unexpected, the organic contingency of the counter-conventional opening gambits. No wonder that Suhrawardi was murdered by the local clergy who conspired against him and asked the local governor of Aleppo, a son of Salah al-Din al-Ayyubi, to have him thrown off the top of a citadel. What Suhrawardi achieved in this simple tale, from which example contemporary Iranian artists can learn much, was to seek to change the world by a sign that confuses the comfortable metaphysical conspiracy between the vision and the visible, between the sign and the signified.

Towards a Cinematic (Counter-)Culture

It has been suggested that 'there is no simple division between the cinema that functions as an instrument of dominant ideology, and the cinema that facilitates the challenges to it'.[30] But whatever position on spectatorship we may hold, the fact remains that there is always the historical circumstances of a cinematic (counter-)culture in which visionary theorists may use its own destructive forces to liberate it from its over-extended anxieties. This is practised at a counter-metaphysical and aesthetic level, where the paradigmatic narratives of a culture place and thus animate themselves. There is, of course, a distance, a subliminal space, between the political instruments of power that claim that culture and its metaphysical underpinnings. In an 'Islamic Republic', however, that space is perforce reduced because theocracies cannot but expose, exhaust and thus discredit their own metaphysics. The historical case of the post-revolutionary Iranian cinema vividly demonstrates how under the most brutal forms of censorship, great artists can still manage to engage their culture in an eyeball-to-eyeball conversation, a dialectic of self-negation, a skinning of new hopes out of the shell of encrusted fear. On this point, Iranian filmmakers are not unique in their attempts to use the destructive forces of their culture against its deadly proclivities. In his study of Hans-Jürgen Syberberg's *Hitler* (1977), Anton Kaes has noted:

> Syberberg wants to use film to find a way back to the spiritual home of the Germans, which he believes has been lost to materialism and rationalism. His project is paradoxical: irrationalism, which the Hitler movement had appropriated and exploited, is to be wrested away from its National Socialist associations by means of a film that celebrates irrationalism as the essence of German identity. The attitude necessary for this task simultaneously constructs and demolishes, enchants and disillusions, hypnotizes and alienates: hence the contradictory union of stylistic models from Brecht and Wagner, and vacillation between affirmation and criticism in the presentation of the fascination exercised by fascism. 'Hitler is to be fought', Syberberg says, 'not with statistics of Auschwitz or with sociological analysis of the Nazi economy, but with Richard Wagner and Mozart'.[31]

'Art', Adorno believed, 'is the social antithesis of society'.[32] Similar to such Iranian filmmakers as Bahram Beiza'i, Abbas Kiarostami, Rakhshan Bani-Etemad, or Mohsen Makhmalbaf, and precisely for similar purposes as theirs, Syberberg uses the repertoire of 'Aryan' thematics, Wagner's operas in particular, at the heart of the Nazi propaganda against the enduring memory of that cultural pathology.[33] Unaware of this innate inevitability of the function of art, certain even sympathetic critiques of Salman Rushdie have argued that he acted irresponsibly in subverting the enduring metaphysical assumptions of his inherited culture. One such critique has argued that ...

> ... the task of such a political actor [that is, an artist who wishes to be socially relevant] is creative and patient engagement with issues and involvement in genuine debate with those who need it most but happen to live beyond the pale of intellectual or intellectual's culture. Far from an invitation to docility and compromise, this is a challenge to undertake the heroic task of modifying one's message in view of its possible effects and consequences: to synthesise artistic creativity and political effectiveness without sacrificing one for the sake of the other. The price for becoming socially relevant and politically influential is to take the long and arduous path of responsibility and adjustment.[34]

However laudable this may indeed appear politically, artistically such formulaic prescriptions as 'artistic creativity and political effectiveness' cannot hold. No great artist can ever calculate the precise measures of one ounce of creativity for a ton of political effectiveness. As much as politics places and posits the art, the art cuts into political legitimacy, not by counter-propaganda, but by subverting its cultural foregrounding. There is thus always a discrepancy, an unbridgeable gap, between the politics of power and the aesthetic subversion. Any compromise in the integrity of those enduring negotiations can dangerously transmute the art from subverting a culture of fear into sub-serving it.

The problem with this entire line of super-imposition of the political on the artistic is the peculiar relationship between the aesthetic and the non-aesthetic, which is constitutional to Adorno's theory of the aesthetic:

> The tendency to perceive art either in extra-aesthetic or preaesthetic fashion, which to this day is undiminished by an obviously failed education, is not only a barbaric residue or a danger of regressive consciousness. Something in art calls for this response. Art perceived strictly aesthetically is art aesthetically misperceived. Only when art's other is sensed as a primary layer in the experience of art does it become possible to sublimate this layer, to dissolve the thematic bonds, without the autonomy of the artwork becoming a matter of indifference.[35]

Art is to be placed, located, at once historically and materially, in order for it to be able to transcend both its history and its materiality. By defying history and materiality, the kind of cine-mysticism that subserves the culture of fear in an Islamic Republic collapses onto itself by being neither art nor mysticism. In its most life-affirming aspects, what we call 'Persian Sufism' sought to transmute the paralysing fear of God, central to the metaphysical nomocentricity of the dominant reading of the Qur'an, into the far more enabling love of God. In the process, monumental figures – such as Attar in allegorical realism, Suhrawardi in philosophical fablism, or Rumi in his transcendental poetic – created art almost despite themselves. It is the sheer power of the narrative, and of the poetic, that takes over in the work of these enduring visionaries, and precisely in that inevitability a liberating art is created. The most troubling aspect of the kind of cine-mysticism that subserves the metaphysics of violence and the tropics of fear at the root of any Islamic republic is neither its literary illiteracy nor its astonishing ahistoricity and immateriality. It is its own unfortunate aesthetic denial of itself. It is, in Adorno's words, 'art aesthetically misperceived'. By aggressively forgetting its own historicity and materiality, its time and place in the world, by opting for a pathological world-rejection, this cine-mysticism has suppressed its other. And 'art is related to its other as is a magnet to a field of iron filings'.[36]

What this life-rejecting, cine-mystical servility to the republic of fear loses is precisely that contingency that an artwork as an artwork is to generate and sustain. 'Nature is beautiful in that it appears to say more than it is'.[37] What precisely is that 'more' is where art raises its flag. 'To wrest this more from that more's contingency', Adorno knew, 'to gain control of its semblance, to determine it as semblance as well as to negate it as unreal: This is the idea of art'.[38] Iranian cinema *collapsing* into mysticism is precisely the opposite of what happened in classical 'Persian Sufism', where mysticism was *elevated* to art. In Adorno's precise phrasing, ...

> Artworks become artworks in the production of this more [that is, from contingency to the semblance of what appears as beautiful]; they produce their own transcendence, rather than being its arena, and thereby they once again become separated from transcendence.[39]

But Adorno fails his own insights when he collapses into the notion that 'only in the achievement of this transcendence [...] are artworks spiritual'.[40] It is heart-breaking to see the co-author of the *Dialectic of the Enlightenment* to speak of the 'spiritual'. Having been privileged and enabled by the Enlightenment, he could never leave the light of the illusion completely to be able to look at it from its shadow. But we in the colonial outpost, by virtue of being written out of the Enlightenment by the very author of *Was ist Aufklärung?*[41] could not but be born, along with our art, in that shadow, where there can be no trace of the 'spiritual' in the sense that European Enlightenment allows a German philosopher who literally had to run from the Holocaust. What Adorno does in this passage is crossing the border of the aesthetic and seeking, once again, refuge in the metaphysical, and all of that because of the fear of the abyss that he senses behind an aesthetics with no metaphysics. We have come from the colonial outpost of that abyss – and retrieved our kind of post-Enlightenment 'spirituality'. It is not fearful. Adorno is equally on dangerous territory when he rightfully points out that the transcendence of the artwork 'is their eloquence, their script'. But right here he falls flat on the minefield of 'but it is a script without meaning or, more precisely, a script with broken or veiled meaning'.[42] This is one of those rare times when one wishes Adorno was less rather than 'more precise'. The wobbling syndrome one notices in Adorno here – 'but it is a script without meaning or, more precisely, a script with broken or veiled meaning' – captures Adorno precisely in the moment of his fear and trembling, when he could not trust his own theoretical wings that he could indeed fly away on his aesthetic theory, that he needed no metaphysical security blanket. There is no, nor is there any need for any, 'veiled meaning' in art. Adorno is too scared to see or say it: art does not mean. It cannot mean. It will not mean. Quite to the contrary: it gently exposes the self-serving, conspiratorial lie of all acts of meaning, of the Terror of the Metaphysical Itself. Art sublates and enables without meaning and minding.

The constitution of the postcolonial unknowing subject must dwell on that suspicion of the metaphysics of meaning, as it basks in the aesthetics of its own transcendence. The cinematic counter-culture that arises from the premise of the idea of *cine-mysticism* offers us a fertile ground where the world of creative imagination touches base with the mythic moments of a living culture that is blessed and condemned to remember its deepest memorial layers as it makes them historical. The idea of fabling the world triggers the domain of verisimilitude, which in turn connects the mythic, the mystical and the metonymic together and brings them to bear on the historical. The point here, as in the previous chapters, is to map and detail the passageways through which enduring mythologies connect distant memories and present histories to craft a collective sub/consciousness in which agential thinking and being is abled beyond the reach of colonial de-subjection. When we reach there, Forough Farrokhzad is waiting for us:

> My share is descending down a rundown stair
> Connecting me to something in loneliness and decay ... [43]

In that loneliness and decay, Farrokhzad's sublime poetry marks the unknowing subject bidding farewell to all the metonymic facilities that had enabled that descending ascent.

PART V

VISIONS IMPERMISSIBLE

10

Visions of the Invisible

Dast ha yam ra dar baghcheh mikaram –
Sabz khaham shod midanam midanam midanam ...

I plant my hands in the little garden –
I shall grow green, I know, I know, I know.[1]

Forough Farrokhzad, '*Tavallodi Digar*/Another Birth' (1962)

As the writing of this book was coming to an end in the fall of 2022, a massive social uprising that was almost instantly code-named '*Zan, Zendegi, Azadi*/ Woman, Life, Freedom' engulfed Iran. Like all other Iranians in and outside their homeland, I was drawn to this uprising. Led mainly by young women and given a poignant feminist twist of a post-Islamist character, the movement demanded a far more radical way of thinking about its historic roots and postcolonial character. The violent interface between a young and defiant society and an aging and recalcitrant Islamism placed the entire sacred claims of the ruling regime to theocratic rule to test. Islamism as a potent case of political Islam, a byproduct of colonial modernity, was coming to an epistemic closure. Neither the republican claims of the ruling state nor the totality of the prerogative it had demanded on Islam was any longer viable. Here we faced not a mere rebellious movement demanding to dismantle the ruling regime. We were at the moment of an historic epistemic rupture. Iranian women were demanding their rights, not only in terms of social justice, but also in terms definitive to the gender politics of a potent social uprising.

It is in this context that in this final chapter I turn to the fateful encounter between the sublime and the sacred on a specifically postcolonial bodily site where the mythic moment has found specific visual registers. Thinking through the artwork of contemporary artists such as Ardeshir Mohassess (1938–2008), Bizhan Assadipour, Shirin Neshat and Jasmine Bouziane, in this final chapter I turn to the site of the physical body as the simulacrum of the metaphysical alterity that it both represents and conceals. Here, the body retrieves its own mythic moment, becomes its own metonymic representation and thus achieves the philosophical simulation of the posthuman unknowing subject. Concerning the posthuman disposition of this fragmented body, we are back in the moment of the mythic recreation of the radically de-framed and freshly knowable world.

Art as Postcoloniality

The significance of the very idea of an 'Iranian cinema' is to a considerable degree in its *ipso facto* postcoloniality. This cinema, at its best, has been *post*-colonial even while Iran has been in the throes of a colonial economic and political condition ever since the very inception of that cinema. From its very beginnings early in the twentieth century, to its sporadic sparkles of promising signs throughout the 1950s, to its coming to full fruition in the 1960s and 1970s, and finally to its global recognition as a major force in the 1980s and 1990s, Iranian cinema has heralded a mode of postcolonial modernity beyond the colonially conditioned reception of the project. If this observation is true about contemporary Iranian art in general, it is particularly correct about cinema because of its cultivated visual affinity with the global art forms it has seen and incorporated. Cinema was *modern* from its very inception. It was not *modernised*, as in the case of the claim on Persian prose or poetry. The constitutional affinity of Iranian cinema with the colonial modernity of the art form in its global disposition has been a characteristic which could not have been shared by other contemporary arts in Iran, because the barrier of language could never be trespassed by any act of translation. From Ezra Pound to T. S. Eliot, from Mallarmé to Rimbaud, and from Heine to Rilke, authors and poets were either not translated into Persian, or else translated to no particular effect. Poets such as Pablo Neruda, Nazim Hikmet, or Nizar Qabbani were perhaps exceptionally important in the works of some prominent Iranian poets. The works of Balzac and Zola, Hemingway and Faulkner, Silone and Pirandello were indeed translated into Persian, but were far too limited in their effect on the general reading public. The best works of poetry and fiction were printed in about 1,000 copies. No more than 10,000 or 20,000 people could claim to have actually read these books. These figures could not compete with the hundreds of thousands who swarmed to movie theatres to see not just commercial films but also such critically acclaimed features as Mehrju'i's *Cow* (1969), or Makhmalbaf's *Gabbeh* (1997). Cinema had a far-reaching audience that was both caused and conditioned by its visuality.

A key strategic significance of cinema in constituting its postcoloniality is its ocularcentrism. As the inheritor of a deeply auditory culture, Iran has had a phenomenally spectacular experience in beginning to imagine itself visually. There is, of course, a rich visual culture integral to Iranian cultural history. There is the Persian miniature painting which, despite its glorious achievements in the sixteenth century under the Safavids, has remained a highly restricted art, always limited to its aristocratic milieu. The coffeehouse paintings, on the contrary, were far more accessible to a mass audience. There were, of course, a variety of live performing arts, from *Ta'ziyeh* to *Rohozi*, from *Pardeh-dari* to *Naqqali*. But constitutional to all these demonstrative and performative art forms has been an irreducible vocal cord so that, even when a painting is seen or a play watched, it is still the words that matter the most, whether written or spoken. Visions of the invisible world of imagination could never stand alone on the ocularcentric authority of their own. Cinema, however gradually and haltingly, taught Iranians the autonomous authority of the visual. It showed them how to watch. Retrieving the vast repertoire of visual and performing arts in its own immediate history, the cinematic arts that that Iranian encounter with colonial modernity made possible coincided with the formation of an active and boisterous public sphere in which visions of otherwise invisible facts and phenomena became possible.

Against the Jargon of Authenticity

It has been argued and demonstrated that the philosophical discourse of European modernity has been quintessentially ocularcentric.[2] The critic of this European modernity, as a result, has assumed anti-ocularcentric orientations. From Heidegger's 'turn' to poetry to French post-structuralist thought, these discourses have demonstrably identified modernity with ocularcentrism and sought to dismantle the former via a philosophical disengagement with the latter. The problem we face with the rise of ocularcentrism in societies that were physically or mentally colonised is this: while the project of modernity has been ocularcentric and its postmodern critique is leaning towards an auditory substitute, in colonial societies we have had pre-modern aural traditions giving way to a European ocularcentric modernity, with the qualification that, as with the project of modernity itself, we have received this ocularcentrism via colonialism.

The modernist reception of ocularcentrism in cultures such as Iran's will have to be examined in the context of the visual tradition that existed prior to that reception. Because of certain dominant themes in the Islamic conception of 'vision', cultures under its authority have a proclivity towards veiling more than just the women. 'Veiling' is a phenomenon that needs to be understood in a much wider context. Consider, for example, the following assessment of Frithjof Schuon about the nature of 'Truth' in an Islamic context:

> 'Veil' (hijab) and 'quintessence' (lubab): two words which are opposite in meaning, both as symbols and doctrinal expressions, and which refer respectively to the outward and inward, or to contingency and necessity.[3]

In Schuon's assessment, 'veiling' is a constitutional aspect of Islamic metaphysics.

> We have mentioned [...] the often indirect character of Arab rhetoric [...]. The Gospel injunction not to cast pearls before swine nor to give what is sacred to dogs [...] indicates at the same time [...] a specifically Semitic trait: direct and naked truth is both too precious and too dangerous, it intoxicates and it kills, and it runs the risk of being profound and of inciting revolt; it is like wine which must be sealed, and which Islam prohibits, like woman who must be covered, and whom in fact Islam veils.[4]

Against this presumed culture of concealment, so that the assumption of the hermeneutic 'discovery' of the concealed can constitute the 'Truth' thus revealed, an ocularcentric movement cannot but constitute a mobilised counter-discourse, emancipatory in all its aspects. Iran's, as indeed Islam's, has been a culture of interpretation, of revealing what is hidden, of *ta'wil*, *tafsir*, *istinbat*, *istidrak* and so on, all having to do with the hidden meanings of the Qur'an being extracted from its surface wordings. The Qur'an is believed to have seventy layers of meaning concealed under its surface.

Every one of those layers of meaning has in turn another seventy layers of meaning. Libraries of Qur'anic commentary have been written, pages and pages on every word and every letter of the Holy Text. The whole world, not just God's Divine Words, is a mystery that needs to be unravelled. Sa'di, one of the greatest poets of Iran, authored a poem in which he proclaims:

> The leaves of the green trees
> In the eyes of the intelligent
> Are each like a book
> On every page of which the knowledge of the Divine.

Against this culture of fixation with interpretation and search for hidden meaning, ocularcentrism – a disarming attention to the visible, the outward appearance and the tangible, the whole productionist metaphysics of it notwithstanding – is nothing but refreshingly emancipatory. The cultivated ocularcentrism thus played itself against the prevalence of the real and metaphoric veiling that was supposed to conceal a quintessence. A visual culture of nakedness was a critical way out of a persistent metaphysics of concealment. Against a metaphysics of interpretation, an aesthetics of the revelation can begin to make the surface more real than its presumed concealment of a hidden intention. In Sohrab Sepehri's poetry, as well as in Forough Farrokhzad's, both anticipating the cinema of Abbas Kiarostami and much more, this aesthetics of the surface was carried to its most poetic conclusions.

If the colonially conditioned ocularcentrism in the particular case of Iran was conducive to a postcolonial emancipation, then the whole question of art and its political implications assume a larger significance. Art can, of course, be as colonially conditioned as any other aspect of a colonised society. But the creative imagination at the root of any art is constitutionally subversive. Here Bakhtin's theory of 'the carnivalesque' is extraordinarily crucial for understanding not just the demonstrative aspect of art but, far more important, its critical creativity in envisioning the invisible, imagining the impossible. Not just a medieval carnival *à la* Rabelais,[5] and not even the mere creative heteroglossia of the novel, but as we may learn from Bakhtin for cinema (a task performed marvellously by Robert Stam in his *Subversive Pleasure*),[6] any creative act of verbal, visual, or dramaturgical dimensions can constitute a creative site where heteroglossia reigns supreme. This heteroglossia constitutes a tension, a creative zone of contestation, between centrifugal and centripetal forces. The centrifugal forces constitutional to a work of art register the dominant economic, political and cultural conditions that define its creation. Here, the conditions of coloniality and patrimonialism are paramount in placing an Iranian work of art in much of the nineteenth and twentieth centuries. But, and here is the rub, it is constitutional to a work of art to balance dialogically and subversively these centrifugal forces by centripetal forces that de-centre, dis-organise, de-rail, ex-pose, out-manoeuvre, dis-mantle and de-construct the authority of the forbidding 'no'. In its negationality, art is thus quintessentially substitutional for the politics of power, even while produced under a condition of coloniality. The heteroglossia mark of art, *ipso facto*, without any stated manifesto and by virtue of its subversive presence, engages in a defiant usurpation of the dominant ideology. Cinema, far more effective than the novel, constitutes a carnivalesque occasion that even itself is not in full control of its consequences. Participation in this carnival is by virtue of spectatorship, of the closed doors, the turned-off lights, the projected imageries and ultimately of the vicarious participation in the lives, thoughts, sentiments and actions of the fictive but un-really real characters.

The inversion of the power-basing strategies central to all patriarchal and colonial conditions is thus the principal driving force that occasions at once the creativity and the subversiveness of art in a society like Iran. That makes art almost *ipso facto* as much a political act as an act of aesthetic emancipation. The emancipatory function I attribute here to the aesthetic act is obviously at odds with notions of the aesthetics that give it subsidiary or cosmetic significance, or at best make it subsequential to epistemological and/or metaphysical foregrounding. Adorno and Horkheimer's critique of the Enlightenment already had within it a critique of the instrumental reason that separated aesthetic and epistemic realms. In his theory of aesthetics, Adorno had argued for a cognitive status inherent in the aesthetic act.[7] The emancipatory and revolutionary potentials of the aesthetic act are precisely in its non-metaphysical foregrounding, in its irreducibility to positive propositions and ultimately in its pregnancy with uncontrollable consequences.

The Publicity of the Spectacle

Out of control, or what appears to be out of control, is the principal rhetorical device of the carnivalesque occasion. When it comes to capturing the carnivalesque potentials of the public spectacle, no one comes close to Ardeshir Mohassess (1938–2008) and his orchestration of the bizarre to reveal the otherwise blatantly concealed.

Mohassess became the satirical choreographer of a whole visual tapestry of evident realities. These 'realities' were so obvious that Mohassess had to resort to visual satire to reveal their treacherous hiding habits. Their being 'evident' revealed the palpability of the ridiculous in the very midst of tragedy. Through Mohassess' comic narration, the dislocating forces of colonial modernity became brutally evident. His piercing eyes saw far beyond the rapidity of images that left the inner contradictions of a colonially vitiated modernity uncharted. The kinds of debunking evident in Mohassess' work became the touchstone of measuring the translucent time. The parodic debunking of the dominant is the principal mode of operation in the carnivalesque, whereby whatever is considered sacred is profaned, serious is ridiculed, supreme is lowered, lowered is raised, dominant is subverted. The parodic debunking is one means at the disposal of the visual carnivalesque, whereby the ancestral and the colonial are counter-narrated. The result of this counter-narration is that the patriarchally and colonially constituted subject are actively and creatively de- and re-subjected. Here, it is crucial to keep in mind that the purely *aesthetic* forces of the parodic debunking must oppose and de- and re-subject a mode of subjection occasioned by the *material* forces dominant in a society, from its economic conditions to its enduring cultural suppositions. To be thus political, art need not be 'instrumental', as Adorno feared it would become. Art is, in Adorno's own words, 'the social antithesis to society'.[8] In Mohassess' caricatures,

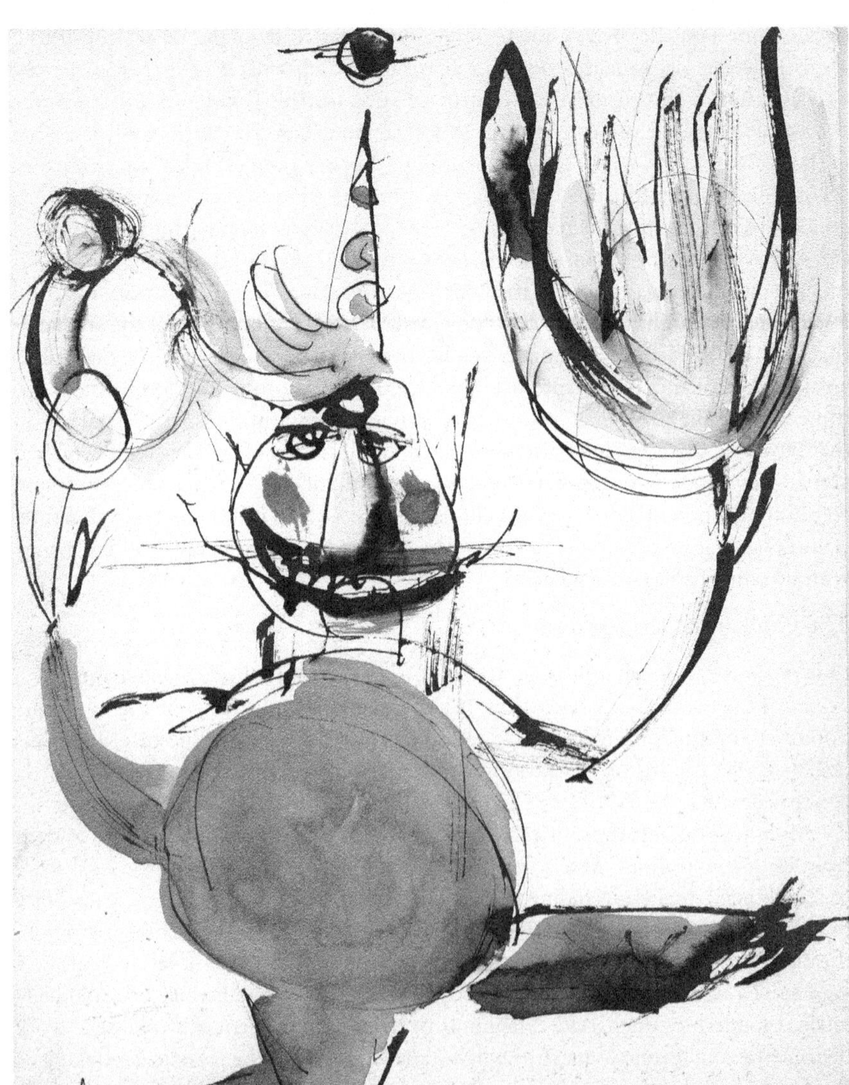

Figure 10.1 *Ardeshir Mohassess, 'Untitled # 5, 0000-22', watercolour and ink on paper, 12' × 9' (no date). (Photo: The Ardeshir Mohassess Trust)*

once again, that parodic antithesis assumes the effective modes of a visual orchestration of the pathetic, from the hidden place of the sublime.

At once plaintive and ridiculous, Mohassess' depiction of the world that he sees leaves no room for exaggeration. His parodic deflation has a matter-of-factness to it that leaves one with a sense of 'yes, of course, but how come I didn't notice it before'. The result is that the lugubrious sensation of tragedy never collapses into self-pity in Mohassess. One laughs at these possibilities. But the laughter is far more enabling than paralysing.

Counter-Imagining the Moral

Central to my arguments in this chapter, as indeed in the entirety of my book, is a critical assessment of Iranian film, fiction and poetry for its active counter-imagining of the moral and political totalitarianism that have marked its social and cultural history. The sacred certitude of Shi'ism, the secular absolutism of the colonially mediated project of modernity, and all other totalitarian tendencies in between, have charted modern Iranian history against a gridlock of final and total solutions for an increasingly shrinking world. The smaller the world gets, the more the terms of moral and political subjugation to the economic logic of global capitalism and (neo)colonialism intensify, and the more final and absolutist become the ideological 'solutions' to its problems. The fear of all utopias has been evident in much of twentieth-century literature, particularly in such visionary warnings as Aldous Huxley's *Brave New World* (1932) and George Orwell's *1984* (1949). Colonised or semi-colonised societies such as Iran were doubly subject to the nightmare of dehumanisation, constitutional to not only the totalitarian tendencies of the twentieth century but also the project of colonialism in particular. Aspects of Iranian art in much of the twentieth century, which has been simultaneously against the jargon of ancestral authenticity and anti-colonial, have successfully challenged both the totalitarian tendencies and the colonially constituted subjectivities. These tendencies and subjectivities are rooted at once in the domestic 'traditions' of Persian patriarchy and Islamic (Shi'i) clericalism, both instigated by the colonial modernity they have faced. The three principal articles of Huxley's *Brave New World* – 'Community, Identity and Stability' – are the hallmarks of the twentieth-century totalitarianism, whether capitalist or socialist, secular or sacred. It is not accidental that, in Huxley's nightmarish vision, art is completely eradicated. Art dreams the forbidden, speaks the banned, imagines the censured. Against all material odds, art makes the politics and the aesthetics of re-subjection possible. While for decades the rampant lumpenism of Iranian cinema subserved the combined ferocity of Persian patriarchy and Shi'i clericalism, the best of Iranian cinema, which came to life after much hesitation in the 1960s, subverted those forces by imagining the politics and aesthetics of alternative moralities, while at the same time actively re-subjecting the colonially constituted Iranian person.

The re-subjection via the visual – the way in which, for example, Mohsen Makhmalbaf has done it repeatedly but perhaps most effectively in the 'Birth of an Old Woman' episode in his *Peddler* (1986) – works via a public spectacle that must loudly and clearly announce itself. Through the effective use of the bizarre and the grotesque, Makhmalbaf has repeatedly managed to question radically the very constitution of Iranian subjectivity. The way in which the dominant modes of subjectivity are challenged is via the existing remissive occasions constitutional to every culture. In Philip Rieff's theory of the sacred order of interdictions that form the subject, 'there are two kinds of remissive motifs. First, those remissions which subserve – that is, support – the moral demand system of which they are a part; second, those same motifs, expanding their jurisdiction in the system of action, can become subversive of that system'.[9] Art can subserve the dominant order by supporting fantasies, and yet art can subvert the same dominant order by alternative substitutional fantasies. Which fantasies are mobilised is determined by the modes of response to the conditions of tyranny in which the artists live. The most enduring energy of the presence of the spectacle in the Iranian visual art of modernity has been the social and psychological effects of living under the conditions of tyranny. At once real and perceived, the condition of tyranny is debilitating in terms beyond politics. Consider the incapacitating realities that reflect themselves in Kambiz Derambakhsh's cartoons.

The satirical brutality evident in such images is in their sheer relentlessness and repetition. In precisely their relentlessness and repetition, the image qualifies political protest beyond the aging fact of life – beyond the protest for bread remains the deadline of aging and death. This is how political protests engulf, inundate and saturate the living memories of a people. Growing up under tyranny is to internalise fear beyond reality or measurement – punctuated only by aging and dying. Oscillating between the extreme poles of hatred and fear, fact and fantasy, anger and laughter, growing up with tyranny robs entire generations of people of their ability to think straight through the a/moral parameters of the colonial modernity we had inherited.

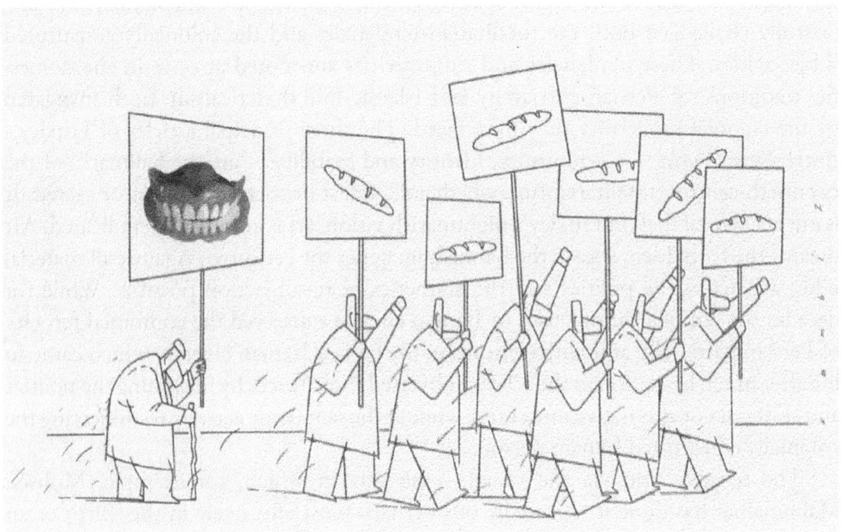

Figure 10.2 *Kambiz Derambaksh, untitled (no date). (Photo: Public domain, fair use)*

Cinema, at its best, was our eye onto the world. With it we looked not just at the world but through the world at ourselves. The colonially constituted modernity has effectively been translated into a brutal mode of political protest that beyond the actuality of its existence assumed metaphysical proportions in our captive mind and the mortality of our existence. Much of the simplicity we now notice in Iranian cinema, in the cinema of Kiarostami in particular, is a formal reaction against the moral confusion and depravity caused by that tyranny. Far more than merely political, the tyranny was (and is) cultural, deeply rooted in the power-based production of the ancestral roots in Persian patriarchy and Shi'i (Islamic) clericalism. While Kiarostami's cinema has been a counter-metaphysical un-doing of the tyrannical roots of that metaphysics, Beiza'i's cinema has been the active pursuit of the same ends, but in precisely those mythic and metaphysical terms. Kiarostami sought to eradicate that metaphysics by making us see through the transparency of the real, while Beiza'i made us negotiate with the inevitable brutalities of that metaphysics and its mythic foregrounding by transforming us into their operating realms. In both their diagnosis and prognosis, we were in effect seeking to pacify our temptations to exist, in E. M. Cioran's words, beyond the violence of our being 'Iranian'.

Being Iranian

The violence of being 'Iranian', in patriarchal and colonial terms beyond our control, transfixed generation after generation of Iranians unto a mode of subjectivity whose material sources were beyond our control and whose ideological forces we had to fight in their own terms. Figural self-mutilation in the Iranian graphic art, perhaps as best represented in the work of Bidjan Assadipour, became a paramount example of strategic re-subjection, available as a modicum of the ability to challenge that violence.

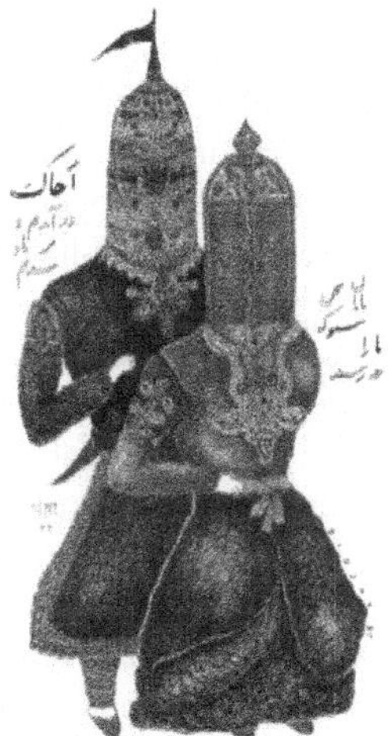

Figure 10.3 *Bidjan Assadipour, 'Dust thou art and unto dust thou shall return' (no date). (Photo: Public domain, fair use)*

The body, in this metaphoric act of re-subjection, is defaced and self-mutilated – heads cut off, throats cut, limbs severed, eyes gouged out, tongues and ears pierced – as the most blatant sign of defiance against a power-based constitution of subjectivity and personhood. This figural defacing and self-mutilation, bordering on a kind of pictorial masochism, visually substitutes for what physically would be impossible. The figural masochism defaces and disfigures the body and physically mutilates the most evident site of cultural inscription. The bodily site carries on it, from the most ancient to the most recent, the certainties and anxieties of a culture. In the Iranian graphic art of the 1960s through the 1990s, as evident in the work of Ardeshir Mohassess and Bidjan Assadipour, among scores of others, the physical mutilation of the figural body is visually the most evident masochist defence against the cruelties of a fatherly fear. Gilles Deleuze's study of *Masochism* (1967) radically challenged the psychoanalytically perceived conceptions of both sadism and masochism and sought to dismantle the very supposition of sadomasochism.[10] In his radical revision of masochism, principally predicated on a re-reading of Leopold von Sacher-Masoch's own *Venus im Pelz* (*Venus in Furs*, 1870), Deleuze suggested that through the mechanism of *contract*, in the act of masochism, there is a bodily substitution of the son for that of the father: '[i]t is not a child but a father that is being beaten'.[11] Here, in arguably the most significant aspect of Iranian graphic arts, defacement and bodily mutilation came to represent that climactic moment in cultural rebellion against patriarchy and its colonial substitutes. The threat of the paternal presence, the very dominant fact that cultures are mandated by the figures, dead or alive, of the father, real or symbolic, the monarch or the mollah, animates much of contemporary Iranian art, its force and ferocity as powerful as that of the colonial presence. Cultures with masochistic traits ('masochistic' *not* in its received clinical definition, but instead in its radically revised literary reading by Deleuze) confront their sons and fathers on the site of the figurative body, chief among any number of other symbolic sites. Fathers, monarchs, chiefs of police, mollahs and military officers are all the threatening custodians of a patriarchal culture that in their presence constitute a threat of youthful attempts against their authority. Art in general, and the visual arts in particular, became the symbolic site of this battle between patriarchy and its discontent. In the realm of poetry, too, the assassination of Naser al-Din Shah (1822) and the subsequent downfall of the Qajar dynasty coincided with the collapse of Persian classical prosody and the rise of modernist poetry. The *kulturkampf* that thus results has no conclusive evidence in the course of its operation. Instead, the battle rages and constitutes the most energetic source of agitation in the culture. The figural body is substituted for the physical body, and then it is mutilated as the bodily substitution of the father, in order to release the son from the horror of his presence and the fear of his return, thus making possible a new, 'father-less' person. 'The masochist', in Deleuze's words, 'thus liberates himself in preparation for a rebirth in which the father will have no part'.[12] The result is one of the most aggressive forms of first de-subjection and then re-subjection in contemporary art, a task to which the best of Iranian visual arts, not least Iranian cinema, is dedicated. One of the principal reasons behind the restrictions imposed on the presence of women in the Iranian visual arts is precisely the tacit alliance between sons and mothers against the fear of the father. In Deleuze's assessment, '[t]he masochist's experience is grounded in an alliance between the son and the oral mother [...]'.[13] The alliance is necessary and precarious:

> What are the masochistic defenses against both the reality and the hallucination of the father's aggressive return? The masochistic hero must evolve a complex strategy to protect his world of fantasy and symbols, and to ward off the hallucinatory inroads of reality.[14]

To procure a mode of fictive operation that protects the son against the fear of the father, according to Deleuze, the mechanism of a 'contract' is devised:

> A contract is established between the hero and the woman, whereby at a precise point in time and for a determinate period she is given right over him. By this means the masochist tries to exorcise the danger of the father and to assume that the temporal order of reality and experience will be in conformity with the symbolic order in which the father has been abolished for all time. Through the contract, that is through the most rational and temporally determinate act, the masochist reaches toward the most mythical and the most timeless realms ...[15]

What the abundance of figural self-mutilations in modern Iranian graphic art points to is precisely this attempt to exorcise the overwhelming presence of the father. The strategy works through an approximation of the temporal order of reality and the symbolic dis-ordering of that order. In the work of art, as in the masochist's 'contract', all the received anxieties, whether patriarchal or colonial, are subjected to a figurative dis-ordering, so that at least in the publicity of the work of art the patriarchal and colonial universality of the subject is challenged.

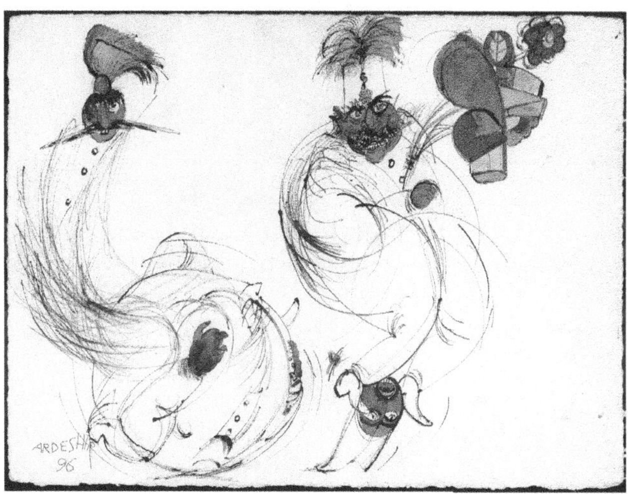

Figure 10.4 *Ardeshir Mohassess, 'Untitled' (1996). (Photo: Courtesy of Metropolitan Museum of Art)*

Self-Spectatorship

What makes this rather general thematic trait in Iranian art more important in the case of visual arts, and cinema in particular, is the close bordering, as evident in Assadipour's figure, between defacement, self-mutilation and self-spectatorship. While defacement and self-mutilation points to the confrontational anxieties about patriarchy, the self-spectatorship points to the much more fundamental problems of being subject of the gaze. In his phenomenology of 'shame', Jean- Paul Sartre located the physical presence of the body within the existential parameters of the existence of Others. 'By the mere appearance of the Other, I am put in the position of passing judgment on myself as an object, for it is as an object that I appear to the Other. Yet this object which has appeared to the Other is not an empty image in the mind of another'.[16] From here arises the most destabilising reality of merely being-in-the-world, the fact that we cannot see ourselves, that we are subject to the Other's gaze. Figural decapitations such as those abundant in Assadipour's work metaphorically remove this source of profound anxiety and make possible a mode of vicarious self-spectatorship.

A few crucial consequences are contingent on this mode of figural self-spectatorship. The most immediate dislocation caused by figural self-spectatorship is the de-objectification of the colonial Self as the object of the Other's gaze. This is

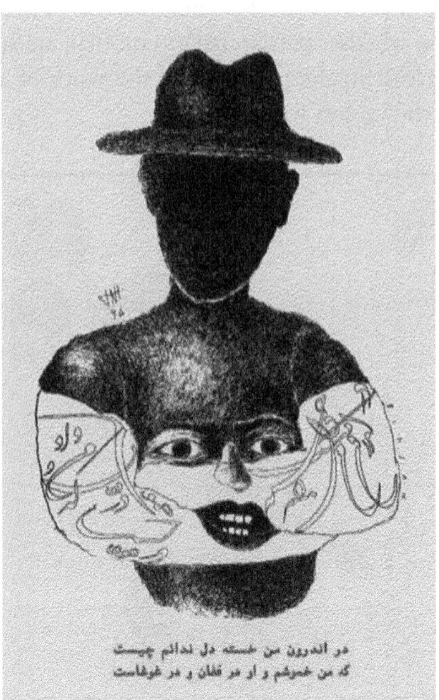

Figure 10.5 *Bidjan Assadipour, 'I can't tell who is inside my wounded heart/that I am so silent and yet it is in constant commotion' (no date). (Photo: Public domain, fair use)*

by far the most revolutionary event that a visual counter-culture can launch against both patriarchy and colonialism. De-objectification of the subject opens up a whole spectrum of possibilities, by freeing the culturally constituted person from their historically mandated parameters. The wide range of emotive responses affiliated with 'shame', as Sartre understood it, is hereby put under erasure by making the figure of the person freed from the evidence of involuntary objectification. The categorical condition of what Sartre calls 'shame' needs to be carefully unpacked here. In the case of an 'Iranian', as a historical construct, 'shame' here means a state of anxiety which is generated by the combined effect of the patriarchal stare, which is permanent and demanding, and the colonial gaze, which is transitory but debilitating. The combined effect of the patriarchal stare and the colonial gaze is a kind of objectification of the subject by an Other which is at once permanent and swift, transcendental and debilitating. The visual act of self-spectatorship subverts the authority of that generalised and amorphous Other, via the figural defacement and decapitation, so that the emancipatory act of de-objectification can produce the possibility of an entirely different historical person and persona. The visual mechanism of this de-objectification is an equally violent reversal of the gaze. Figural decapitations visibly remove the obstacle of inability to look at oneself by making the fixed location of the eyes mobile, migratory, dislocated and severed from the body.

Here we reach by far the most significant function of the visual and performing arts in contemporary Iranian culture, a significance which is derived directly from the graphic art of self-mutilation/self-spectatorship – in the collective works of Ardeshir Mohassess, Bidjan Assadipour and Kambiz Derambaksh, among others. In the metaphorically severed head, we have the most visible simile of the constitution of the cinematographer camera as a severed head with which we can begin to look at ourselves, a revolutionary phenomenon entirely impossible if we were limited to our naked eyes and to the fixed position of our head.

The camera-as-our-severed-head pans and tilts, stops and moves, in measures and manners entirely impossible before. The reversal of the gaze, in graphic acts figuratively and in cinema multifariously, robs the singular authority of the patriarchal/colonial Father/Other, whether it is embedded in the permanence of the patrimonial stare or in the sharpness of the colonial gaze, from its most effective advantage. Reversing the gaze is to free the (would-be) subject from the look of the Father/Other, to dismantle the memory of its historical objectification, to give authority and autonomy to what by virtue of the gaze (both the patriarchal and the colonial) was constituted as a 'thing'. The birth of the person as an autonomous self and a sovereign subject is thus contingent on this reversal of the gaze. The debilitating anxieties associated with shame and self-alienation are thus reversed, and the apprehension of being looked at is turned around.

Here again we may need to take account of the ocularcentrism at the heart of this perspective on both the centrality of the gaze and its attempted reversals in much of colonial history. Martin Jay's identification of Sartre's view of the gaze as part of a movement in much of post-War French thought has pointed out an anti-ocular direction against the primacy of 'vision' in much of post-Platonic thought.[17] The joint projects

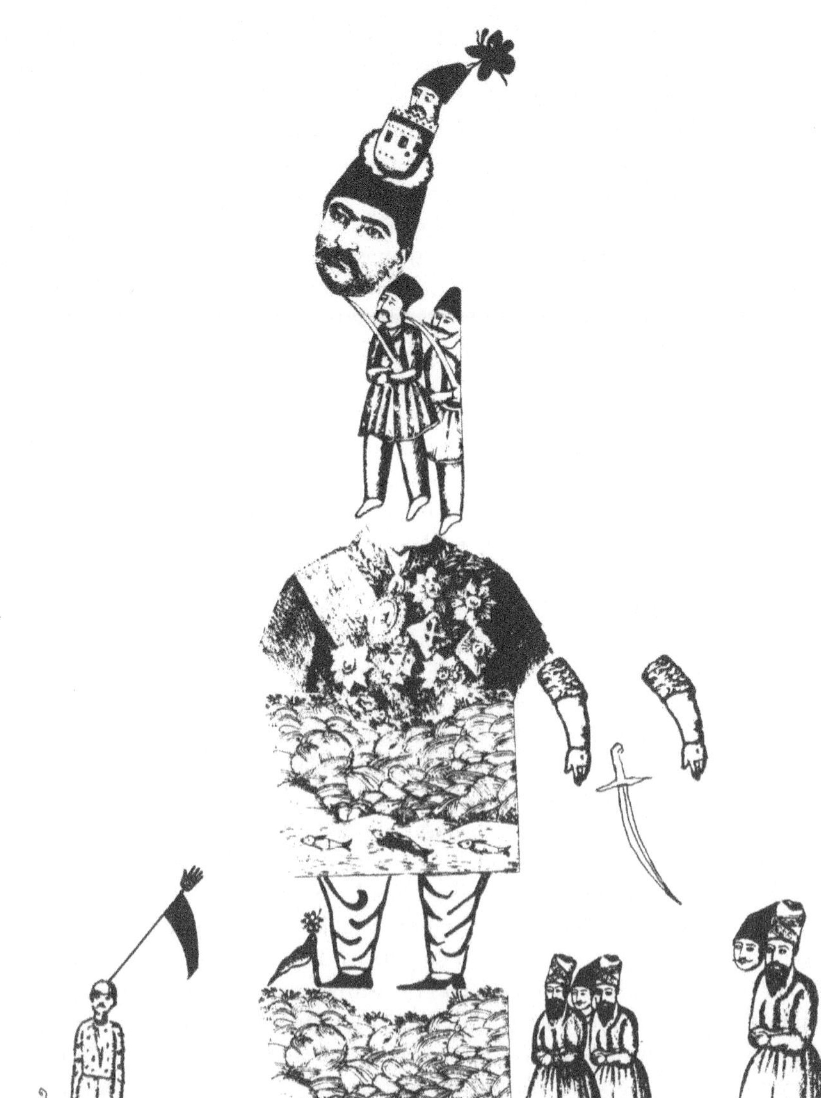

Figure 10.6 *Ardeshir Mohassess, 'In honor of the commander who loved nature and who was killed in the heart of nature by his servants' (1987). (Photo: Courtesy of Mage Publishers)*

of the European Enlightenment and capitalist modernity are the more immediate sites of this prejudice. On the extended colonial site of this modernity, the operation of the visual and the productionist metaphysics assume far more sinister apparitions. Within a newly constituted cinematic culture, the ocularcentric movement can both constitute and take full advantage of the psycho-social consequences of gazing. The idea of the camera as the severed head turns the ocularcentrism of cinema into its advantage. From Nietzsche to Foucault, Jay has documented a radical critique of ocularcentrism in an attempt to investigate the site of an auditory set of metaphors. Heidegger's later attention to poetry, Jay has argued,[18] might be pointed out as an indication of seeking auditory as opposed to visual sites as alternative modes of understanding. A privileging of 'interpretation' rather than 'observation' has been suggested to exist at the root of this critique of ocularcentrism.[19] None of these critics of ocularcentrism, however, can negate the extraordinary function of the reversal of the gaze against a history of patriarchy and colonialism combined, a history which has *ipso facto* constituted the contemporary Iranian subject.

The Aesthetic as Liberating the Subject

In the received 'technologies' of subject-formation, as Foucault called them, there is a potential for liberation which must be attended to without any undue concern with perpetuating ocularcentrism. In *Discipline and Punish* (1975), Foucault theorised the notion of the gaze as the particular mode of visual domination. Through the systematic modification of the mechanics of punishment and control, a panoptic surveillance is constituted, in response to which the subject is effectively constituted for the uses of capitalist modernity. Through the power of the gaze, which for Oriental subjects was grafted somewhere between the point of the colonial officer's gun and that of the Orientalist's pen, the colonised is subjected as an object. The same mechanism is equally operative in the working of all patriarchal cultures. Whether friendly with the colonial role, as the late Mohammad Reza Shah's was, or hostile to it, as Ayatollah Khomeini's appeared, both Persian monarchy and Shi'i patrimonialism constitute their subject as either 'Iranian' or 'Shi'i' by objectifying it to a transhistorical gaze. The entire spectrum of Perso-Islamic morality might in effect be read for the clinical cure of the person who is evidently assumed to be 'sick' and in dire need of moral therapy. The effective mechanism of clinical observation, central to Foucault's *The Birth of the Clinic* (1963), is to constitute the subject as 'ill' and in need of therapy. From the medieval Persian treatises on ethics to modern clinics and hospitals, the subject-as-ill is central to the discursive constitution of the un/knowing subject.

Thus, by far the most significant consequence of self-spectatorship has to be the sheer possibility of re-constituting the patriarchally and colonially constituted subjectivity of the Iranian 'person'. Here, and in a condition of fragile patriarchy and potential postcoloniality, we need to think more rigorously through Foucault's notions of resistance, not least because as much as he thought about power, he scarcely theorised the condition of coloniality. Moving away from his analysis in *Discipline and Punish* (1975), by the time he wrote *The History of Sexuality, Volume One* (1976), Foucault considered the site of resistance integral to 'the dense web' of power-relations.

Whether in a Marxist separation of the two sites of power *and* resistance, or in the later Foucauldian coagulation of the two, the effective possibility of postcoloniality identifies the creative corner of art as the location of potential re-subjection where at least the terms of emancipation can be actively visualised. The object of all patriarchal disciplines and colonial orders is what Foucault in *Discipline and Punish* unabashedly called 'the soul'. This 'soul', however, is a construct, a product, a manufactured outcome of the technologies of disciplinary punishment, panopticon surveillance, systematised supervision and so on. The manufacturing of this 'soul' is 'the machinery by which the power relations give rise to a possible corpus of knowledge, and knowledge extends and reinforces the effects of this power'.[20] Here, Foucault is effectively summarising the history and effect of Orientalism as *the* form of knowledge that constituted the colonial disposition of the Oriental subject, as documented by Edward Said in *Orientalism* (1978). The creative re-constitution of the patriarchally and colonially manufactured self/soul (subject) is perforce facilitated by the possibility of the returned gaze.

The Colonial Modernity of Being Iranian

The constitution of 'the Iranian' subject as a both patriarchal and colonial construct is a peculiar achievement of European colonial modernity. The active subjection of 'the Iranian' was a direct consequence of the colonially mandated project of Orientalism, which in turn had read the enduring patriarchal sources of Iranian culture. As a form of positivist knowledge, 'Orientalism' framed the existence of something called 'the Iranian' or 'the Persian' within the more general context of its production of 'the Orient' – and there was no oppositional force to read that heritage differently. Against this discursive formation of the Oriental subject, one can point to the articulation of the project of 'Orientalism' by Edward Said as one particularly palpable case in a kind of counter-discourse mobilised to confront the colonially constituted subject in the metropolitan centres of power. The whole gamut of postcolonial theory and practice in and outside the academy might also be considered as a more general movement against the colonial constitution of the Oriental subject as an object of the colonial gaze. But what critical thinkers such as Edward Said, Gayatri Spivak, Homi Bhabha and others have theorised has for a far longer period of time been practised in the realm of creative imagination. From the nascent nationalism and socialism of the early nineteenth century to the militant Islamism of the late twentieth century, in the domain of political theory and practice the constitution of the political subject has been persistently challenged in terms domestic to that Orientalism, while the parameters of patriarchal culture were being simultaneously strengthened. From nationalism over socialism to Islamism, the most sacrosanct parameters of patriarchy have stubbornly persisted and been renewed and recast. Even in the most democratically disposed versions of socialism, let alone the most patrimonially modulated forms of nationalism and Islamism, patriarchal traits have been the principal parameters of the dominant political culture. Only in the open-ended realm of the creative imagination has the patriarchally/colonially constituted 'Oriental' subject been a point of critical re-constitution.

Looking Back

In the work of two brilliant photographers, Shirin Neshat (Iranian) and Yasmine Bouziane (Moroccan), the simultaneity of this counter-discourse is particularly evident. By collapsing the culturally sanctioned binary opposition between piety and sensuality, Shirin Neshat has targeted one of the most vulnerable blind spots of Iranian (and Islamic) political culture. The lifted hand that points to the lip allows for the fingers to silence the lips while also letting the lips kiss the fingers. Asceticism and sensuality here corrode each other in a negating tension. The ascetics of silence and the sensuality of a suggested kiss are here the subtextual prelude of a hand that pictures two iconographic opposites of Shi'i patrimonialism – the supreme invocation '*Ya Qamar-e Bani-Hashem*' – and materiality – one of the most famous poems of Forough Farrokhzad. Masculine Shi'ism as ascetic inhibition and feminine poetics as sensual emancipation here embrace each other on the back of a single hand. In this single move, Shirin Neshat embraces the im/possibilities of two iconographic opposites. Through their matrix of inhibitions, cultures make it impossible for juridically mandated masculine piety to border on the suppressed sensuality of the feminine. An ascetics of denial is at the root of the jurisprudence of piety operative in Shirin Neshat's paternalistic culture. In the same culture, however, the subversive theo-eroticism of Persian Sufism has always experimented dangerously with the im/possibilities of that border. While in the realm of the literary, from Rumi's musical poetics in the thirteenth century to Sohrab Sepehri's material aesthetics in the twentieth, we have witnessed shattering encounters of the sensual with the pious, in visual terms we have never seen what it means to have the two universes collide. It is through her perceptive grasp of the nature of feminine piety in an Iranian/Islamic universe that Shirin Neshat can detect and convey the seductive energy of the clasp where the sacred and the sensual meet. The palpable affection with which Shirin Neshat embraces such evident opposites is one crucial source of the precision of her visual bordercrossings, wherein the whole spectrum of patriarchally/colonially constituted subjectivity of not only the feminine Muslim but, perhaps even more important, the very masculinity of 'Islamic' culture is counter-imagined. 'Tradition' and 'modernity', 'the Prophetic' and 'the Poetic', 'the sacred' and 'the sensual', and ultimately 'home' and 'exile' collapse into an overwhelming embrace summoned by Shirin Neshat's loving hands, seen and shot through her sensual counter-gaze.

Yasmine Bouziane, quite independent of any influence by Shirin Neshat, equally photographs the body that mocks. The mocking bodies of Yasmine Bouziane have learned how to forget themselves and master a new memory. Yasmine Bouziane photographs in jest for generations of Orientalised and domesticated bodies: Orientalised, that is, by the exotic imagination of the colonial Europe, domesticated by the patriarchal gaze of such resistance to colonialism that could only begin with the body of 'the Muslim woman' as their first and last battleground. Between patriarchy and colonialism, the body of the 'Muslim Woman' has been invested with a certain kind of memory. Yasmine Bouziane's task is to mock that memory and thus erase it, displace it, replace it with other possibilities. In battles for 'dignity', which is always yet to be defined, the body of women becomes the battleground for the clash of cultures. If the so-called 'Westernised' and the 'Fundamentalists' are fighting for two ideals of Algeria, why not just fight over their differences on the streets, in the barracks, in the mosques, or movie theatres? Why on the body of women? The body of the woman, by virtue of its being targeted as a battleground, becomes the site of cultural contestation. Her legs are no longer to walk, her hands to handle things, her eyes to see, her lips to taste. Every single organ of the body becomes something else, the physical carrier of a symbolic reference far beyond itself. Her body, by virtue of its being thus targeted, becomes the metaphoric substitution of all that a culture wants to be, or does not want to become. Yasmine Bouziane has the uncanny ability to hold a culture precisely at the moment when it *wants to be something (else).* The possibilities of her photographs never collapse into dead certainties. They always flirt with the borderlines of living suggestions, charged innuendoes, multiple implications. She does not dare to commit herself but makes a virtue out of her fears. She is an artist of borderlines, the wide and accommodating margins of two cultures, two genders, two nations, two sexes, two languages, two eroticisms, two tyrannies, two gazes. She has crafted for herself a borderline which is elusive, transparent, maybe there, maybe not. Is she French or is she Moroccan, is she European or is she Arab? What are the differences, who sets the parameters? Why do they matter? Her anxieties are the trepidations of an urban bourgeoisie that was never either completely here or completely there. The subject of Bouziane's photographs is an Arab in Paris and a French in Tangier. If she were an Arab in Tangier and a French in Paris, there would not be anything to photograph. This strange mutation, this supreme ironic output of colonialism, is what makes picturing as mimicking possible.

The bordercrossings of Shirin Neshat and Yasmine Bouziane, their visual mobilisation against colonialism *and* patriarchy with one and the same strike, points to the tension that holds together and separates from each other the sacred and the sensual. 'Just as ethical religion, especially if it preaches brotherly love', Weber concluded in his *Sociology of Religion*, 'enters into the deepest inner tensions with the strongest irrational power of personal life, namely sexuality, so also does ethical religion enter into a strong polarity with the sphere of art'.[21]

The Aesthetic and the Sacred

Both in its rooted affinity with the sacred and its modern distance from it, art has always had a contentious relationship with the authority of the sacred. Art can either subserve, in Philip Rieff's terms,[22] or subvert the sacred. But even as it subserves it, as perhaps best exemplified in Rumi's lyrical poetry or Bach's cantatas, there is something palpably dangerous to the authority of the sacred lurking beneath the piety of art. In both Rumi and Bach, there is a transmutation of the fearful into the beautiful, in order to make it comforting. 'Religion and art are intimately related in the beginning', Weber noted. 'That religion has been an inexhaustible spring of artistic expressions is evident from the existence of idols and icons of every variety, and from the existence of music as a device for arousing ecstasy or for accompanying exorcism and apotropaic cultic actions'.[23] That affinity, however, is bound to shatter. Because, as

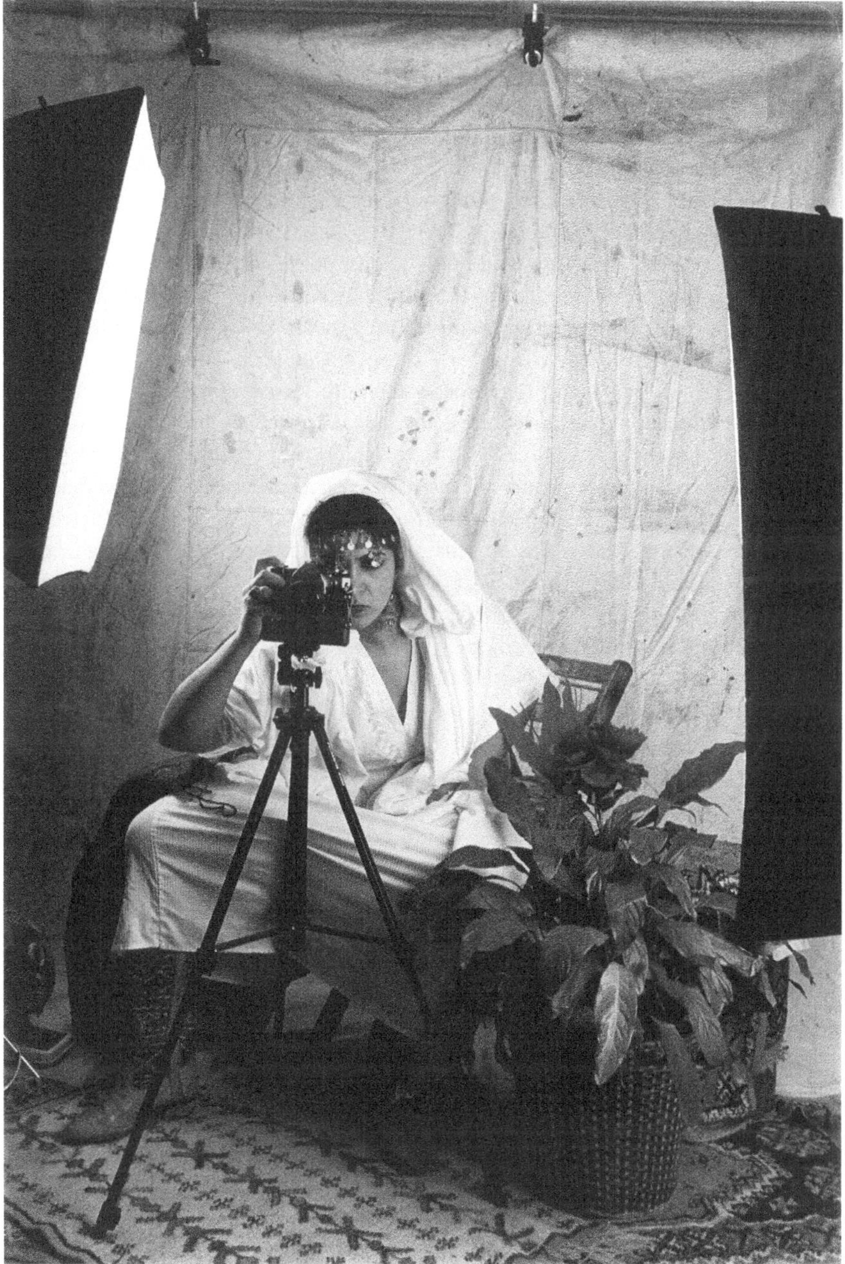

Figure 10.7 *Yasmine Bouziane, 'Self-Portrait' (no date). (Photo: Courtesy of Yasmine Bouziane)*

Weber noted, 'the more art becomes an autonomous sphere, which happens as a result of lay education, the more art tends to acquire its own set of constitutive values, which are quite different from those obtained in the religious and ethical domain'.[24] The authority of the sacred has historically taken advantage of the aesthetic power of the beautiful. As Gadamer has noted, 'the rejection of iconoclasm, a movement that had arisen in the Christian church during the Sixth and Seventh centuries, was a decision of incalculable significance. For the church then gave a new meaning to the visual language of art and later to the forms of poetry and narrative'.[25] But by the time of Hegel, we were already told that art for us is 'a thing of the past'. By the time Gadamer acknowledges this and tells us in his essay on 'The Relevance of the Beautiful' that 'we must work out a new legitimisation for art', we are already in the realm of the post-sacred aesthetics.[26]

In the realm of Islamic culture proper, the tension has never been any less contentious. The seventeenth-century art historian Qadi Mir Ahmad Qomi in his *Golestan-e Honar/The Flowerbed of Art* (circa 1591)[27] gives a glimpse of the narrative devices that Muslim theorists and practitioners of art have created to legitimise the viability of visual art, in particular against specific doctrinal inhibitions. The carefully crafted text of Qomi demonstrates how Muslim artists have tried to trace the legitimacy of their craft to the centrality of the sacred Text of the Qur'an and of Prophetic Traditions in the sacrosanct documents of Islam itself. Through the conventional opening gambit of *bira'at-e istihlal*, a literary technique whereby all the dominant themes of the proceeding text are metaphorically plotted in the convocational passage in praise of God, the Prophet Muhammad and other Muslim saints, Qomi seeks to achieve something far more significant. Here, *bira'at-e istihlal* functions like the overture of a musical composition where all the major melodic leitmotifs of the piece are introduced. Qadi Ahmad Qomi's ingenious use of the *bira'at-e istihlal* technique is that, in the disguise of praising God, he narratively transmutes the very act of creation of the world into an act of art. Notice how he does this:

> In the Name of God, the Merciful, the Compassionate
>
> O Thy Name the Very Beginning
> Of the Book of the Everlasting,
> The very Ornament of Every Page
> Of the Layers of Heaven.
>
> The Scribe of the Eternal
> Has written the Page of Thy Majesty
> By the Pen of the Ceaseless
> Upon the Tablet of the Infinity.
>
> Most sincere Praise and Gratitude is worthy of that Artist (Sane') Who has painted the colorful page of the heavens with the black and white of 'Thou causest the night to pass into the day, and Thou causest the day to pass into the night' [from Qur'an, III: 27]. And infinite grace and adulation is worthy of He who wrote: 'Nun. By the pen and that which they write (therewith)' [from Qur'an,

XVIII: 1], the One Who has composed the Book of the turning heavens with the colorful pages of Spring and Fall.[28]

If you notice, the terms 'beginning' (*dibacheh*), 'book' (*divan*), 'ornament' (*arayesh*), 'page' (*safheh*), 'pen' (*kelk*), 'tablet' (*lawh*) and so on all are technical expressions specific to the art and craft of calligraphy and painting. Far more important is the narrative transmutation of the very act of creation into an act of art. God has 'painted' the universe in the way an artist paints on a canvas. In the opening poem, God is not only 'The Painter' but also 'The Painted'. He is both He Who Ornaments the Book of Existence and Its Ornamentation. Upon the Tablet of Time – that is, as long as existence has or will have existed – He has written, in beautiful calligraphic letters, as it were, His authority. God is called an 'artist', a '*sane*", He who creates, the world being His artwork ('*son*'). The firmament, the pages of the universe, is the canvas on which He has painted with the two primary colours of Black and White, which is a Qur'anic reference to His creation of Night and Day. He is the One who swears by the pen in the Qur'an, and by that which the pen writes or draws (*yastarun*). The ultimate metaphor of artistic creation in this opening passage is God's 'painting' of the turning pages of the heavens with the changing colours of spring and fall.

In the realm of the verbal arts, too, there are emphatic Qur'anic and Prophetic inhibitions of poetry. 'As for poets', we read in the Muslim Holy Text, 'the erring follow them. Hast thou not seen how they stray in every valley, And how they say that which they do not?' (Qur'an, XXVI:224–26). There are repeated Prophetic traditions that corroborate these statements by considering poetry *nafth ash-Shaitan*, 'what Satan has spit out', and warning Muslims that '[v]erily it would be better for a man to have his belly filled with pus until it destroys him than to fill himself with poetry'.[29] When one considers these Qur'anic and Prophetic injunctions against poetry and then compares them with the poetic avalanche in Arabic, Persian, Turkish and Urdu, one is bound to conclude that these inhibitions have been invitations to transgress. We will never understand anything from the inner contradictions of Islamic culture if we fail to understand that, if anything at all, this culture is the dialectical outcome of a persistent historical conversation between its doctrinally sanctioned inhibitions and the socially manifested transgressions against those inhibitions.

The more art becomes autonomous, the more it constitutes a danger to the sacred assumptions of a culture. It is through the sacred assumptions of a culture and its material conditions that its members draw their identities. How can art then be instrumental in an historically material form of re-subjection? How can art, the mere work of the imagination, constitute a counter-discourse to a subjectivity which is formed by the relations of power constitutional to the material basis of a culture? How can the pen that draws combat the sword that is already drawn? How can there be an historically material consequence to the creative imagination of artists inorganic in their social presence? Here, we can borrow from Gadamer's transcendental aesthetics not unlike the way Marx drew from Hegel. 'The ontological function of the beautiful', Gadamer concludes in his 'Relevance of the Beautiful', 'is to bridge the chasm between the ideal and the real'.[30] Gadamer works his way towards this conclusion via a reading of Plato's *Phaedrus*, a text in which the human souls get a glimpse of the heavenly order of the cosmos, before they are once again entrapped in the confusion and anarchy of their earthly life. They are subsequently given the chance of re-experiencing that all-but-forgotten heavenly order via their experiences of love and beauty. 'It is by virtue of the beautiful that we are able to acquire a lasting remembrance of the true world'.[31] Translating Gadamer's reading of Plato into an historically material language, the discrepancy between the ideal and the real is filled by the creative imagination of artists who, inorganic as they might be, still can inventively compensate for the power that has constituted a servile and compromised subject and the counter-mobilisation that must dream of emancipation.

To be sure, no artist and no power of imagination can compensate for the historically material forces present in the instruments of power. But the mobilisation of a counter-discourse in the site of cultural contestations can always act to erode beyond the hegemony of the institutions of power and take to task the historical formation of their economic and political underpinnings. For Foucault, in both sexuality and in the arts (as in fact before him for Max Weber), there are such re-constitutive forces that can modify a dreary existence. Art can, or at least so Foucault hoped, become constitutional to a struggle against the institutionalised mechanisms of subservient subjection, whether it is instrumentalised in state apparatus, penal codes, or cultural mores. In Foucault's rhetorical question 'But couldn't everyone's life become a work of art?'[32] there is already an evident answer. Living life as a work of art is not to take the configuration of one's historically constructed subjectivity for an unchanging quintessence. Contrary to Sartre's notion of 'authenticity', Foucault proposes the notion of 'creativity'[33] as one's attitude towards one's self. But in Foucault's theorisation of the mechanism of re-subjection, there will always remain a strong element of inorganic intellectualism that cannot fully account for the absence of material forces, at a general societal level, conducive to the effective mobilisation of a counter-discourse. If re-subjection is not to remain a limited, if not futile, exercise on the part of privileged (and thus inorganic) intellectuals, then material forces, or at least the massive mobilisation of a counter-discourse to which there is wide access, are necessary. The case of the Islamic Revolution in Iran is a perfect example of how active mobilisation of a counter-discourse which even can go so far as to initiate and bring to successful fruition a revolution cannot *ipso facto* initiate an enduring re-subjection beyond that subjectivity which was colonially and patriarchally constituted. The counter-discourse of the Islamic Revolution, to which Foucault was in fact quite attracted, was at once radically anti-colonial and yet deeply patriarchal – and thus its patriarchy became colonially fortified. The Islamic Republic that it brought about has remained rhetorically anti-colonial but patriarchal in the most recalcitrant sense of the term. But even its rhetorical anti-colonialism is severely limited by its location within a political economy of ideas and materials beyond its control. Iran more than ever remains a single-product economy, almost entirely dependent on oil export, and commercially nothing but a peg on the production belt of global capitalism to which it gives oil and from which it buys consumer goods.

More than forty years after the success of the Islamic Revolution, the Iranian bourgeoisie is more jaundiced and pettier than ever, and there is no sign of a politically significant revolutionary working class. In the absence of local productive means and relations, and in the shadow of a massive global economy which is no longer conducive to the formation of revolutionary labour movements and a bourgeoisie whose threatened economic interests leaves no room for protecting even its own civil rights and liberties, economies such as Iran's are in no shape to produce either a progressive bourgeoisie or a revolutionary labour movement. So, what exactly has been the result of the massive mobilisation of an Islamic counter-discourse launched against the colonially constituted Iranian subjectivity? Nothing. Both because of strong patriarchal elements in the counter-discourse of the Islamic ideology and the overwhelming power of global capitalism, the Islamic Revolution has failed to make the slightest advancement in reconstituting the colonially crafted Iranian subjectivity. The same predicament is applicable to the generation of self-proclaimed 'secular' – both nationalist and socialist – counter-discourses, mostly produced by inorganic intellectuals, which has resulted in no revolutionary and enduring reconfiguration of the colonially conditioned 'Iranian' subjectivity.

So, once again: what is the function and the place of art in emancipating the materially captive subject of a patriarchally and colonially constituted modernity? This book is the sustained course of reflecting on that prospect. The site of the physical body in this final chapter functions like the simulacrum of the metaphysical alterity that retrieves its mythic moment, transforms into its own metonymic representation and stages the philosophical simulation of the unknowing subject. On the posthuman disposition of this fragmented body, we retrieve the radically de-framed and freshly renewable world – all from the vantage point of a plant-animal-human evident in Farrokhzad's poem:

> I plant my hands in the little garden –
> I shall grow green, I know, I know, I know.
> Sparrows will lay eggs in the interdigit grooves of my fingers –
> I will hang a pair of earrings on my ears
> From two pairs of twin red cherries –
> And upon my nails I will stick the petals of Dahlia.[34]

Conclusion
Mashya and Mashyana Unearthed

Zendegi shayad an lahzeh-ye masdudist keh negah man
Dar ni-ni chashman-e to khod-ra viran misazad …

Life is perhaps that impassable moment
When my gaze destroys itself
In the pupil of your eyes –
Wherein lies a feeling
That I will mix
With understanding the moon
And grasping darkness.[1]

Forough Farrokhzad, '*Tavallodi Digar*/Another Birth' (1962)

I have guided you through a winding journey, from ancient myths to recent mythologies, asking you to join me asking: *Quis custodiet ipsos custodes?*/Who watches the watchers? We are the watchers, and that which we watch is watching us back. What we watch is watching back. What we are gazing at is gazing back. We become the product of that which is the product of our own gaze. When the Fourth Wall is thus collapsed, we become the sum total of that which we have looked at for a long time, not knowing it was looking back and shaping what and who we think we are. This is what has preoccupied me throughout this book – how we become the unknowing subject of that which we knowingly watch and is unknowingly watching us back. I am not just watching Hamlet or reading Seyavash; Hamlet and Seyavash are watching me back, and something of Hamlet and Seyavash remains in me as I become the unknowing subject of their metonymic gazes. As I mapped out in some detail in my Introduction, the intermediary function of such metonymic tropes in the visual and performing arts constitutes my unknowing subjectivity by facilitating the mnemonic interface between distant myths and contemporary arts, which in turn we might read as the purgatorial conduits between the mythic foregrounding of aging cultures and their renewed metonymic resurrections. This dialectic is where the postcolonial philosophy of the unknowing subject announces itself.

Who therefore is the person who stands behind the 'I' of the beholder – a man, a woman, something in between, or something beyond? What does this designation mean, signify, determine? Is gender-fluidity a recent discovery of human nature, or is it perhaps an ancient truth? At what cost have we lost that wisdom? Does raising such a question belong to a limited 'Gender Studies' project, or does it have larger philosophical implications – by de-gendering the knowing subject and thinking towards a liberated, amorphous and unknowing subject? If we were to raise such questions not in a generic abstraction – and falsely assume it to be universal – but in specific cultural settings, say, in the US, or Europe, or Australia, or else somewhere in Asia, Africa, Latin America, or in India, China, Egypt, or Iran, would responses to such questions vary? And if so, to what effect? Where would we locate the textual and material evidence to help us raise such questions? Could celebrated works of art chart our pathway to thinking through such questions – what is shimmering in a film, a work of fiction, or a piece of poetry, the visual and performing arts of a nation, of any people, that might reveal more than we have been prepared to interpret? If we were to assume a certain subterranean continuity between a people's ancient and unfolding mythologies and their winding contemporary aesthetic proclivities, can we perhaps find our way from that premise? Does the fluidity of gender articulations they entail lead us towards the prospects of a postcolonial philosophy of the de-gendered and de-racialised subject, rooted instead in the lived or forgotten experiences of a people, at the centre of which stands an imperceptive moral agency, an *unknowing subject*, within which dwells an intuition of transcendence, and to which forced and violent gender and racial identity is but a dimmed bodily allusion? Who watches the watcher? Who stands, sits, or sleeps behind the 'I' of the beholder? We become Black or White, Male or Female, knowing or unknowing, by virtue of the works of art we choose to celebrate, and in those very works of art lurk the shimmering prospects of our liberations. This premise and that promise have been at the roots of my book.

It is time for me to bring the ideas I have put forward throughout this book to a conclusion. I have taken my time and leisurely walked you through a plethora of Iranian films, fiction and poetry, teasing out of them ideas and sentiments that I have in turn used to build a political, moral and philosophical argument to posit the prospects of a liberated unknowing subject – formed beyond the condition of coloniality we have inherited. At the writing of this conclusion late in the fall of 2022, a massive social uprising code-named '*Zan, Zendegi, Azadi*/Woman, Life, Freedom' engulfed Iran around the central idea of recasting an entire political culture in a specifically post-patriarchal register. My prolonged and quiet preoccupation with the postcolonial unknowing subject and a transnational public sphere upon which it was formed suddenly found pronounced contemporary responses. Defying mandatory veiling as the singular insignia of a political patriarchy formed as an Islamic Republic, this uprising demanded an entirely different look at the centrality of gender politics in a post-Western polity. The terms of my sustained critique of the European colonial subject-formation and my careful cruising through Iranian visual and performing arts to oppose and end it were now all acting themselves out in the streets of Iran. The critique had not just anticipated history, but it was now reading it in decidedly post-patriarchal terms.

My Philosophical Mother is a Poet

In an interview, the celebrated French philosopher Jacques Derrida (1930–2004) was asked, if he were to choose a philosopher as his mother, who would that philosopher be.[2] Derrida, the master deconstructionist, was visibly dumbstruck by the curve ball of that most simple question thrown at him; after a moment of visible bewilderment, he finally said no philosopher could be his mother, and that was precisely behind his critique of phallogocentrism. Could that revelatory moment when a towering European philosopher could not identify his philosophical mother and indeed confessed no philosopher could ever be his mother be a clear indication that the European knowing subject could have never been anything but a male interlocutor? And if so, has then a tilted epistemic axis from Socrates and Plato to Heidegger and Derrida defined what it means to be a European philosopher – to be a knowing subject? And if so, how would a de-Europeanised knowing subject look like and be, a subject that begins and ends before and after that gender-specific male knowing subject at the heart of the self-universalised European philosophy? In another interview conducted in German with Hannah Arendt (1906–75), the interviewer asks the eminent German thinker how she felt about being in the circle of philosophers, to which she too immediately objected and said she was no philosopher at all but ('if anything at all') a political theorist.[3] Neither Derrida could imagine a philosopher mother, nor could Arendt see herself as a philosopher. How could a woman be a philosopher in this vastly masculinist domain, not by any deliberate design or patriarchal conspiracy, but simply by the sheer masculinist anonymity of what has designated itself as the 'European' knowing subject being implicitly and thus subconsciously presumed to be a man? In this book I have taken these and similar questions and asked them in a world farthest removed from the answers habitually given to them, wondering, if indeed the European philosopher is categorically a white heterosexual male interlocutor of truth, then what would happened if we were to reverse and topple all those designations.

As leading feminist philosophers like Luce Irigaray and others have long since recognized, the European knowing subject is categorically masculinist and childless. In her *Speculum of the Other Woman* (1974), among other works, she reads Plato, Aristotle, Descartes, Kant, Hegel and Freud through the phallocentric logic of their blindness and insights.[4] The history of European philosophy thus emerges as an assembly of anxious men repressing their maternal and feminine instincts, fearing for their paternal posterity and thus casting their metaphysics of solitary and ascetic masculinity onto the foundation of their unexamined universality. I thought we needed to move to a domain faraway from these knowing subjects, towards the mythic moment outside the European provenance where the knowing subject was not yet gendered and where pure verisimilitude and metonymic aesthetics posited a mnemonic, amorphous and, above all, unknowing subject behind any and all gendered binaries.

I have invited my readers to shift domains and begin again – to decentre 'Europe' and start anew – farthest removed from the motherless European knowing subject, when two eminent thinkers (a man and a woman) could not think of a philosophical mother – to themselves or to their progenies. I have invited you to abandon for a moment the mind-boggling question of how, if not born to any mother, did the curious figure of 'the European philosopher' surface on this earth, in our philosophical consciousness. I have invited you to another domain where thinkers, like all other human beings born to their body and souls and mind, will have to have a mother and a father, even before their parents had parted ways and gendered into one solid thing or another. Imagine, I have asked you, a gender-fluid philosopher: where would they hang their hat and say they are home, and they cannot do or be otherwise?

'Typical', we read in an enthusiastic review, dated 25 May 2021, of a major exhibition of Iranian art and culture at the Victoria and Albert Museum in London. 'You go for months without any culture, then 5,000 years of it come along at once. That's what the V&A's luxury coach tour of a blockbuster promises, and delivers, including quite brilliant recreations of Iran's two most renowned sites, Persepolis and Isfahan'.[5] This exhibition must have been years in the making and cost a fortune to curate. 'Epic Iran shows there is a cultural history that connects the country as it is today with the people who lived here five millennia ago. To put this in perspective, that's like telling the story of Britain from before Stonehenge to the present and hoping it all connects up somehow. But in Iran, it does'. There is, of course, an element of truth in what we read in this review. But how does this 'somehow' work exactly– how does the life of a people today connect with those distant and immemorial pasts – in Iran or in Britain, if we fathom and measure them from Persepolis or from Stonehenge? In this book I have sought to offer one detailed answer to that question.

The V&A exhibition raises a serious theoretical, imaginative and above all philosophical issue: how and in what particular terms might we connect the dots that the curators of this splendid show have spotted for us in their exhibition halls? What if chronology or nationalism or even old-fashioned imperial narratives do not suffice to account for the longevity of a civilisation? What if all we see and read and feel and fear and desire and repress in contemporary film, fiction and poetry are *metonymic substitutes* for much older and more ancient mythologies, long since forgotten, except through this modern unearthing of deeply buried archetypes of normative and moral imagination. In this book I have taken as a prototype the Zoroastrian myth of creation, in which we encounter two mythic characters, Mashya and Mashyana, the would-be (but not the) Adam and Eve of Persian mythology, the first original proto-human beings emerging from a plant from which the rest of humanity would eventually spring. What happened to such mythologies, I have wondered, as form, as epistemes, as mnemonic devices, as iconic archetypes of undying fears and fantasies? Might we then not consider the plethora of visual, performing, literary and poetic arts as their metonymic substitutes and simulacra, their return of our collectively repressed? What if our modern mythologies are not that modern? Based on much earlier sources, Ferdowsi had composed his *Shahnameh* in the year 1010, and ever since successive illustrated copies of the epic have been produced at royal courts from India over Iran to Central Asia, the Caucasus and Anatolia. From there scholars have produced major critical editions, cinematic adaptations, oral declamations, theatrical performances. What holds these dots together? What happens when ancient myths from time immemorial reach the evident contemporaneity of our aesthetic sensibilities? This book is a testament to that prospect.

I have suggested the distance between hidden and forgotten mythologies and their latter-day metonymic gestations as an unexplored philosophical inroad into how we are to read our contemporary facts, fictions and mythologies of who and what and wherefore we all are – how, in short, our *mnemonic subjectivity* is formed. Using the archetypal example of Iran as an ancient civilisation with a sustained course of continuity all the way to our own time (we could equally use Chinese, Indian, Aztec, or Egyptian examples), in this book I have offered a philosophical reflection on the iconic interface between what we see and feel today when entering an exhibition hall in the V&A or any other museum or art gallery, and what we have otherwise deeply buried in the forgotten layers of our collective un/consciousness from time immemorial. This is the story of Mashya and Mashyana unearthed, an exploration of when and where ancient myths become metonymic and mnemonic in varied forms of contemporary cultural and aesthetic representations, a philosophical inquest of our contemporary whereabouts in the vicinities of our ancient habitats – all under the overwhelming spell of a fear of fascism, a politics of despair, a gendered (absence of) subjectivity, endemic to postcolonial polities and societies. Put differently, under the extended shadow of the European sovereign, all-knowing subject, made possible at the expense of de-subjecting the world at large, how might a *postcolonial de-gendered unknowing subject* be imagined, enabled and empowered on these planetary possibilities?

The immediate timeframe of my book that has formed its political thrust is Iran of the last one-hundred years, when an aging Qajar monarchy (overthrown in 1925) gave birth to the robust young monarchy of the Pahlavis (dismantled in 1979) and then succumbed to an aging Shi'i theocracy (belligerent but still triumphalist), resonating fear of fascism throughout this past century. But at the same time, the distant memories of time immemorial resonate under the skin of these last one-hundred years, as has the fear of a pending fascism informed the political urgency of my book, as I have navigated ancient Iranian mythology, as well as their metonymic surfacing in contemporary Iranian film, fiction and poetry, and as I have dwelled on a philosophical meditation of what all of this may mean when we look at it from the vantage point of a *postcolonial unknowing subject* – de-gendered, de-racialised, liberated from false binaries, freely floating signifier of unknowingly knowing the unknown.

How do I know that unknown? The answer is simple: if I were to be asked who my philosophical mother is, I would immediately say Forough Farrokhzad – and the extended roots of her poetry in the metonymic recollections of the myth of Mashya and Mashyana.

Overcoming the European Sovereign Subject

My purpose in writing this book has been to pave the path towards a radical overcoming of the sovereign European knowing subject, through an aesthetic articulation of the postcolonial unknowing subject, actively engaged in a hermeneutic of misunderstanding European colonial modernity. At the heart of my book, therefore, I have planted a provocative retrieval of the ancient Iranian myth of creation to enable a fresh new way of rethinking a de-gendered subject through contemporary art and culture. This I have proposed as a critical reflection on how cultural continuities and civilisational endurance defy, overcome, collate and correct the course of history and expose the flawed logic of chronological periodisation – allowing the myth of 'the West' to overshadow 'the Rest'. As a detailed study of contemporary Iranian visual and performing arts with reference to their global contexts, this book has sought to explore their hidden themes of gender and sexuality, self and society, home and exile, solitude and liberation, mysticism and philosophy. But such a systematic decoupling of false binary oppositions is preparatory to clear the way towards a radical articulation of a metonymic unknowing subject. An exploration of the world of Iranian film, fiction, poetry and drama has fortuitously offered the wellspring of modern mythologies of selfhood and personhood, rooted in hidden and unexplored subterranean visions of a de-gendered alterity we had not yet seen or assayed. This exploration of the ways in which the ancient Iranian myth of creation resurfaces in contemporary film, fiction and poetry stages the metonymic allusions that overcome the fear of fascism and the politics of despair. The extension of this aesthetic of liberation and deliberation paves the way towards the prose of a historicity that writes its own philosophical purpose. This articulation of the groundwork for a postcolonial metaphysics of the *unknowing subject* I offer as the counter-force to the colonial violence of the European all-knowing sovereign subject, mapping the prospect of a condition of decoloniality from the grounded facts and aesthetic experiences of lived and imagined realities.

I began the long and determined path of this thinking with recalling and recasting the distant birth of Mashya and Mashyana in the Mazdaian myth of creation, and from there I gently moved towards its varied metonymic gestations that have enabled a reading of gender-fluidity, on the premise of which we can begin to posit a mode of de-gendered subjectivity hitherto unknown or rare on the postcolonial philosophical horizons. The designation of the iconic *loci* of gendered humanity as Men and Women, or Feminine and Masculine, soon become coterminous with the dialectic of Self and Society, Home and Exile, or Mysticism and Philosophy, in reading the archetypal formations of a living culture that were before or beyond the colonial constitution of gendered subjectivity. This trajectory of thinking soon found its own prose and ultimately led to the prospects of a postcolonial counter-metaphysics through mnemonic subjectivity on the battlefield of literary and dramatic pure verisimilitude. These terms, ideas, concepts and horizons began to take shape, and soon the prospects of a semblance of subjectivity persuasively suggested itself. That prospect, in turn, enables us to overcome the crisis of the European subject that has been colonially exported and conditioned around the globe. The unknowing subject that thus emerges on the decolonial site moves towards a liberation philosophy that we are now able to fathom.

Based on this theoretical premise, I have then sought to detail how the passage from distant mythologies to contemporary film, fiction and poetry, and from there to the prospects of a postcolonial person marks the contours of an *unknowing subject* that has already overcome the impossibility of being-colonially-in-the-world. If we begin to think of this unknowing subject at the epicentre of a self-decolonising world, dwelling as this subject does on a hermeneutic of misunderstanding colonial modernity, the gender-fluidity of those distant mythologies will find a renewed aesthetic significance in our reading of contemporary arts. At the dawn of a decolonial liberation philosophy, that unknowing subject and their hermeneutics of misunderstanding have already announced themselves. But it still needed to be theorised.

In his *Prison Notebooks* (1929–35), Gramsci takes a look at Kant's statement in his *Groundwork of the Metaphysics of Morals* (1785) – 'act only on that maxim whereby you can at the same time will that it should become a universal law' – and wonders if everyone can say the same thing. He concludes that not everyone can say so, because first the person who says so must have achieved what Gramsci calls 'cosmopolitan enlightenment and the critical conception', which means that, like the German philosopher's, his subjectivity has assumed universality. In this book I plan to go upstream from both Kant and Gramsci and ask if I (as a Muslim, an Iranian, a misplaced 'immigrant', a stateless person with nomadic subjectivity) can partake in the iconic Cartesian moment of *cogito ergo sum*. As soon as I ask that question, I suddenly find myself in the company of a generation of Latin American and Caribbean philosophers such as Enrique Dussel, Walter Mignolo, Maria Lugones, Aníbal Quijano and Nelson Maldonado-Torres, which has placed a potent *ego conquiro* at the heart of the colonial conquest that had enabled and empowered that *ego cogito*.[6] But here, too, I wish to plant two upstream stages of *ancient mythology* and *aesthetic metonymy* before I reach the stage of a postcolonial *philosophy of the unknowing subject* – a mode of subjectivity that is always already mnemonic. In this book I have sought to detail and unpack that move from myth to metonymy to the unknowing mnemonic subject – a subject that must always remember worldly agency to fathom, form and frame it.

In *One Hundred Years of Solitude* (1967), Gabriel Garcia Marquez tells us the story of the fictitious town of *Macondo*. Similarly, *Yoknapatawpha* County is a fictional Mississippi place that William Faulkner (1897–1962) created based on a Chickasaw word and, primarily, on Lafayette County, Mississippi. In Guillermo del Toro's *Pan's Labyrinth* (2006), we are placed in the immediate aftermath of the Spanish Civil War, during the early Franco period. This real world fuses into a mythical world centred on an abandoned labyrinth and a mysterious faun, with whom the main character, Ofelia, interacts. Exactly one-hundred years ago come 2025, in 1925, the last feudal monarchy of Iran, the Qajar dynasty, collapsed and thereafter commenced the turbulent history of contemporary Iran in the grip of both colonial modernity and domestic tyranny of a subsequent monarchy and a militant theocracy that followed it – bidding their odds against the enduring legacies of the foreign and militant nativism they both faced. The history of Iran of these last one-hundred years of solitude and society (1925–2025) is no less surreal than those of *Macondo* or *Yoknapatawpha*, or no less magical than *Pan's Labyrinth*. The only difference is the incapacity of a banal political historiography that has failed to come to terms with the magic of that reality. The task at hand is not to abandon historiography and to start writing fiction – and there are plenty of wonderful works of fiction on that score, two of the best being Houshang Golshiri's *Prince Ehtejab* (1969) and Mahmoud Dolatabadi's *The Colonel* (circa 1980s). The task at hand is to rethink the components of the prose of our historiography, where the *Macondo* of Marquez, the *Yoknapatawpha* of Faulkner and the *Pan's Labyrinth* of Guillermo del Toro all come together to give us a clue as to how to reimagine and recast all other national histories on the borderlines of enduring ancient myths, their subsequent aesthetic metonymies, the fear of fascism and the postcolonial philosophy of the unknowing mnemonic subject they have occasioned and entailed. My book has been a preliminary step in that direction.

The Prose and Poetics of a *Longue Durée*

To start imagining that history, I have offered the proposition that there are three underlying facts definitive to the course of European militant modernity in much of the colonial world: a resurgent ancient mythology that demands and exacts attention in the face of the unknowable world that the postcolonial person faces, a fundamental fear of fascism in the contemporary politics of despair, and the effervescence of metonymic art and literature navigating and animating that fear. Within that epistemic triangulation dwell the prospects of a postcolonial philosophy of the unknowing subject. The anxiety-ridden constitution of gender and sexuality is the acid test and the defining leitmotif of the interface among these three facets of the postcolonial articulation of a traumatised Self and a triumphant Other. Who and what and why and wherefore is a Man, a Woman, a Child, what constitutes masculinity or femininity, and the passageways and byways and intersubjectivity between the two – these all lie at the heart of how the ideas of selves and societies, home and exile, mysticism and philosophy are creatively configured. If we were to consider the wide spectrum of this aesthetic modernity as metonymic for far more ancient mythic origins, then the character and contour of these works of art become definitive to a philosophical meditation that is the *modus operandi* of critical thinking in the world beyond the reach of European modernism or realism. The trajectory of this particular line of thinking – from the traces of ancient mythology, over their metonymic resurgence in contemporary arts and the fear of fascism that frames this entire wide spectrum or recollections, to the philosophical meditations they occasion – has never been either identified in that order nor assayed in this *longue durée* historical cosmogony which I have proposed in this book. The prose that this study had required and produced, as a result, has traversed from critical reflections on ancient mythologies, over aspects of literary criticism and issues in cultural studies, and finally to philosophical meditations on the prospects of an unknowing postcolonial subject.

Given the texture and disposition of that critical trajectory, the prose and purpose of this book had to explore a fusion of philosophical and aesthetic criticism, in order to map out the contours of how to think about contemporary cultures outside the purview of what calls itself 'Western aesthetics'. Theories of myth, metonymic poetics and political mythology all come together to frame and occasion this postcolonial meditation on the core question of what in this book I have identified as 'the unknowing subject'. Seen as the aesthetic resurfacing of more ancient traits, these cultural forms (film, fiction, poetry) conceal more than they reveal. I have used the examples of Iran and its environs to make a larger hermeneutic claim on the whole idea of aesthetics as the platform of a robust interface between a postcolonial philosophy of the subject and the critical edges of the politics that occasion and frame it. My purpose here has been to use the rich and diverse body of work in Iranian film, fiction and poetry, with necessary references to drama and visual arts, to show how the constitution of a human being as human, a self within a society, a miasmatic gender with attributive sexuality – men, women, feminine, masculine, home, exile *etcetera* – is only the tip of the iceberg in a potent and pervasive dismantling of the *metaphysics of identity* towards *an aesthetic of alterity*. That aesthetic is emblematic, mnemonic, pointing to a philosophy of the unknowing subject that has been waiting for our theoretical encounter.

My intention through this appositive dialectic has been to show how not *identity* but, in fact, *alterity* – not what we are, but what we wish to become, or fear ever to be; not what we know, but what we fear we may never know; not what we think we understand, but what we in fact positively misunderstand – is at the roots of this body of work. From this premise I have then moved towards the articulation of a world of *pure verisimilitude* that embraces, informs and enables the world of visible and tangible realities (the truth) that form the material culture of any historical civilisation. By thus *enframing* the metaphysical roots of Iranian culture, I have moved towards an *in-dwelling* that works through the particularities of a Brechtian *Verfremdungseffekt*, or what the Russian formalist theorist Viktor Shklovsky called '*Ostranenie*' – making the familiar foreign in order to make the foreign familiar. Among many other examples, I have consistently offered the work of Abbas Kiarostami and his systematic breaking of the Fourth Wall in the same vein, working towards an aesthetic framing of what it means to be human. That aesthetic framing is the premise of my articulation of a postcolonial subjectivity beyond the reach of colonial de-subjection – a condition that does not wait for a postcolonial moment to envision decoloniality, but that in fact detects the seeds of decoloniality in the very condition of coloniality. We in the former colonies were all overdue for such a theorisation. My in-dwelling in Iran is fully aware of the larger screen of a moral imaginary beyond Iranian or even Islamic borders. Misunderstanding the European project of colonial modernity as if it were a programme of global liberation is the premise of the prose and poetics of the *longue durée* I have sought to detail in this book.

The Battlefield of Pure Verisimilitude

My overarching argument here has been to show how in our contemporary film, fiction and poetry, we are on the battlefield of *pure verisimilitude*, where the entire culture, rooted as it is in its most ancient mythologies or most recent traumas, is being recast, re-imagined, re-mythologised, re-aestheticised, including but not limited to its issues of gender and sexuality, selfhood and otherness, identity and alterity, homeliness and uncanniness. Even more emphatically than the mystique of gender and sexuality would allow, in the formation of the ideas of selves and society, society and solitude, fact and fiction, home and exile, the realm of pure verisimilitude works through a dialectic that never results in a synthesis, but always remains at the level of pure speculative aesthetics. From the meandering formation of the genders of men, women and the miasmatic spaces in between, all the way to the domains of solitude and mysticism – as in Iranian cinema perhaps best evident in the works of Amir Naderi and Daryoush Mehrju'i – the ideological *cul de sac* of the politics of despair and fear of fascism have paradoxically given way to an emancipated aesthetics. There is an economic foregrounding for this political dead-end and aesthetic liberation. Because of the labour- and raw-material-intensive economy of places such as Iran, or most other countries around it, as a spot on the world economic system, the fruits of abused domestic labour go directly to the Eurocentric globalised capital and thus do not allow for active formations of a formidable labour force or an entrenched national bourgeoisie, except in the oil industry – where, in fact, it led to the nationalisation of the industry by Mohammad Mosaddegh in the 1950s, which in turn resulted in the US and UK military coup that toppled his government. This incorporation of domestic labour and raw material in the global economy of power and hegemony results in a regimented society between disorganised labour and the comprador bourgeoisie it enriches, coterminous with ideologically fractured politics and, in turn, a highly formalised aesthetic space over-compensating for such frustrated formations of selves and societies – which remain in a constant state of flux and negotiations, where gendering and sexuality are in a state of fluidity, where facts and fictions collide and collude, forming varied constellations of *assemblages* that are always in a state of mutability and impermanence. To this defining space must be added the force of Persian lyrical poetry that has always been amorphous and gender-fluid in a context where it can be read as allegorically fragmentary, socially inconsequential and politically potent but inconclusive. Through the active introduction of the catalytic force of mythologies – ancient and modern – my book as a result has dwelt on a dialect between the poetics of politics and the politics of the open-ended aesthetics of liberation, thriving far more on the formations of metonymic *others* than articulation of allegorical *selves*, gazing at all its allegorical alterities rather than fixating with its metaphysical identities.

At the centre of my project in this book has therefore been the overriding question: how do cultures cohere and connect beyond, beneath, above and over their manufactured periodisation into ancient, medieval and modern – all on the European model? What if much that we see and read and feel and fear and desire and repress in contemporary film, fiction and poetry are really metonymic substitutes for much older and more distant mythologies of origins, long since forgotten except through their metonymic gestations up to the recent unearthing of deeply buried and yet resurgent archetypes of normative and moral imagination? Might we not be collectively dreaming in our works of art, especially when terrified of a rising politics of despair, what we had feared and fantasised, desired and repressed, at the dawn of our humanity, when the elemental forces of our collective un/conscious were being formed? How can a person be the unknowing subject of their repressed fears and desires, or too vividly remembering the inaugural myth of their worldly wonders? This is not to diminish or dismiss very real and very recent traumas, or the human capacities for more urgent and immediate mythologies. This is just to open the frames of their references.

The active recasting of ancient mythologies throughout the ages up to and including our own is therefore central to my arguments in this book. In the sublime artistic work of the contemporary Iranian artist Nasser Oveissi (born 1934), such as in his series of women and horses – 'Shirin and her Horse' is one potent example – we have one of the most compelling cases of the visual re-mythologisation of the ancient metaphors of vegetal, animal and human transmutations in a boldly erotic visual text that alludes back to the Zoroastrian myth of creation, from the androgynous Kayumars and its (his, her, their) progenies Mashya and Mashyana. Borrowing the formal structure of the European Orientalist tradition of the odalisque and mixing it with the Persian iconic tradition of the Khorshid Khanom/Lady Sun leitmotif, this whole genre of Oveissi's work invokes a fusion of mytho-erotic sensibilities. In this series, integral to the *Saqqa-khaneh* movement of the 1960s and 1970s, Oveissi recasts the myth of Mashya and Mashyana in the potent eroticism he borrows from both Persian and European leitmotifs, while in his own subconscious repertoire he appeals to a very ancient 'hermaphroditic' myth. The artwork therefore generates and sustains tension between its formal allusion to an Orientalist genre, its invocation of the Lady Sun, as well as its ancient roots in an Iranian myth of creation, its militant juxtaposition of the erotic and the politics (a fusion that is poetically best evident in the works of Ahmad Shamlou).

In this book I have therefore worked primarily through the mythic and aesthetic constitution of selves and society, gender and sexuality, and the formations of the domains of foreign and familiar, as evident in the varied evidence of Iranian film, fiction and poetry – for that wide spectrum gives the prose of this book an element of necessary urgency and contemporaneity that it needs. However, I have also sought to connect these contemporary materials to the archetypal figures of *male* and *female* that emerged in the more ancient archetypes of Mashya and Mashyana in Persian mythologies. Through these reflections that bridge classical and modern, mythical and historical, I have mapped out a hermaphroditic re-reading of the figures of *man* and *woman*, as well as the twin *loci* of self and society, foreign and familiar, as they are reconceived and recast in Iranian film, fiction and poetry – the archetypal repertoire

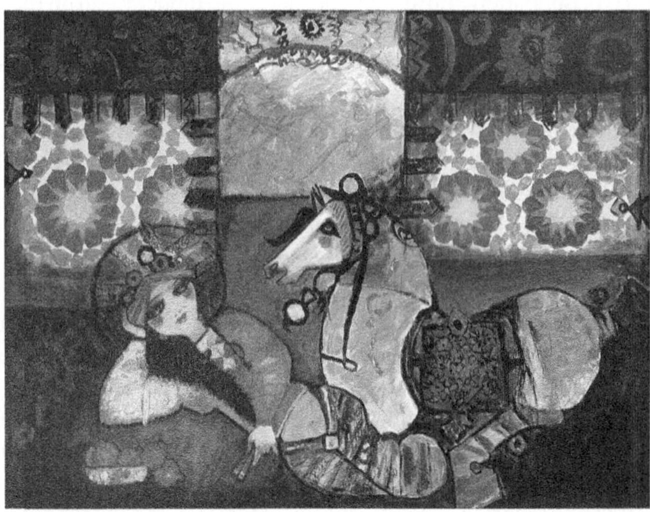

Figure C.1 *Nasser Oveissi, 'Shirin and her Horse' (no date). (Photo: Nasser Oveissi Family)*

of a living culture. I, of course, mean the term in the sense of questioning the social construction of gender binaries and not as referring to the so-called 'ovotesticular disorder', an intersex condition in which a person is born with both ovarian and testicular tissue. To be sure, I need to acknowledge the Greek and Latin origins of the term 'hermaphrodite' and then carry it into its Iranian domicile. We have the term 'hermaphrodite' from the Latin Hermaphroditus, which comes from Ancient Greek Hermaphroditos, which derives from Hermaphroditus, the son of Hermes and Aphrodite in Greek mythology. Extended to its Iranian dominion, the idea implied in this term becomes far more archaic – extending from the cosmic to the vegetal, animal and human – and connects the birth of Mashya and Mashyana to their distant and long-since deceased 'parent' Kayumars who was murdered long before the birth of their distant offspring. I therefore use the term 'hermaphrodite', or the fusion of Mashya and Mashyana, not in reference to any biological disposition of being intersexed, but in overcoming the social construction of *man* and *woman*, and the emotive universe they generate in the space between. I have then taken the terms *man* and *woman*, *male* and *female*, as the iconic referents to the formation of other key binaries, self and society, self and other, mysticism and philosophy, home and exile, and so on. I have done so all within the mythic universe of Iranian cosmogonic imagination. This, in turn, generates a realm of pure verisimilitude upon which is then negotiated the terms of a mnemonic subjectivity.

From Mazdaian Myth to Metonymic Subjectivity

I therefore needed to turn to the inaugural myth of our humanity in its Iranian gestation. In the Introduction I shared how, according to the Zoroastrian creation myth as described in the *Bundahishn*, Ahura Mazda's sixth creation is Kayumars, who was neither male nor female. The Evil Spirit or Ahriman (Angra Mainyu) dwelt in the Absolute Darkness, seeking to destroy all that Ahura Mazda had created. It sent the demoness Jeh to kill Kayumars. Upon his death, the moon captured his seed, and from his corpse grew a rhubarb plant, the seeds of which were the origin of all plant life, and from the branches of which grew Mashya and Mashyana. That myth of origin has been central to my argument in this book, for through that myth, I have re-read enduring aspects of contemporary Iranian cultural effervescence as a subconscious archetypal urge to recapture that mythic moment of creative gender-fluidity in varied aesthetic, poetic and literary terms. The mythic domain of these archaic figures is where the verisimilitude of forms and archetypes dwell and agitate. Conscious or otherwise, so I contend, Iranian artists, poets and literati have been hard at work recasting the archaic terms of their very ancient culture in very modern terms. The archaic lexicography of what it means to be human, to be a man, a woman, a child, a person, a society, to be at home, or to be in exile are all the results of an active aesthetic (metonymic) interface with very ancient and deep-rooted archetypes hidden from the naked eye. A critical task of this book has been to bring such aesthetic remembrances to fuller consciousness.

Ancient Iranian mythologies have never been left to rest in distant times and become forgotten memories, but have been systematically, consistently and without interruption traveling across history as they were renewed and remembered – from the pre-Islamic into the Islamic periods, thus effectively overriding this dubious periodisation of Iranian history. The translation of Pahlavi sources into Arabic and Persian early in Islamic history by such towering figures as Ibn Muqaffa' (died ca 756/759) eventually led to the composition of Ferdowsi's masterpiece, *The Shahnameh*, early in the eleventh century as the prime example of actively and creatively remembering and recasting ancient mythologies, legends and histories – all from a distant past directly into a palpable present. The canonical presence of the *Shahnameh* and other pre-Islamic sources throughout the last 1,400 years has sustained the course of this varied and procreative remembrance. The extraordinary philosophical oeuvre of Shahab al-Din Yahya Suhrawardi (1154–91) in the twelfth century gave bold philosophical twists to that historical memory – and in that way, it had rendered them in epic narrative almost a century earlier. While Ferdowsi's *Shahnameh* inaugurated numerous other epics in subsequent centuries, equally rooted in pre-Islamic legends and myths, Suhrawardi's philosophical edifice, too, was extended into the works of succeeding generations of philosophers such as Shams al-Din Muhammad ibn Mahmud Shahrazuri and Qutb al-Din al-Shirazi in the thirteenth and fourteenth centuries. The thrust of these mythological attestations in epic and philosophical prose continues apace to our own time. In his *Spiritual Body and Celestial Earth: From Mazdean Iran to Shi'ite Iran* (1960/1977), the eminent French scholar Henry Corbin has mapped out in detail the link between the Mazdaian mythological traditions all the way to the later and contemporary Shi'i philosophy of the sixteenth through the twentieth centuries. What we are witnessing here is a dual contraction of time and space, between ancient mythology and later philosophy, a fusion of all manners of projected dualism of past and present, East and West, masculine and feminine, home and exile, self and society, abstractions and figurations. The figure of Kayumars in the *Shahnameh* and his subsequent succession of representations in manuscript illustrations (especially in the Timurid and Safavid eras) is key iconic evidence linking the ancient mythology to ever more contemporary iconic gestations. These manuscript illustrations and the texts they illuminate are the enduring evidence of the visual and poetic arts that have been the metonymic registers of those ancient mythologies. These sources inform and animate the very visual vocabulary of generations of Iranian artists, poets and filmmakers, all the way to our own time. A filmmaker like Bahram Beiza'i, an artist like Nasser Oveissi, a poet like Mehdi Akhavan-e Sales, or a novelist like Mahmoud Dolatabadi, among scores of other contemporary and current artists, are all living testimonies of such uninterrupted continuities. More recently, in 2020, Suhrawardi's allegorical stories of the twelfth century have even been re-narrated as children's stories.[7] We therefore are not talking about ancient mythologies that we need to unearth out of nowhere.

The de-gendered disposition of Kayumars, which literally means 'Mortal Life', places the inaugural person, who was the creation of Ahura Mazda, at the primordial moment when it (he, she, it, they) lived as a spirit before it assumed the corporeal form of a handsome young person. After a short life, Kayumars is poisoned by Ahriman at the instigation of the arch-demon Whore Jeh. But from Kayumars' seed eventually

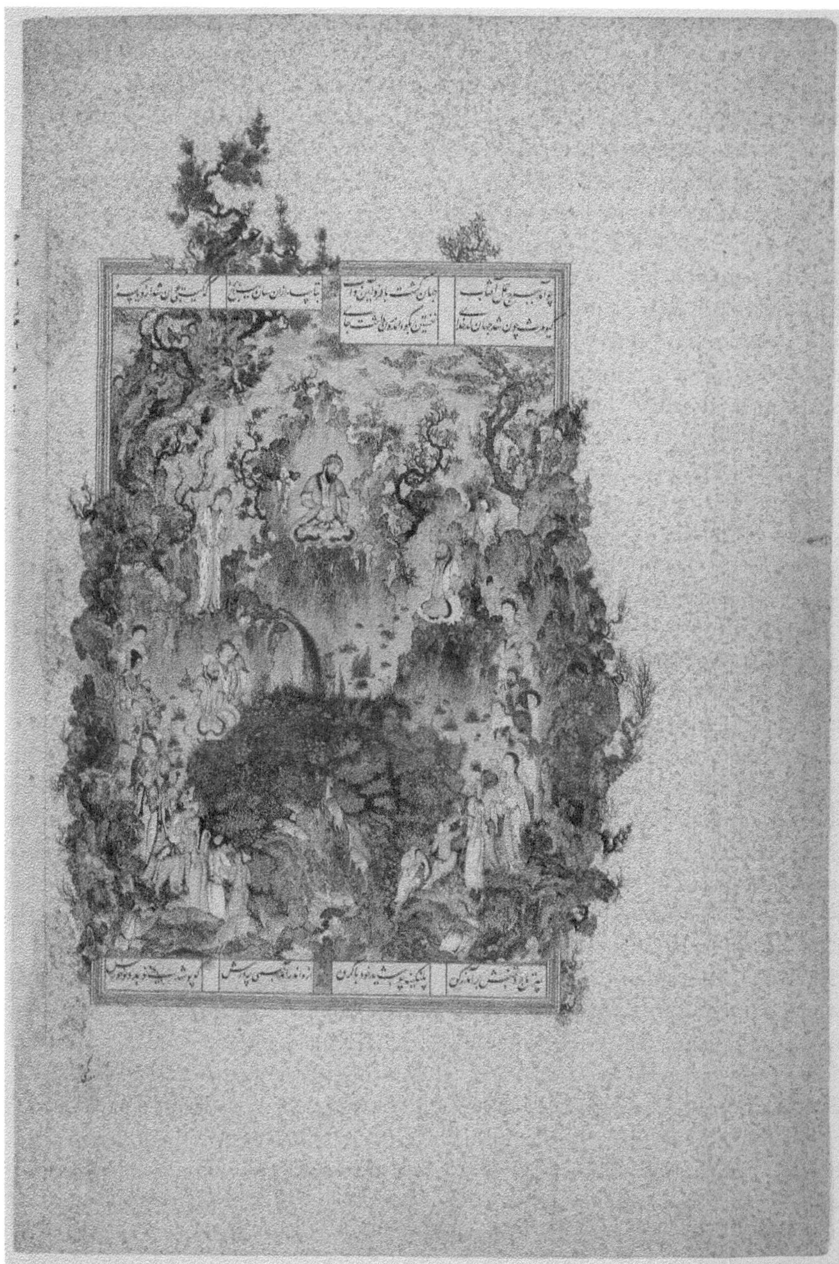

Figure C.2 *'The Court of Kayumars', painting by Sultan Muhammad, Iran (ca 1522). (Photo: Courtesy of Aga Khan Museum)*

grew the rhubarb plant, the stem of which developed into the first human couple, the parents of the human race, Mashya and Mashyana. This inaugural moment of gender-fluidity – from the Divine Will to the proto-human to plant to the first couple – determines the amorphous disposition of being human at its very inception. Today much has been written by scholars of gender-fluidity, such as Judith Butler and others, about the manner in which gendering is seen as the product of performative practices, all determined by the dominant heteronormativity. But seen from the vantage point of this ancient myth, as well as its consistent historical recasting in the visual and performing arts, gendering can also be seen as part of a far more overarching fragmentation of the human species, from immortal to mortal, from animal to vegetal, and from vegetal to de-gendered and then re-gendered species, from which the dialectic of being and non-being, divine and human, good and evil, self and other, solitude and society rises in a more extended mythic dominion.

This reading of a sustained course of inaugural mythic, subsequent metonymic and, ultimately, philosophical meditations that I have proposed in this book was foreshadowed by the sociological imagination of thinkers in other fields – such as George Herbert Mead and Erving Goffman, who had already theorised selfhood and personhood long before Judith Butler's articulation in a specifically gendered sense. Thus read and projected, the Zoroastrian myth of creation gives gendered bifurcation a far more mythic disposition, while Butler takes it towards a more moral and epistemological formation of the knowing subject in Lacan's symbolic order. Much of such theorisations remains ahistorical, evidence-free, deeply and subconsciously Eurocentric, entirely oblivious to the vastly diversified cultural contexts of the world outside the European (Christian) imaginary. The gender-fluidity we encounter in the case of Mashya and Mashyana and their subsequent gestations all the way to the contemporary stages much larger conditions of moral and material fluidity that under patriarchal, masculinist and specifically colonial settings assumes far more radical implications in the contemporary arts – where the platform is set for the rise of *an unknowing (metonymic and mnemonic) subject*, a subject that could always defiantly know through a hermeneutic of misunderstanding but was always already colonially pre-empted from knowing, and therefore a decolonised subject of that which is unknowable to the European sovereign subject – the blind spot of its condition of coloniality. The unknowing subject has been pre-empted from the European colonising epistemology, it did *cogito* alright, but there was no *ergo* follow-up to enable any *sum* – as it were. Therefore, it was not, for it could not have been – although it could think. Ontologically pre-empted while epistemologically agitated, the colonial subject became the agent of its own unknowability. The unknowing subject has always been known to itself, unknown to the Cartesian stipulation, and therefore it became the subject of the unknowable to that very same Cartesian epistemology. Because of its metonymic and mnemonic disposition, the decolonised unknowing subject was and remains the blind spot of the European sovereign all-knowing subject – and from that vantage point, invisible to the European knowing subject, the postcolonial person became the unknowing subject of the world beyond the European blind spots. We can see them, we have always seen them, in our rearview mirrors, as it were, but they cannot see us; they have never seen us, for they had (willy-nilly) written us out of history. The unknowing subject is therefore a point of postcolonial privilege, made of a point of colonial denial. The aesthetics and poetics of this postcolonial person is the metonymic (mnemonic) passageway between its mythic past and its philosophical presence. Since they were denied being the knowing subjects of a knowable world, they have become the unknowing subjects of a renewed knowable world.

Semblance and Subjectivity

What I have therefore proposed and explored in this book takes the anxiety-ridden question of gender-fluidity upstream from its current post-structuralist (heavily Eurocentric) formations and places the crucial ideas of philosophers such as Baudrillard regarding *simulacrum* and *simulation* in a more specific historical context and begins to decentre 'Europe' towards a more global understanding of gender-fluidity and its related issues of a de-gendered, de-racialised, de-centred, amorphous and unknowing subject formation and historical agency. It also places the thinking of other philosophers such as Roland Barthes regarding modern mythologies against the background of far more ancient formations and their contemporary metonymic gestations. Barthes is after mapping and navigating the contours of modern bourgeois mythologies. Here I am after the metonymic allusions to subconscious myths, embedded as they are in contemporary works of art as the sites of subconscious revolt against endemic colonial de-subjection. This in and of itself de-Hellenises our literary and aesthetic consciousness of myths and mythologies – in specifically Indo-Iranian, but potentially any other worldly context. As we turn to the varied spectacles of contemporary Iranian art and culture and tease out their metonymic allusions, we will see how Guy Debord's notion of 'the society of the spectacle' might consider the dialectic between ancient mythologies and their contemporary mnemonic manifestations more seriously. The same holds true for Walter Benjamin's theorisation of fragments as allegories – for here mythological fragments (as in their memorial recollections) carry the seeds of their later full-bodied metamorphic offspring within themselves. At the same time, we will see how Adorno's philosophical reflections on the centrality of *semblance* and *subjectivity* is cast upon a whole new mode of mimetic possibilities, evident, for example, in the Shi'i passion play of *Ta'ziyeh*. We have solid evidence of making such links in the extraordinary scholarship of the French scholar Henry Corbin who had detected such transmutations from Mazdaian to Shi'i philosophical traditions. The point here, however, is not to conduct any form of cultural archaeology, but to see how under a sovereign politics of despair and fear of fascism the metonymic transmutations of old mythologies enable a contrarian mode of philosophical thinking – predicated on an amorphous and unknowing subject always in the blind spot of the European sovereign subject. While in Nazi Germany the mythic dispositions of culture (as later diagnosed and theorised by Ernst Cassirer) were driven in specifically fascist directions, here I propose precisely the opposite direction in decidedly liberating possibilities. The porous borderline between 'Europe' and 'non-Europe' on which I write this prose is precisely where the local and global begin to open up to alternative readings of interstitial universalities – on which premise I, as a thinker, am an always itinerant and nomadic subject.

In the exquisite visual repertoire of Abbas Kiarostami, more specifically in his series *Roads and Rain* (2007), we find a potent passageway connecting the implied mythic and manifest metonymic allusions at the heart of his artworld.[8] Evident in the photographic work of Abbas Kiarostami dwells a composite vision of reality, compatible with his cinematic oeuvre, in which the digitised fragmentations of the image exacerbate their metonymic power of simulacra and simulation – where the unknowing subject becomes as amorphous as what they see. Here we have palpable visual evidence of the allegorical power of the digitised visual fragments that enable a mode of semblance and subjectivity which is self-contained within the visual register – forming a world of pure verisimilitude akin to the mythic inauguration of any and all cultures. While in his cinema, as I have demonstrated earlier in my work, his brand of Actual Realism dwells on the uncanny disposition of the familiar, in his later photography he dismantles the totality of that realism into spatial and narrative fragmentations that are disallowed to coagulate to represent anything other than their own disjointed allegorical self-referentiality. This is how his visual repertoire becomes the homely habitat of the unknowing (both metonymic and mnemonic) subject. Although there are other Iranian artists such as Parviz Kalantari or Ardeshir Mohassess who in their respective work exude such pure verisimilitude, the global audience afforded to Kiarostami has enabled a far more potent exposure of this aspect of his artworld.

I have arrived at the idea of that amorphous and unknowing subject from an angle predicated on Walter Benjamin's work, but with a crucial difference. In his *Origin of the German Trauerspiel* (1925–28), Benjamin sought to demonstrate how Baroque tragic drama is constitutionally different from Classical Greek tragedies.[9]

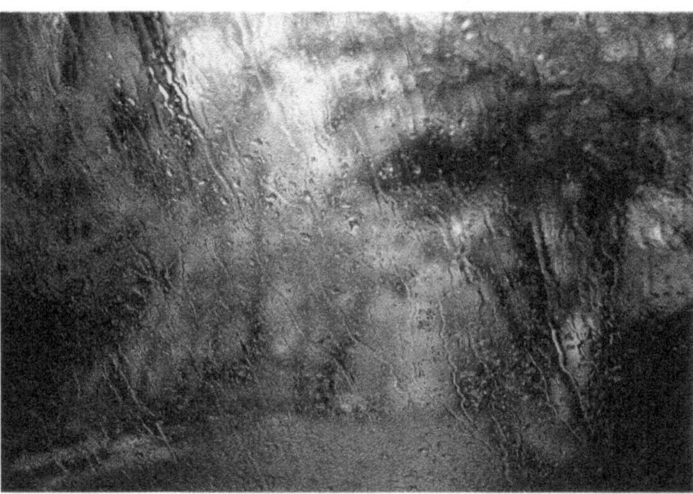

Figure C.3 *Abbas Kiarostami,* Roads and Rain *(2007). (Photo: Courtesy of Kiarostami Foundation)*

This he proposed by way of placing the tragic hero inside the historical fluidity of the traumatised European subject. The classical hero he proposed is fated, the Baroque hero he had unearthed is historical, circumstantial, therefore agential and perforce vulnerable. The classical hero is predestined, the Baroque hero's free will is pitted against those of his fellow characters, engaged in a Bakhtinian (we might add) dialogical act of heteroglossia, if we were to read Benjamin via Bakhtin. Benjamin therefore detected a melancholic disposition in the Baroque hero, dwelling in the debris of a ruined historical landscape that, in turn, becomes allegorical for the rest of (European) humanity. In this book I have proposed to read the Persian Passion Play (*Ta'ziyeh*) as a counter-example of what Benjamin was seeing in German tragic drama, and from there to move (with Corbin's reading of Mazdaism/Shi'ism together) the concomitant mimetic crisis of contemporary art as a metonymic transmutation of ancient mythologies into imperceptive allegories of the unknowing subject. Neither the limited Eurocentricity of Benjamin, nor the binary opposition he posits between Classical Greek and historical Baroque should distract our attention from the fact that, in the historicity of the latter, he has indeed detected a thematic fact that becomes even more acute once we shift the scene to colonial and postcolonial sites.

With the androgynous gender-fluidity of this unknowing subject, the philosophical legacy that this epistemological leitmotif implicates could not be binary, as evident in the fact that the subject pronouns in Persian are not gender-specific. That crucial disposition of the unknowing subject entails an entirely different relationship with the unknowing self and the prospects of a freshly knowable world. Towards the colonising European world, we decolonised postcolonials could not but have a negative dialectic that has enabled us to come to ourselves through a hermeneutic of misunderstanding, in which our colonisers have failed to locate us anywhere except on the dark side of their Enlightenment.[10] The auxiliary extensions of this gender-fluidity do not remain limited to gender issues and are extended to the corollary concepts of self and society, home and exile, solitude and communion, what philosophy is and how it is different form theology or mysticism. A whole cosmogony of social and moral being is at stake here – the particulars of a full human being. The signifier is therefore liberated from a fixed obedience to any fixed signified. The sustained history of Suhrawardi's philosophy of Illumination (*Hikmah al-Ishraq*) is the singular site of this philosophical adventure that, as Henry Corbin has documented in detail, extends all the way from its Mazdaian origins to its varied Shi'i manifestations. As I have proposed here, the link between the myth of origin and this philosophical prospect of a de-gendered unknowing subject is metonymic and mnemonic and has worked through contemporary film, fiction and poetry – which, in turn, as I have demonstrated in this book, opens up whole new horizons of coming to terms with the robust mysteries of this body of art.

The archival material with which I have worked is therefore by necessity threefold: (1) a substantial portion of the material comes from the Iranian visual, performing and literary arts; these sources are then made to converse with the implied and hidden hermeneutics of both; (2) European and (3) Islamic philosophical traditions brought together through a negative dialectic that best suits an itinerant nomadic subject. There has therefore been no primacy to any one of these sources in my thinking.

The unfolding core of my critical thinking has determined the direction of its own discourse and thematically moves from one to the other. Central to this unfolding remains the hermeneutic link between mythic memories and their metonymic meanderings – with the ancient Zoroastrian myth of creation of Mashya and Mashyana as the threshold of this sustained spectrum. I have taken the aesthetic power of Iranian visual and performing arts – cinema, in particular – as the mnemonic labyrinth through which ancient mythologies are remembered and thus resurface and inform the effervescence of modern and contemporary arts. In this respect, the chapters on Bahram Beiza'i's iconic film *Bashu: The Little Stranger* and my extended interview with him are at the epicentre of this book. Historically framed, film, fiction and poetry run through the veins of this study, while the metonymic links between myth and philosophy have held its theoretical body together. The consistent articulation of the amorphous and unknowing subject at the heart of this passage towards a future philosophy of a still knowable world remains the zenith of my journey.

Pivoting towards a Liberated Subject and a Liberation Philosophy

This journey has therefore pivoted towards a philosophy of decolonial liberation, through a radical reconsideration of gender-fluidity as an amorphous subject; thus, it has been quite necessary to keep in mind a critical corrective lens at this juncture. To a European or Europeanised mind, any invocation of a mythic moment in the configuration of any contemporary culture even outside Europe seems reminiscent of the German philosophical tradition of the last two centuries that speculated on the presumed mythical origins of cultural (Germanic) identity – and the horrid havoc that such thoughts wrought on modern history. Equally fraught would be to read such a prose as a rehabilitation of those perilous German philosophies speculating on the 'cultural spirit' of nations as the foundation for a philosophy of cultural interpretation. These are entirely European anxieties – and rightly so. My turn to a mythic moment like that of Mashya and Mashyana moves in precisely the opposite direction and is to dismantle the tyranny of a gendered, racialised, colonised, classed and irreversibly Europeanised knowing subject that has violently stared down the world. I locate the philosophical provenance of this act of critical thinking within the larger context of Latin American (particularly Argentinian) Philosophy of Liberation and decoloniality, widely articulated by philosophers such as Enrique Dussel, Walter Mignolo, Maria Lugones, Aníbal Quijano, Nelson Maldonado-Torres and others, with whose work I feel philosophically most at home. This project could not be assimilated backwards, either into the 'Area Studies' *cul de sac* on one side, or European philosophical anxieties on the other. My thinking in this book and many others is deeply embedded in the thought of the Congolese philosopher V. Y. Mudimbe in his *Invention of Africa: Gnosis, Philosophy, and the Order of Knowledge*, the Japanese philosopher Kojin Karatani, perhaps best in his *Isonomia and the Origins of Philosophy*, and the Bengali philosopher Ranajit Guha in his *History at the Limit of World-History*. Even in the European (Germanic) context is it important to recall the rise of the Frankfurt School in the immediate aftermath of the collapse of Nazism in Germany, to pivot towards a Critical Theory that would seek to salvage the defiant humanity of a people against the terror of their own perilous mythologies. If there is one pivotal text that informs the way I read modern and contemporary art in relation to deeply rooted mythologies, it would be the Mexican filmmaker Guillermo del Toro's *Pan's Labyrinth* (2006), to which I alluded earlier and where the political defiance against fascism assumes a compelling mythic semiotics.

Particularly important in this philosophical pedigree has been the work of Argentinian feminist philosopher María Lugones (1944–2020) and her seminal idea of the 'coloniality of gender', which identifies the condition of European coloniality as the principal culprit in the superimposition of gender binaries at the service of capitalist modernity.[11] Lugones' work is particularly crucial to be juxtaposed against the current Iranian feminist proclivity that, as perhaps best represented in the work of Afsaneh Najmabadi, deliberately and consciously chooses to disregard, side-step and downplay the centrality of coloniality and chase after insular and domesticated theatres of such changes.[12] These nativist scholars are squarely located within a very limited 'Qajar specialist' and lack historical imagination of any larger theoretical significance. Exactly in the opposite direction, Lugones is integral to a whole movement of decoloniality reading, as she examines the current articulations of race, gender and sexuality in the shadow of European colonialism. As Deleuze and Guattari have demonstrated in their *Anti-Oedipus: Capitalism and Schizophrenia*, the violent act of subjectivation within the daddy-mummy-baby triumvirate is a larger capitalist project that reaches around the globe via the colonial enterprise. My concern, therefore, has commenced upstream from the stage of aggressive gender-formation and through the trope of gender-fluidity goes back to a mythic moment that hovers over cultural production. I decidedly work through a body of evidence in the visual and performing arts with exaggerated proclivity towards staging heteronormativity. Through the thicket of that heightened masculinity and its binary femininity I have worked my way backward towards the spectre of gender-fluidity from which they are running away. Through their staging of too much protestation I have excavated the apparition of gender-fluidity they are trying to deny and conceal, but in fact paradoxically affirm and reveal. In two masterpieces of Iranian cinema, Mohammad Reza Aslani's *Chess Game of the Wind* (1976) and Bahram Beiza'i's *Bashu: The Little Stranger* (1986), the patent absence of a *paterfamilias* stages the condition of this narrative fluidity. In this book, such staging of gender-fluidity is not an end unto itself, for it is the opening gate to the emancipation of the decolonised unknowing subject.

That unknowing subject emerges from the ground zero of colonial de-subjection. Gendering bifurcations and the de-subjection of the colonised person were coterminous on the colonial site and went hand in hand. The forced division of the polyamorous, polyandrous and androgynous body into binary formations of the mommy-daddy-baby unit conducive to economic and consumer productivity was primarily a capitalist and ultimately colonial practice of dividing the body and ruling and appropriating its labour. The myth of monogamous heteronormativity was the grandest scheme of colonial modernity. Recalling and recasting the originary myth of creation with Mashya and Mashyana, as I have done in this book, demythologises the mythic cornerstone of European colonial modernity. The metamorphic conception of the vegetal, animal and human at the heart of this myth of origin becomes historical through the metonymic staging of works of art where the subconscious actively revolts against the colonised superego. This lineage of the metonymic aesthetic back to the unruly subconscious mythic becomes totemic, linking the emerging gender-fluidity to an allusion to the repressed mythic past. Here Rumi's famous poem in the *Masnavi* is crucial – for long before the advent of European colonial modernity, right here in this seminal passage in Rumi's masterpiece, we see the elemental fusion of our existential materiality.

Az jamadi mordam-o nami shodam ...

I died to the inanimate and became vegetal
I died to the vegetal and became animal –
I died to the animal and became human –
So why should I fear – when did I diminish from dying?
Next move and I shall die to human –
So I can rise among the angels –
Even from the angels I must jump over the brook
'Everything dies except His Face'.[13]

In these contexts, my turn to the Iranian myth of creation has therefore not been in search of any speculative philosophy marking the 'national spirit' through which we might understand contemporary Iranian art. This is a peculiarly European anxiety, given their history of such terrorising mythologies. In the twentieth century and in the wake of the rise of Nazism, the eminent German philosopher Ernest Cassirer wrote poignantly about the dangers of such mythic disposition in national historiographies. This legitimate European anxiety is not the urgent moment of decoloniality that informs my kind and pedigree of critical thinking. The mythical disposition of the creation story for me is at the service of the theoretical thrust towards the articulation of the mnemonically disposed unknowing subject, which is targeted precisely against the speculative philosophies of any presumed 'national spirit'. The same is true about the link between Cassirer and decolonial and postcolonial thinking, which I have already examined, by dismantling the proto-fascist proclivities of the politically depleted militant Islamism, in *The Emperor is Naked: On the Inevitable Demise of the Nation-State* (2019); there, I extend Cassirer's seminal posthumous book, *The Myth of State* (1946) to the predicament of post- and decoloniality. Following that study, my project here is to face and dismantle the fear of fascism embedded in the European sovereign subject, by turning the mystical proclivities of fascism against itself. Cassirer's turn to mythological thinking was to expose them at the root of modern European totalitarianism – which project proved useful when I did the same with the militant Islamism that the European colonial project had occasioned and exacerbated. In doing so, my thinking was closely informed by the second volume of Cassirer's *Philosophy of Symbolic Forms*, which is on 'Mythical Thought'. The German turn to mythical fascism was rooted in the German economic woes after World War I. I did the same with the Muslim turn to militant Islamism, which was a nativist reaction to the European colonial domination of the Muslim world. To Cassirer's Enlightened European imagination, this turn to mythical thought was an aberration and quite surprising. To us on the colonial edges of that Enlightenment, it is not. The turn to barbaric fascism or militant nativism are two sides of the same coin – occasioned by the condition of European coloniality in and outside itself.

Ernst Cassirer was too much enamoured by 'the rational' in European thought, which he thought had gone awry with fascism. On the colonial edges of the self-same capitalist modernity, we have no such illusions about European rationalism – as Adorno and Horkheimer discovered the hard way at the conclusion of the Jewish Holocaust. The task at hand is not to consider mythical thinking as an aberration, as European philosophers have – the task is to see how that mythical thinking can be turned against colonised and de-subjected minds and the fascism they enable. The philosophy of liberation in which my project is located begins from the ground of coloniality up; in my case, it posits the prospects of an unknowing subject that is mnemonic in its mythic, heroic and historical worlds in which such a liberation might take place. If from poets and philosophers extending from Ferdowsi and Suhrawardi over Rumi to Mehdi Akhavan-e Sales and filmmakers like Bahram Beiza'i have turned to primordial myths to ascertain their place in the world, then thus must also be located my theorisation of their practice. At the epicentre of capitalist modernity, any claim to the myth of origin is actively racialised, and as such supremacist, triumphalist, total and self-centring. At the colonial edges of the self-same project, ancient mythologies and their metonymic gestations are defiant, de-racialised, de-gendered, de-colonial, decentred and, as such, fragmentary, allegorical, merely mnemonic. They never get into a person, a persona, a movement, or an ideology, for they are a will to resist power and oppose any will to power. They are mnemonically amorphous.

To see how this mythic disposition of cultures can be turned against totalitarian proclivities of a solitary 'European' knowing subject, my book is to be read not just in a post-Orientalist key, but equally so in a post-Saidian register. The anxieties of the so-called 'Area Studies' prose have long been overcome by the philosophically potent prose in which I have written this book. The question of gender-fluidity, at the very heart of this book, and its Iranian provenance is embedded in the intertwined formation of *Mashya and Mashyana* itself – the supreme mythic signifier of gender-fluidity in its Iranian provenance, as I have re-articulated it on these pages. But neither the Iranian provenance nor the organising issue of gender-fluidity should ethnicise or localise my larger epistemological project at the expense of enabling the powerful mythic, metonymic and philosophical appeal of the project – which invokes Aeschylus' *Prometheus Bound* and Shelly's *Prometheus Unbound* at one and the same time and takes them to uncharted territories. The specificity of my textual evidence (the archive through which I work) is therefore meant to buttress my argument in this direction on solid evidentiary grounds in the visual and performing arts. To the degree that I use the Iranian cultural provenance, I do so not as an end in itself, but as the prolonged historical body of evidence to map out my more urgent philosophical project of articulating the theoretical primacy of the unknowing subject – which is my main and most potent theoretical contention in this book. I have dwelled on aspects of Iranian literary and visual and performing arts by way of teasing out their embedded and implied theoretical thrust in decidedly philosophical terms, positing their repressed universal contingencies. Pivoting towards a liberation philosophy, if I were to take my cues from the work of the Argentinian philosopher Enrique Dussel and the Mexican muralist Diego Rivera together, requires unearthing ancient mythologies at the roots of the aesthetic metonymies that make the radical contemporaneity of our lives resonate with enduring relevance.

My turn to the mythic disposition of cultures reverberating in the aspects of Iranian visual and performing arts on a global scene is not limited to the myth itself, but its metonymic and mnemonic manifestations in contemporary art, for no philosophy of liberation is possible without liberating the knowing subject at the aesthetic centre of this art – and that is impossible without liberating that knowing subject from the binary violence of gendering knowledge. Mashya and Mashyana are the floating signifiers of time immemorial that have animated the visual, performing and literary arts at the heart of this book. I am not entirely oblivious to the terrifying political consequences of such European invocation of distant mythologies from faraway cultures. In an earlier book, *Persophilia: Persian Culture on the Global Scene* (2015), I have dealt extensively with at least one such theme in German Romanticism and its penchant for Persian mysticism. A recent study, titled *The Longing for Myth in Germany: Religion and Aesthetic Culture from Romanticism to Nietzsche*, by George S. Williamson has done extensive work in that domain and alerted us to how a particular brand of German Romanticism was heavily inclined towards myth – especially in the works of Herder, Schelling, Wagner and Nietzsche. This was a massive social movement in Germany itself that perhaps inadvertently paved the way from romanticism to mysticism and the rise of Nazism, a development I have addressed on multiple occasions and mapped out in my *Persophilia*. But even there I have already discussed how, when such mythologies of distant origins come back from Europe to Iranian or any other postcolonial sites, they in fact dismantle that mysticism in specifically Dionysian terms. We must morally, imaginatively and philosophically decentre 'Europe', historicise it to its localised specificities, if we ever are to tease out the violently hidden and repressed universal alterities to European Enlightenment modernity and its philosophical pedigree. That pedigree has been the roadmap for my thinking through a liberation philosophy.

Mythos as Inheritance

Let me now conclude with a question that is at the heart of this book. At the centre of this emancipatory retrieval of the mythic moment in its contemporary aesthetic gestations is the key question of how we exactly inherit the past, why we would inherit the past – say, in this case, the myth of Mashya and Mashyana? Why bother? What is the impetus, hence the pitfalls, of asking such questions and retrieving such distant memories?

The experience of coloniality, from any close encounter (India or Algeria) or its tangential implications (Iran or Turkey), is a drenched and soaked purgatory through de-subjection, of denial of agency, of being philosophically written out of Europeanised global history, and as such an act of deliberate and designed cultural amnesia, foregrounding the historical trauma of nations and the fragility of their historical inheritance. This is the reason why Frantz Fanon rightly believed decolonisation means the complete replacing of one 'species of men' for another. That colonial inheritance is not given. It is cultivated – always, as I have argued in this book mnemonically, for it is metonymically mitigated. But what does that exactly mean? By positing a prolonged thrust pivoting between the mythos of vanquished empires and the cultural memory of postcolonial nations I have sought a way out of the predicament of colonial de-subjection – not just in this but in much of my other work, too. I am, of course, not proposing a 'precolonial' origin to cultural mythologies of the present – instead I am offering a *longue durée* vision of lived realities, of cultural memories, of collective recollections. I am less concerned with postcolonial identity than I am with decolonial alterity, and as such my thinking crosses paths with the concept of 'inheritance' in such European philosophers as Jacques Derrida, as it does with the German philosophical tradition of the last two centuries, suggesting a link between mythical origins of cultural identity. My project, however, should not be assimilated backward into such European predicaments, for the simple fact that I live and read and think and write from a contrarian condition of coloniality that was squarely within the European philosophical blind spots. They could not see us, except as de-subjected subjects of their globalised empires. European political upheavals and philosophical controversies therefore – from the rise of their fascism over the absence of their postcolonial remorse to their own current crisis of the subject – are meaningless in the colonial site, albeit theoretically quite edifying to behold. I am therefore happily traversing uncharted territories, mapping a decolonised postcolonial subject that will have to come to terms with what that proposition might actually mean.

The postcolonial condition is not merely a temporal or spatial domain (yesterday we were colonised in India and Algeria and today we are liberated in Latin America and North Africa) but an entirely epistemological and ontological proposition. The term 'precolonial', when placed before 'postcolonial', falsely temporalises the condition of coloniality, which in turn offers a limited reading of that condition and privileges and fetishises the passing instance of European colonialism and gives it metaphysical authority and authenticity – as if it was the end and purpose of the entire global history. This was an unfortunate, perhaps inadvertent, consequence of the groundbreaking works of pioneering thinkers such as Césaire, Fanon, Said and especially Homi Bhabha. As a result, massively varied and deeply complicated historical cultures are silenced, pacified and neutralised under the rubric of 'precolonial', or 'premodern', or even 'early modern'. In my work I have never yielded that authority to 'Europe' or, even worse, to 'the West', or to the instrumental reasoning of its 'modernity' that first spelled calamity for the world at large, long before it came back to bite its own populations in the back. But even if not temporal, then the thematic link between the atemporal moment of myth and the threshold of postcolonial philosophy for me is the mitigating metonymic power of contemporary art – which has remained largely under-theorised until now. This purgatorial disposition of the metonymic power of art in my thinking (as perhaps best evident in the *Saqqa-khaneh* movement in contemporary Iranian art) remains definitive to this book and protects and distinguishes it from being read as a commentary on European philosophers or European traumas, such as the rise of fascism. As a postcolonial thinker, I have a contested claim on European philosophical thinking, which is inevitably my contested inheritance, too. The metonymic thrust I propose as definitive to the substance of this purgatorial passage therefore absolves the so-called 'precolonial' mythic into the emerging parameters of philosophical postcoloniality.

The question therefore persists in a different epistemic gestation: in what particular ways do we, in fact, inherit the past – not just time immemorial as the fragmented relics of this past that moves from the *mythic* over the *heroic* to the *historical* (as I have read them successively in my recent book on the *Shahnameh*)[14] – but also as it complicates our immediate colonial inheritance? In his *Specters of Marx*, Derrida dwells on what precisely such an 'inheritance' of the Marxist tradition of critical thinking might be – where the inheritance becomes something proactive, forward-looking and regenerative. Samir Haddad in his seminal text *Derrida and the Inheritance of Democracy* (2013) and before that in his insightful essay on 'Arendt, Derrida and Inheritance of Forgiveness' (2007) draws attention to the idea of an 'inheritance' of the past as an aporetic prelude to the opening horizons of a future.[15] The issue of 'inheritance', as outlined by Derrida and Haddad, obviously implicates the postcolonial thinker in that contested inheritance of colonialism itself as we seek to dismantle it. The archival evidence with which I work is the *locus classicus* of that contested inheritance, both a byproduct and an antidote to that inheritance, a pharmakon (as in Derrida's reading of Plato's *Phaedrus*) at once deadly and yet miraculous in its restorative powers. My way of thinking towards that end is to dwell confidently in the archival material with which I work – mostly from literary, visual and performing arts outside the archival comfort zones of European thinkers. This archive is far more solid than speculative in how such a spectrum of 'inheritance' acts itself out from the vantage points of the aesthetic intuition of transcendence – turning the lemon of colonialism into the lemonade of postcoloniality. More specifically, I work through the metonymic power of art and not the aporetic foregrounding of texts. Such aesthetic evidence in any body of art and the artworld they implicate are completely lost to Derrida and his articulation of the aporias of futurity. My way of thinking will have to account for those massive bodies of artistic evidence – because I think (and given my postcolonial location I must think) from the ground up, and at the radical epistemic moment where I dwell, much of this evidence has been read (mostly with an anodyne prose of film and art criticism) with a grain of positivistic Orientalism and thus with the force of an alienating exotica that has robbed them of their philosophical resonances. My book seeks to restore a paradoxical philosophical twist to that inheritance.

Paramount in this worldly rendition of the contemporary is the temporal instantiation linking the mythic to the heroic to the historical. In my *Shahnameh: The Persian Epic as World Literature* (2019), I have detailed this temporal instantiation extending from the distant *mythic* over the emerging *heroic* to the evident *historical*, both internal to the narrative logic of the Persian epic and also emblematic of an Iranian historical consciousness. But I have not left that trajectory just in temporal periodisation and framed it as a simultaneous instance in which all the registers are concurrently present and dialogical – from (1) *the world* in which the epic is created, over (2) *the world* the epic creates, to (3) *the world* in which the epic is read. This epistemic triangulation puts an entirely worldly disposition to the three 'intentions' that Umberto Eco has articulated in the dialectics of his hermeneutics: (1) the intention of the author, (2) the intention of the text, and (3) the intentions of the reader. The moment of myth in this reading does not remain stationary in time immemorial. It travels towards and through the heroic and enters deeply into the historical, and this mobility is, of course, a two-way street in which the historical and the heroic also feed and loop back to the mythic. The circular time feeds and animates itself, and thus my metonymic reading of visual and performing arts at once invokes and alludes to the mythic moment that dwells in its own radical contemporaneity. In short, my turn to the myth of Mashya and Mashyana is not merely heuristic, but it is also epistemic in the immediate grasp of our otherwise radical contemporaneity. In the moment of that contemporaneity, I am not nostalgic for any ancient myth. I am critically recollecting an inheritance which my colonial existence has radically sought to eradicate to the de-subjected me. That myth is not the occasion of my re-subjection. The critical exercise of claiming it as integral to my critical thinking is.

This temporal simultaneity has crucial consequences for how to remember (inherit) this cycle of mythic-heroic-historical past/present, which is very much at the roots of the question of inheritance. Can we extract ourselves from our colonial inheritance, or are we condemned and privileged to live through it, or could we by way of overcoming and reclaiming that inheritance turn it against itself? There is no pure or pious space for the postcolonial, except through the colonial. But the colonial is not the entirety of our memorial and immemorial inheritance – nor should it be fetishised out of historical proportions. Much of the inheritance of Fanon and Said – as indeed their own thoughts – are caught up in that trap. One is a dispossessed Palestinian and the other a misplaced Caribbean, and as such they had no choice but to forge ahead against their 'West'.[16] This is not the case about critical minds deeply rooted and fully conscious of the civilisational (literary and philosophical, in particular) traditions that this 'West' could not possibly even fathom, let alone eradicate. Said and Fanon and the whole postcolonial movement they generated altogether gave too much power to this 'West'. 'The West' was a powerful illusion, backed by the mighty power of colonialism it promoted – but still an illusion nevertheless that could not entirely rewrite global history. Neither the inheritance we have received from Fanon and Said, nor the inheritance of the 'Western colonialism' they boldly dismantled could possibly rewrite the factual, cultural, literary, philosophical inheritance of far richer and far more potent worlds that we continue to inherit from Asia, Africa and Latin America, which have survived their savageries. I write from the depths of Iran, as Mudimbe did from the depths of Africa, Dussel and Mignolo from Latin America, Guha from India, Karatani from Japan. We are no longer beholden to the illusion of 'the West'. Said and Fanon were, precisely in their bold defiance of this very 'West'. No assumption of inheritance outside that defiance can pave the way towards a democratic future. The idea of 'democracy to come' must by definition dwell on the interface between these two colonial and memorial legacies. As a text and a context, the structure of colonialism is itself aporetic – for it has enabled a postcolonial thinker to discover and dismantle its irresoluble contradictions.[17]

My theorisation of the purgatorial function of the aesthetic as an intuition of transcendence through its metonymic trajectories banks on that impossibility and turns it against itself. Here we may turn to the work of those who are not sharing such a solid jurisprudence of 'inheritance'. A good counter-example to Derrida would be the exquisite text of Laura U. Marks, *Hanan al-Cinema: Affections for the Moving Image* (2015), which is a bravura performance in teasing out the philosophical disposition of film and other visual arts in the Arab world – entirely outside the European inheritance, colonial or hegemonic.[18] Marks effectively de-inherits the Derridean inheritance. Here, Marks commands an immense archive of works and watches and reads them counter-intuitively. She comes at these texts 'from the left field', as it were, unexpectedly, with a fresh and joyous take that is entirely outside the purview of the established (inherited) scholarship. There is a Dionysian (Nietzschean) quality to her penchant for the sensual. Equally relevant is her other book, *The Skin of the Film: Intercultural Cinema, Embodiment, and the Senses* (2000), where we discover her uncanny insights into the invisible, the inaudible and the transmutant. This whole book, chapter after chapter, is on memory – especially when a filmmaker leaves her homeland and finds a place somewhere in between her senses. As evident in Laura Marks' work, the issue of 'inheritance' that Derrida raises is indeed crucial but not definitive or inhibitive of an entirely different sense of contemporaneity – where nomadic bordercrossings become the liberating move against the aporias of self-contradictions. There is an aporia at work here, to be sure, of the itinerant theorist philosopher making her familiarities foreign, by making the foreign she has inherited profoundly familiar – in which process the claim of inheritance has indeed become a transformative performance.

If we place Laura Marks next to Derrida and then bracket them both with the bold and brilliant work of Susan Buck-Morss (a Frankfurt School philosopher) – say, her *Hegel, Haiti, and Universal History* (2009) or, before that, her *Thinking Past Terror: Islamism and Critical Theory on the Left* (2003) – we would be directed towards de-fetishising the territorial claims of that Derridean 'inheritance'.[19] In her *Touch: Sensuous Theory and Multisensory Media* (2002), Laura Marks has already mapped out the space of physical sensuality as the site of cinematic discovery. This is a deeply erotic and embodied encounter with the visual. Many of the films she examines are not part of any particular canon – she has discovered them on her own and with and through them reads them in an unsettling way. Perhaps the most compelling aspect of her work is when she turns to Walter Benjamin's take on translation between languages to speculate on the translation between visual arts and critical prose. A similar Benjaminian de-similitude might be thought between Derrida or Levinas and their postcolonial interlocuters. A similar gesture is evident in Laura Marks' other book, *Enfoldment and Infinity: An Islamic Genealogy of New Media Art* (2010), where she comes at the history of Islamic art from an entirely unexpected angle – linking classical Islamic thought to the aesthetics of the new media. Laura Marks did not 'inherit' experimental film and video of the Arab world, or the Islamic genealogy of the new media; she earned them by the most potent theorisation she offered them in any language anywhere.

Whence therefore the inheritance, and where to find, inherit, or transform it? In what I have offered in this book, the mythic is already inherited in both the heroic and the historical. This is simultaneous, not consecutive – that has been my key proposition, from my book on the *Shahnameh* to this work. This is not Judeo-Christian Biblical, this is Indo-Persian epic. In the Judeo-Persian legacy, the Hebrew Bible and the Persian epic had come together, as in Classical Antiquity of the Greco-Roman legacies Xenophon and Aeschylus had already inherited their *Persians* and their *Cyropaedia*. My take on the question of inheritance of the colonial past would therefore pivot towards the active and rooted de-fetishisation of the condition of 'Western' coloniality, cutting it to its historical size and stripping it of the undue metaphysical and meta-narrative power Fanon, Said *et al.* had invested in it – as I began to prepare the groundwork for it in my *Europe and Its Shadows: Coloniality after Empire* (2019) – and thus dismantling the 'inheritance' it has helped to form and fashion. My work is unlike Derrida's or Laura Marks' or even Susan Buck-Morss' – but it presumes them as solid platforms to posit the position of the metonymic power of art flowering to sublate the archetypal myths we have inherited and a postcolonial philosophy of the subject geared towards the blind spots of the unknowing subject becoming fully and historically aware of itself, thus becoming historically agential, not despite but through the condition of European colonial modernity. These are all by way of safeguarding the prose of this mode of thinking from being assimilated backwards into the European philosophical inheritance, for better or for worse, which as a postcolonial thinker I embrace playfully, not blindfolded. The root of my theoretical prose is inspired by the Latin American philosophy of liberation, while fully aware of the European self-universalisation it takes to task, but it does not take it too seriously because of the agential power my rootedness as an Iranian Muslim thinker has enabled.

The unknowing subject towards which I (thus located) have worked in this book is the undoing of the masculinist, sovereign European knowing subject, not from within the Heideggerian *Dasein* (where no non-European has entry), but decidedly from the postcolonial without. The postcolonial unknowing subject, as I have read and written it here, de-frames and re-frames the knowable colonised world. From Marx and Freud to Heidegger, Lacan and Foucault, the European sovereign subject has been systematically dismantled, its totalising sovereignty made suspect, and yet the masculinist shadow of its sovereignty kept looming supreme in the colonised world. By opposing the physical and epistemic violence of European colonialism, from Fanon to Said an entire generation of postcolonial thinkers became the paradoxical extensions of that European sovereign subject, corroborating its political power, sustaining its moral imagination and enabling its agential audacity to conquer (*ego conquiro*) and to know (*ego cogito*). The prospect and proposition of the postcolonial unknowing subject located within a hermeneutic of misunderstanding begins on the premise of dismantling that European sovereign subject, by undoing its masculinist gendering of its global conquest, discrediting its white supremacy forestructure, before proceeding to articulate the de-racialised gender-fluidity of the unknowing subject. The unknowing subject thus restores to the world its renewed strangeness, de-familiarises its colonially familiarised realities. Through what the Russian formalist Viktor Shklovsky called

'*Ostranenie*' and what based on his theorising of Chinese theatre Bertolt Brecht called *Verfremdungseffekt*, this renewed de-familiarisation of the knowable world unveils and reveals it to the liberated, decolonised, unknowing subject. My thorough citation of this unknowing subject on the site of Iranian visual and performing arts is an iteration that could very well be performed on any number of other world cultures, from Egypt to India to China to Latin America. On these sites we are no longer engaged with any 'indigenous' alterity just to question the universality of Europe. We are long past that particular anxiety. We are instead positing a universal citation systematically violated and concealed under the colonial gaze of that presumed but flawed universality. The theorisation of this unknowing subject on any non-European site should not be assimilated backwards, either to a gestation of European sovereign subject or an act of indigenous nativism. We are to be the forerunners of a future philosophy – even beyond Nietzsche's imagination – predicated on the robust and healthy disposition of a de-racialised, de-gendered and always unknowing subject. Here we happily borrow as we wish, from the Freudian *uncanny* to Schklovsky's *Ostranenie*, to help us point towards a creative confiscation of the inheritance of coloniality to read the colonially ravaged world we have inherited against itself.

I have therefore sought to plunge my readers deep into the visual and performing arts of a vast and variegated postcolonial culture, marking the metonymic passageways between repressed but unforgotten mythologies of origin and the prospects of a postcolonial philosophy of the unknowing subject. The condition of coloniality that had de-subjected the postcolonial person hereby reverses itself and, through a version of what Vattimo calls *il pensiero debole* (Weak Thought), the unknowing and de-gendered subject has already arrived at the threshold of decoloniality. If we consider Kant's *Critique of Pure Reason* as the constitution of the (European) knowing subject, his *Critique of Practical Reason* as the constitution of the knowable (colonised) world and his *Critique of Judgment* as the interface between the two, then the system is full and foreclosed to the non-European colonised subject. Against the totality of that self-referential and impenetrable system, the liberation philosophy of the postcolonial subject must necessarily dwell on the fact of discovering the knowable world by an unknowing subject. My book is a tribute towards that aspiration – the substance of it promised in these two simple lines by Forough Farrokhzad:

> And thus it is
> That someone dies,
> And someone remains:
> For no pearl-diver will ever find a pearl
> In a pathetic brook headed towards a swamp![20]

Notes

Introduction

1. Abbas Kiarostami, 'My Best Shot', *The Guardian*, 29 July 2009, available online at: https://www.theguardian.com/artanddesign/2009/jul/29/photography-abbas-kiarostami-best-shot.
2. See Judith Butler, *Gender Trouble: Feminism and the Subversion of Identity* (London: Routledge, 1990).
3. For a pioneering essay on how Kiarostami breaks the Fourth Wall, see Roxana Hadadi, '"Do We Film or Not?" Abbas Kiarostami's Through the Olive Trees and Smashing the Fourth Wall', *Bright Wall/Dark Room*, 69 (1994), available online at: https://www.brightwalldarkroom.com/2019/03/18/through-the-olive-trees-1994/.
4. For more on *Hurqalya* and the philosophical tradition it represents, see Henry Corbin, *Avicenna and Visionary Recital* (New York: Pantheon Books, 1960), p. 260, where he says it is in *Hurqalya* 'that our visionary recitals take place – that is, in the world of the celestial Angels-Souls who preserve the archetypes of prophetic visions and mystical visions'.
5. For further reflections on Shirin Neshat's earliest art, before her later (more problematic) work, see my essay, 'Bordercrossings: Shirin Neshat's Body of Evidence', in Hamid Kashmirshekan (ed.), *Contemporary Art, World Cinema, and Visual Culture: Essays by Hamid Dabashi* (London: Anthem: 2019), pp. 145–66.
6. Forough Farrokhzad, '*Tavallodi Digar*/Another Birth', in *Tavallodi Digar/Another Birth* (Tehran: Morvarid, 1962), pp. 156. My translation.
7. For more on the idea of '*Ittihad-e Aqil wa Ma'qul*/Unification of the Intellectual and the Intellection' and its philosophical origins, see Zahra Mostafavi, 'Moqayeseh Negaresh-e Mulla Sadra va Ibn Sina dar Mas'aleh-ye Ittihad-e Aqil wa Ma'qul/Comparison of the Perspectives of Mulla Sadra and Avicenna on Unification of the Intellectual and the Intellection', *Kherad-nameh Sadra*, 36 (Summer 1383/2004), pp. 27–37.
8. See Viktor Shklovsky, 'Art, as Device', translated and introduced by Alexandra Berlina, *Poetics Today*, 36:3 (September 2015), available online at: https://warwick.ac.uk/fac/arts/english/currentstudents/undergraduate/modules/fulllist/first/en122/lecturelist2017-18/art_as_device_2015.pdf.
9. Mohammad Monavvar al-Mihani, *Asrar al-Tawhid fi Maqamat al-Sheikh Abi Said*, edited by Mohammad Reza Shafi'i Kadkani (Tehran: Agah Publishers, 1987), vol. I, p. 228.
10. I have addressed the centrality of body in our reading of our contemporary culture in my *Corpus Anarchicum: Political Protest, Suicidal Violence, and the Making of the Posthuman Body* (New York: Palgrave, 2012).
11. For a collection of essays on the dramaturgical aspects of *Ta'ziyeh*, see Peter Chelkowski (ed.), *Eternal Performance: Ta'ziyeh and Other Shiite Rituals* (London: Seagull Books, 2010).

12. Farrokhzad, '*Fath-e Bagh*/Conquest of the Garden', in *Tavallodi Digar/Another Birth*, p. 116. My translation.
13. Farrokhzad, '*Asheghaneh*/Lovingly', in *Tavallodi Digar/Another Birth*, p. 46. My translation.
14. For a close reading of Rakhshan Bani-Etemad's erotic camerawork, see my chapter on her cinema in my *Close Up: Iranian Cinema: Past Present Future* (London: Verso, 2001), Chapter Six (pp. 213–43).
15. Ahmad Shamlou, '*Bagh-e Ayeneh*/Garden of Mirror' (1339/1960), in *Collected Poems* (Giessen: Bamdad Verlag, 1988), vol. 1, p. 508.
16. Erving Goffman, *The Presentation of Self in Everyday Life* (Edinburgh: University of Edinburgh Social Sciences Research Centre, 1956), Preface [n. p.].
17. Goffman, *The Presentation of Self in Everyday Life*, p. 2.
18. See Jena A. Zelezny, 'Judith Butler: Performativity and Dramaturgy', *Performance Philosophy* (2010), available online at: http://performancephilosophy.ning.com/profiles/blogs/judith-butler-performativity-and-dramaturgy.
19. Erving Goffman, *Frame Analysis: An Essay on the Organization of Experience* (Boston: Northeastern University Press, 1974), p. 21.
20. Goffman, *Frame Analysis*, p. 138.
21. Ibid. p. 139.
22. See Sunera Thobani, 'The Secularity of Empire, the Violence of Critique: Muslims, Race, and Sexuality in the Politics of Knowledge-Production', *Hypatia*, 32:3 (Summer 2017), pp. 715–30.
23. Thobani, 'The Secularity of Empire, the Violence of Critique', p. 729.
24. See Nelson Ernesto Coelho Jr and Luis Claudio Figueiredo, 'Patterns of Intersubjectivity in the Constitution of Subjectivity: Dimensions of Otherness', *Culture & Psychology*, 9:3 (September 2003), pp. 193–208, available online at: https://www.researchgate.net/publication/257340511_Patterns_of_Intersubjectivity_in_the_Constitution_of_Subjectivity_Dimensions_of_Otherness.
25. Coelho Jr and Figueiredo, 'Patterns of Intersubjectivity in the Constitution of Subjectivity', p. 12. Emphasis added.
26. I have addressed this issue in some detail in my book *Can Non-Europeans Think?* (London: Zed Books, 2015).
27. Martin Heidegger, 'Question Concerning Technology', in Martin Heidegger, *Question Concerning Technology and other Essays*, translated and with an Introduction by William Lovitt (New York: Harper, 1977), p. 12.
28. Heidegger, 'Question Concerning Technology', p. 19.
29. Giorgio Agamben, 'What is an Apparatus', in Giorgio Agamben, *'What Is an Apparatus?' and Other Essays*, translated by David Kishik and Stefan Fedatella (Palo Alto: Stanford University Press, 2009), p. 12.
30. See Henrik Gustafsson and Asbjorn Gronstad (eds), *Cinema and Agamben: Ethics, Biopolitics and the Moving Image* (London: Bloomsbury, 2014), p. 4.
31. Abbas Kiarostami, 'My Best Shot'.
32. Judith Butler, *Bodies That Matter: On the Discursive Limits of 'Sex'* (London and New York: Routledge, 1993), p. 95.
33. Maulana Jalal al-Din Rumi, *Masnavi*, edited by R. A. Nicholson (Tehran: Amir Kabir, 1363), vol. II, p. 277. With slightest variation from Nicholson's editorial choices.
34. See Hamid Dabashi, *Corpus Anarchicum: Political Protest, Suicidal Violence, and the Making of the Posthuman Body* (New York: Palgrave, 2012).

35. See Ehsan Yarshater, *She'r-e Farsi dar Ahd-e Shahrokh ya Aghaz-e Enhetaṭ dar She'r-e Farsi/Persian Poetry during the Reign of Shahrokh, or the Beginning of the Decline of Persian Poetry* (Tehran, 1955); Ehsan Yarshater, 'The Theme of Wine-Drinking and the Conquest of the Beloved in Early Persian Poetry', *Studia Islamica*, 13 (1960), pp. 43–53; and Sirus Shamisa, *Shahed Bazi dar Adabiyat Farsi/Pederasty in Persian Literature* (Tehran: Ferdows, 1381). For the most recent scholarship on the subject, see Fateme Montazeri, 'Who Says Only Men Have a Beard? Revisiting the Question of Gender Ambiguity in Persian Poetry', *Anthropology of the Middle East*, 16:2 (Winter 2021), p. 128–47.
36. For more on this theory, see Umberto Eco, *The Open Work*, translated by Anna Cancogni, introduction by David Robey (Cambridge: Harvard University Press, 1989).
37. There are two entries in *Encyclopedia Iranica* about Kayumars. One is under 'GAYŌMART' by Mansour Shaki, available online at: https://iranicaonline.org/articles/gayomart-; the other is under 'GAYŌMARD (ARTICLE 2)' by Carlo Cereti, available online at: https://iranicaonline.org/articles/gayomard. Both these entries and their references are the most reliable sources on the subject.
38. See 'GAYŌMART', in *Encyclopedia Iranica*.
39. Farrokhzad, '*Tavallodi Digar*/Another Birth', p. 156. My translation.

Chapter 1

1. Forough Farrokhzad, '*Ayeh-ha-y Zamini*/Earthly Verses', in *Tavallodi Digar/Another Birth* (Tehran: Morvarid, 1962), p. 89. My translation.
2. See Ali Akbar Akbari, *Lumpenism* (Tehran: Sepehr Publications, 1973). Although this study was conducted before the Islamic revolution of 1977–79, much of its observations and conclusions remain valid in the post-revolutionary period. All English translation I cite in this chapter are my own from the original Persian of this text.
3. See Mas'ud Zavvarzadeh, *Seeing Films Politically* (Albany: State University of New York Press, 1991), p. 1.
4. Zavvarzadeh, *Seeing Films Politically*, p. 1.
5. Akbari, *Lumpenism*, p. 9.
6. Karl Marx, *The Communist Manifesto*, in David McLellan (ed.), *Karl Marx: Selected Writings* (Oxford: Oxford University Press, 1977), p. 229.
7. Akbari, *Lumpenism*, p. 23.
8. Ibid. pp. 23–24.
9. For a pioneering essay on the practice of '*ayyari*', at the root of all these concepts, see Mohammad Ja'far Mahjoub, 'A'iyn-e Ayyari', *Sokhan*, 20:10 (1349/1970). See also Kazem Kazemini, *Naqsh-e Pahlavani va Nehzat-e Ayyari* (Tehran: Bank-e Melli Iran, 1343/1964).
10. For an essay on the manifestations of these themes in Persian popular romances, see William Hanaway Jr, 'Formal Elements in the Persian Popular Romances', in Javad Haidari (ed.), *Review of Nationalities: Iran* (Collegeville, MN: St. John University Press, 1971). For an excellent Persian source on the genre of '*futuwwat-namah*', see Mawlana Hossein Va'ezi Kashefi Sabzevari, *Futuwwat-Namah Soltani*, edited by Mohammad Ja'far Mahjoub (Tehran: Bonyad-e Farhang-e Iran, 1349/1970).
11. For the complete story of Samak Ayyar, see Faramarz ibn Khodadad ibn Abdullah al-Kateb al-Arjani, *Samak Ayyar*, edited and annotated by Parviz Natel Khanlari (Tehran: Entesharat Agah, 1362/1983), six volumes.
12. For the pre-Islamic origin of the idea and practice of '*Luti-gari*', see Mehrdad Bahar, *Barrasi-ye Farhangi-Ijtema'i Zurkhaneh-ha-ye Tehran* (Tehran: Shura-ye 'Ali-ye Farhang

va Honar, 2535/1355/1976). If the assumption that the origin of Iranian masculinity and masculine '*Luti-gari*' indeed goes back to Mithraism, then we have a whole new angle on their misogynistic traits, because as manifested among the Roman soldiers' conversion to Mithraism, the sect was violently anti-woman.

13. See Parviz Natel Khanlari, *Shahr-e Samak* (Tehran: Agah Publishers, 1364/1985), pp. 69–100.
14. See Khanlari, *Shahr-e Samak*, p. 74.
15. See Ibid. p. 74.
16. For examples from *Samak Ayyar*, see ibid. p. 74.
17. Quoted in ibid. p. 90.
18. See Gayatri Chakravorty Spivak, 'Imperialism and Sexual Difference', in Clayton Koelb and Virgil Lokke (eds), *The Current in Criticism: Essays on the Present and Future of Literary Theory* (West Lafayette: Purdue University Press, 1986), pp. 319–37.
19. Spivak, 'Imperialism and Sexual Difference', p. 319.
20. Ibid. p. 320.
21. Ibid. p. 320.
22. Ibid. p. 320.
23. Akbari, *Lumpenism*, p. 30. For a more comprehensive study of the political function of the *Jahels* (also known as *Lutis*), see Willem M. Floor, 'The Political Role of the Lutis', in Michael Bonine and Nikki Keddie (eds), *Modern Iran: The Dialectics of Change and Continuity* (New York: SUNY, 1981).
24. This relationship between the intellectuals and Iranian lumpenism is completely absent from Al-e Ahmad's two-volume examination of intellectuals in Iran. See Jalal Al-e Ahmad, *Dar Khedmat va Khiyanat-e Roshanfekran* (Tehran: Khwarazmi Publishers, 1357/1978), two volumes. To my knowledge, Akbari was the first to have noted and examined this link. For a full discussion of Al-e Ahmad's ideas, see my *The Last Muslim Intellectual: The Life and Legacy of Jalal Al-e Ahmad* (Edinburgh: Edinburgh University Press, 2021).
25. For a detailed study of Gramsci's idea of 'hegemony' and its relationship to those of Machiavelli, see the excellent work of Benedetto Fontana, *Hegemony and Power: On the Relation between Gramsci and Machiavelli* (Minneapolis: University of Minnesota Press, 1993).
26. See Antonio Gramsci, 'The Intellectuals', in *Selections from the Prison Notebook*, edited and translated by Quintin Hoare and Geoffrey Nowell Smith (New York: International Publishers, 1971), pp. 3–25.
27. See Gramsci, 'The Intellectuals', p. 7.
28. Ibid. p. 5.
29. Ibid. p. 6.
30. Ibid. p. 7.
31. See Edward W. Said, *Representation of the Intellectual* (New York: Pantheon Books, 1994), pp. 52–53.
32. See Hamid Dabashi, *Brown Skin White Masks* (London: Pluto, 2011).
33. Akbari, *Lumpenism*, p. 116.
34. Ibid. p. 119.
35. For a study of the origin of the Jahels' clothing mannerism, see Amir Ethbati, 'Az Kolah Makhmali ta Pashneh Tala'i', *Film*, 92 (Tir 1369/July 1990), pp. 25–29.
36. In his pioneering study of the genre of 'Jaheli' cinema, Hamid Naficy has distinguished between a 'Luti' as a positive character and a 'lat' as a negative one. See Hamid Naficy,

'Guneh-ye Film Jaheli dar Cinema-ye Iran', *Iran Nameh*, 10:3 (Summer 1992), pp. 537–52. (Naficy published the same essay three years later in a different journal, in *Goftegu* [Spring 1474/1995], pp. 135–50). Naficy's distinction is impressionistic, untenable and predicated on a nostalgic conception of something he calls 'authentic Iranian culture' (p. 537). This presumed 'authenticity' itself is predicated on a flawed (borderline racist) assumption, according to which the victory of Dash Akol over Kaka Rostam in both Sadeq Hedayat's and Mas'ud Kimia'i's *Dash Akol* is 'the victory of non-Iranian and alien elements over the authentic Iranian culture' (p. 537). To consider the presumed victory of foreigners over Iranians as the victory of 'Evil' over 'Good' and of 'Pollution' over 'Authenticity' (p. 538) is the xenophobic foregrounding of troubling politics. For a more balanced essay of Naficy on *Dash Akol*, see his 'Iranian Writers, the Iranian Cinema, and the Case of Dash Akol', *Iranian Studies*, 18:2–4 (Spring-Autumn 1985), pp. 231–51.

37. See Ali Akbar Dehkhoda, *Loghat-nameh*, c. v. 'Luti'. For a preliminary study of paedophilia among the Sufis, see Peter Lamborn Wilson, *Scandal: Essays in Islamic Heresy* (New York: Autonomedia, 1988), pp. 93–121.
38. One of the issues of the monthly journal *Film* was dedicated to the examination of 'Jaheli' films. See *Film* (Tir 1369/July 1990), pp. 15–36. Naficy's 1992 essay, considers the views expressed in these essays as unduly condemnatory and not 'deep and objective' (p. 539). Naficy equally dismisses Akbari's *Lumpenism* as having missed the point of Jaheli films that Naficy celebrates as expressive of 'authentic Iranian culture'.
39. See Ali Akbar Dehkhoda, *Loghat-nameh*, c. v. 'Jahel'.
40. For a critical examination of the image of women in Persian literature, see Farzaneh Milani, 'Ro'ya'i az Gozashteh ya Zan-e Ro'ya'i dar Athar-e Hedayat', *Iran Nameh*, 5:1 (Autumn 1365/1986), pp. 81–97. For an examination of the image of women in Iranian cinema, see Hamid Naficy, 'Zan va Mas'aleh-ye Zan dar Cinema-ye ba'd az Enqelab', *Nimeh-ye Digar*, 14 (Spring 1991), pp. 123–69. See also Behzad Eshqi, 'Tasvir-e Bazhguneh-ye Zan-e Zeshtkar dar Cinema-ye Lumpeni-ye Iran: Vasile-'i bara-ye Ertezaq-e Baj-Khor-ha va Vaseteh-ha', *Mahnameh-ye Cinema-'i-ye Film*, 92 (Tir 1369/July 1990), pp. 21–24.
41. Farrokhzad, '*Ayeh-ha-y Zamini*/Earthly Verses', p. 89. My translation.

Chapter 2

1. Forough Farrokhzad, '*'Porsesh*/Question', in *Tavallodi Digar/Another Birth*, p. 52. My translation.
2. See Nastaran Musavi et al. (eds), *Zan va Cinema/Women and Cinema* (Tehran: Roshangaran Publications, 1376/1997), p. 5. All translations are mine.
3. For more details, see Shahnaz Moradi Kuchi, *Zanan-e Sinema-gar-e Iran/Iranian Women Filmmakers* (Tehran: Noruz Honar, 1379/2000).
4. For more details, see Anonymous (ed.), *Aramaneh va sinema-ye Iran/Armenians and Iranian Cinema* (Tehran: Film Museum of Iran, 1383/2004). I am grateful to my friend and colleague, the distinguished Armenian filmmaker and theater director Arby Ovanessian, for both giving me a copy of this book and for his handwritten notes correcting some of the data gathered in this extraordinary volume.
5. For more on Bibi Khanom Astarabadi and her *Ma'ayeb al-Rejal*, see its critical edition by Afsaneh Najmabadi, *Bibi Khanum Astarabadi's Ma'ayeb al-Rejal: Vices of Men* (Chicago: Midland Press, 1992). For another critical edition, plus the text of *Ta'dib al-Niswan*, see Hasan Javadi et al. (eds), *Ta'dib al-Niswan va Ma'ayeb al-Rejal/Disciplining of Women and Vices of Men* (Bethesda: Jahan Books, 1992).

6. For more on Taj al-Saltaneh, see her memoir, *Crowning Anguish: Memoires of a Persian Princess* (Washington DC: Mages, 1996).
7. For more on Parvin E'tesami, see Heshmat Moayyad (ed.), *Once a Dewdrop Accosted a Rose: Essays on the Poetry of Parvin E'tesami* (Costa Mesa: Mazda Publishers, 1994), including my essay in this volume, 'Of Poetics, Politics and Ethics: The Legacy of Parvin E'tesami'.
8. For an excellent essay on the image of women in Iranian cinema, see Najmeh Khalili Mahani, 'Women of Iranian Popular Cinema: Projection of Progress', *Offscreen*, 10:7 (31 July 2006), available online at: http://www.offscreen.com/biblio/phile/essays/women_of_iran/.
9. For more on the revolutionary role of Tahereh Qorrat al-Ayn in the Babi movement, see Abbas Amanat's *Resurrection and Renewal: The Making of the Babi Movement in Iran, 1844–1850* (Ithaca: Cornell University Press, 1989), pp. 328–30. See also my *Shi'ism: A Religion of Protest* (Cambridge: Harvard University Press, 2012), pp. 159–206.
10. See Farzaneh Milani, *Veils and Words: The Emerging Voices of Iranian Women Writers* (Syracuse: Syracuse University Press, 1992).
11. Milani, *Veils and Words*, p. xiv.
12. Ibid. pp. xi–xii.
13. Ibid. p. 5.
14. This pioneering essay later became the first chapter in Chandra Talpade Mohanty, *Feminism without Borders: Decolonizing Theory, Practicing Solidarity* (Durham: Duke University Press, 2003), pp. 17–42.
15. In the singular work of Forough Farrokhzad, the visual and the verbal come together in her brief but entirely ingenious career in which she published four collected volumes of her poetry and directed a film pioneering in Iranian cinema, *The House is Black* (1963). For more details, see the chapter on her career in my *Master and Masterpieces of Iranian Cinema* (Washington DC: Mage Publishers, 2008), Chapter One.
16. For an account of Ghazaleh Alizadeh's life, work and death, see the narrative given by her friend Reza Qassemi, 'Khakestar Shodan-e Tireh-ye Kamyab/The Turning to the Ash of the Rare Progeny', *Noqteh*, 6 (Summer 1375/1996). For an electronic version of this essay, see http://www.rezaghassemi.org/maghaleh14.htm. I am grateful to the distinguished Iranian publisher and civil rights activist Shahla Lahiji for sharing with me her intimate knowledge of the circumstances surrounding Ghazaleh Alizadeh's death.
17. Gayatri Chakravarty Spivak, 'Can the Subaltern Speak?' in Cary Nelson and Lawrence Grossberg (eds), *Marxism and Interpretation of Culture* (Chicago: University of Illinois Press, 1988), p. 307.
18. For a short biographical note in English on Zahra Kia Khanlari and a sample of her fiction, see John Green and Farzin Yazdanfar (eds), *A Walnut Sapling on Masih's Grave and Other Stories by Iranian Women*, Foreword by Evelyn Accad (Portsmouth: Heinemann, 1993), pp. 97–112.
19. For short biographical sketches and samples of Simin Daneshvar's short stories, see Green and Yazdanfar, *A Walnut Sapling on Masih's Grave*, pp. 62–82; Soraya Sullivan (tr.), *Stories by Iranian Women since the Revolution*, Introduction by Farzaneh Milani (Austin: Center for Middle Eastern Studies, The University of Texas at Austin, 1991), pp. 16–35; Simin Daneshvar, *Sutra and Other Stories*, translated from the Persian by Hasan Javadi and Amin Neshati (Washington DC: Mage Publishers, 1994); Simin Daneshvar, *Daneshvar's Playhouse: A Collection of Stories* (Washington DC: Mage Publishers, 1989); and Heshmat Moayyad, *Stories from Iran: A Chicago Anthology 1921–1991* (Washington DC:

Mage Publishers, 1991), pp. 111–28. See also Simin Daneshvar, *Savushun: A Novel about Modern Iran*, translated from the Persian by M. R. Ghanoonparvar, Introduction by Brian Spooner (Washington DC: Mage Publishers, 1990). There is another English translation of *Savushun* by Roxanne Zand, as *A Persian Requiem* (New York: George Braziller, 1992). For a discussion of Simin Daneshvar's fiction, see Milani, *Veils and Words*, pp. 181–99. For a more detailed study of her relationship with her husband, see my *The Last Muslim Intellectual: The Life and Legacy of Jalal Al-e Ahmad* (Edinburgh: Edinburgh University Press, 2020), Chapter Three. For more on Fatemeh Sayyah, see my chapter on her in my *Reversing the Colonial Gaze: Persian Travelers Abroad* (Cambridge: Cambridge University Press, 2019), Chapter 12.

20. For more on Goli Taraghi and samples of her stories in English, see Sullivan, *Stories by Iranian Women*, pp. 58–70; Green and Yazdanfar, *A Walnut Sapling on Masih's Grave*, pp. 157–72; Franklin Lewis and Farzin Yazdanfar (comp. and tr.), *In a Voice of Their Own: A Collection of Stories by Iranian Women Written Since the Revolution of 1979* (Costa Mesa: Mazda Publishers, 1996), pp. 3–22; and Moayyad, *Stories from Iran*, pp. 363–80. See also Goli Taraghi, *A Mansion in the Sky and Other Short Stories*, translated by Faridoun Farrokh (Austin: University of Texas Press, 2003). For a translation of her 'Hibernation', see Goli Taraghi, *Winter Sleep*, translated from the Persian by Francine T. Mahak (Costa Mesa: Mazda Publishers, 1994).
21. For more on Shahrnoush Parsipour and a sample of her writing, see Shahrnoush Parsipour, *Women Without Men*, translated by Kamran Talattof and Jocelyn Sharlet (Syracuse: Syracuse University Press, 1998); Moayyad, *Stories from Iran*, pp. 437–78; and Lewis and Yazdanfar, *In a Voice of Their Own*, pp. 42–50. The prominent Iranian artist Shirin Neshat has also made a film version of Shahrnoush Parsipour's *Women without Men*.
22. For more on Mahshid Amirshahi and a sample of her work, see Moayyad, *Stories from Iran*, pp. 381–402.
23. For more on Moniru Ravanipour, see Moayyad, *Stories from Iran*, pp. 479–90; and Lewis and Yazdanfar, *In a Voice of Their Own*, pp. 51–68. See also Moniru Ravanipour, *Kanizu*, translated by Hirad Dinevari et al., edited with an Introduction by M. R. Ghanoonparvar (Costa Mesa: Mazda Publishers, 2004); and Moniru Ravanipour, *Satan's Stone*, translated by M. R. Ghanoonparvar (Austin: Texas University Press, 1996).
24. Ghazaleh Alizadeh, *Khaneh-ye Idrissi-ha* (Tehran: Tirazheh, 1991–92), vol. 1, p. 7. My translation.
25. For a critical study of intellectual 'nativism' in Iran, see Mehrzad Boroujerdi's *Iranian Intellectuals and the West: The Tormented Triumph of Nativism* (Syracuse: Syracuse University Press, 1996). This is an important study, but I believe, in view of the globalised eradication of local and regional cultures, the entire notion of 'nativism' and the derogatory attitude towards it need to be critically re-examined.
26. See Edward Said, *Humanism and Democratic Criticism* (New York: Columbia University Press, 2004), p. 47.
27. Said, *Humanism and Democratic Criticism*, p. 35.
28. Ibid. p. 33.
29. Ibid. pp. 32–34.
30. See Edward Said's 1995 Afterword in his *Orientalism* (London: Penguin Books, 1995), p. 340.
31. For more details, see Hamid Dabashi, *The World of Persian Literary Humanism* (Cambridge: Harvard University Press, 2012), Chapter Six.

32. See Gauri Viswanathan, *Masks of Conquest: Literary Study and British Rule in India* (New York: Columbia University Press, 1989), p. 10.
33. Said, *Humanism and Democratic Criticism*, p. 39.
34. Ibid. p. 44.
35. Ibid. p. 53.
36. For more details on my reading of the cover of *Reading Lolita in Tehran* and the picture from which it was cropped, see my essay 'Native Informers and the Making of the American Empire', *Al Ahram Weekly* (1 June 2006).
37. See Ralf Dahrendorf, *Society and Democracy in Germany* (New York: W. W. Norton and Company, 1967), p. 385.
38. See William Kornhauser, *The Politics of Mass Society* (New Brunswick: Transactions Publishers, 1959/2008), p. 32.
39. Alexis de Tocqueville, *Democracy in America* (New York: Vintage Books, 1945), vol. 2, p. 340. Throughout *Democracy in America*, Tocqueville makes many other similar observations: 'Despotism, then, which is at all times dangerous, is more particularly to be feared in democratic ages' (p. 109). Tocqueville's insights into the functioning of democracy in the United States were of course the prelude to his systematic theorisation of French colonialism in Algeria and elsewhere. For a quick critique of his positions on Algeria, see Hassane Sohbi, 'Tocqueville and Colonialism in Algeria', *Review of Middle East Studies*, 45:1 (Summer 2011), pp. 50–52. For a longer and more sympathetic reading of Tocqueville's advocacy of French imperial project, see Ewa Atanassaw, 'Colonization and Democracy: Tocqueville Reconsidered', *American Political Science Review*, 111:1 (February 2017), pp. 83–96. For a more balanced review, see John W. P. Veugelers, 'Tocqueville on the Conquest and Colonization of Algeria', *Journal of Classical Sociology*, 10:4 (November 2010), pp. 339–55.
40. Tocqueville, *Democracy in America*, p. 110.
41. See Ferdinand Tönnies, *Community and Civil Society*, edited by Jose Harris (Cambridge: Cambridge University Press, 2001).
42. Kornhauser, *The Politics of Mass Society*, p. 32.
43. See Hannah Arendt, *The Origin of Totalitarianism* (New York: Harcourt, Brace, 1951), p. 317.
44. It is not just expatriate scholars such as Farzaneh Milani who have this tendency towards metaphysical generalisation of veiling in Iran and/or Islam (Milani, *Veils and Words*, p. 5). Similarly generic and trans-historic attribution of veiling as quintessential to Iranian culture are to be found also in Hamid Naficy's 'Veiled Voice and Vision in Iranian Cinema: The Evolution of Rakhshan Bani-Etemad's Films', *Social Research*, 67:2 (Summer 2000), as well as in his 'Veiled Voice and Vision in Iranian Cinema: The Evolution of Rakhshan Bani-Etemad's Films', in Murray Pomerance (ed.), *Ladies and Gentlemen, Boys and Girls: Gender in Film at the End of the 20th Century* (New York: State University of New York Press, 2001), pp. 36–53. Both Milani and Naficy take their cues and borrow these ideas from a much earlier ethnographic work of William O. Beeman, *Language, Status and Power in Iran* (Indianapolis: Indiana University Press, 1986), who also believes in this essential conceitedness of Iranian society.
45. Farrokhzad, '*Porsesh*/Question,' p. 52. My translation.

Chapter 3

1. Forough Farrokhzad, '*Divar-ha ye Marz*/Border Walls', in *Tavallodi Digar/Another Birth*, p. 54. My translation.
2. See Zavvarzadeh, *Seeing Films Politically*, p. 1.
3. See Partov Nuri Ala, *Do Naqd/Two Critiques* (Tehran: Agah Publishers, 1985), pp. 47–68.
4. Nuri Ala, *Do Naqd/Two Critiques*, p. 48. All the English citations from the Persian original of this and all other sources are mine.
5. Ibid. p. 49.
6. Ibid.
7. Ibid. p. 51.
8. Ibid. p. 53.
9. Ibid.
10. For a study of the eroticisation of the 'European woman', see Mohammad Tavakoli-Targhi, 'Imagining Western Woman: Occidentalism and Euro-Eroticism', *Radical America*, 24:3 (1990), pp. 73–87. This is an excellent documentation of the active eroticisation of the 'European Women', despite the fact that Tavakoli-Targhi's basic theoretical assumptions that there was parity between the Orientals and the Occidentals, and that 'the field of vision and meaning were contested' (p. 73), or even more important, that 'in the interplay of Eastern and Western looks, there was no steady position of spectatorship, no objective observer, and no mastery of knowledge' (p. 73), are all categorically flawed. What sustained the colonisers' gaze was power. What animated the colonials' look back was a severe case of *ressentiment*. Tavakoli-Targhi remains completely oblivious to this crucial distinction and as a result assumes a parity of gazes which is entirely ahistorical and inaccurate.
11. I have discussed in theoretical detail the metaphysics of this corporeal body in my essay 'Bordercrossings: Shirin Neshat's Body of Evidence', in Hamid Keshmirshekan (ed.), *Contemporary Art, World Cinema, and Visual Culture: Essays by Hamid Dabashi* (London: Anthem Press, 2019), Chapter Five.
12. See the towering Shi'i jurist and theologian Sheikh al-Ta'ifah Muhammad ibn al-Hasan al-Tusi, *Tamhid al-'Usul*, translated, with an Introduction and Annotations by 'Abd al-Muhsin Mishkat al-Dini (Tehran: Anjuman-i Hikmat va Falsafah-yi Islami Iran, 1358/1979), pp. 14–18.
13. I have addressed this corporeality of the body and its posthuman disposition in my *Corpus Anarchicum: Political Protest, Suicidal Violence, and the Making of the Posthuman Body* (New York: Palgrave Macmillan, 2012).
14. See Nuri Ala, *Do Naqd/Two Critiques*, p. 52.
15. For the significance of the concept of *ressentiment* in Nietzsche's work and his preference of the French over its German equivalent, see Walter Kaufmann's Introduction to Nietzsche's *Genealogy of Morals*, in Walter Kaufmann (ed.), *Basic Writings of Nietzsche* (New York: The Modern Library, 1992), pp. 441–46. For Scheler's take on Nietzsche's idea of *Ressentiment*, see Max Scheler, *Das Ressentiment im Aufbau der Moralen* (Frankfurt am Main: Vittorio Klostermann, 1978).
16. See Kaufmann (ed.), *Basic Writings of Nietzsche*, p. 472.
17. For a deeply flawed reading of this anxiety, see the analysis of Mehrzad Boroujerdi in *Iranian Intellectuals and the West: The Tormented Triumph of Nativism* (New York: Syracuse University Press, 1996). Boroujerdi's analysis places the rise of modern Iranian intellectuals in their response to what he calls 'the West', at the expense of a more

historically necessary breakdown of that myth of the 'West' into its economic and cultural constituents. He takes 'the West' at face value. For my most recent dismantling of the myth of 'the West' and the 'Islam' it had occasioned, see Hamid Dabashi, *The End of Two Illusions: Islam after the West* (Oakland: The University of California Press, 2022).

18. See Ernst H. Kantorowicz, *The King's Two Bodies: A Study in Mediaeval Political Theology*, with a New Preface by William Chester Jordan (Princeton: Princeton University Press, 1981). See in particular Kantorowicz's argument on '*dignitas non moritur*', pp. 383–450.
19. For an account of the Persian theory of Kingship, see al-Ghazali, *Counsel for Kings*, translated by F. R. C. Bagley (London: Oxford University Press, 1964). See particularly Chapter I in Part II, 'On Qualities Required in Kings', pp. 47–53.
20. Hamid Naficy characterises Dash Akol as representing an 'authentic Iranian'. See Hamid Naficy, 'Guneh-ye "Film Jaheli" dar Cinema-ye Iran: Barresi-ye Sakhtari-ye Film Dash Akol', *Iran Nameh*, 10:3 (Summer 1992), pp. 537–52. In Naficy's reading, Dash Akol represents 'a symbol of ancient Iran, one of the old *Javanmards* and *Lutis* who with their inner purity, power of their arm, and their social dignity constituted the cement of their society' (p. 537). Kaka Rostam, Dash Akol's arch enemy, Naficy identifies as '*lat*' and '*rajjaleh*' – that is, as lumpen. Naficy even offers a rather xenophobic distinction between the two protagonists of the story: 'The victory of Kaka Rostam over Dash Akol is not only the victory of the Lats over the Lutis but the victory of non-Iranian and foreign elements over the authentic Iranian culture. Both Hedayat's story and Kimia'i's film are a eulogy mourning this transition from Good to Evil and from Authenticity to Pollution' (p. 537).
21. For the original version of Hedayat, see Sadeq Hedayat, 'Dash Akol', in *Seh Qatreh Khun/ Three Drops of Blood* (Tehran: Amir Kabir, 1341/1962), pp. 43–62. For an account of the 'true' story of Dash Akol, see Ebrahim Golestan, *Gofteh-ha/Statements* (London: Rozan, 1998), p. 140. Golestan was one of the first to write enthusiastically on behalf of Kimia'i's lumpenist cinema. He later changed his mind. See '*Seyr-e Soqut-e yek Emkan*/ The Declining Trajectory of a Possibility' in the same book, pp. 139–51.
22. See al-Tusi, *Tamhid al-'Usul*, pp. 19–25.
23. See Nuri Ala, *Do Naqd/Two Critiques*, pp. 57–58.
24. Ibid. p. 58.
25. See Sigmund Freud, *On Creativity and the Unconscious: Papers on the Psychology of Art, Literature, Love, Religion* (New York: Harper Colophon Books, 1958), p. 2.
26. See al-Tusi, *Tamhid al-'Usul*, pp. 26–30.
27. See ibid. p. 31.
28. See Freud, *On Creativity and the Unconscious*, pp. 187–205.
29. Ibid. p. 187.
30. Ibid. p. 187.
31. Ibid. p. 188.
32. See Nuri Ala, *Do Naqd/Two Critiques*, pp. 60–61.
33. See Mojtaba Minovi's Introduction to Muhammad ibn Ali Muhammad al-Zahiri al-Samarqandi, *Sandbad-nameh*, edited and annotated by Ahmad Atash (Tehran: Ketab-e Farzan, 1362/1983).
34. A modern classic in Persian on this issue is Reza Barahani's *Tarikh-e Mozakkar/Masculine History* (Tehran: Negah Publishers, 1351/1972).
35. al-Samarqandi, *Sandbad-nameh*, p. 25.
36. Ibid. p. 330.
37. See Nuri Ala, *Do Naqd/Two Critiques*, p. 65.

38. See Naficy, 'Guneh-ye "Film Jaheli"' dar Cinema-ye Iran' (1995), p. 146, where in a self-censored language he briefly discusses the theme of homosexuality in *Snake Fang*.
39. See Luce Irigaray, *Ce sexe qui n'en est pas un* (Paris: Minuit, 1977). For an English translation, see *This Sex Which is Not One*, translated by Catherine Porter with Carolyn Burke (New York: Cornell University Press, 1985).
40. See the article on 'JEH' in *Encyclopedia Iranica*, available online at: https://www.iranicaonline.org/articles/jeh.
41. Farrokhzad, '*Divar-ha ye Marz*/Border Walls', p. 54. My translation.

Chapter 4

1. Forough Farrokhzad, '*Tanha Sedast keh Mimanad*/Only the Sound will Last', in *Iman Biavarim beh Aghaz-e Fasl-e Sard/Let Us Believe in the Commencement of the Cold Season* (Tehran: Morvarid Publications, 1973), p. 93–94. My translation. Farrokhzad died in an automobile accident in 1967. This poem was published posthumously in 1973.
2. The earlier drafts of this chapter have appeared on previous occasions, most recently as 'An Artistic Perspective: Women of Bahram Beizai's Cinema', in Firoozeh Kashani-Sabet and Beth S. Wenger (eds), *Gender in Judaism and Islam: Common Lives, Uncommon Heritage* (New York: New York University Press, 2014), pp. 311–40. The original title of the essay was 'Mythmaker, Mythmaker, Make me a Myth: Women of Beizai's Cinema'. This is a revised and expanded version of that chapter.
3. See Shahla Lahiji, *Sima-ye Zan dar Athar-e Bahram Beiza'i: Filmsaz va Film-nameh-nevis/The Figure of Women in the Cinema of Bahram Beiza'i: Filmmaker and Scriptwriter* (Tehran: Roshangaran Publishers, 1993), p. 38. This is a pioneering and comprehensive study of the place of women in Beiza'i's cinema from the perspective of an activist who has championed the cause of women's rights in Iran under intolerable conditions.
4. For a short discussion of the various theories of myth, see Lauri Honko, 'The Problem of Defining Myth', in Alan Dundes (ed.), *Sacred Narrative: Readings in the Theory of Myth* (Berkeley: University of California Press, 1984), pp. 41–52.
5. Theodore W. Adorno, *Aesthetic Theory*, newly translated, edited, and with a Translator's Introduction by Robert Hullot-Kentor (Minneapolis: University of Minnesota Press, 1997), p. 5.
6. Adorno, *Aesthetic Theory*, p. 5.
7. Georges Bataille, *The Absence of Myth: Writings on Surrealism*, translated and with an Introduction by Michael Richardson (London: Verso, 1994), p. 48.
8. See Max Weber, 'Science as a Vocation', in H. H. Gerth and C. Wright Mills (transl. and eds), *From Max Weber: Essays in Sociology* (New York: Oxford University Press, 1946), p. 155.
9. See Åke Hultkrantz, 'An Ideological Dichotomy: Myth and Folk Beliefs Among the Shoshoni', in Dundes (ed.), *Sacred Narrative*, p. 165.
10. On the quantitatively reducible number of variations on a single myth see, for example, the astonishing discovery of Anna Birgitta Rooth, professor of Ethnology at the University of Uppsala. She found out about the North American creation myths that all of the 300 myths she had collected could squarely be divided into no more than eight archetypes. See Anna Birgitta Rooth, 'The Creation Myth of the North American Indians', in Dundes (ed.), *Sacred Narratives*, pp. 166–81.
11. Susan Taslimi's acting in this film is frightfully real, among the very few performances in recent memory that make me hesitant in my otherwise perfect celebration of Iranian

cinema's turn away from professional actors. Golab Adineh is another such visceral actor. Fatemeh Mo'tamad Aria, except for her fatal mistakes of entrusting herself to third-rate directors in recent years, is still among the few extraordinary professional actors who have weathered well the perfectly correct turn of Iranian cinema away from professional actors.

12. Lahiji, *Sima-ye Zan dar Athar-e Bahram Beiza'i*, p. 49. My translation from the original Persian.
13. See, for example, G. S. Kirk, 'On Defining Myths', in Dundes (ed.), *Sacred Narrative*, pp. 53–61, as an articulation of such choices.
14. See Roland Barthes, *Mythologies*, selected and translated from the French by Annette Lavers (New York: Hill and Wang, 1972), p. 28.
15. Barthes, *Mythologies*, p. 28.
16. In one way or another, most readers of Beiza'i fall into this trap. For good examples, see Lahiji, *Sima-ye Zan dar Athar-e Bahram Beiza'i*, pp. 48–60; Baqer Parham, *Negahi beh Film-ha-ye Bahram Beiza'i*', in Anonymous (ed.), *21 Sal: Az Amu Sibilu ta Mosaferan: Moruri bar Athar-e Bahram Beiza'i beh Bahaneh-ye Jashnvareh-ye Vinnale* (Vienna: Markaz-e Esha'eh-ye Iranshenasi, 1995), pp. 38–48; Zhaleh Amuzegar, 'Raz-ha-ye Ostureh dar "Mosaferan"', in Zaven Qukasian (ed.), *Dar-bareh-ye 'Mosaferan'* (Tehran: Roshangaran Publishers, 1371/1992), pp. 29–33. The unexamined binary opposition between myth and history is central to all these diverse readings of Beiza'i. In the absence of any critical attention to the place and function of the mythical in Beiza'i's cinema, Parham, for example, comes to the outlandish conclusion that *Bashu* is 'parenthetical' to Beiza'i's cinema! See Anonymous, *21 Sal*, p. 39. It is not. It is, in fact, typical, as I have detailed it in this chapter.
17. Bataille, *The Absence of Myth*, p. 48.
18. See Lahiji, *Sima-ye Zan dar Athar-e Bahram Beiza'i*, pp. 54–60. Lahiji has a similarly 'motherly' reading of *Perhaps Some Other Time*. See Lahiji, *Sima-ye Zan dar Athar-e Bahram Beiza'i*, p. 66. In both these cases, Lahiji's laudable social concerns about the fate of Iranian mothers dulls her critical reading of Beiza'i's cinema.
19. These are motif-index A 625 and motif-index A 625.1 in Stith Thompson's *Motif-Index of Folk Literature: A Classification of Narrative Elements in Folktales, Ballads, Myths, Fables, Mediaeval Romances, Exempla, Fabliaux, Jest-Books, and Local Legends* (Bloomington: Indiana University Press, 1955–58).
20. See Alan Dundes' editorial note in Dundes (ed.), *Sacred Narrative*, p. 182.
21. For the full version of Professor Numazawa, see K. Numazawa, *Die Weltanfänge in der Japanischen Mythologie* (Paris and Lucerne: Librairie de Recueil Sirey, 1946). For a short version of it, see Dundes (ed.), *Sacred Narrative*, pp. 182–92.
22. K. Numazawa, 'The Cultural-Historical Background of Myths on the Separation of Sky and Earth', in Dundes, *Sacred Narrative*, p. 191.
23. Ibid. p. 191.
24. Ibid. p. 192.
25. Ibid.
26. See Dundes (ed.), *Sacred Narrative*, p. 183.
27. Stith Thompson, *Motif-Index of Folk Literature*: Myth-type A 1255, A 1225.1, and A 1234.1.1.
28. Bataille, *The Absence of Myth*, p. 48.
29. Th. P. Van Baaren, 'The Flexibility of Myth', in Dundes (ed.), *Sacred Narrative*, p. 222.

30. The best collection of essays on Beiza'i's *The Travelers* is to be found in Qukasian, *Dar-bareh-ye 'Mosaferan'.*
31. Shaykh Ahmad Ahsa'i, 'Physiology of the Resurrection Body', in Henry Corbin, *Spiritual Body and Celestial Earth: From Mazdean Iran to Shi'ite Iran* (Princeton: Princeton University Press, 1977), p. 180. Except for minor modification, I use Corbin's translation of his extract from *Kitab Sharh al-Ziyara*. Corbin's book contains excellent excerpts from the works of Suhrawardi in the twelfth century to Sarkar Agha in the nineteenth, on the issue of 'body', which is of concern to me here.
32. Ahsa'i, 'Physiology of the Resurrection Body', p. 180.
33. Ibid. p. 181.
34. Ibid.
35. For the centrality of all these Aristotelian references in Islamic astronomy, see George Saliba, 'The Role of the Astrologer in Medieval Islamic Society', *Bulletin d'Études Orientales*, 44 (1992), pp. 45–67. For more detailed accounts, see George Saliba, *A History of Arabic Astronomy: Planetary Theories during the Golden Age of Islam* (New York: New York University Press, 1994.)
36. L. V. Vaglieri and G. Celantano, 'Trois Epitres d'Al-Kindi', *Annali, Instituto Orientale di Napoli*, 34 (N.S. 24) (1974), p. 537, as quoted in George Saliba, 'The Development of Astronomy in Medieval Islamic Society', in Saliba, *A History of Arabic Astronomy*, p. 55.
37. Ahsa'i, 'Physiology of the Resurrection Body', pp. 182–84.
38. Ibid. p. 183.
39. Ibid.
40. Ibid. p. 184.
41. Ibid. p. 185.
42. Farrokhzad, '*Tanha Sedast keh Mimanad*/Only the Sound will Last', pp. 93–94. My translation.

Chapter 5

1. Forough Farrokhzad, '*Aftab Mishavad*/The Sun Rises', in *Tavallodi Digar/Another Birth*, p. 12. My translation.
2. For a critical assessment of the Green Movement in its local, regional and global contexts, see my *Iran, the Green Movement and the USA: The Fox and the Paradox* (London: Zed, 2010).
3. See Max Weber, 'Politics as a Vocation', in H. Gerth and C. Wright Mills, *From Max Weber: Essays in Sociology*, p. 78.
4. Ervand Abrahamian's *Khomeinism: Essays on the Islamic Republic* (Berkeley: University of California Press, 1993) is an insightful collection of essays tracing the formation of an ideology of violence that continues to define the Iranian political culture.
5. See Georges Sorel, *Reflections on Violence*, translated by T. E. Hulme, Introduction by Edward A. Shils (London: Collier Books, 1950).
6. Kenneth Katzman, *The Warriors of Islam: Iran's Revolutionary Guard* (Boulder: Westview Press, 1993), goes a long way in demonstrating some of the salient features of the post-charismatic institutionalisation of violence.
7. Katzman, *The Warriors of Islam*, p. 1.
8. Ibid. p. 49.
9. I have addressed the specificities of Iranian realism in Hamid Dabashi, *Masters and Masterpieces of Iranian Cinema* (Washington DC: Mage Publishers, 2007).

10. See Fredric Jameson, *Signatures of the Visible* (New York: Routledge, 1990), p. 6.
11. Jameson, *Signatures of the Visible*, pp. 128–29.
12. See Julia Kristeva, 'Revolution in Poetic Language', in Kelly Oliver (ed.), *The Portable Kristeva* (New York: Columbia University Press, 1997), pp. 32–70.
13. Martin Heidegger, *Being and Time*, translated by Joan Stambaugh (Albany: State University of New York Press, 1996), p. 52.
14. Heidegger, *Being and Time*, p. 25.
15. Ibid. pp. 25–26.
16. Ibid. p. 26.
17. See Afdal al-Din Muhammad Maraqi Kashani, 'The Antecedence of "Thing" over "Existent" (*Pishi-ye 'Chiz' bar 'Hast'*)', in Mojtaba Minovi and Yahya Mahdavi (eds), *Musannafat* (Tehran: Khwarizmi Publishers, 1331/1952), pp. 647–52. The similarity of this twelfth-century Iranian philosopher's concern over the nature of 'thing' and its being different from 'existent' and of Heidegger's concerns boggles the mind. See Heidegger's 'The Thing', in *Poetry, Language, Thought*, translated by Albert Hofstadter (New York: Harper & Row Publishers, 1971), pp. 163–86.
18. Kashani, 'The Antecedence', p. 648. All the translations from the original Persian are mine.
19. Ibid. p. 649.
20. Ibid. p. 650.
21. Ibid. p. 651.
22. Susan Sontag, *Against Interpretation* (New York: Farrar, Straus, Giroux, 1961), pp. 4–5.
23. Sontag, *Against Interpretation*, p. 6.
24. Ibid. p. 6. Emphasis added.
25. Ibid. p. 7.
26. Martin Heidegger, *Being and Time*, translated by John Macquarrie and Edward Robinson (New York: Harper & Row, Publishers, 1962), p. 164.
27. Michael Zimmerman, *Heidegger's Confrontation with Modernity: Technology Politics, Art* (Bloomington: Indiana University Press, 1990), p. 22.
28. Gilles Deleuze and Félix Guattari, *Anti-Oedipus: Capitalism and Schizophrenia*, Preface by Michel Foucault (Minneapolis: University of Minnesota Press, 1983), p. 131.
29. Deleuze and Guattari, *Anti-Oedipus*, p. 131.
30. See H. Cixous and C. Clément, *The Newly Born Woman* (Manchester: Manchester University Press, 1986), p. 63.
31. A good exception is Mary Wollstonecraft's *A Vindication of the Rights of Women* (London: Penguin, 1982). Wollstonecraft's critique remains almost exclusively within the context of the European Enlightenment in which she wrote.
32. See Cixous and Clément, *The Newly Born Woman*, p. 87.
33. Farrokhzad, '*Aftab Mishavad*/The Sun Rises', p. 12. My translation.

Chapter 6

1. Nima Yushij, '*Khaneh-am Abri-ast*/My Home is a Cloud', in Sirus Tahbaz (ed.), *Collected Works of Nima Yushij* (Tehran: Nashr-e Nasher, 1364/1985), vol. 1, p. 620. My translation.
2. *Premiere*, March 1995, pp. 50–51.
3. *The New York Times*, 26 April 1996. Emphasis added.

4. For an account of Lacan's groundbreaking significance in Freudian psychoanalytic, see Stuart Schneiderman, *Jacques Lacan: The Death of an Intellectual Hero* (Cambridge: Harvard University Press, 1983).
5. For Lacan's discussion of the 'mirror' stage, see Jacques Lacan, *Écrits: A Selection*, translated by Alan Sheridan (New York: W. W. Norton & Company, 1977), pp. 1–7. For Gilles Deleuze's critical discussion of the Imaginary and his preference of the Crystal, see Gilles Deleuze, *Negotiations* (New York: Columbia University Press, 1995), pp. 62–67.
6. The earliest signs of Lacan's concern with the centrality of language in the formation of the subject and the distinction between the Imaginary and the Symbolic is already evident in his doctoral dissertation. See Jacques Lacan, *De la psychose paranoiaque dans ses rapports avec la personalité* (Paris: Édition du Seuil, 1975).
7. One of the best discussions of Lacan on the Oedipal is in Jacques Lacan, *Le Séminaire de Jacques Lacan*, texte établi par Jacques-Alain Miller (Paris: Édition du Seuil, 1991), pp. 99–166.
8. For an excellent translation of Al-e Ahmad's *Nun wa al-Qalam*, see Jalal Al-e Ahmad, *By the Pen*, translated by Mohammad Reza Ghanoonparvar (Austin: Texas University Press, 1988).
9. For an account of the centrality of language in Lacan's theory of subject-formation and a counter-argument informed by Noam Chomsky's linguistics, see Joseph H. Smith, *Arguing with Lacan: Ego Psychology and Language* (New Haven: Yale University Press, 1991).
10. The 'name' of the father is constitutionally a 'literal' move, as opposed to an 'imaginary' one. As a result, literary cultures have an elective affinity with the Oedipal. For an excellent reading of Lacan's preoccupation with the 'literal', as opposed to the 'imaginary' in the formation of subject, see the excellent essay by Jean-Joseph Goux, 'Lacan Iconoclast', in Alexandre Leupin (ed.), *Lacan and the Human Sciences* (Lincoln: University of Nebraska Press, 1991), pp. 109–19. Lacan's attention to the Imaginary is of course particularly disturbing to the verbal underpinning of the metaphysical. For a theological debate with Lacan's conception of 'the Law of the Father', see Charles E. Scott, 'The Pathology of the Father's Rule: Lacan and the Symbolic Order', in Edith Wyschogrod, David Crownfield and Carl A. Raschke (eds), *Lacan and Theological Discourse* (Albany: State University of New York Press, 1989), pp. 76–96. For Lacan's own account, see his 'The Agency of the "Letter" in the Unconscious or Reason since Freud', in Lacan, *Écrits*, pp. 146–78.
11. Susan Sontag, *Against Interpretation* (New York: Farrar Straus Giroux, 1961), p. 7.
12. An excellent example of how Beiza'i becomes a victim of such over/interpretations of his own ingenious visuality is his conversation with Zaven Qukasian about *Travelers*. See Qukasian (ed.), *Dar Bareh-ye 'Mosaferan'*, pp. 89–169. On many occasions, Beiza'i instinctively resists such over/interpretations (p. 99). At other times, he is drawn completely into in effect aggravating it (pp. 100–1).
13. In his 'L'ordre symbolique de Jacques Lacan a la lumiere du symbolique d'Ernst Cassirer', Steve G. Lofts has linked the Lacanian conception of the Symbolic through Lévi-Strauss' theory of the myth to Cassirer's philosophy of the symbolic form. See Steve G. Lofts and Paul Moyaert (eds), *La Pensée de Jacques Lacan: Questions historiques – Problemes théoriques* (Leaven-Paris: Édition de L'Institut Supérieur de Philosophie Louvain-la-Neuve, 1994), pp. 83–105. This link is central to my argument here. See also Ernst Cassirer, *The Philosophy of Symbolic Forms* (New Haven: Yale University Press, 1923–29/1996), 4 vols; and Hans Blumenberg, *Work on Myth*, translated by Robert M. Wallace (Cambridge: MIT Press, 1979/1988).

14. See Frederic Jameson, 'Imaginary and Symbolic in Lacan: Marxism, Psychoanalytic Criticism, and the Problem of the Subject', *Yale French Studies*, 55–56 (1977), pp. 338–95.
15. See Bataille, *The Absence of Myth*, p. 48.
16. On the notion of '*il pensiero debole*', or 'weak thought', see Gianni Vattimo, *The End of Modernity* (Baltimore: Johns Hopkins University, 1985), pp. 79–89.
17. For a brilliant essay on the visual ethics of the Islamic Republic censorial policies, see Azar Naficy, 'The Veiled Threat: The Iranian Theocracy's Fear of Female', *The New Republic* (22 February 1999), pp. 24–29.
18. On the significance and function of veiling and its aesthetic manipulation, see my essay on Shirin Neshat's photography, 'The Gun and the Gaze: Shirin Neshat's Photography', in Shirin Neshat, *Women of Allah* (Torino: Marco Noire Editore, 1997), pp. v–ix.
19. There is an excellent study on the metaphysical underpinning of the Lacanian conception of subject-formation in Joël Sipos, *Lacan et Descartes: La tentation métaphysique* (Paris: Presses Universitaires de France, 1994). See, in particular, Sipos' discussion of the subject as 'Science or metaphysics' in Part One, pp. 1–47.
20. See Luce Irigaray, *Speculum of the Other Woman*, translated by Gillian C. Gill (Ithaca: Cornell University Press, 1974/1985). See, in particular, 'The Blind Spot of an Old Dream of Symmetry', pp. 11–132.
21. Lacan's discussion of the centrality of phallus is in Lacan, *Écrits*, pp. 281–91 ('The Signification of the Phallus').
22. Irigaray, *Speculum of the Other Woman*, pp. 88–90.
23. See Deleuze and Guattari. In his Preface to this book, Foucault called it an 'introduction to the Non-Fascist Life' (p. xiii), referring precisely to its anti-Oedipal counter-Symbolic. The constitution of the counter-Symbolic in the Iranian (Islamic, colonial) context invariably assumes creative manifestations.
24. For a full descriptive account of Orientalist painting and the place of the Odalisque in it, see Mary Anne Stevens (ed.), *The Orientalists: Delacroix to Matisse – The Allure of North Africa and the Near East, Catalogue Published on the Occasion of the Orientalist Exhibition at the National Gallery of Art, Washington, DC* (London: Royal Academy of Arts, 1984). For two excellent critical accounts, see Alain Grosrichard, *The Sultan's Court: European Fantasies of the East*, translated by Liz Heron, introduced by Mladen Dolar (New York: Verso, 1998); and Linda Nochlin, *The Politics of Vision* (New York: Harper and Row, 1989). Between 1919 and 1929, Matisse alone painted some fifty canvases depicting harem (Persian, Hindu, Moorish) odalisques. In 1922, a large colonial exhibition opened in Marseilles, marking a peak of Orientalist painting in France. Soon after, Léonce Bénédite, President of French Orientalist artists and director of the Luxembourg, bought *Odalisque in Red Harem Pants* for the museum, the first ever of a Matisse painting to be hung in a Paris Museum.
25. A good contemporary example of the centrality of a re-constitution of masculinity in national liberation movements is in the Palestinian case. Joseph Massad has critically examined this issue in his 'Conceiving the Masculine: Gender and Palestinian Nationalism', *Middle East Journal*, 49:3 (Summer 1995), pp. 467–83. Massad rightly locates the engendering of national liberation movements in the Enlightenment project.
26. See Mohammad Tavakoli-Targhi, 'Imagining Western Women: Occidentalism and Euro-Eroticism', *Radical America*, 24:3 (July-September 1990), pp. 73–87.
27. Tavakoli-Targhi, 'Imagining Western Women', p. 76.

28. I have categorically questioned this privileging of the European part of these travellers' sojourns abroad. See my *Reversing the Colonial Gaze: Persian Travelers Abroad* (Cambridge: Cambridge University Press, 2019). These travellers were going around the globe and recasting the world. Europe was a small part of their itinerary.
29. See Jenny Sharpe, *Allegories of Empire: The Figure of Women in the Colonial Text* (Minneapolis: University of Minnesota Press, 1993), pp. 61–69.
30. Fanon was among the first critical thinkers to have detected this symbolic significance of veiling for and against the logic of colonialism. See Frantz Fanon, 'Algeria Unveiled', in *A Dying Colonialism* (New York: Monthly Review Press, 1965), pp. 35–64.
31. See Deleuze and Guattari, *Anti-Oedipus*, p. 51.
32. Ibid. p. 51.
33. As an example of the bourgeois feminism targeting Bani-Etemad, see the review of *The May Lady* by Mihan Bahrami, 'A Few Thousand Years of Wandering', *Gozaresh-e Film*, 9:117 (15 Azar 1377/6 December 1998), p. 71. Bahrami is terribly incensed as to why Forough Kia is so entangled in the web of her social boundaries and finds her love affair with Amir Rahbar rather ridiculous and socially irrelevant. She accuses a filmmaker who has spent a lifetime documenting the most brutal realities of Iranian society as socially unconscious! The kind of sensibilities that Bahrami represents in this review is symptomatic of a whole generation of bourgeois feminism out of touch with the working class.
34. See Julia Kristeva, 'Revolution in Poetic Language', in Kelly Oliver (ed.), *The Portable Kristeva* (New York: Columbia University Press, 1997), pp. 32–34.
35. For an English translation of the story of Seyavash in the *Shahnameh*, see Ferdowsi, *The Legend of Seyavash*, translated with an Introduction and Notes by Dick Davis (London: Penguin Classics, 1992).
36. See Kristeva, *Revolution in Poetic Language*, pp. 32–39.
37. Yushij, '*Khaneh-am Abri-ast*/My Home is a Cloud', p. 620. My translation.

Chapter 7

1. Forough Farrokhzad, '*Iman Biavarim beh Aghaz-e Fasl-e Sard*/Let us Believe in the Commencement of the Cold Season', in *Iman Biavarim beh Aghaz-e Fasl-e Sard/Let us Believe in the Commencement of the Cold Season*, p. 21. My translation.
2. This chapter is a revised version of an essay that first appeared as 'Davandeh/The Runner', in Gönül Dönmez-Colin (ed.), *The Cinema of North Africa and the Middle East* (London: Wallflower Press, 2007), pp. 81–90. I am grateful to Gönül Dönmez-Colin for inviting me to write that essay. I have an even earlier take on Amir Naderi's *The Runner* in my book *Masters and Masterpieces of Iranian Cinema* (Washington DC: Mage, 2007), pp. 221–52. All these takes are preliminary to the much more developed arguments in this chapter.
3. For a critical assessment of the link between Avicenna's and Ibn Tufail's versions of the story of Hay ibn Yaghdhan, see Dimitri Gutas, 'Ibn Ṭufayl on Ibn Sīnā's Eastern Philosophy', *Oriens*, 34 (1994), pp. 222–41.
4. For a comparative study of Ibn Tufail and Defoe, see Lamia Mohamed Saleh Baeshen, 'Robinson Crusoe and Hayy Bin Yagzan: A Comparative Study' (Doctoral Dissertation, University of Arizona, 1986), available online at: https://repository.arizona.edu/bitstream/handle/10150/183936/azu_td_8704754_sip1_m.pdf?sequence=1&isAllowed=y.
5. Farrokhzad, '*Iman Biavarim beh Aghaz-e Fasl-e Sard*/Let us Believe in the Commencement of the Cold Season', p. 21. My translation.

Chapter 8

1. Mehdi Akhavan Sales, '*Qasedak*/Dandelion', in *Collected Works* (Tehran, 1397/2018), vol. 1, p. 571.
2. Shahab al-Din Yahya Suhrawardi, 'A Tale of Occidental Exile', translated by W. M. Thackston Jr, in *The Mystical and Visionary Treatises of Suhrawardi* (London: Octagon Press, 1982), pp. 100–8.
3. I have discussed the question of 'exile' and the idea of 'new organicity' in some detail in my *Post-Orientalism: Knowledge and Power in a Time of Terror* (New Brunswick: Transactions, 2009), Chapter 1 (pp. 1–16) and Chapter 7 (pp. 229–70).
4. For a full account of Rosi Braidotti's articulation of the idea, see *Nomadic Theory: The Portable Rosi Braidotti* (New York: Columbia University Press, 2012).
5. For a pioneering study of filmmakers in exile, see Hamid Naficy, *An Accented Cinema: Exilic and Diasporic Filmmaking* (Princeton: Princeton University Press, 2001).
6. For a short biographical sketch, see the entry 'SHAHID SALESS, Sohrab' in the *Encyclopedia Iranica*, available online at: https://www.iranicaonline.org/articles/shahid-saless-sohrab.
7. For a series of excellent essays on various aspects of Shahid-Saless' cinema, see Azadeh Fatehrad (ed.), *The Films of Sohrab Shahid-Saless: Exile, Displacement and the Stateless Moving Image* (Edinburgh: Edinburgh University Press, 2020). Before that we also have another major volume in Persian, Ali Dehbashi (ed.), *Ketab-e Yadnameh-ye Sohrab Shahid-Saless/The Festschrift of Sohrab Shahid-Saless* (Tehran: Sokhan Publishers, 2015).
8. This part of the chapter first appeared as an essay for a catalogue that, on occasion of a major retrospective, the Museum of Cinema in Torino, Italy, had published on Amir Naderi's cinema in 2005. Only the Italian translation of the essay was published in that catalogue. I am grateful to Grazia Paganelli for having invited me to write that essay. The English original of the essay is here slightly reworked for this chapter.
9. I have explored this aspect of Naderi's cinema in detail in my chapter on his work in my *Masters and Masterpieces of Iranian Cinema*, pp. 221–52.
10. David Ng, 'Noises Off: Seeking Solace in the Ambient Sounds of the City', *Village Voice* (29 March 2004).
11. Ng, 'Noises Off'.
12. Ibid.
13. See David Ng, 'An Artistic Orphan in the Big City,' *Salon.Com* (11 June 2003), available online at: http://www.salon.com/ent/movies/int/2003/06/11/naderi/index_np.html.
14. See Ronnie Scheib's review of *Sound Barrier* in *Variety* (4 May 2005).
15. See Jared Rapfogel, 'Lakes in Lower Manhattan: The 4th Annual Tribeca Film Festival, April 19–May 1, 2005', *Senses of Cinema* (June 2005), available online at: http://www.sensesofcinema.com/contents/festivals/05/36/tribeca2005.html.
16. Rapfogel, 'Lakes in Lower Manhattan'.
17. Ibid.
18. Ibid.
19. See Theodore Adorno, *The Culture Industry* (London: Routledge, 2001).
20. See Walter Benjamin, 'The Work of Art in the Age of Mechanical Reproduction', in *Illuminations* (New York: Schocken, 1969), pp. 217–52.
21. Benjamin, 'The Work of Art in the Age of Mechanical Reproduction'.
22. Ibid.

23. Ibid.
24. See Andrew Delbanco, *Melville: His World and Work* (New York: Knopf, 2005).
25. Akhavan Sales, '*Qasedak*/Dandelion', p. 571.

Chapter 9

1. The first much shorter version of this chapter was in the form of a short essay I called 'Fictive Transparency of the Real: Perils and Promises of Cine-Mysticism in Iranian Cinema,' in Chua Lawrence (ed.), *Nuae No. 2: Collapsing New Buildings* (New York: Kaya/Muae, 1996), pp. 152–60. That publication however no longer seems to be in print.
2. Farrokhzad, '*Tavallodi Digar*/Another Birth,' p. 156. My translation.
3. See Roland Barthes, *Sul Cinema* (Genova: Il Melangolo, 1994), p. 170.
4. See Gianni Vattimo, *The Transparent Society*, translated by David Webb (Cambridge: Polity Press, 1992), p. 28.
5. See Shaykh Farid al-Din 'Attar Nishaburi, *Tadhkirat al-Awlia*, edited, annotated, with an Introduction by Muhammad Estelami (Tehran: Zavvar Publishers, 1347/1968), p. 5. My translation from the original Persian.
6. Vattimo, *The Transparent Society*, p. 31.
7. Ibid. p. 31.
8. Ibid.
9. See Stephen Vlastos (ed.), *Mirror of Modernity: Invented Traditions of Modern Japan* (Berkeley: University of California Press, 1998).
10. For a translation, see Farid ud-Din Attar, *The Conference of the Birds*, translated with an Introduction by Afkham Darbandi and Dick Davis (London. Penguin Books, 1984).
11. Attar, *The Conference of the Birds*, p. 219. I have made a slight modification in this extraordinarily successful translation.
12. Cinematic adaptations of the Greek dramatic mechanism of *deus ex machina* are to be found in such early Indian films as D. G. Phalke's *Raja Harischandra* (1913) in which Lord Shiva interferes in human affairs in order to resolve an otherwise un-resolvable dilemma of the hero. See Brigitte Schultze, 'D. G. Phalke's RAJA HARISCHANDRA in British India of 1913: Pioneering National Cinema under Colonial Rule', *Kintop 3: Jahrbuch zur Erforschung des frühen Films* (1994), pp. 173–89.
13. For a short version of the script of *Travelers*, see Qukasian, *Dar Bareh-ye 'Mosaferan'*, p. 17–22.
14. Such as Jamshid Arjomand in '*Mosaferan, Gozaresh-e Band-e Ajal*?/Travelers: Undoing of the Fate's Knot?' in Qukasian, *Dar Bareh-ye 'Mosaferan'*, pp. 23–28.
15. See Alireza Tavana, 'Barresi-ye Tatbiqi-e "Mosaferan"', in Qukasian, *Dar Bareh-ye 'Mosaferan'*, pp. 39–62.
16. For a comprehensive and insightful reading of the role of women in Beiza'i's cinema, see Shahla Lahiji's *Sima-ye Zan dar Athar-e Bahram Beizai* (Tehran: Roshangaran Publishers, 1993).
17. See Robert Stam's reading of Bakhtin and Nietzsche in a theoretical translation of the idea of 'the carnivalesque' for cinema in *Subversive Pleasures: Bakhtin, Cultural Criticism, and Film* (Baltimore and London: The Johns Hopkins University Press, 1989). The third chapter is particularly important in this respect.
18. See Jamshid Arjomand, Zhaleh Amuzegar, and Soheila Najm's essays, all centred around the fear of death, and then compare them with Beiza'i's own comments in his conversation

with Zaven Qukasian, in Qukasian, *Dar Bareh-ye 'Mosaferan'*, pp. 89–69. As Beiza'i puts it himself, '*Travelers* is a very simple film in praise of life and new hopes' (p. 89).

19. Zaven Qukasian's otherwise excellent interview with Bahram Beiza'i is marred by such unexamined assumptions as 'our Eastern and myth-making mind, having grown up with such ideas, is more prone to accept this last scene [that is, the final sequence of Mahtab and her family entering the room and bringing the mirror]' (Qukasian, *Dar Bareh-ye 'Mosaferan'*, p. 117). The narrative logic and the visual rhetoric of *Travelers* is made so masterfully that understanding the last sequence needs no such empty abstraction as 'our Eastern and myth-making mind'. As Beiza'i himself puts it, 'let me repeat, it is not important that someone believes the last sequence. It is enough if one likes it and shares the hope – which is an old hope of all humanity – that is hidden in it' (p. 117). Or even more emphatically, referring to Hamlet, he points out: 'Don't you think that the spirit of Hamlet's father is really a reflection of his own thoughts? The spirit in fact says the sort of things that Hamlet wants to hear. This point is far more important than our asking whether or not a spirit can appear to someone and speak to him. You see that the mind cannot be separated into East and West ... ' (p. 118).
20. My translation of Sohrab Sepehri's '*Neshani*/Address' from his *Hasht Ketab* (Tehran: Tahuri Publishers, 1977), pp. 358–59.
21. Mawlana Jalal al-Din Rumi, *Mathnawi*, edited by R. A. Nicholson (Tehran: Amir Kabir, 1984), vol. 1, pp. 86–87; verses 1399–1407.
22. See Attar, *The Conference of the Birds*, p. 9.
23. Adorno, *Aesthetic Theory*, p. 78.
24. '*U*' in Persian is not gender-specific – in English we have no choice but opt for he or she – thus 'he-ness' for '*u'i*'. I have opted for my own translation of this passage to try to bring out the evident suggestiveness of the original. A far more readable, but alas not entirely accurate, translation of the whole treatise is to be found in W. M. Thackston Jr, *The Mystical and Visionary Treatises of Suhrawardi* (London: The Octagon Press, 1982). The translation of 'The Sound of Gabriel's Wing' is on pp. 26–34.
25. Thackston, *The Mystical and Visionary Treatises of Suhrawardi*, p. 109.
26. Thackston's translation of Suhrawardi in Thackston, *The Mystical and Visionary Treatises of Suhrawardi*, p. 26. For the original, see Shahab al-Din Yahya Suhrawardi, *Majmu'eh Musannafat Sheykh Ishraq*, edited, annotated, with an Introduction by S. H. Nasr, with an additional Introduction in French by Henry Corbin (Tehran: Académie Impériale Iranienne de Philosophie, 1977), pp. 207–23.
27. Thackston, *The Mystical and Visionary Treatises of Suhrawardi*, p. 27. Suhrawardi, *Majmu'eh Musannafat Sheykh Ishraq*, pp. 209–10. I have made some necessary corrections in Thackston's translation.
28. Here I have found Thackston's translation in Thackston, *The Mystical and Visionary Treatises of Suhrawardi*, p. 32, unusable. I have translated the passage anew, with particular attention to Suhrawardi's own anxiety in constituting Gabriel between the subjugation of the mortal being to generation, corruption and decay, and the Divine immunity to such a cycle. See the original in Suhrawardi, *Majmu'eh Musannafat Sheykh Ishraq*, p. 220. I have also opted for an alternative reading of the last sentence of my translation from that preferred by S. H. Nasr in his critical edition. I prefer one of the manuscript variations that would translate as 'constitutional to his being' rather than 'constitutional to being'.
29. See Thackston, *The Mystical and Visionary Treatises of Suhrawardi*, pp. 26–28; Suhrawardi, *Majmu'eh Musannafat Sheykh Ishraq*, pp. 208–10.

30. Judith Mayne, 'Paradoxes of Spectatorship', in Linda Williams (ed.), *Viewing Positions: Ways of Seeing Films* (New Brunswick: Rutgers University Press, 1994), p. 156.
31. Anton Kaes, *From Hitler to Heimat: The Return of History as Film* (Cambridge: Harvard University Press, 1989), p. 68.
32. Kaes, *From Hitler to Heimat*, p. 66.
33. Ibid. pp. 63–64.
34. See Ahmad Sadri, 'Adjusting to the World According to Salman Rushdie,' in Carol Becker (ed.), *The Subversive Imagination: Artists, Society, and Social Responsibility* (New York: Routledge, 1994), p. 181.
35. Adorno, *Aesthetic Theory*, p. 6.
36. Ibid. p. 7.
37. Ibid. p. 78.
38. Ibid.
39. Ibid.
40. Ibid.
41. For a collection of passages on Kant's position on 'the Negro', see Emmanuel Chukwudi Eze (ed.), *Race and the Enlightenment: A Reader* (Oxford: Blackwell, 1997), p. 38–78.
42. Adorno, *Aesthetic Theory*, p. 78.
43. Farrokhzad, '*Tavallodi Digar*/Another Birth,' p. 156. My translation.

Chapter 10

1. Farrokhzad, '*Tavallodi Digar*/Another Birth,' p. 156. My translation.
2. See David Michael Levin (ed.), *Modernity and the Hegemony of Vision* (Berkeley: University of California Press, 1993).
3. See Frithjof Schuon, *Sufism: Veils and Quintessence* (Bloomington: World Wisdom Books, 1979/1981), p. 1.
4. Schuon, *Sufism*, pp. 6–7.
5. See Mikhail Bakhtin, *Rabelais and His World*, translated by Hélene Iswolsky (Bloomington: Indiana University Press, 1984).
6. See Robert Stam, *Subversive Pleasures: Bakhtin, Cultural Criticism, and Film* (Baltimore: The Johns Hopkins University Press, 1989).
7. See Adorno, *Aesthetic Theory*, particularly pp. 175–97.
8. See ibid. p. 8.
9. See Philip Rieff, 'Toward a Theory of Culture', in *The Feeling Intellect: Selected Writings*, edited and with an Introduction by Jonathan B. Imber (Chicago: The University of Chicago Press, 1990), p. 325.
10. See Gilles Deleuze, *Masochism* (New York: Zone Books, 1991).
11. Ibid. p. 66.
12. Ibid.
13. Ibid. p. 67. 'Oral mother' is one among a triple typology that Deleuze has constructed.
14. Ibid. p. 65.
15. Ibid. p. 65–66.
16. See Jean-Paul Sartre, *Being and Nothingness*, translated and with an Introduction by Hazel E. Barnes (New York: Gramercy Books, 1956), Part 3, p. 221.
17. See Martin Jay, *Downcast Eyes: The Denigration of Vision in Twentieth Century French Thought* (Berkeley: University of California Press, 1993).

18. See Martin Jay, 'Sartre, Merleau-Ponty, and the Search for a New Ontology of Sight', in David Michael Levin (ed.), *Modernity and the Hegemony of Vision* (Berkeley: University of California Press, 1993), pp. 143–85.
19. See Georgia Warnke, 'Ocularcentrism and Social Criticism', in Levin, *Modernity and the Hegemony of Vision*, pp. 287–308.
20. See Michel Foucault, *Discipline and Punish: The Birth of the Prison*, translated by Alan Sheridan (New York: Pantheon, 1979), p. 29.
21. See Max Weber, *Sociology of Religion*, translated by Ephraim Fischoff, Introduction by Talcott Parsons (Boston: Beacon Press, 1922), p. 242.
22. See Rieff, 'Toward a Theory of Culture', p. 325.
23. See Weber, *Sociology of Religion*, p. 242.
24. See Ibid. p. 243.
25. See Hans-George Gadamer, *The Relevance of the Beautiful: And Other Essays* (Cambridge: Cambridge University Press, 1986), p. 15.
26. Ibid. pp. 3–4
27. See Qadi Mir Ahmad Qomi, *Golestan-e Honar/The Flowerbed of Art* (Tehran: Manuchehri Publishers, 1351/1972).
28. Qomi, *Golestan-e Honar/The Flowerbed of Art*, p. 3.
29. See Christoph Bürgel, '"Die beste Dichtung ist die lügenreichste": Wesen und Bedeutung eines literarischen Streits des arabischen Mittelalters im Lichte komparatistischer Betrachtung', *Oriens*, 23 (1974), pp. 7–102, for further details on these traditions.
30. Gadamer, *The Relevance of the Beautiful*, p. 15.
31. Ibid. p. 15
32. See Michel Foucault, 'On the Genealogy of Ethics: An Overview of Work in Progress,' in Paul Rabinow (ed.), *The Foucault Reader* (New York: Pantheon Books, 1984), p. 350.
33. See Rabinow, *The Foucault Reader*, p. 351.
34. Farrokhzad, '*Tavallodi Digar*/Another Birth', p. 156. My translation.

Conclusion

1. Farrokhzad, '*Tavallodi Digar*/Another Birth', p. 156. My translation.
2. The video of this interview is available online at: https://www.youtube.com/watch?v=-TKRimlH5ZU.
3. The video of this interview is available online at: https://www.youtube.com/watch?v=dsoImQfVsO4.
4. See Luce Irigaray, *Speculum of the Other Woman*, translated by Gillian Gill (Ithaca: Cornell University Press, 1985). See, in particular, her discussion of the Phallic Order in Chapter One, 'Women, Science's Unknown', pp. 13–24.
5. See Jonathan Jones, 'Five Thousand Years of Mystical Magnificence: Epic Iran at the V&A', *The Guardian*, 25 May 2021, available online at: https://www.theguardian.com/artanddesign/2021/may/26/epic-iran-five-thousand-years-mystical-magnificence-epic-iran-va-review.
6. See Enrique Dussel, *Philosophy of Liberation* (New York: Orbis Books, 1985), p. 3.
7. See Fereydoun Amu Zadeh Khalili (ed.), *Ketab Majmu'eh Qesseh-ha-ye Nakoja-abad/The Book of the Collection of Stories of Utopia: Based on the Ideas and Stories of Suhrawardi for Children* (Tehran: Nashr-e Sales, 1399/2020), 6 vols.
8. For this series of Abbas Kiarostami's photographs, see this piece in *The Guardian*: https://www.theguardian.com/artanddesign/gallery/2009/may/19/abbas-kiarostami-photo

graphy-exhibition. For his own reflections on these photographs, see: https://www.theguardian.com/artanddesign/2009/jul/29/photography-abbas-kiarostami-best-shot.

9. For the most recent translation of Benjamin's seminal text, see Walter Benjamin, *Origin of the German Trauerspiel*, translated by Howard Eiland (Cambridge: Harvard University Press, 2019).
10. See Walter Mignolo, *The Darker Side of Western Modernity: Global Futures, Decolonial Options* (Durham: Duke University press, 2011).
11. For a collection of her essays, see María Lugones, *Pilgrimages/Peregrinajes: Theorizing Coalition Against Multiple Oppressions* (Lanham: Rowman & Littlefield Publishers, 2003).
12. See, for example, Afsaneh Najmabadi, *Women with Mustaches and Men without Beards: Gender and Sexual Anxieties of Iranian Modernity* (Oakland: University of California Press, 2005), pp. 5–6, where she completely dodges and dilutes the central question of coloniality.
13. Rumi, *Masnavi*, vol. III.
14. See Hamid Dabashi, *The Shahnameh: The Persian Epic as World Literature* (New York: Columbia University Press, 2019).
15. See Jacques Derrida, *Specters of Marx: The State of the Debt, The Work of Mourning and the New International* (London: Routledge, 2006); Samir Haddad, *Derrida and the Inheritance of Democracy* (Bloomington: Indiana University Press, 2013); and Samir Haddad, 'Arendt, Derrida, and Inheritance of Forgiveness', *Philosophy Today*, 51:4 (Winter 2007): pp. 416–26.
16. I have dealt extensively with the exhausted power of this illusion in *The Future of Two Illusions: Islam after the West* (Oakland: University of California Press, 2022).
17. For a full discussion of the Derridean concept of 'aporia', minus the theoretical *loci* of coloniality, see Haddad, *Derrida and the Inheritance of Democracy*, pp. 7–22.
18. See Laura U. Marks, *Hanan al-Cinema: Affections for the Moving Image* (Cambridge: MIT Press, 2015).
19. See, for example, Susan Buck-Morss, *Hegel, Haiti, and Universal History* (Pittsburgh: University of Pittsburgh Press, 2009).
20. Farrokhzad, '*Tavallodi Digar*/Another Birth', p. 156. My translation.

Index

Note: *italic* denotes illustration

EU Authorised Representative:
Easy Access System Europe Mustamäe tee 50, 10621 Tallinn, Estonia
gpsr.requests@easproject.com

Printed and bound by CPI Group (UK) Ltd, Croydon, CR0 4YY
01/04/2026
02082098-0002